THE COLLECTED WORKS OF

LALA LAJPAT RAI

VOLUME TWO

THE COLLECTED WORKS OF

LALA LAJPAT RAI

VOLUME TWO

Chief Editor
B.R. Nanda

MANOHAR
2003

First published 2003

ISBN 81-7304-480-5 (Series)
ISBN 81-7304-517-8 (Volume 2)

Published by
Ajay Kumar Jain for
Manohar Publishers & Distributors
4753/23 Ansari Road, Daryaganj
New Delhi 110 002

Printed at
Lordson Publishers Pvt. Ltd.
Delhi 110 007

CONTENTS

उप-राष्ट्रपति, भारत
नई दिल्ली
VICE-PRESIDENT
INDIA
NEW DELHI

FOREWORD

Lala Lajpat Rai ranks among the outstanding leaders of modern India and occupies a distinctive place in the galaxy of world personalities who fought for the freedom of their peoples. A contemporary and colleague of Mahatma Gandhi, Lokmanya Tilak, Pandit Motilal Nehru and Gopal Krishna Gokhale, Lala Lajpat Rai got a place in the national lexicon as one of the triumvirate (Lal, Bal, Pal) of the extremist fame in the Indian nationalist struggle in 1905 during an all-India agitation against the partition of Bengal. Lalaji made his first foray into politics in 1888 when he was only 23 years old and wrote a series of 'Open Letters' to Sir Syed Ahmed Khan which appeared in the Urdu weekly *Koh-i-Noor* of Lahore. In these letters he profusely quoted from Sir Syed's earlier writings to prove his *volte face* concerning his earlier views on Hindu-Muslim unity and Indian nationhood and all what he had preached before the Indian National Congress was founded.

These 'Open Letters' shot young Lajpat Rai to instant national fame so much so that A.O. Hume, the founder of the Indian National Congress, got them published in English and circulated. When Lajpat Rai arrived at Allahabad in 1888 to attend the Congress session, Ajudhianath and Madan Mohan Malaviya had come to receive him at the railway station.

Lalaji's public life spanned the last decade of the nineteenth century and first three decades of the twentieth century which was a period of political and economic upheavals in human history. It was a period when capitalism and militarism were the dominant forces shaping the destiny of nations and empires. A virulent revulsion against empires and imperialism was felt by Lalaji instinctively. He thought that a transformation in the world system was not possible by eliminating one or two empires or by substituting one empire by another but by abolishing all of them. Until imperialism in all its forms was obliterated there was little hope, he added, of coming into being of a just world order. Having a cosmopolitan outlook, Lalaji looked forward to the emergence of a free Asia and Africa. He empathised with the people of South Africa in their fight against racial discrimination.

While in his teens Lala Lajpat Rai came under the spell of Arya Samaj and its founder Swami Dayanand. It is from them that he imbibed his first lesson in patriotism and pride in his cultural heritage. His contact with Mazzini's writings further gave a boost to his resolve to undergo sufferings and privations for the country's freedom and national unity. And to tell the glorious saga of Italian Risorgimento to the youth of his country, Lajpat Rai penned inspiring biographies of Mazzini and Garibaldi in his Great Men of the World series. During this period the other biographies he wrote were of Shri Krishna, Shivaji, Swami Dayanand and Guru Datta Vidyarthi, a scholar of Sanskrit, and later he wrote a biography of Asoka.

Love for the country and passionate concern for freedom remained the twin motivating and propelling passions throughout his life. Though an ardent nationalist, he considered the good and well-being of the whole humanity as the final touchstone of every nationalist endeavour. What with Mazzini's influence his idea of nationalism immunized him against a parochial self-aggrandizing nationalism on the one hand, and, on the other, against a vague cosmopolitanism.

Admittedly, the goal of Indian nationalism, according to Lalaji, was a world civilization in which the ideas and civilization of every nation could find place. He thought that an increased diversity in the world and an emphasis on diversity of culture could help dismantle the structures of imperialism and hegemonism. He said, 'The world is good and beautiful only with its diversity.' Though he found diversity inevitable in the new world order, he noted, it was not possible to survive in isolation. Communication and interdependence had become compulsory among nations and peoples. He saw the Indian nationalist struggle in world perspective and realized the importance of enlisting the support of other countries in putting pressure of world public opinion on Britain. He formed close contacts with British Labour and Irish nationalist organizations and sought to bring Asian and British Labour closer to each other.

The reform of the Hindu society remained his abiding mission and the removal of untouchability and discrimination in any form anywhere topped his agenda. He called untouchability a blot on Hinduism and an affront to God who resided in every being. Right from his early days he crusaded for its total abolition, and in 1913, presiding over the Depressed Classes Conference, he said: 'We must float or sink with them (untouchables). In their strength is our strength; and in their weakness our fall.' He believed that education would bring about their awakening and make them conscious of their rights and responsibilities. He also gave utmost importance to the cause of the youth, women and children and worked from many platforms for their welfare.

Politics, to Lalaji, was a dynamic and ever-changing phenomenon. He did not believe in absolutes, nor was he wedded to any rigid ideology or dogma.

On questions of vital importance he kept an open mind. He applied canons of strict reasoning not only to political, social and economic issues but also to matters of religion. He opined that 'Reason, rationalism, science and religion have all to be brought into the field before a substantial breach is made in the citadel of superstition and deep-rooted prejudices.' In the controversy between the social reformers and revivalists he opposed the extreme, rigid postures assumed by them. He believed in the process of growth and preserving the national character by assimilating the finest in India's cultural heritage with the best in modern civilization. Since in the Indian context the social questions were so much intertwined with religion that the problem of advancing social reform merely by legislation was a delicate one, he sought the cooperation of all agencies of social reform, science, religion and men of conscience and reason.

Though Lajpat Rai had become *bete noire* of the British bureaucracy very early, he really got involved in the Congress work only at the turn of the century. By 1905 he had come to be recognized as an all-India leader. In May 1907 his deportation to Burma by the Government without a trial created a grave political crisis. The Minto-Morley correspondence amply prove how unwarranted it was, for which the perpetrators of this grievous wrong had to regret later. When he was released, Lalaji found the Indian National Congress torn by a conflict between the moderate and extremist groups. When the extremist group proposed his name for Presidentship of the Congress in 1907 he, with his characteristic self-abnegation, declined the honour in the hope that it might help prevent a split in the party.

In the years preceding the First World War, he remained active in the Congress both in the provincial and national spheres. In 1905 Lajpat Rai was deputed as a Congress delegate to educate British public opinion on the Indian situation. Lajpat Rai visited England in 1908 for the second time and delivered lectures to the Indian students, the British intelligentsia and the working class. In 1914 he again undertook a tour of England, the United States and Japan. In fact, when the war broke out he was in England. He knew that he was likely to be clapped into prison on return to India, and therefore opted for voluntary exile in the United States in order to mobilize public opinion in that country in favour of India's struggle for freedom. In 1920 he returned to India and was accorded a hero's welcome and was elected to preside over the historic Calcutta session of the Indian National Congress. At the session he feelingly spoke on the agony of Punjab, reacting sharply to the ruthless oppression by the British bureaucracy resulting in the Jallianwala Bagh massacre. Soon he came round to Mahatma Gandhi's programme and leadership at the Nagpur Congress session (1920) at which non-violent non-cooperation was accepted as an instrument of struggle. His collaboration with Mahatma Gandhi and his countrywide campaigning evoked unprecedented public response and transformed the

Congress from an upper-class body into a mass movement, thereby changing the very complexion of the nationalist struggle. But in the wake of the Chauri Chaura incident in February 1922, Gandhiji called off civil disobedience and the movement declined. What with factional and communal tensions the mid-twenties were a dismal period in Indian politics. However, there was a political revival in 1928 and Lajpat Rai actively canvassed support for the Nehru Report on the future constitutional set-up of the country. At this time, forgetting all his differences with Motilal Nehru, he was cooperating with him fully both inside and outside the Central Legislative Assembly. When the 'all-white' Simon Commission visited India, he was in the forefront of the agitation for its boycott. It was while he was leading a demonstration against the Commission outside the Lahore railway station that he was assaulted by the police and suffered injuries which led to his death. Lalaji's life had epic dimensions. All his life he lived a hero and in death too he was crowned a martyr. Paying a touching tribute to Lajpat Rai, Gandhiji feelingly wrote in *Young India* of 22 November 1928: 'Men like Lajpat Rai cannot die so long as the sun shines in the Indian sky.'

There was hardly any Indian leader, with the exception of Gandhiji, whose public activities covered such a wide range as those of Lalaji. As Gandhiji put it, 'It is impossible to think of a single public movement in which Lalaji was not to be found.' In 1886 he was associated with the founding of the D.A.V. College at Lahore and out of his income from a lucrative practice at the District Court in Hissar and the Chief Court at Lahore he contributed a lion's share to it. In 1899-1900 when a dreadful famine raged in Punjab, the Central Provinces, Rajputana and the United Provinces, Lajpat Rai planned and implemented the relief work on an extensive scale. He set up several orphanages for deserted children and orphans at many places. To help the downtrodden and the depressed in the Hindu society he spearheaded many campaigns and set up the Kumar Ashram at Meerut to provide free education. From the very beginning Lalaji emphasized the growth of trade and industry and wanted the Congress to hold industrial conferences during its annual sessions. He founded institutions like the Punjab National Bank and the Lakshmi Insurance Company and favoured setting up of indigenous outfits to give a boost to export by Indian traders as against the British entrepreneurs who were making huge profits in the absence of any competition. Lalaji was a great exponent of free and compulsory education, and to inculcate patriotism and nationalism among the youth he delineated a model of national education. He established the Tilak School of Politics for the political training of students and the Servants of the People Society to enlist and train life members vowed to work selflessly for the country.

Lajpat Rai approached the communal problem in a rational and practical manner. He emphasized the need for concentrating on economic and other interests which were common to various communities rather than harping on their sectarian differences. Setting aside their communal bickerings, he said, their foremost passion should be to 'combine to fight our poverty and ignorance—the common enemies of the whole mankind'. He said since India was not exclusively Hindu, its prosperity and future depended on the reconciliation of Hinduism with the greater 'ism'—the Indian nationalism. In the same vein elsewhere he remarked: 'India is neither Hindu nor Muslim, not even both. It is one. It is India. Let us live and die for each other, so that India may live and prosper as a nation.' He appealed both to the Hindus and Muslims to take pride in the achievements of their common heroes and saints: 'If mother India had an Asoka, she had an Akbar too; if she had a Chaitanya, she had a Kabir also. For every Hindu hero, we can cite a Muhammadan hero. We may be as proud of Syed Ahmed Khan as of Rammohun Roy and Dayanand.' What India needed, according to Lalaji, was more of nationalism and tolerance than orthodoxy and bigotry. To resolve the communal tangle his prescription was to integrate the different religions as much as possible by emphasizing the points on which they agreed, by eliminating non-essentials, by restricting the essential differences within the narrowest limits and finally by removing all barriers to free social intercourse between the communities.

To foster the spirit of true nationalism among the people, Lalaji did not favour in the least the idea of annihilation of all nationalities or communal identities but wanted their coming together in a free and equal association, removing all impediments that tended to create a sense of segregation, anomie and alienation among the various groups constituting the nation. For this he favoured correlation of interests sustaining all classes and sections in the nation for the development of a national ethos, a national will and the self-evolving of a higher loyalty, i.e. nationalism.

In the future constitution of India Lalaji enjoined granting of religious liberty to all religious denominations subject only to such restrictions as were inevitable for the maintenance of law and order. To this, he thought, must be added the absolute religious neutrality of the state. This may be seen perhaps as the earliest enunciation of the idea of a secular state in the Indian context.

Realizing the pluralist character of the Indian nation, Lajpat Rai pointed out that the differences among the communities and castes were quite real and to evolve a sound and effective system of governance they must not be ignored. With a deep insight into the nature of the communal problem of India, Lalaji pleaded for accommodating the interests of the different communities within the framework of a united India. Understanding the psychology of communalism, he was willing to make reasonable concessions intended to save Indian polity from disintegrating under the pressure of communal strain. According to him, the character of Indian polity was to be composite, reflective of regions as well as communities. He strongly resisted sectarian trends, which were being boosted by the British, the revivalists and other communal leaders. Had his line of thinking been accepted, the partition of the country could have been averted.

In a memorial tribute published in *Young India*, Gandhiji wrote: 'He (Lajpat Rai) was sincerely desirous of promoting and achieving Hindu-Muslim unity. He wanted not Hindu Raj but he passionately wanted Indian Raj; he wanted all who called themselves Indians to have absolute equality.' The constitution of free India that Lalaji envisaged was to be secular in outlook, federal in structure and pluralistic in character. The ideals of social justice, equality of opportunity, freedom and democracy were to be the imperatives of the polity after India gained freedom.

Among the leaders of the freedom struggle, Lalaji was a widely travelled person and befittingly called the 'cultural ambassador of India'. Realizing the importance of world public opinion, Lalaji undertook these travels to publicize India's case in America, Britain and other countries as well as at international assemblies like the International Labour Organization and the World Parliaments Union at Geneva and the World Migration Conference in London. During these visits he came in contact with many British, American and other statesmen and opinion leaders and made an abiding friendship with some of them. He corresponded with many British leaders like Ramsay MacDonald, Col. Josiah C. Wedgwood, William Wedderburn, Sir Henry Cotton, Henry M. Hyndman, George Lansbury, Benjamin Spoor and the Webbs. He also established rapport with Keir Hardie, Fredrick Mackarness, V.H. Rutherford and other Labour leaders.

Lalaji also founded and edited newspapers and journals and was a prolific writer and builder of institutions. He launched the English weeklies, *The Panjabee* and *The People*, and the Urdu daily, *Bande Mataram*, and made them powerful instruments of national awakening. He founded the Indian Home Rule League of America in October 1917 and launched *Young India*, a monthly, as the official organ of the League. He also set up the Indian Information Bureau in New York with himself as its Director to serve the cause of India's freedom. During his enforced stay in America, besides travelling from coast to coast and delivering lectures on the Indian situation, he authored some of his notable books—*The United States of America*, *England's Debt to India*, *National Education* and *Young India*. His *Unhappy India*, published in 1928, contained by far the best and most scathing refutation of Miss Mayo's scurrilous attacks on Indian society as given in her book, *Mother India*.

To realize a peaceful international order Lalaji emphasized the need for building up self-governing communities free from every form of exploitation with all segments of society enjoying equal opportunities of good life and growth. Mutual cooperation, respect for each other's culture and interaction on terms of equality were the pre-requisites of a just international order, and to achieve this, he said, democracy, political and social, at all levels was to spread and inform the world order. He envisioned a pivotal role of free India in the emerging international system which was to be that of an active, cooperative and constructive member of the global fraternity—a role in the cause of world peace the realization of a truly democratic world order.

I trust the publication of this series of the *Collected Works of Lala Lajpat Rai* edited by Shri B.R. Nanda, noted historian of modern India, and biographer of Gandhi, Nehru and Gokhale as the Chief Editor and Dr Madan Gopal Gandhi, an eminent social scientist and litterateur as the Editor, will contribute to a better understanding not only of Lala Lajpat Rai's life and work but also of some important phases in India's struggle for freedom.

New Delhi
25 July, 2002

Krishan Kant

(KRISHAN KANT)

EDITORIAL NOTE

This volume covers the period from 1901 to 1906 which witnessed a great spurt in Lajpat Rai's political activities. As we saw in the previous volume, after his spectacular entry into national politics with his "Open Letters to Sir Syed Ahmed Khan" and his presence at the Allahabad session of the Indian National Congress in 1888, Lajpat Rai took only sporadic interest in nationalist politics. Perhaps his hands were too full during this period with his legal practice at the Lahore Chief Court and his involvement in religious, educational and social reforms. But an additional reason may have been the lackadaisical manner in which the Congress seemed to be conducting its affairs. In 1901 in an article in the *Kayastha Samachar* of Allahabad, Lajpat Rai described the annual sessions of the Congress as "annual festivals of educated Indians" in which the political work done was of "doubtful and ephemeral character". The size of the annual gathering, he wrote, was so unwieldy, that it "precluded the very idea of serious work whether in the shape of deliberation, discussion or action." The delegates could not make the best use of the time at their disposal owing to the lengthy programme of speeches and resolutions. The lack of a sense of responsibility in a majority of members was shown by the fact that they did nothing during the year. They were doing little to check the growing poverty of the people and dispel ignorance which was the crying need of India.

Since its foundation in 1885, the Congress had met every year during the Christmas week, and demanded legislative and administrative reforms such as enlargement of the size, elective proportion and functions of the legislative councils, extension of trial by jury, grant of commissions to Indians in the Army, reduction in military expenditure and equitable adjustment of financial burdens between India and Britain. Neither the ideal of self-government nor the modest reforms as steps towards it had struck a chord in the British rulers of India. Lord Dufferin, during whose viceroyalty the Congress was founded, doubted the possibility of applying constitutional reforms to a conquered country "inasmuch as self-government and submission to a foreign sovereign are incompatible terms." In 1900 Lord Curzon assured the Secretary of State for India that "the Congress was tottering to its fall." Three years later, Lord Ampthill, the Governor of Madras, described the session held in that city as a "great failure". Most British officials in India saw Congress leaders as a small and selfish minority who were out to feather their own nests and did not really mean what they said, and whose demands in any case could not be entertained without shaking the foundations of British rule. With such an attitude on the part of British bureaucracy in India, and a Tory government in power in Britain through 1890s, the Congress went on repeating the same demands every year and doubts began to be voiced on the wisdom of its strategy.

Eight years before the publication of Lajpat Rai's article in *Kayastha Samachar*, Aurobindo Ghose had charged leaders of the Congress with lack of vision, courage and earnestness. The Congress leaders did not like this criticism, but some of them themselves had a sense of frustration and futility. Things looked really bleak until 1904, when British politics took a hopeful turn. The Conservative party found itself in difficulties and the days of Balfour ministry seemed numbered. A general election was on the cards. The Bombay session of the Congress (December 1904) unanimously decided to depute a few Congress representatives to England to put forward the claims of nationalist India before the British electorate, the parliamentary candidates and political leaders in that country. Sir Henry Cotton, who presided over the Bombay Congress session, and Sir William Wedderburn, Chairman of the British Committee of the Congress, stressed the urgency of despatching Indian delegates as the imminence of a general election offered excellent opportunity for focussing attention on Indian grievances. Early in April 1905 it was agreed that Lajpat Rai, as the representative of Indian Association of Lahore, and Gokhale, as the representative of Bombay Presidency Association, should visit England as delegates of the Indian National Congress. In the event Gokhale's departure was delayed and only Lajpat Rai was able to leave on 13 May.

Before sailing from Bombay Lajpat Rai paid a flying visit to Poona. Gokhale received him at the Poona railway station and took him to his residence. Next day, Lajpat Rai called on Tilak and was invited to dinner. He hit it off with both the Maharashtrian leaders—a rare achievement as they were considered rivals in national politics.

Lajpat Rai immensely enjoyed his month-long voyage and sent detailed and lively accounts of it to Lahore for publication in his weekly paper *The Panjabee*. Throughout his travels abroad he continued to share with the readers of this paper his experiences and reflections not only on his own political work, but on every subject under the sun. His intellectual curiosity was insatiable. For example, in England he noticed the spirit of patriotism in the people. "The English child never forgets his country", he wrote. "If there is anything which is most prominent and patent on the face of every institution it is an Englishman's love for his country and its political institutions. I have seen books in primary schools which aim at impressing on English boys how precious liberty is." Of France he wrote : "It is more advanced than England in science and technology. The French language is understood in almost all countries of Europe. Perhaps it would not be wrong to say that France is more liberal and open-minded as regards new ideas, techniques and methods than England. England believes in following the beaten track. Englishmen do not take easily to innovations of any kind, conservatism being their national trait."

After arrival in London in June 1905, Lajpat Rai called upon Sir William Wedderburn and other members of the British Committee of the Indian National Congress. He was told that the committee was pressing for Gokhale's presence in England, but meanwhile it was for Lajpat Rai to brief English politicians and British political associations on the Congress stand. Herbert Roberts, a Liberal M.P., arranged for Lajpat Rai to hold informal discussions with members of the House of Commons, who were interested in Indian affairs. Sir William Wedderburn was present when Lajpat Rai presented the Congress case. The same afternoon Lajpat Rai was in the visitors' gallery of the House of Commons. He was shocked to see the House suddenly empty when the time came to debate the Indian budget. However, he appreciated the courage with which a few members voiced Indian grievances against heavy odds. He noted that these "friends of India" were dubbed as "faddists, little Englanders, misguided philanthropists" by the authorities and the people in general.

In his speeches to English audiences, Lajpat Rai took the line that in spite of the fact that India was considered "a jewel in the crown", it hardly received any attention at the hands of British parliamentarians and statesmen. The British Parliament was neglectful of Indian affairs; ministers and members joined hands in putting the debate on the Indian budget "at the fag end of the session and vied with each other in fleeing from the House when the budget came up for discussion." As a result, the administration of India was left to the British officials posted in India. Lajpat Rai appealed to the British public to take interest in the affairs of India and through the imminent general elections influence the government in the right direction. He referred to recent enactments in the teeth of Indian opposition by Lord Curzon which alienated the people of India, such as the Official Secrets Act, the Universities Act, and the Universities Validating Act. He pointed out that the people of India themselves had very little say in the management of their own affairs. There was no Indian on the Viceroy's Executive Council and the Indian representation in the Legislative Councils was wholly inadequate. Englishmen were wont to boast of their work of "civilising India", but did they know that more than 90 per cent of the population of the country was illiterate, and the first failure of rains brought the whole population in the affected regions to the verge of starvation? He asserted that so long as there existed in India a ruling class separate and distinct from the ruled, it was futile to hope for any improvement in the condition of the people.

Sir William Wedderburn was so impressed by Lajpat Rai's performance in England that he deputed him to visit the United States to put across the grievances of Indian people and their demands for constitutional reforms. On

30 August, Lajpat Rai wrote home: "I am going to America on duty. I have been really doing the work of 'sappers and miners' here, and I am required to do the same work in America. I would gladly do any work that is likely to be of any use to my country, however troublesome it may be."

During his month-long stay in the United States, Lajpat Rai was even more blunt in his speeches and writings than he had been in England. He held England responsible for the poverty and backwardness of India, and asserted that famines and other woes of India were the direct consequence of British policies of exploiting India as a market. The British were, he charged, running Indian industries and controlling exports so that British goods and commerce could have the whole field to themselves.

Lajpat Rai's work in England and the U.S.A. was appreciated by the Congress leaders. For him it was certainly a great distinction to be coupled with Gokhale as an advocate of Indian nationalism in the heart of the British Empire. However, after his return to India he did not boast about his work, but drew lessons for himself and his country from what he had witnessed. He was impressed by the intense desire for political liberty and freedom that filled the people of European countries he had visited in which the "press, the pulpit and the platform were all ringing with the cries of away with the tyrants and autocrats who stood in the way of democracy". In contrast, the political scene in India was marked by "apathy, want of earnestness, timidity and the consequent failure of the political agitation." "What sacrifices do we undergo to deserve what we want?" he asked. "Anything more than the trouble of attending the annual sessions of the Congress?"

Even before leaving for England, Lajpat Rai had flayed the policies of Lord Curzon, and especially the partition of Bengal. His foreign trip had convinced him that not much could be expected from appeals to the British political parties whether they were Liberal or Conservative. And a direct appeal to the British electorate had its own limitations, because of its preoccupation with domestic issues. He was convinced that ultimately the people of India had to depend on their own efforts, if they wanted to improve their lot.

In December 1905 at the Banaras Congress over which Gokhale presided Lajpat Rai spoke strongly on the partition of Bengal. "Lord Curzon had done a great service to India," he said, "by provoking the lion in his own den and rousing him to a sense of consciousness of his being a lion." "There are times, gentlemen," he added, "when I am inclined to pray that from time to time God might be pleased to send Viceroys like Lord Curzon to this country, in order to awaken the people of this country to a sense of their responsibility." The partition of Bengal had raised the political temperature in the country. At the Banaras session there were currents and undercurrents of discontent. The young radicals (who later came to be known as Extremists) were sharpening their knives. The Subjects Committee which decided the resolutions for the plenary session got bogged down on the very first resolution welcoming the Prince of Wales (later King George V) to India. Lajpat Rai objected to the resolution on the grounds that India was suffering from famine and smarting under Curzon's repressive measures and was in no mood to stage a pageantry for the royal couple. The Prince was invited to the Banaras session of the Congress but had not responded. Bal Gangadhar Tilak supported Lajpat Rai, but the original resolution of welcome to the Prince was passed by a majority in the Subjects Committee. Lajpat Rai and his supporters threatened to oppose the resolution in the plenary session. For twenty years the Congress leadership had scrupulously kept the royal family out of politics; it did not want to tarnish its image in England just when a Liberal government had come to office.

There was much excitement in the Congress camp on the night of 27 December and the local Congress leaders even feared a riot. On the following day just before the plenary session was scheduled to begin, Gokhale sent for Lajpat Rai and made a "personal appeal" to him not to oppose the resolution and sought his assistance in persuading Tilak and the Bengali Extremists to exercise a similar restraint. While the controversial resolution was being debated in the plenary session, the opponents of the resolution stayed out of the Congress pavilion; some Bengali delegates had to be forcibly kept out by Lajpat Rai and S.S. Bapat, an adherent of Tilak. On his part, Gokhale was sporting enough to agree that the Congress records would not show the resolution as having been passed unanimously.

The tensions released by the partition of Bengal had been contained at the Banaras Congress session. But the battle lines between the Congress Old Guard led by the adherents of Pherozeshah Mehta and the emerging Bengal-Maharashtra-Punjab Extremist alliance had been drawn. A clash had been avoided by Gokhale's acumen, patience, tact and his personal equation with Lajpat Rai, and the latter's influence over Tilak.

In the few months preceding the Banaras Congress session Lajpat Rai had been able to establish a rapport with Gokhale. He had been his teammate for the education of British public before the general elections. He was aware of the tension between Gokhale and Tilak. His own political views were closer to those of Tilak, but he was perceptive enough to realise that Gokhale's ability, patriotism and charisma were great assets for the mainstream Congress movement, and that any division in the Congress ranks would only make the party play into the hands of the British rulers.

From 1905 onwards, Lajpat Rai became increasingly involved in nationalist politics. He did not break his links with the Arya Samaj and the D.A.V. College.

When there was a famine or a catastrophe such as the earthquake in the Kangra valley, he hastened to throw himself into relief operations. There was, however, no doubt about the growing primacy of the nationalist politics in Lajpat Rai's thoughts and activities.

The material published in this volume has been drawn from G.K. Gokhale's papers, records of the Home Department (Political) and *Report of the Indian Famine Commission*, 1901 in the National Archives of India. The newspapers and journals that have been consulted are—*The Panjabee, The Tribune*, *The Hindustan Review*, *Kayastha Samachar*, *The Hindustan Review and Kayastha Samachar, Selections from the Vernacular Newspapers Published in the Punjab*, *India* (London), *Abhyudaya*, a Hindi weekly, and *Zamana*, an Urdu monthly. Some of the speeches, articles and letters have been reproduced from *Reports of the Proceedings of the Indian National Congress,* V.C. Joshi (ed.), *Lala Lajpat Rai—Writings and Speeches*, Volume I, *Lala Lajpat Rai—The Man in His Word*, Lal Chand Falak (ed.), *Europe, America ke Safar ke Halat*, and J.S. Dhanki (ed.), *Perspectives on Indian National Movement—Selected Correspondence of Lala Lajpat Rai.* Prof. S.R. Mehrotra has made available to us a copy of a letter written by Lajpat Rai to William Wedderburn.

I am grateful to the Directors and staff of the Nehru Memorial Museum & Library and the National Archives of India for extending full cooperation to us.

I acknowledge with thanks the support provided by the Ministry of Tourism and Culture to the project.

I would like to express my appreciation of the contribution made by my colleagues in the project—Madan G. Gandhi, Sangam Lal, A.K. Avasthi, S.L. Manchanda and Ritu Bhagat. The typescript of the volume was prepared by Saroj Kumar Bindhani.

The English translation of the Hindi material has been done by Prof. S.C. Narula and of the Urdu material by Shri Jai Ratan and for the first volume of this series also this work was undertaken by them as also by Shri J.P. Uniyal who translated from Hindi for which I thank them.

I am specially thankful to Shri Satya Paul, Secretary of the Servants of the People Society, for taking keen interest in this project and extending all help and cooperation, whenever required. He was assisted by Shri R. Mani.

B.R.N.

1
THE INDIAN NATIONAL CONGRESS

1. Defects of the Congress and Remedies[1]

The date fixed for the celebration of the annual national festival of the educated Indians is drawing near and it is, I think, time to spend a few hours and devote a few thoughts to its programme, and see if there is any possibility of some serious business being gone through, at the next meeting, along with the usual festivities.[2] I purposely call it a festival, because as hitherto conducted it is at best only a festival—an occasion on which some educated Indians put on their best dresses, take a trip to one of the best cities in India, and after a year's hard struggle in life enjoy a few days' holiday, and derive the greatest pleasure they can from seeing sights, meeting friends, making acquaintances, exchanging greetings, purchasing presents, etc., in short, giving themselves up as completely as circumstances permit to mirth and merriment. Some of them enjoy all the fun at the cost of others. There are others who make name and add to their fame, if they are already on the ladder, by uttering plausibly-worded platitudes and well-disguised commonplaces in the shape of speeches. Even the last are losing their charm, as platitudes have become too common, and the commonplaces too apparent, to delude any longer the people who are possessed of even ordinary intelligence and share a little, at least, of common sense. I do not know if the Anglo-Indians are much to be blamed, if they judge the prosperity of British India by the appearance and evidently rich surroundings of the Congress. The delegates mostly look well-to-do people who can spare enough money for taste, elegance and show. The decorations, receptions, furnishings, etc. are done on a scale which can hardly lend weight to our contention of being perhaps the poorest people on the face of the globe. This so-called political work done after all this fuss is of such a doubtful and ephemeral character as to raise serious doubts in the minds of even enthusiasts—whether we are not frittering away our energies in trifles and, besides wasting away our own time and money, keeping the nation in delusion and under false hopes. I am not prepared to deny that even as festival alone the annual meeting is not without its value and should not therefore be altogether given up. Let me assure you,

1. *Lala Lajpat Rai—The Man in His Word* (Madras, 1907), pp. 225-41; originally published in *Kayastha Samachar* (English monthly published from Allahabad) of November 1901.
2. The reference was to the forthcoming Congress session to be held at Calcutta in December 1901.

   After attending the Congress session at Bombay in 1889 Lajpat Rai's enthusiasm for the party had abated and since then he had attended only two annual sessions—one in 1893 and another in 1900—both held at Lahore.

my brethren of the Congress, that by saying these unpleasant things, I mean no offence to anybody. I am one of you, and all that I have said above applies to me with equal, perhaps greater, force than to anybody else. Nor do I mean there are no exceptions. There are honourable and good men amongst us who can be truly called patriots but their number is so small that I will prefer to make no exception. The truth is that till now we have not realised the full significance of this "patriotism". We have been taking it easy, and never realised in our heart of hearts that patriotism is a cult requiring the most rigid and ascetic course of life from its devotees. It is only one degree lower than the absolute self-denial of a sannyasi. What I am anxious for is to see if it is not possible to achieve better and more laudable results from this annual gathering of the best and most intelligent of the educated Indians. As at present conducted, its principal defects are:

(1) Its unwieldy size which precludes the very idea of serious work whether in the shape of deliberation, discussion or action.

(2) The anxiety to speak in the name of all Indians, a good many of whom think otherwise, and repudiate all sympathy with it. This attempt at forced union is mostly at the bottom of the discontent which at present prevails even amongst those who have all along supported it, and who think that till now the Congress agitation has been a mere waste of energies, funds and opportunities.

(3) The want of sense of real responsibility amongst its members, which results in total inactivity during the course of the year.

(4) The failure to afford the opportunity of comparing notes and exchanging views, by which the unity of the nation, or at least of its principal components, may be really furthered and definite progress in this direction may lead to more exertion towards the same end.

This is mainly due to the mismanagement of the short time that is at the disposal of the delegates owing to the lengthy programme of speeches and resolutions, etc.

(5) Failure to take some practical steps to check the growing poverty of the country and to dispel ignorance, which is still the crying need of India.

(6) Its unbounded but unreasonably mistaken confidence in its power to enforce the redress of the grievances, to extort political privilege by the passing of resolutions and the making of speeches, which result in misleading the nation to place unjustifiable faith in the over-efficacy of the Congress agitation, and fails to impress upon them the necessity of a stupendous preparation attended with great sacrifices and mighty efforts before even one step can be gained in the ascent to political progress. The temple of freedom is not easily opened unto those who claim admission into it by simply knocking at its gates. Mere aspiration is no guarantee of success. The intending worshipper or claimant for admission must show his mettle by sacrifices and trials before he can obtain

the status of a pilgrim, because the goddess of liberty is so jealous of its sanctity that it would admit none but those tried of unquestionable sincerity, devotion and faith.

I will stop for the present and suggest remedies which in my opinion are calculated to remove the defects and which might be considered by Congressmen before they meet at Calcutta, and then adopt or reject them with such modifications or alterations as to them seem desirable.

Under clause (1) I will suggest that the sitting of the general assembly be shortened, as much as may be possible to do, at once. In no case should it exceed two days with a maximum sitting of 5 hours every day at the most. The programme might be something as follows:

(a) Welcome by the Chairman of the Reception Committee who will in it propose the President elect as the nominee of the Indian Congress Committee.[3]

(b) Speech of the President.

(c) Omnibus resolution including all matters and subjects upon which the Congress has, by the end of the preceding year, pronounced definite views and upon which public opinion in this country is practically settled.

(d) Resolutions upon new subjects that have cropped up during the course of the year, which the Indian Congress Committee have recommended for inclusion in the Congress programme, and upon which there is a practical unanimity of opinion between Indians of all classes, creeds and shades of opinion.

(e) Such other subjects recommended by the Indian Congress Committee upon which there is a likelihood of a difference of opinion.

In the general assembly no speaker, whether the proposer or the supporter, should be allowed to exceed the limits of 10 or 15 minutes respectively, except the Chairman of the Reception Committee, the President or the proposer of the resolution or amendment falling under clause (e).

This will leave the different committees, sub-committees and other special conferences, already organised or to be organised, sufficient time to devote to serious work requiring discussion and deliberation; as, for example, the Indian Congress Committee should every session devote at least some hours to the question of starting political organisations in places where there are none, and perfecting those which already exist, 2ndly, the education committee and, 3rdly, the industrial committee. With the work of these two latter we will deal under clause (5).

Under clause (2) I will suggest (a) total discontinuance of all such practices

3. The Indian Congress Committee, which was constituted during the Lucknow session of the Congress in 1899, consisted of 45 members and acted as the executive committee of the Congress.

as are, if at all, adopted, encouraged or connived at to bring in such people to the Congress as are otherwise either not eligible for its membership, or do not possess sufficient interest therein, or are of no use to it, except in increasing the number of delegates from a particular class. It should be the business and duty of every Congressman to jealously maintain the honour, the dignity and the prestige of the Congress, and nothing should be allowed or encouraged which has even the least semblance of being dishonourable, undignified, or likely to lower its reputation or to lessen its sense of self-respect.

(b) The number of subjects upon which there is any likelihood of a reasonable friction existing, or coming into existence, between members belonging to the different religious nationalities in India, ought to be reduced to a minimum, if there is still any room for the same, in the agenda paper of the general assembly, such subjects being reserved for separate treatment by the inclusive organisations of these nationalities. This will lead to the necessity of a Hindu political or a semi-political congress or conference being organised, and the sooner it is done the better. As at present situated, the absence of such an organisation places the Hindus at a distinct disadvantage, and takes away from them the chances of a united action or of a united expression of opinion upon matters, which affect the unity, prosperity, the well-being and generally the interest of Hindus all over India. In order to leave no room for doubt as to the necessity for this step I will be more specific. In my opinion it should be the business of such a Hindu congress or conference to support and take, as far as possible, such steps which might conduce to their unity and strength as a religious nationality as, for instance, the language question, the question of characters, the advisability of having common text-books, the teaching of Sanskrit language and literature all over India, the taking of steps which might lead to the protection of Hindu orphans from the hands of the proselytising agencies of other denominations and, if necessary, to record a protest against those confidential circulars of the Government, which aim at the favouring of other communities to the loss of the Hindus. In my humble opinion it is futile to attempt at a chimerical and premature union of the various religious nationalities that are to be found in India, the principal of which are the Hindus, the Mohammedans and the Christians. The wisest course will be to wait for a physical union and to aim at the same. This is impossible to achieve till these nationalities have had a free hand to strengthen themselves, and to exhaust all means by which they can do so at no cost to the other or others. A physical union presupposes a common danger and a conviction that they cannot overcome it or meet it but by uniting and combining against a common foe. At present this conviction is wanting, and there is still lurking in the mind of at least one community, that they can crush the other or others. So long as one community looks the other down and talks of it with contempt, it is ridiculous, nay suicidal, for the latter to try to force a union and make advances which are liable to be misconstrued as the outcome of fear, or of expediency, or of treachery. I quite agree with a talented writer in the *Kayastha Samachar* that the springing up of so many castes or conferences against the Hindus is a menace to the development of the idea of Hindu nationality and might lead to harm. He has, I think, done a distinct service to the cause of Hindu nationality by giving public expression to an idea, which has been causing a serious anxiety to many a lover of the idea of Hindu nationality or to many a Hindu nationalist. It is time that the leaders and promoters of these conferences took note of the warning so judiciously given—not to destroy the fabrics which they have constructed, but to so mould and guide them as to make them instrumental in the eventful construction and building up of Hindu nationality. Theirs should be the attempt to destroy the sub-castes, to bring about a fusion of the different sub-divisions in castes, and to eventually bring round Hinduism to its four original castes. There will be ample time then to think and talk of the evils of caste system, and modifications in the latter, to suit the requirements of the time. Then the conferences can be used to spread education amongst the backward classes and to bring them to the level of the time, but their promoters ought to proceed very carefully, lest in their efforts to unite the sub-divisions of a caste they create permanent schisms between the different main castes, and create barriers amongst them, impeding the fructification and the realization of Hindu nationality. It is therefore far immature and far before the time to talk of marriages between the different castes of Hindus as it is futile to think of bringing about a complete political union of Hindus and Mohammedans at once.

The Mohammedans think that the Hindus are physically inferior to them, and wanting in certain qualities—energy, pluck, boldness, fearlessness, stamina, character, capacity to command and ability to take a stand—which go to make a good, effective and capable administrator. But, in short, the Mohammedans think that they belong to a race of rulers, and their fellow-subjects, the Hindus, having been in slavery so long, cannot claim an equality with them in the scale of nations. Even the otherwise amiable Sir Syed[4] talked of Hindus with

4. Syed Ahmed Khan (1817-1898); an eminent Muslim leader, scholar, educationist and politician who first supported the Congress but later turned against it; started career as a judicial officer under the East India Company in 1838 and retired as a Subordinate Judge in 1878; made Honorary Fellow of Royal Asiatic Society in 1864; founded Translation Society in 1864 which later was renamed as the Scientific Society; started *Aligarh Institute Gazette*, a bi-lingual (Urdu and English) weekly, in 1866 and *Tahzib-al-Akhlaq* (*Social Reformer*) in 1870; founded the Mohammedan Anglo-Oriental College in 1875 which later became the Aligarh Muslim University; member, Indian Legislative Council, 1878-82; knighted in 1888; works include *The Causes of the Indian Revolt* and *Indian Mussalmans*.

contempt. The result is that every Mohammedan, be he a *julaha* or a *penya* or the like, thinks that he can dominate over the Hindus and claim a superiority over them in the art of governing. The latter, on the other hand, retort that, as a nation, they have never displayed cowardliness, always proving equal to the occasion whenever necessity forced them to take up arms and assert their dignity as men, as is abundantly evident from the history of the Rajputs, the Sikhs and the Mahrattas, and that the physical inferiority of certain of their sections, even if admitted, is so much counterbalanced by their intellectual and moral superiority over their rivals that, in this age of science and art, they think they are sure to win the race and acquire qualification which alone can confer a political status in these days of learning and knowledge.

This is not the occasion to discuss how far these claims are well-founded, but it is a fact that a large class of educated Mohammedans keep aloof from the Hindus and suspect their organisations and agitations as likely to prejudice them in the race for progress and advancement. They think they have better chances of political prosperity as a separate nationality and in keeping aloof from the majority who are Hindus. There are a good many far-seeing men amongst them who can read the signs of the times and think that this game won't pay, but the number, on the other hand, is preponderant, because in the case of the leaders especially, and of other newly-educated young Mohammedans generally, personal benefit which follows this line of policy lends great weight to the other arguments and considerations by which their present political attitude aspires to be actuated. All welcome therefore to those who are prepared to foresee the future and join with the Hindus in the struggle for political rights. Let therefore be a general assembly which can voice the joint aspirations of such Hindus, Mohammedans and Christians by all means, but let not this general assembly stand in the way of Hindu progress and, in the name of a higher, though at present impracticable, impulse, lull them to sleep over their interests as such, make them forego the opportunities of furthering their own unity, *inter se*, and neglect the placing of it on a firm, sound and unassailable basis. Once wisely led, no power in the world can stand in their way, retard their progress and stifle their aspirations. The Hindus have existed as a nation since times to which the memory of man runneth not, in weal or woe they have maintained their individual existence and have, from time to time, given to the world lessons in religion and morality, which even today when the sun of European civilization is at its zenith shine in the splendour of their purity and in the grandeur of their truth. Are they then to die as a nation in this twentieth century of the *Vikram* era? True, that just now we are in a very sad plight and if judged by the national vices that have crept into our society, and by their national weaknesses which are too numerous to be mentioned here, the last ray of hope often disappears and turns the most hopeful optimist into a disappointed pessimist. It is only in unity that the safety of the Hindus lies. No wise or prudent Hindu can therefore neglect the opportunities of seeking the safety. Let them once make up their mind to be a united nation and to continue as such. Let them once be inspired by a living faith in their future, and by a conviction that when God has willed the individuality of a nation and given it a mission to perform. He has at the same time given the people constituting that nation the means, power, and capacity, by which they can successively resist all those forces which tend to disintegrate or disorganise them, and which trace their existence as a nation.

True, that our selfishness and estrangement from national interests is simply indescribable. There have been and there are Hindus who have now and then sold the nation and its interests to the enemy, and aggrandised themselves at the cost of the former, still to a close and thoughtful observer who can feel the pulse of the nation and who has a mind and capacity to read the signs of the time; enough of life and vitality seems yet to be left in Hindus to enable the latter to respond to skilful treatment and kind and devoted nursing. Skill and devotion must therefore be put forth for this purpose by the whole Hindu community or at least by the thinking portion of it. It is on these grounds therefore that I suggest the formation of a Hindu congress or conference to meet annually at the place of the Congress, and to discuss only such matters and devise such measures as are likely to further the cause of Hindu unity and otherwise tend to the well-being and prosperity of the Hindus as such. Of course, such an assembly should only consist of, not a very large number of men, say 100 of the best and the most representative of Hindus. One word about the Social Conference. The Indian Social Conference as at present constituted is no more a Hindu organisation than the Congress. You might as well call the latter also a Hindu Congress. It is as powerless to do anything for the Hindus exclusively as the latter. In the anxiety to give it a national character the Mohammedans and Christians have been allowed to take part in its deliberations, and resolutions have been altered and weakened, nay rendered meaningless, in the attempt to make them acceptable to all. Here again Hindu interests, as such, have been sacrificed for a false idea of nationality and in the attempt to achieve it at once. For example, what on earth have the Christians and Mohammedans to do with the *Shuddhi* movement? The *Shuddhi* movement, which aims at the purification and readmission of all Hindu apostates to the Hindu fold, is a purely Hindu movement, in which the Hindus alone are interested. The same may be said of the resolution dealing with orphans. At the last Conference both these resolutions had to be modified into vague generalities which deprived the propositions of much of their force and effect, and rendered them incapable of producing any impression either on the public or on the Government. Then the Conference is a gathering and an assembly of advanced Hindus and does not represent the orthodox portion of the community who are still in an overwhelming majority over their English-educated brothers. Then again, the Conference, as at present constituted, cannot ventilate the grievances of the Hindus and is not in a position to speak for them. Hence the necessity of a general Hindu organisation with its provincial branches all over India. The functions and constitution of the provincial branches will be similar to those of the many Islamic *anjumans* already existing in the country, and without criticising the policy of the Government in the abstract, without passing resolutions on abstract political propositions, these Hindus organisations will confine themselves to concrete objects and tangible grievances. As such, the country will not be deprived of the valuable assistance which it can get from the cooperation of those Hindus who are in the employ of the Government and who in fact constitute the pick and the cream of the nation. I have been rather too long on this part of the subject but the importance of the point necessitated a full expression of my views. Thereupon clause (2) requires no further comments.

Under clause (3) I will suggest that only responsible and really working men should be selected as members of the Indian Congress Committee. Men whose interest in the movement is confined to annual visits ought not to find a place on this Committee. One of the best methods of testing one's earnestness in a particular cause is to see if he is prepared to spend his money for the same. I will therefore repeat the proposal that was made at the last meeting of the Congress at Lahore by one of the Punjabi delegates, and which was unceremoniously dismissed at the general meeting and ridiculed in the meeting of the Subjects Committee by two of our "revered" leaders, that every member of the Indian Congress Committee should be required to pay at least Rs. 5 a month towards the funds of the Congress. The Provincial Committees, moreover, ought to see that only such men are placed on this Committee who take a real interest in the political reform movement, and who are prepared to undergo some amount of sacrifice in the cause of the country's political progress. Members who fail to attend even one meeting in the course of the year ought to be disqualified for re-election. Clause (4) does not require any further comment. The remedies suggested under clause (1) will remove this complaint.

Under clause (5) I will suggest that the least that should be undertaken at once is the employment of a paid officer whose business should be to go round and collect information on both these heads. I am glad to find that the Indian Congress Committee have decided to pass a resolution whereby it is proposed to ask the Government to undertake an industrial survey of the country. This is a right move, no doubt, but the mere passing of the resolution does not advance us one inch in the cause which we have at heart. In my opinion we ought to be prepared to give a more substantial proof of our earnestness by voting a certain amount of money to be spent in the coming year by ourselves on the object in question. One year's experience will give us sufficient ground to judge of the usefulness of the project and will strengthen our demand. I am afraid I have already exceeded the limits of an ordinary article and must stop here for the present.

2. Grievances of Punjab Delegates and Reaction of the Congress[1]

I

I daresay you and your readers will like to know of the protest which was entered by the Punjab delegates at the last meeting of the Indian National Congress against the abolition of the Indian Congress Committee at Calcutta in 1901.[2] Well, I propose to give you an account of the impressions formed by me of the last meeting of the Congress and in the course of the same will make mention of the protest also. I reached Bombay at night on the 25th of December 1904 and was accommodated at the house of a local Arya Samajist in accordance with the arrangements kindly made for us by Swamis Vasheshra Nand and Nitya Nand. With me were my friends L. Dwarka Das, L. Tek Chand, L. Jagan Nath and L. Debi Parshad. Early in the morning on the 26th we went to the Congress camp near the Colaba railway station and found that with the exception of Dr. Ram Kishen from Amritsar no other Punjabi was staying there. We had expected that some letters would be waiting there for us but finding none we had to return rather disappointed. In the reading room pavilion we found a good number of the last issue of the *Panjabee* which had evidently been sent to my address and opened there in my absence. From the camp we proceeded to the rooms of the Presidency Association and there met Mr. Ganpat Rai and Mr. Sinha. Mr. Sinha told us that Sir Henry Cotton[3] was very anxious to meet

1. Article written in two parts and published in *The Panjabee* of 6 February and 6 March 1905 respectively.
2. At the Calcutta session of the Congress held in 1901 the Indian Congress Committee was completely ignored and no elections to it were allowed. Protesting against this, the Punjab delegates to the Bombay Congress held in 1904 and threatened to secede from the Congress. They also protested against the non-adoption of a Congress constitution so far which, they thought, was necessary for the smooth running of the organization.
3. (1845-1915); I.C.S.; served in Bengal for several years and thereafter at the Centre; after retirement in 1902 took active part in the Congress and became its President in 1904; active member of British Committee of the Indian National Congress; M.P. 1906-10; works include *Memorandum on the Land Tenures of Bengal* (1884), *India in Transition* (1885) and *Indian and Home Memories* (1911).

the Punjabees and hear their grievances and that he had several times enquired for them. At about 12 noon we entered the Congress *pandal* which was a splendid structure made to accommodate a good number of people and tastefully decorated. To the right of the *pandal* seats had been assigned for the Madras delegates, and behind them for those of the United Provinces of Agra and Oudh and also for Punjab. We found that a goodly number of these seats had been occupied by the Bombay delegates as their seats being in the background some of them were very anxious to get to the front. The gentlemen of the Reception Committee had, however, to point this out to them and it was not till after a good deal of pressure that they made room for those for whom the seats were meant. We were glad to observe that unlike Calcutta the good sense of the Bombayites eventually prevailed and they submitted to the orders of the authorities in-charge. Thus it was not without some difficulty that all our friends from the Punjab could get proper seats. A little after we learnt from Mr. Roshan Lal, Bar-at-law, that he and Mr. Ganpat Rai had seen Sir Henry Cotton who was very anxious to see the Punjab delegates, to hear their grievances and to explain matters to them. Mr. Roshan Lal added that Sir Henry Cotton said that he had full sympathy with the demand of the Punjabees but that on talking over the matter with Mr. Dadabhai Naoroji[4] and other leaders of the Congress they were of opinion that the time had not yet come to give a constitution to the Congress. We concluded therefrom that the question had thus been practically decided and our protest was not likely to bear any fruit. Soon after, we were treated to a magnificent speech from Sir Pherozeshah Mehta.[5] Sir Pherozeshah is an old, experienced and accomplished speaker and knows how to crush those who differ from him under the weight of strong pungent remarks, both sarcastic as well as witty. Be it said to his credit that he is unsurpassably frank and open. He knows not how to mince matters or to conceal his real thoughts by the use of cumbersome, vague platitudes which may mean nothing or anything.

4. (1825-1917); popularly known as Grand Old Man of India; taught mathematics and natural philosophy at Elphinstone College, Bombay, 1854; Dewan of Baroda, 1873; member, Bombay Legislative Council, 1885-87; President, Indian National Congress, 1886, 1893 and 1906; member, British Parliament, 1892-95; member, Royal Commission on Indian Expendiure, 1896; works include *Poverty and Un-British Rule in India* (1901).
5. (1845-1915); barrister of Bombay; thrice Chairman of Bombay Corporation; one of the founders of the Bombay Presidency Association; founder-member of Indian National Congress and its President in 1890; member, Bombay Legislative Council, 1887-89 and 1893-94; President, Bombay Provincial Conference, 1892; member, Imperial Legislative Council, 1894-96 and 1898-1901; Vice-Chancellor of Bombay University.

Autocratic and self-opinionated, witty or whatever may be said of him, he is what he is and what he means to be. There is not much beating about the bush in the man. He speaks out his mind plainly and strongly and gives it hot to those who do not agree with him, though at times he softens the sting of his cutting sarcasm by an admirable use of well-chosen wit. In his speech he has plainly told the people what in his opinion is the real function of the Congress. After refuting the charge often brought against the Congress that they are only spasmodically wasting their energies and that the Congress is nothing more than a *tamasha* where a lot of money is wantonly thrown away, by explaining that they do not spend much on the spectacular side of the business and that what little is spent in that way is justifiable, he proceeds to say:

> But if you realise it clearly and fully, there is no purpose more important, no mission more sacred, than the one that the Congress fulfils in the three short days to which it confines its sessions. It would be absurd to say that the Congress meets to deliberate on, discuss and decide, all the important subjects with which it deals. That task must be and is largely performed in the course of the year by such institutions as we may possess for forming Indian public opinion, in the common intercourse of social life, in local bodies more or less active, in the native press which is undoubtedly daily growing more and more capable and potent. At the end of the year we all meet together from different parts of the country, representatives of the people, not selected, it is true, by any authoritative or scientific process, but still representative in all the various ways in which virtual representation works itself out in the early stages of its progressive development, representatives who are of the people and in immediate touch and contact with them, representatives realizing in themselves the wants, the wishes, the sentiments, the aspirations of the people, representatives whose education has qualified them to ponder over grave questions of policy and principle in their application to the administration and government of this country in all their complex relations of a foreign rule, representatives into whom education has instilled an earnest, devoted, and enlightened loyalty to the British Crown and a keen solicitude for the safety and permanence of the British Empire in which, they are firmly persuaded, lie implanted the roots of the welfare, the prosperity and the good government of this country. I say we delegates, representatives of the people, meet together at the end of the year to give voice to the public opinion of the country taking shape and formulating throughout the year, to present our Petition of Rights, our Grand Remonstrance, our appeal and our prayer for a firm and unfaltering grasp of a policy of wisdom and righteousness, for the reversal of retrograde measures inconsistent with such a policy

> and for the adoption of means steadily ensuring the gradual development of free political progress. 'Broadening slowly down from precedent to precedent.'
>
> Such an appeal and such a prayer can be most effectively offered at a great gathering like this by the unanimous voice of delegates assembling from all parts of the country.

You may allow me to add that after a careful study of the matter and on closely observing the sentiments and attitude of several other Congress leaders this seems to be the ruling idea in the Congress camp now. Several other leaders spoke to us in the same strain and denied in so many words that the Congress had any constructive or educational mission. Herein, in fact, we find the crux of the whole opposition to the idea of having any constitution for, or giving any permanent organisation to, the Congress. I reserve a statement of my own views on the question for a future occasion and begging your pardon for this digression will proceed with my account. Sir Mehta gave a bit of his mind to the new scheme of Bengal politicians who have of late been attempting to place the industrial revival problem in the forefront of patriotic work and saying rather openly that the sort of political agitation we have been carrying on in the past cannot of necessity carry much benefit or bear much fruit. It may be in the recollection of your readers that Mr. A. Chaudhri of Bengal, who presided at the last sitting of the Provincial Conference in Bengal, sounded a note of warning against our pinning much faith on impotent political agitation consisting of speeches and resolutions only.

In his anxiety to give an emphasis to his idea of subordinating more agitation to more solid work, Mr. A. Chaudhri is believed to have said rather plaintively that using the word in its true sense a subject race could have no politics. However strange this may appear to Sir Mehta and other great men of his thinking and so as to be characterised as a homily, we are afraid the remark was only too true in the present political state of this unfortunate country. However, more of this in its proper place. Sir Mehta's reply to this was both characteristic and pungent. He characterised the thesis as "utterly unhistoric and unmanly," and proceeded to beg the pardon of his Bengali friends in order to tell them how he regarded them. In his opinion they were "the Esaus of Bengal ready to sell their birthright for a mess of pottage." In a preceding sentence he had even insinuated that they (his Bengali friends) were perhaps "endeavouring to coax their European friends to help them by specious professions of giving up their favourite vice of excessive political agitation and turning out reformed characters." A voice from the Bengal camp protested against these insinuations and Sir Mehta in his own unsurpassably clever manner did not fail to express satisfaction at it. It was thus that the Chairman of the

Reception Committee at Bombay disposed of those friendly critics with whom he did not agree and who he knew were still with the Congress and in fact were present, Mr. A. Chaudhri himself being present as a delegate. The speech, it need not be said, was a masterpiece and was very eloquently delivered in a clear resonant voice. Whatever one may think of Sir Mehta's views about the mission of the Congress and its methods of work and whatever view one may hold of his crushing intolerance of those who happen to differ from him, there cannot be the least doubt about the great and extraordinary abilities that are centred in him. A man of his talents is bound to gain influence wherever he happens to move. It is no wonder therefore that according to the *Times of India* the Bombay Corporation is nothing more than Sir Mehta and that Sir Mehta is really the Bombay Corporation. The unbounded influence which Sir Mehta commands in Bombay, both in official as well as unofficial circles, is a fitting testimony to his towering intellect and to his versatile genius. If there was ever a man whom a habit of fearless expression of his views and a bold defiant criticism of his opponents and adversaries had placed at the highest pinnacle of power which is possible for all Indians to achieve that man is Sir Pherozeshah Mehta. No wonder then that in the Congress he is supreme and his word is law. Even the "Esaus" of Bengal, altogether smarting under his arrows, did not dare even whisper a word of indignation or protest at the rather merciless dissection they had been subjected to in the address of welcome given to them as delegates by the Chairman of the Reception Committee. We had an occasion to see several Bengali delegates and talked to them on the subject of the Indian Congress Committee; we found that they were very indignant at this treatment of their leaders and that there were a large number of Bengal delegates who agreed with us in the matter of the Indian Congress Committee, but to our surprise and astonishment we experienced latterly that these Bengalis who are so loud in denouncing the acts of Government were entirely without a tongue to protest against the oppressive attitude of their own leaders. Men who are so impatient of the "capital I" in Lord Curzon[6] have to say nothing but to listen in mute admiration to the "capital I" of the Indian National Congress. However, to return to our narrative, the speech of the Chairman of the Reception Committee was followed by the election of the President and his inaugural address, after which came on the election of the Subjects Committee. We had in the morning drafted the protest, which the Indian Association of the Punjab had instructed us to lodge. In a private meeting of the Punjab delegates held in the *pandal* itself to elect our members for the Subjects Committee we got that protest

6. George Nathaniel Curzon (1859-1925); Under-Secretary of State for India, 1891-99; Viceroy of India, 1899-1905; Lord President of the Council and member of the War Cabinet, 1916-18; Foreign Secretary, 1919-24.

signed by as many as were present there. Then ensued a discussion as to whether we should send in any names for the Subjects Committee at all. Some of us were of opinion that our only business was to enter a protest and that, as the matter had apparently been already decided, there was no chance of our protest making any impression and that therefore we should only delegate one of us to attend the meeting of the Subjects Committee, hand over the protest and hear the decision and retire. Mr. Roshan Lal had told us that Mr. Kelkar[7] of the *Mahratta* had represented our case very strongly and forcibly before Sir Henry Cotton and that he had expressed an opinion that the time had not come to give a constitution to the Congress. However, as there seemed to be considerable difference of opinion amongst the delegates on the question of electing members for the Subjects Committee we eventually decided to proceed formally and put Rai Sahib Murli Dhar[8] in the chair. On the matter being put to vote it was decided by the majority that we should elect the following gentlemen to attend the Subjects Committee in order to enter our protest against the abolition of the Indian Congress Committee and to act on the said Committee—Rai Sahib Murli Dhar, Lala Dharam Dass, Mr. Ganpat Rai, Mr. Roshan Lal, Pandit Rambhaj Dutt[9] and Dr. Parma Nand. Consequently, these gentlemen attended the meeting of the Subjects Committee held on the 26th. I declined to work on the Subjects Committee for reasons which need not be mentioned here. Our delegates presented their protest and the President promised that a full and patient hearing shall be given to what we may have to say on the subject in the meeting of the Subjects Committee to be held the next day. We were much gratified to learn the next day that on being asked to give names of speakers from the Punjab on the various resolutions to be proposed on the 27th December Rai Sahib Murli Dhar declined to speak or to take active part in the proceedings unless some satisfactory decision was come to in the matter of our protest. So our delegates maintained a firm attitude. Early the next morning it was agreed that I also should attend the meeting of the Subjects Committee to be held that day and open the discussion. In the very early part of the proceedings we were informed by Mr. V. Raghavachariar of Madras that he had made an engagement

7. N.C. Kelkar (1872-1947); a close associate of B.G. Tilak and editor of *Mahratta*, 1897-1919, and of *Kesari*, 1897-99 and 1901-31; President, Bombay Political Conference, 1920; member, Central Legislative Assembly, 1923 and 1926.
8. A distinguished lawyer of Punjab; attended, with Lajpat Rai, Allahabad Congress in 1888 and Bombay Congress in 1904; one of the organisers of Punjab Political Conference held at Ambala in 1906.
9. (1866-1923); a prominent leader of Arya Samaj in Punjab; played an important role in establishing Hindu Sahayak Sabhas to unify Hindu politicians of Punjab; member of Indian National Congress; edited two journals in association with his wife, Sarala Devi Choudharani.

with Sir William Wedderburn[10] to see us and hear what we had to say. In the meantime we discussed the matter over with the Hon'ble Pandit Madan Mohan Malaviya[11] and Lala Ganga Parshad.[12] Both of these gentleman expressed their agreement with our views and said that we must insist on having the Indian Congress Committee reappointed but should not insist on having the same members and the same strength as before. We said we were quite willing to accept a smaller committee. We then met Sir William Wedderburn and represented our grievance to him. He gave us a very patient hearing and expressed his views also, from which we gathered that in this matter at least we could not expect much help from that quarter. When coming out of the tent where this interview took place we met Sir Pherozeshah Mehta who asked us whether we were now satisfied. On our expressing that we had a firm faith in constitutional methods of work and that in our opinion the Congress was not likely to achieve much unless it was converted into a permanent organisation and worked under some sort of constitution, he plainly and unambiguously repeated what he had said in his speech about the real functions of the Congress. We understood him to deny the educational mission of the Congress, or that it was a permanent organisation. Coming to the question of the abolition of the Indian Congress Committee, he charged Mr. Nundy[13] and Lala Harkishen Lal[14] with not having proposed its re-election at the Calcutta session and that it was their fault that the matter did not come up before the Congress at all. He thought we had all been put up by Lala Harkishen Lal who had in his turn been put up by Mr. Nundy. We tried to disabuse him on this point and told him that although widely differing from Lala Harkishen Lal in other matters we considered this

10. (1838-1918); joined Indian Civil Service in 1860 and served in Bombay Presidency till 1867; Judge, Bombay High Court, 1885; President, Indian National Congress, 1889 and 1910; member, Royal Commission on Indian Expenditure, 1895-1900; Chairman, British Committee of Indian National Congress; M.P., 1893-1900.
11. (1861-1946); educationist and politician; edited *Hindustani*, *The Indian Union* and *Abhyudaya*; member, U.P. Legislative Council, 1902-12; President, Indian National Congress, 1909, 1918 and 1933; member, Imperial Legislative Council, 1910-20, and Central Legislative Assembly, 1924-30; member, Indian Industrial Commission, 1916; founded Nationalist Party in 1926; founder of Benares Hindu University, and its Vice-Chancellor, 1919-39; President, All India Hindu Mahasabha, 1923, 1924 and 1936; President of Sanatan Dharm Mahasabha; attended Second Round Table Conference in 1931.
12. (1863-1914); journalist and politician; founder-member of Indian National Congress; founded *The Indian Union* in 1886; member, U.P. Legislative Council.
13. Alfred Nundy; barrister and journalist; editor of *The Tribune*, 1898-1908.
14. (1864-1937); taught mathematics at Government College and Oriental College, Lahore; started legal practice in 1913; floated Punjab National Bank, People's Bank and Bharat Insurance Company; Chairman, Reception Committee of Lahore Congress, 1909; arrested under the martial law in Punjab in 1919; Minister in Punjab, 1921 23.

to be a matter of principle, and that too of great importance, and so were of one mind with him on this subject. Sir Mehta possesses a charming personality and one requires a very strong faith in his own views to resist the spell of his influence. I reserve the account of that night's proceedings of the Subjects Committee so far as our protest is concerned for another letter as the mail is about to close.

II

The Congress sitting till late on the 27th, the meeting of the Subjects Committee could not be convened until after 6 P.M. My friends, members of the Committee from the Punjab, having obtained the permission of the President for myself and others, we went in to find hardly any seats being available for us, so great was the rush. Immediately after, the President announced that the first business to be done that night was the hearing of the Punjab protest, and he called upon the Punjab delegates to open their case. My friends having already selected me for the duty I was asked to come in the centre and say what I wanted to say. I began by giving a brief history of the agitation for a constitution to be given to the Congress and pointed out that as far back as 1890 it was decided to have one and that subsequently the subject was from year to year before the Congress until at the Poona Congress session a committee was appointed to consider and discuss and submit a report to the Congress. This report, I pointed out, laid before the Congress in 1899 at Lucknow, was unanimous and was signed by all the different provincial leaders, including amongst others Mr. Surendranath Banerjea[15] and Mr. Mudholkar,[16] that it was read out in the meeting as the 1st item of business, though its consideration was postponed to the next day in order to allow full discussion over it and full consideration of the report in the Subjects Committee; that, eventually, the proposed constitution having been fully discussed and properly considered was, with certain modifications which were generally agreed to, put from the Chair[17] and carried with acclamation.

15. (1848-1925); joined I.C.S. in 1871 and dismissed in 1874; founder of Calcutta Indian Association (1876); founded *The Bengalee* in 1878 and edited it for a number of years; "moderate" leader of Congress and its President in 1895 and 1902; member of Bengal Legislative Council for several years, member, Imperial Legislative Council, 1913-20; Minister for Local Self-government in Bengal, 1921-23; works include *Nation in the Making*.
16. R.N. Mudholkar (1857-1921); lawyer and Congress leader of Central Provinces; Congress delegate to England in 1890; secretary, Reception Committee of Amraoti Congress, 1897; presided over C.P. and Berar Provincial Conference held at Raipur in 1897; sided with "moderates" after the split in the Congress in 1907; President, Indian National Congress, 1912.
17. R.C. Dutt (1848-1909); I.C.S. and first Indian economist to write on Indian agrarian problems;

This constitution, I said, was not the result of any impulse, neither was it framed in a hurry or carried by any chance vote, but was the deliberate decision of the Congress arrived at after careful sifting of all the pros and cons and after a very thoughtful discussion of the matter amongst the leaders as well as the general body of the Congressmen; that it was in accordance with this constitution and the rules mentioned therein that an Indian Congress Committee was appointed to manage the affairs of the Congress; and that this constitution was subsequently confirmed and acted upon by the Congress in its session of 1900 at Lahore, where a new committee was selected. In support of my contention I read passages from the speech of Mr. Mudholkar delivered at the Lucknow Congress in 1899. I then briefly referred to the work done by and the meetings held of the Indian Congress Committee in 1900 and 1901 and observed that the Indian Congress Committee could not be said to have had a fair trial, and that therefore the way in which it was silently buried at the Calcutta session was, to say the least, unconstitutional and high-handed. I added that the Punjab was not pledged to any particular committee or to any particular men, but what it wanted was an executive committee to supervise and be responsible for all political work in the country, and that the control and guidance of the Indian National Congress should vest in a properly constituted body rather than in individuals, however able, high-minded or self-sacrificing they may be. In justice to the chairman and the members I must say that I was patiently and attentively heard, as well as the two gentleman who followed me. These latter, viz. Lala Dharma Das and Dwarka Das, supported me in two short speeches. The chairman thereupon said that he having engagements elsewhere could not see the evening's business through. He, however, expressed his opinions, sympathising with the aspirations of the Punjab, but pointing out the practical difficulties in giving effect to them, and left the meeting, leaving Sir William Wedderburn to take the chair. Thereupon Mr. Krishna Swami Iyer[18] of Madras proposed an amendment which was seconded by Sir Pherozeshah Mehta himself to the effect that a new committee may be appointed to reconsider the whole matter and submit their report to the next Congress.

In proposing and seconding this amendment, they said that they could not see their way to accept the proposal of the Punjab delegates on the ground of

---

resigned from I.C.S in 1897 and taught Indian history at University College, London; President, Lucknow Congress, 1899; returned to India in 1904; Dewan of Baroda State, 1909; member, Royal Commission on Decentralisation, 1907; translated *Rigveda* into English and wrote several books including *Peasantry of Bengal, History of Literature of Bengal* and *History of Civilisation in Ancient India*.

18. (1863-1911); lecturer of law at Madras Law College, 1890-95; close associate of Gokhale; member of A.I.C.C.; member, Madras Legislative Assembly, 1907; Judge, Madras High Court, 1910; member, Governor's Executive Council, 1911.

its being impracticable, but that they had no objection, for the sake of harmony, to have the whole matter reconsidered and decided anew. Sir Pherozeshah Mehta further explained the circumstances under which the reappointment of the Indian Congress Committee was not moved at the Congress session at Calcutta, and I must confess that some of the facts stated by him which were not known to me before went a great deal against our case. Though I was not convinced that even those facts could justify the entire ignoring, out of existence, of the Indian Congress Committee, but, in fairness to Sir Pherozeshah, I must inform my brothers of the Punjab that in the light of those facts the non-appointment of the Indian Congress Committee at Calcutta did not appear to be an act of high-handedness as I thought before. Sir Pherozeshah explained that the Committee had been appointed only for one year and that it was the duty of those who were in favour of its continuance to propose its reappointment, and that notwithstanding the permission from the Chair but their spokesman refrained from doing so fearing certain exposures which were bound to follow. He also explained that the passing of the original resolution framing the constitution of the Congress at the session of 1899 was also due to a pressure from the Punjab and N.W.P. delegates who were in an overwhelming majority. It need not be said that the speech was delivered with that usual frankness which generally characterises Sir Pherozeshah's utterances and therefore had its effect. It being very late at this time no reply was attempted and the amendment was carried by a majority including some Punjab delegates. In fact, no dissenting votes could be counted on one's fingers. Now, to come to the opinions and impressions I have formed, I will put them here categorically: (1) I think it would be un-patriotic on the part of the Punjab to impair the unity of the movement by seceding from it; (2) that it will be impolitic and suicidal in the interests of the Punjab itself to do so; (3) that instead of dictating a constitution to the Congress, the Punjab will do better by forming a provincial organisation and working it properly, manfully, and, above all, with a spirit of sacrifice, because let me tell my Punjabee friends clearly that the most crushing fact advanced by Sir Pherozeshah against the case put forward by the Punjab was the total inactivity of the Punjab in matters political; (4) that although I do not agree with that part of the Congress programme which is confined to begging and beseeching only, still it cannot be denied that the educational and political value of the Congress is immense, and without it and besides it there is no other platform upon which all Indians can stand as brothers and workers in the same cause. I do not agree with that school of Congressmen who maintain that the only business of the Congress is to focus the public opinion of the country and to give expression to it at the end of the year. My opinion is that the Congress can and must do some constructive work as well. But those who are for it should lead the way by practical and actual work.

3. Repressive Measures in Bengal[1]

Mr. President,[2] brother delegates, ladies and gentlemen, I am afraid I cannot deliver a speech in the strain which we have been hearing on the resolution of the "Partition of Bengal" and the present resolution before you.[3] I give it my heartiest support on two grounds. You have been hearing of the misfortunes of our brethren of Bengal. I am rather inclined to congratulate them on the splendid opportunity which an all-wise Providence, in His dispensation, has afforded to them by heralding the dawn of a new political era for this country. I think the honour was reserved for Bengal, as Bengal was the first to benefit by the fruits of English education. Bengal, up to this time—excuse me for saying that—the Bengal lion, by some cause, had degenerated into a jackal, and I think Lord Curzon has done us a great service by provoking the lion in his own den and rousing him to a sense of consciousness of his being a lion. I think no greater service could have been done to India, to the cause of India or to Bengal, by any other statesman. There are times, gentlemen, when I am inclined to pray that from time to time God might be pleased to send Viceroys like Lord Curzon to this country, in order to awaken the people of this country to a sense of their responsibility in this matter. Gentlemen, I believe, and I believe earnestly, that the political struggle has only commenced, and it was only in the fitness of things that when the Congress attained its majority, the attaining of that majority should have been preceded by a manly and vigorous protest on the part of the people of this country. It is only in the fitness of things that the movement's coming to age of majority should have been preceded by a vigorous and manly declaration of its approaching manhood. I think in the circumstances like ours, in conditions like ours, we are perfectly justified in taking the attitude that our brethren of Bengal have taken.[4] What else was left for you? It has been explained that all possible things that could be done in the name of constitutional agitation

1. Speech at Benares Congress, 29 December 1905. *Report of the 21st Session of the Indian National Congress, Benares, 1905.*
2. G.K. Gokhale
3. While supporting the Congress resolution moved by Surendranath Banerjea protesting against the partition of Bengal "in the face of the strongest opposition on the part of the people of the province" and appealing to the Government of India and the Secretary of State to "reverse or modify the arrangements", Madan Mohan Malaviya had moved another resolution protesting against the repressive measures adopted by the Government in Bengal.

   Bengal had been partitioned by Curzon on 16 October 1905 by carving out Eastern Bengal and Assam as a separate province with a Muslim majority.
4. The swadeshi and boycott movements had been started by the people in Bengal. See also *post*, section 2, item 1.

have been exhausted. What was the example given to you by your fellow-subjects in the other parts of the Empire. Englishmen have been our teachers in all branches of human knowledge. Englishmen have given us constitutional rights. Is it not perfectly right to take a page from the book of the Englishmen on the methods of constitutional agitation and adopt those methods which will be appreciated by themselves? Now let us see what Englishmen in England do. I do not say that our conditions allow of our exactly copying or imitating them, but surely we have a right to adopt that spirit, understand that spirit and follow it. Let me tell you what are the methods adopted by Englishmen in England when they have a grievance to be listened to by the Government. The method, which is perfectly legitimate, perfectly constitutional and perfectly justifiable, is the method of passive resistance. Although I am not at the present moment quoting any Social Democrat or Labour man, I must admire them; I have great respect for them. I must tell you that the message which the people of England wanted to send to you through me was the message that in our utterances, in our agitations and in our fight and struggle for liberty, we ought to be more manly than we have been heretofore. An Englishman hates or dislikes nothing like beggary. I think a beggar deserves to be hated. Therefore, it is our duty to show Englishmen that we have risen to the sense of consciousness, that we are no longer beggars and that we are subjects of an Empire where people are struggling to achieve that position which is their right by right of natural law. Gentlemen, in every age people were arbiters of their destiny, but we are not so at the present moment. We are perfectly justified in trying to become arbiters of our own destiny and in trying to obtain freedom. I think the people of Bengal ought to be congratulated on being leaders of that march in the van of progress. I rather envy them. I am rather jealous of them; at the same time I am proud of them. They have begun the battle, they have begun the fight and they have begun it in right manly style. They have effaced all those taunts, they have effaced all those insinuations against them of being timid and cowardly; they have exhibited a manliness, they have exhibited a spirit in this battle which has to be commended to other provinces of India. If the other provinces of India will just follow their example, I say the day is not far from distant sights. But if you simply go there as a beggar without the consciousness of your power, of your right to demand your rights, you go there simply to be rejected. If, therefore, you want to be heard, and you want to be heard with respect, you must approach with determination, with evidences of determination, with signs that you are determined to achieve your rights at any cost. Unless you do that, the goddess of liberty is very jealous, she shall never allow you to approach her, and she shall never allow you to enter her portals. You must remain outside because you are profane: you cannot enter because you are not sufficiently pure; you must purify yourselves through the ordeals of fire and self-sacrifice.

The goddess of liberty is the most sacred goddess in the world and before you can approach her, you should show by your life, life of self-denial, that you are fit to enter her temple. What have we been doing to be fit to approach that temple? I am afraid that our record is extremely poor and extremely humiliating; it is extremely bad to look at. But there are signs of the rising sun. And if the people of India will just learn that lesson from the people of Bengal, I think the struggle is not hopeless. We are just awakening to a sense of our duty and a sense of responsibility to the motherland. It may be that with the consciousness of that strength we may tread the right way, the right path in the struggle for freedom. I have only to say one word about that part of the resolution which deals with repressive measures. I think the repressive policy of this Government is very encouraging. A Government commanding 2,60,000 or 5,00,000 soldiers stooping to strike us by striking at our boys! I say what have these wise statesmen of Government come to! Are they not displaying disgraceful weakness, a weakness of which the people are conscious? It will be difficult for them to remain where they are. What would people conclude that this mighty Government, with so many guns and cannons, with so many armies and with such an array of statesmen, have begun to fight with boys. I say that as friends of order, as friends of peaceful progress, as friends of the present Government, because we are not ungrateful, we advise them to eschew these weak methods, disgraceful methods, and reassert their manliness by pursuing paths of righteousness. If we were to adopt the methods of revolutionaries, if we were to adopt the same secret methods which the Government of Lord Curzon has adopted in pushing forth the partition scheme, if we were to adopt the same methods which the Government of India and bureaucratic rulers are adopting in dividing people against people, in setting the Hindu against the Mohammedan, the Hindu against the Sikh, it will be a dangerous game. I say that the Government is giving weapons which are sharp but which are disgraceful and which show signs of weakness. I, therefore, say that it is a dangerous game which the Government is playing. It might injure them at any moment. Therefore, as friends of the Government, as friends of order, we warn the Government against treading this path of danger and difficulty. Let the Government remember, and let you, gentlemen, also remember that people once awakened and awakened rightly cannot be put down. It is impossible for the Government of India, after a century of British rule, after a century of liberal education, after having put the books of Burke,[5] Bain[6] and

5. Edmund Burke (1729-1797); British statesman, orator and writer; initiated impeachment of Warren Hastings; works include *Thoughts on the Present Discontents* (1770), *Conciliation with America* (1775) and *Reflections on the Revolution in France* (1790).

6. Alexander Bain (1818-1903); Scottish philosopher and associate of J.S. Mill; wrote several books on speculative psychology, including *Mind and Body* (1872).

Mason[7] in our hands, to put us down like dogs and slaves. That is impossible. The Bengalis have just now shown, they are only now showing, that the task is impossible even for a mighty government like the British Government. Therefore, wisdom requires, statesmanship requires, that people should be governed on right lines, on liberal principles, on those democratic principles which are just now stirring the whole world. The wave of democracy is out. I defy any government in the world where there is any just civilization to keep the people out of their rights for any length of time. The history of Europe is before you. What is the fate of autocratic methods? We pray our Government not to adopt those methods. As my friend the Chairman has been telling English audience, the British Government is foolish in following Russian methods. We are great admirers of British rule. As people who are benefited by that rule we call upon the Government not to trample underfoot the best traditions of British rule, but to retrace those steps and not leave the people of this country under the impression that their Government is going to adopt nothing better than Russian methods. If these methods continue, gentlemen, what will be the difference between the Russian Government and the British Government? There will be nothing left for the people of this country to be loyal to the British Government if these things are taken away—if the rights of meetings, if the rights of petitions and if the rights of constitutional agitation are taken away from us. Let my governors tell me what shall be left to us to be loyal to them? Why shall we be loyal to them? I, therefore, say that it is in their own interests that they ought to retrace their steps and follow the noble example which has been set by some of their noblest statesmen, and remedy the state of things that exist.

One word more and I have done. I see the time is going fast. No, I am not going to break the rule. I think I have already exceeded the limits. There is only one word I should like to say. If you have adopted this manly and vigorous policy, be prepared for the logical consequence. Don't conceal your heads, don't behave like cowards. Once having adopted that manly policy, stick to it till the last. Glorify yourselves as I have told you. Is it not a matter of shame for us that this National Congress in the last twenty-one years should not have produced at least a number of political sannyasis that could sacrifice their lives for the political regeneration of the country? Now that the Congress has come to a stage when it could become a father, a parent, I earnestly appeal to you to let it have its legitimate offspring, a band of earnest missionaries to work out the political regeneration of the country. There is no use of our talking aloud, there is not much use of our showing signs of discontent and disaffection unless

7. A.E.W. Mason (1865-1948); British novelist; works include *Four Feathers* (1902), *The Broken Road* (1907) and *At the Villa Rose* (1910).

we are true to ourselves, true to our noble country, true to the motherland, true to the cause of political regeneration and political agitation. If you show, in a few years, to our rulers that we are steadfast in our determination, that we are steadfast in our devotion to our cause, I assure you that there is no power in the world that can prevent you from going forward.

4. To Editor of *The Panjabee*[1]

Lahore
10 January 1906

Mr. Editor,[2]

Permit me to enter a respectful protest against the first editorial note published in your issue of today relating to my humble self.[3] Without making myself liable to a charge of ingratitude I think I must inform you that I entirely disapprove of remarks like the one under reference. The reasons are obvious. Firstly, complimentary notes like this are beside the mark and liable to be misunderstood. Secondly, they are likely to cause mischief. Thirdly, they put me in a false position. You are not perhaps aware that some gentlemen have been circulating very much exaggerated reports of my interest in your paper and that is another reason why complimentary notes like this should not be indulged in. I shall feel extremely obliged to you if you will kindly avoid doing so in the future, as comments like these are likely to injure me as well as the cause which I and you both have so much at heart.

Now a word or two about my speech.[4] There again I am afraid your observations are based upon a misapprehension. I could not have promised to supply you with my speech in manuscript, for the simple reason that I have none, nor ever had it in manuscript.[5] What I said to Lala Jaswant Rai[6] was that

1. *The Panjabee*, 13 January 1906.
2. K.K. Athavale, a journalist from Poona and the editor of *The Panjabee*.
3. The editorial note read: "Lajpat Rai, the acknowledged leader of a Punjab, made a very stirring speech in the last Congress session, which we learn from a private source was pronounced by such a master of elocution and oratory as Mr. S.N. Banerjea as the epoch-making speech of the session."
4. The reference was to his speech delivered at the Benares Congress on 29 December 1905 on the resolutions protesting against the partition of Bengal and the repressive measures adopted by the Government of Bengal. For the speech see *ante*, item 3.
5. In a note printed along with Lajpat Rai's letter, the editor apologised for having conveyed the "impression that he (Lajpat Rai) had ever had in his possession a manuscript of his speech before or after delivery".
6. (1882-1972); educationist, businessman, social worker and philanthropist of Lahore; taught

I might try to reproduce it, though I was not confident that I could, and I am afraid there does not seem to be much chance of the attempt being successful.

Lajpat Rai

Sanskrit at D.A.V. College, Lahore, 1902-04; proprietor and printer of *The Panjabee*, 1904-09; sentenced to six month's imprisonment in the case against *The Panjabee* for publishing an article against a British official in 1907; founded D.A.V. High School at Hissar in 1918 and Lakhpat Rai High School at Karachi in 1923; started Jaswant Rai Sugar Mill at Meerut in 1935; founded Jaswant Rai Churamani Trust at Lahore in 1943; after 'partition' shifted to Meerut and founded Sushila Jaswant Rai Women's Hospital in 1954 and later Churamani Vishnu Devi Hospital at Hissar.

5. To G.K. Gokhale[1]

Lahore
22 January 1906

Dear Mr. Gokhale,[2]

Yours of the 15th to hand. Thanks. I cannot, however, accept your kind offer of paying for the pictures you took for me to England. I know the price won't be trifling and I must not allow you to encroach upon your slender income in this way. Please do write to the Bombay friend to send the bill to me direct.

As for the *Panjabee* I have spoken to the proprietor and he has promised to see me at once. I have been away for about ten days on a piece of business to Karachi and it was there that I happened to read the controversy about the Prince of Wales' resolution.[3] But for the promise I had given you I would have sent the exact resume of the whole affair to the press. I am sorry that the *Mahratta*

1. G.K. Gokhale Papers (microfilm), National Archives of India (henceforth N.A.I.)
2. (1866-1915); life-member, Deccan Education Society; eminent "Moderate" leader of the Congress; honorary secretary of Deccan Sabha; served as secretary of the Bombay Provincial Conference for several years as well as of the Servants of India Society; member, Bombay Legislative Council, 1899-1901; member, Imperial Legislative Council, 1901-15; President, Indian National Congress, 1905; member, Royal Commission on Public Services in India, 1912.
3. The resolution moved by Gokhale on 28 December 1905 at the Subjects Committee meeting of the Benares Congress offering a "royal and dutiful" welcome to the Princess and Prince of Wales (later George V) on the occasion of their visit to India was opposed by Tilak, Lajpat Rai and several leaders of Bengal. Lajpat Rai said that to call the Prince of Wales at this time when a severe famine prevailed in the country and people were dying of hunger was a "bureaucratic

and the *Panjabee* ever noticed it. It should have been entirely ignored or the whole thing should have been given out. Now what is your advice in the matter? I am not in the least afraid of letting the whole truth go before the public but I would not take any step in the matter without your permission. What do you think of the attitude of the *Gujarati*?[4] Does it really want a greater split in the Congress camp? Something within me often rebukes me that I am not doing my duty to my country properly. I often pray for light, though till now I have not found much. I do not see a clear path and am often perplexed what to do. Can you help me by your wise counsels? I know you are very busy but if you can find some time to jot me a few lines, I shall feel deeply grateful.

Yours sincerely,
Lajpat Rai

---

subterfuge, the intention of the inviters being to allay political unrest by diverting public attention to a gala show." However, on the persuasion of Gokhale, he, along with his group, did not attend the meeting the next day when the resolution was passed.

4. A Gujarati newspaper published from Bombay.

6. To G.K. Gokhale[1]

Lahore
30 January 1906

Dear Mr. Gokhale,

Yours of the 25th to hand. Thanks. Is it not strange that my feeling about Mr. Tilak's[2] letter[3] should have been the same as yours?

I have decided to follow your advice.

With kindest regards,

Yours very sincerely,
Lajpat Rai

1. G.K. Gokhale Papers (microfilm), N.A.I.
2. B.G. Tilak (1856-1920); educated at Poona and taught at Fergusson College; outstanding politician and nationalist and "extremist" leader of the Indian National Congress; founded and edited *Kesari* (Marathi) and *The Mahratta* (English), 1881; sentenced to eighteen months' imprisonment for sedition (1897-98), and deported to Burma (1908-14); founded Home Rule League in 1916; author of *Shrimad Bhagvad Gita-Rahasya* (*Karma Yoga Sastra*) and several other scholarly books on Indian history and philosophy.
3. Not available

7. To G.K. Gokhale[1]

Lahore
3 March 1906

Dear Mr. Gokhale,

Some mischievous people with whom I have had extensive differences in the Arya Samaj have been trying to give out in the columns of the vernacular press in this province that during the last session of the Indian National Congress I tried to spread libellous remarks about your work in England and attempted to create difficulties in your way in guiding the proceedings of the Indian National Congress.[2] The first charge was that I had actually said something to the effect that "you had injured the Indian political movement by confining your work in England to special or limited circles". It was originally insinuated that I had used these words in the meetings of the Subjects Committee. When this was contradicted by Babu Ganga Prasad Verma and others then the charge was repeated that some such words or anything reflecting discredit on you was said by me sometime not specified or known to anybody. I have been called upon by these gentlemen to contradict this but I have till now refrained from doing so as, on principle, I am very much opposed to the carrying on of personal controversies in the press. They injure the cause. The gentlemen opposite have also condemned the movement, i.e. the Indian National Congress. You will thus see the awkward position in which they have put me. Although I owe no explanation to these critics, I think I owe you an assurance that I did nothing of this sort and that the whole thing is a fabrication. You know too well that I felt a little hurt by your remarks about the Social Democrats in the Subjects Committee and I did express dissatisfaction with the same to our friend Mr. Devdhar.[3] You yourself referred to this the next day when we were talking over the Prince of Wales resolution[4] and then the matter ended there. I can sincerely assure you that I did not say anything anywhere which could in the least be considered as disparaging to you. I remember to have, perhaps, said

1. G. K. Gokhale Papers (microfilm), N.A.I.
2. The reference was to the Benares session of the Congress held in December 1905 under the Presidentship of Gokhale.

   Lajpat Rai and Gokhale had gone to England as Congress delegates to propound the cause of India at the time of the general election to be held there. Lajpat Rai had left for England in May 1905 and returned to India in November. For details see *post*, section 4.
3. Gopal Krishna Devadhar (1877-1935); journalist, and personal assistant to G.K. Gokhale; one of the founders of the Servants of India Society; did relief work during Mopla riots in 1921; President, All India Social Conference, 1929 and 1933.
4. See *ante*, item 5, fn. 3.

that those people who represented that Mr. Gokhale confined his work in England to some special circle are belittling him and are injuring the Indian political movement. I am writing all this to you as this is the second time when attempt has been made to create bad blood between you and me. I hold such a high opinion of your goodself that I have had no apprehension of these attempts making any impression on you, but still acting on the maxim "forewarned forearmed", I take this liberty of assuring you that I feel really honoured by and proud of this fact that I had an occasion of serving my country in company with yourself. I am proud of the fact that in connection with the work of the Congress deputation to England my name has been associated with yours. Some capital is attempted to be made of my intimacy with Mr. Tilak and of your alleged differences with him. In justice to Mr. Tilak let me assure you that he has never spoken to me anything in any way disparaging to you. I hold Mr. Tilak in great esteem but that is no reason why I should go about discrediting your noble sacrifices in the cause of your country. As for myself, I honour both and feel a genuine pride of claiming the goodwill and friendship of both.

The latest insinuation is that I created difficulties in your way in the matter of the Prince of Wales resolution. How far that is true and how the differences about the resolution ended is well known to you. Please excuse the encroachment on your valuable time which I thought was necessary for the maintenance of friendly relations between us. A reply to this with permission to use to me if necessary will highly oblige.

Yours sincerely,
Lajpat Rai

8. To William Wedderburn[1]

Lahore
11 September 1906

Dear Sir William,

Your kind letter of the 23rd August to hand. Many thanks for the same.

I shall try to act up to your wishes but am not confident whether my efforts are likely to be very effectual.[2] Bengal is just now in great ferment and seems

1. From a copy in Dadabhai Naoroji Papers, Dadabhai Naoroji Memorial Prize Fund, Mumbai, and courtesy: S.R. Mehrotra, Shimla; also published in J.S. Dhanki (ed.), *Perspectives on Indian National Movement—Selected Correspondence of Lala Lajpat Rai* (New Delhi, 1998), p. 20.
2. Referring to the growing differences between the "moderates" and "extremists" in the Congress,

to be full of the new school. The backward provinces are however dull. I hope the Bengal leaders will be equal to the occasion. Whatever way my sympathy may go I am very strongly in favour of the unity and solidarity of the Congress being maintained. I hope I will do nothing which might displease you. Let me subscribe.

Your admirer,
Lajpat Rai

Wedderburn, in his letter of 23 August, had written that Morley had, in his budget speech, referred in a sympathetic way to the Congress, and added, "my object in writing is to say that and hope you will use your influence with impulsive friends and keep the Congress on its present lines, at any rate, until Mr. Morley has had time to get his feet on firm ground".

9. To G.K. Gokhale[1]

Lahore
4 October 1906

Dear Mr. Gokhale,

Yours of the 20th September to hand. To me the developments in Bengal look to be extremely silly.[2] I think both parties are to blame in the matter. However, what do you propose to do? Mr. Naoroji's formal selection as President will stop all agitation and all quarrels about the Presidentship.

May I ask you to give me some definite ideas as to what political work can be done by the district political associations of any province? I have been asked to make a sort of programme for such bodies. Will you help me by your valuable advice in the matter or may I refer them to write to you directly? What line will you advise me personally to adopt with regard to political work? You know my sympathies are in the direction of self-help and self-reliance. I can devote the most of my time to political work if I can once determine what to do in that line.

Hoping to receive a full reply at an early date,
I remain

Yours sincerely,
Lajpat Rai

1. G.K. Gokhale Papers (microfilm), N.A.I.
2. For Presidentship of the Calcutta Congress to be held in December, Tilak's name had been proposed by the "extremist" group led by Bepin Chandra Pal, Aurbindo Ghose and others. But the "moderates" being opposed to the idea persuaded, with a view to avoiding a contest, Dadabhai Naoroji to accept the Presidentship.

10. Ways to Promote Swadeshism[1]

Mr. Chairman, ladies and gentlemen, the Hon'ble Mr. Madan Mohan Malaviya has explained to you that Swadeshism is the effect of widespread poverty that prevails in this country. Our venerable President and Mr. R.C. Dutt have laboured to make it clear that the prevailing poverty of this country is directly due to that economic muddle which has resulted from the action of Government. In order to remove that economic muddle we have a resolution for self-government in this resolution. But pending the acquisition of that self-government, this resolution tells you or explains the method by which, to a certain extent, you can remove the causes of the poverty which prevails in this country.[2] It is not proper for me to explain at length to you what this resolution consists of. In a few words, I want to give you the different factors of which the resolution as to Swadeshism consist. The first thing which Swadeshism reminds you of constantly is that in the use of articles, in the use of the necessaries of life, you have a duty to perform towards your country and that duty can best be performed by the consumption of India-made articles in preference to foreign commodities. One thing which this resolution calls upon you to do is to encourage the production of all home-made articles. I want to make one observation and that is to free your capital as much as you possibly can. Heretofore, we have been not merely depending upon foreign capital, but what little capital we possessed we have been handing over to foreigners to make the best use they could of it. The first thing to promote Swadeshism is to take our capital into our own hands and to devote it for our own purposes. The next thing to do is to consecrate that capital to the production of home-made industries, to invest it for the service of our country, to be a little more enterprising, to be a little more bold in the application of the capital towards the needs of the country. The third thing to do is to help our young men to distribute these articles which we produce in the country. My friends, in my humble opinion, this resolution has a direct bearing upon the question of education. It is impossible to make Swadeshism a success, unless you can have a good deal of technical education in this country. In the present circumstances,

1. Speech at the Calcutta Congress, 29 December 1906. *Report of the 22nd Session of the Indian National Congress, Calcutta, 1906*, pp. 111-12.
2. The resolution moved at the Calcutta Congress declared that "having regard to the fact that the people of this country have little or no voice in its administration, and that their representations to the Government do not receive due consideration, this Congress is of opinion that the Boycott movement inaugurated in Bengal by way of protest against the partition was, and is, legitimate". It also urged the encouragement of indigenous industries "even at some sacrifice".

it may be difficult for you to extort a great measure of technical education from Government and therefore the best thing to do is to go in for technical education yourselves as much as you can under the national system of education. Some of our men are becoming tired of the present system of education, because the Government service and the learned professions are being overcrowded. There is no room for educated men to earn their bread. Swadeshism and national education combined together will solve that question and that problem. We shall be furthering the cause of education, we shall be removing the cause of poverty and thereby we shall be doing a double service to our motherland which, at the present moment, suffers from so many causes of poverty and ignorance. These two resolutions are related to each other. We must go in for them together. But remember there is one word in this resolution which shows how you can achieve that object and that word is, sacrifice. It has been deliberately introduced in this resolution at the suggestion of Mr. Tilak. I do not say that the spirit was not there, the spirit was, perhaps, already there, but it has been made clear by the introduction of the word, sacrifice. It makes it clear that without sacrifice it is impossible to achieve the end aimed at by Swadeshism. You must be true to your pledges, you must be true to your country and be prepared to incur sacrifice before you can really achieve Swadeshism or before you can really support the cause of education. Therefore, I submit that this resolution, concentrating all those forces that go in for national progress is a general resolution, which combines all those elements of national progress that split them into different departments. It is a resolution which goes in for wholesale national progress combining education as well as material and industrial progress, which also includes the doctrine of sacrifice in the interests of our country. Unless we are going to invest capital and free it from hands of those who give 4 per cent and charge 9 per cent and use it for the production of our own articles and try to encourage the consumption of such articles even at a sacrifice, it will be fruitless to expect any success of Swadeshism. As the time has advanced very late, I shall not tire you. With these few words, I humbly support the resolution before you.

11. Tentative Rules for the Congress[1]

Gentlemen, I do not propose to make a speech in support of this resolution. My friends have already told you that we are adopting these rules tentatively for

1. Speech at the Calcutta Congress, December 1906. *Report of the 22nd Session of the Indian National Congress, Calcutta, 1906*, pp. 135-6.

one year.[2] The Punjab has been very keen on having a constitution. I am glad that the whole Congress is practically unanimous that the time has arrived when a constitution must be framed for the Congress. On that point of necessity for a constitution, there is no difference of opinion; but you must understand that it is not a very easy thing to frame a constitution for a body like the Congress. Therefore, the working of the tentative rules for a year will give us experience for framing a better and proper constitution. Next year, I hope it will be in full working order and in a few years' time we will be able to conduct our business in a more constitutional way than has hitherto been done. I am glad that some rule has been framed in the course of last year, in order to reduce the confusion that now and then attends our discussions. It is absolutely necessary that that confusion should be reduced and I am confident that the adoption of these rules will tend to the reduction of that confusion. Therefore, I commend the adoption of these rules tentatively for one year for your acceptance.

2. The tentative rules laid down, among other things, that in each province a Provincial Congress Committee and District Associations would be organized for "sustained and continuous political work in the province". The system of electing the Congress President and constituting the Subjects Committee was also revised.

2
PARTITION OF BENGAL

1. Punjab's Sympathy with Bengal[1]

We are assembled here today for two-fold purposes, the principal of which is to express our heartfelt sympathy with our brethren of Bengal in their present troubles.[2] As subjects of the same Government and members of the same nationality, it is our duty to speak out when we see that a handful of Government officials are trampling under foot the best traditions of administration which have been established by the British law as made and promulgated by some of the greatest statesmen that England has yet produced. It will be suicidal to sit silent when we see that the Government of law and goodwill is being substituted for a Government by force and by military terrorism. It will be criminal to shut our eyes when we find that British modes of administration are being changed for Russian models and that the hitherto professedly constitutional form of government is being openly converted into an irresponsible military despotism. The highest dictates of loyalty demand that the people of India should speak out their mind at such a juncture and should speak out sufficiently loud and quite unambiguously so as to reach the ears of those who are ultimately responsible for the good government of this country. What is a government if not an embodiment of law? True, it possesses the power of changing the law but only after observing certain forms. So long as the law stands and has not been changed in accordance with the established procedure, practice and constitution, the law is binding both on the Government and the people. It is, therefore, the highest loyalty to protest whenever the people find that the executive is inclined to break the law and to assume a power which the law does not give it. Loyalty to law is loyalty to Government. If it is loyalty to support the Government in all its constitutional functions and to defend it against all attacks made upon it by enemies, it is still greater loyalty to defend the law even against the Government itself. I have, therefore, no doubt that we are perfectly loyal to the law of the land when we protest against the illegal and unconstitutional acts of the Local Governments of Bengal, whereby the latter aim at terrifying the people of those provinces who are carrying on a strictly legal and constitutional agitation against the split of their beloved province

1. Speech at a public meeting held under the auspices of the Indian Association at Lahore on 9 December 1905. *The Panjabee*, 11 December 1905.
2. The people of Bengal had started swadeshi and boycott movements in protest against the partition of the province and the Governments of both the provinces had resorted to repressive measures.

   The partition of Bengal effected on 16 October 1905 led to the creation of Eastern Bengal and Assam as a separate province with a Muslim majority. See also *ante*, section 1, item 3.

into two. What can be meaner than the attempt made to coerce the parents by striking at their children and what can be more ridiculous than the attempt to justify a reign of terror on the ground that some schoolboys were displaying a spirit of rowdyism. That the repressive circulars and proclamations of the Governments in Bengal are illegal have been declared by the highest law officer of the Crown; we mean the Advocate-General of Calcutta.[3]

But, gentlemen, over and above the illegal circulars we have the extra-ordinary procedure of the Government of Eastern Bengal in establishing a reign of military terrorism in Barisal.[4] We have to enter an emphatic protest against the same, because we think that steps like these are not only uncalled for in the present state of things but because we believe that steps like these are direct incentives to those violent methods of agitation which none of us sincerely desires to see being introduced in India. Gentlemen, in my opinion the so-called Gurkha rule in Bengal is a very disastrous affair, full of ominous meaning not only as a dangerous precedent but as a confession of the weakness and resourcelessness of the Government. As an established Government, which has a right to claim the affection and attachment of its people, whose chief security lies in the goodwill of the people and in their belief in its sense of justice and respect for law, could not have committed a greater blunder than a display of military power on an occasion like this. Now it is not my intention to minimise the seriousness of the situation in Bengal. That business best pays the Anglo-Indian press for whom it may perhaps be necessary from a business point of view to ridicule every genuinely Indian movement and by under-estimating its force. It has after all to please its clientele which consist either of Government officials or of Anglo-Indian merchants. The former very naturally do not like to be told of their mistakes and blunders and are not likely to pay for papers which do not sufficiently respect their feelings and prejudices. The Anglo-Indian merchants too are directly interested in belittling the importance of the Swadeshi movement. They have a common cause with the officials. An Englishman is nothing if not businesslike and it is a sign of the times that the business instincts of the average Anglo-Indian do not enable him to see much in advance. It has been the privilege of the Anglo-Indian press from time to time to fix dates for the final dissolution of the anti-partition

3. According to a secret circular issued by R.W. Carlyle, the Chief Secretary of Bengal, on 10 October 1905 to District Magistrates and Collectors, the heads of schools and colleges were to be warned that, in the event of their students participating in the protest movements, their grants-in-aid would be stopped and that the University would be asked to disaffiliate their institutions. Another such circular was issued by the Government of Eastern Bengal and Assam to the Commissioners and district officers.

4. Gurkha forces and the punitive police had been posted at several places in Barisal district.

agitation. So far they have been compelled to postpone it from day to day probably because their clients could not furnish them with sufficient evidence to pronounce the final verdict. This time a final date has been fixed as immediately after the next meeting of the Indian National Congress. Fortunately the postponement is not so long as sometimes happens to be the case in our own Chief Court and we shall not have to wait for long to see the vindication of the great occult powers which the *Pioneer* has of late seemed to acquire in abundance. Now to revert, I was pointing out that though the situation in Bengal is sufficiently serious to deserve the best consideration of British statesmen now at the helm of affairs here and also of the cabinet at home, there is nothing in it which can justify the extraordinary step of handing over a whole town to the military. The people of Bengal have done nothing illegal in resolving on the boycott of English-made goods as a political weapon. Some supporters of the Swadeshi movement may hold that in the interests of the Swadeshi movement itself the step was not perhaps wise but they forget that but for this agitation the Swadeshi movement may never have come to prominence so soon and might have failed to elicit that response which it has now.

Boycott was really started as a political weapon to bring pressure upon the great English nation at home and it has already served the very useful purpose of bringing round Indians to a sense of their duty towards the industrial problem of their own country. So far there is no reason to regret it. It has brought about a healthy change in the economic indifference that prevailed in this country, drawing the attention of the people to the possibilities that lie near at hand of saving the economic ruin of their country and by checking its exploitation without the intervention of the Government, by adopting measures which the Government should have enforced by law and which the same has, hitherto in the interests of the British merchants, failed to do.

While on one hand the Swadeshi movement is calculated to give an impetus to Indian industries and manufactures, the boycott movement on the other hand aims at the protection of the same from unequal and unscrupulous competition from without. It is not our intention to discuss whether the latter view is sound or not when judged by the orthodox standard of political economy, but that it is a perfect weapon to be wielded by a law-abiding people we have no doubt. If so, any attempt to persecute those people who have resolved to use this weapon for political purposes is illegal, unconstitutional and unjustifiable and under the circumstances every Indian, whether he accepts the boycott movement as sound or not, can legitimately sympathise with our countrymen in Bengal in their present trouble and protest against the persecution to which they are being subjected. We know that some Government officials are at the present moment carrying on a nefarious trade by setting class against class and classes against masses. We also know that they have here and there succeeded in winning over some of our Mohammedan brethren to their side but we are not at all discomfited by that because we believe that all this is only natural, in fact, encouraging. This sort of diplomacy is usually one of the last weapons that are wielded in self-defence by tottering despotisms. The Congress agitation was the first articulate protest against English despotism in India. As soon as the protest was made the despotism set itself to the task of dividing the people and fanning class and religious prejudices. Ever since then Mohammedans have been set against Hindus, Sikhs against both, agriculturists against moneylenders and so on. The trade has the great charm of looking at first sight to be a paying one. It is, no doubt, very profitable for those who act as the tools of the Government in spreading this propaganda but that it is in the long run a very dangerous game both for the Government as well as for the people at large is proved by the events that are at present happening in Russia. It contains within itself some inflammable elements which once let loose in the end spare neither friend nor foe. To those who have any doubt in the matter I will commend a serious study of Russian politics within the last century. I, therefore, take this opportunity of appealing to all my countrymen irrespective of caste or creed not to allow themselves to be made the tools of officials in spreading disunion amongst our people.

Beware, gentlemen, of the cunning, wily appeals sometimes flattering, sometimes threatening, sometimes made in the name of religion, sometimes in the name of religious nationality, sometimes pleading in the name of past greatness, and at times setting up the phantoms of a great future separate from the rest of the people of this country. Remember we are inhabitants of one country, breathe the same atmosphere, in our veins runs practically the same blood; we are the common inheritors of a glorious past, united we stand and divided we fall. The present is a critical time in the history of our country. We are just now in the throes of a great crisis. If at this juncture we fail to realise our responsibilities as Indians, we set back the tide of progress by a number of years. I say advisedly for a number of years because I have a firm conviction that our progress as a nation may be impeded but it cannot be altogether stopped. Beware, then, gentlemen, of those creeping counsels of discord and disunion which are often breathed in your ears in words of honey and in accents of affection and sympathy. There are signs on the horizon and all those who have eyes can see the same that the process of disillusionment has commenced and both Hindus and Mohammedans have begun to see far.

My appeal to you does not mean that you should cease to be Hindus or Mohammedans. Nay, if you do that I will cease to respect you. By all means love your respective religions as deeply as you can, try to serve your respective communities to the best of your ability, nay, even exert to strengthen them between themselves but never play in the hands of the common enemy whoever he may be. The British Government, as representative of the British nation, is not our enemy, though we cannot say the same of those who try to divide us, to persecute us, to insult us, to trample upon our cherished rights and privileges. Loyalty to the British Government does not demand loyalty to these latter officials. They are themselves disloyal to their own Government insofar as they try to defy the constitution and the law and thereby weaken British rule in India, and insofar as they alienate the affections and the sympathy of the people from that rule.

When, therefore, I ask you to sympathise with your brethren in Bengal over their misfortunes, I ask you irrespective of your caste and creed, irrespective of your belief in the soundness of the boycott movement, and irrespective of your opinion on the partition of Bengal. One word to my Mohammedan brethren. Suppose, gentlemen, the Government were to extend the same treatment to such of you as are inclined to support the Sultan of Turkey in his troubles with European powers, will you not naturally expect your Hindu fellow subjects to sympathise with you and to support you in your exercise of your constitutional rights and privileges? What is at the present moment being done in Bengal may at any moment be repeated in the Punjab. What is at the present moment meted out to Hindus principally may at any minute be extended to Mohammedans also. It is a question of principle for which we stand, upon which we ought to record a unanimous protest. The principle is our right to carry on a constitutional agitation against what we consider to be high-handed and unjust acts of the Government. The Government has no right to coerce the agitators or repress them so long as they are within the bounds of law. The law is sufficiently strong and comprehensive to punish all breaches of the same and all defiance to constituted authority. And no case has yet been made out for any extraordinary steps or for the intervention of the military. It is a pity that the officials in Bengal should have failed to grasp the situation as well as to apply true statesmanlike remedies. It is a still greater pity that they should have stooped so low as to adopt these petty tactics which are so much in evidence in Bengal just now. To the enemies of England the events in Bengal may give occasion for joy but to the friends of the same they can only afford grounds for feelings of shame.

Gentlemen, it is a matter of real concern to see that the resources of the Government in statesmanship should have fallen so low as to necessitate the use of Gurkhas for intimidating the proverbially timid Bengalee. In his haughtiness and in the security of his office Mr. Fuller[5] could not evidently see

5. J. Bampfylde Fuller who became the first Lieutenant-Governor of Eastern Bengal and Assam on 16 October 1905 resigned from his post on 20 August 1906 as some of his actions were not approved by the Government of India.

the loss of dignity and prestige which his acts were likely to entail. Like ordinary bureaucrats he probably thought it statesmanlike to overawe the people by a show of military strength. If so, we can only pity him as he was greatly mistaken if he thought that this show of militarism was likely to quell the agitation and to bring the people to their knees. Measures like these are always double-edged tools and it is a matter of sincere regret that the Lieutenant-Governor of Eastern Bengal did not profit by a study of history which, as a member of the Civil Service, he must be presumed to know sufficiently well.

In the end, gentlemen, and especially you students, I wish to impress on you the importance of being strictly within the law, and of keeping your heads quite cool and calm. Let your hearts be warm and responsive to every noble sentiment, but keep your heads cool whatever happens and whatever trials you have to undergo and however great the troubles you have to face. With these words I move the following resolution for your acceptance:

> That this public meeting of the citizens of Lahore and its environs records its respectful but emphatic protest against the illegal and unconstitutional measures that are being adopted by the Provincial Governments in Bengal to repress the legitimate expression by the people of their grievances and to put down the Swadeshi movement, and conveys its heartfelt sympathy to the people of Bengal in their present troubles and earnestly entreats H.E. the Viceroy to take early steps to allay the feelings of unrest unhappily prevailing there.[6]

6. The resolution was seconded by Chistie and supported by Rambhaj Dutt Choudhari and Fazal Mohamed Khan and passed unanimously.

2. 16th of October—a Red-Letter Day[1]

We have gathered here to express sympathy with our brethren in Bengal. The dire calamity and misfortune under which our Bengalee brethren are at present suffering is, in a way, of a very cruel nature. We in Punjab, ever since the partition day, have been feeling for our brethren, and it is not once or twice but several times that we have given indications of the sympathetic feelings we entertain for them. But as a matter of formality we all should assemble together on the anniversary of the day on which the partition of Bengal became effective to convey our feelings to our sorely afflicted countrymen of Bengal.

Before dispersing the meeting I would like to make one observation. I am not given to make prophesies. But this I must say that the 16th of October is a red-letter day in the history of India. We have all assembled here to express our sorrow but we have a cause for rejoicing at the same time. The days are fast approaching when the 16th of October will be considered a day of national rejoicing than of national mourning. It is first time in the annals of India that the masses and the misguided people have assembled together to ventilate their grievances. Self-help is written in golden letters on the political banner of India. It is for the first time in the history of India that the people have come to realize the truth of the adage that "nations are by themselves made". If they now begin to act up to this principle we have every reason of rejoicing. Every one of us is now realizing the individual responsibility and our working up to the motto of our national banner will lead us to ameliorate our present backward condition.

1. Speech at a public meeting, Lahore, 16 October 1906. *The Tribune*, 20 October 1906.

3
PROBLEMS OF PUNJAB

1. The Ludhiana Water Works Scheme[1]

Sir, The scheme of the Ludhiana Water Works has for some time past formed a subject of discussion in your columns. The opposition to it, as I originally understood, was based upon the impropriety of private charity being diverted for official or semi-official schemes. It was said that an Indian Deputy Commissioiner[2] at least should not have given the sanction of his name to such a course. But however impolitic or inexpedient such a course was, it is now time, I should think, that all opposition to the scheme should cease. The matter stands thus. The Deputy Commissioner of Ludhiana who happens to be an Indian has set the scheme in motion. He has in a way pledged himself to it and is not prepared to change his opinion. He is acknowledged to be a good, considerate and popular officer. The question which now arises is, whether under the circumstances it is wise and patriotic to continue the opposition. A European officer may have acted high-handedly and in that case people might have cried in vain without making him relax even the smallest muscles of his face. I think it is time that out of love and for the sake of the reputation of an Indian Deputy Commissioner all opposition to the Water Works scheme should now cease. It often happens that a leader takes into his head an idea which does not commend itself fully to all his admirers. It may not be objectionable on the part of the latter to state their objections as to his idea. It may even be permissible to them to put a little pressure upon him to give it up, but surely, if persisted in, the opposition should not be carried further and the decision should be accepted. It is in this spirit, viz., one of loyalty to an Indian officer of unquestionable integrity and ability that I would respectfully ask the opponents of the scheme to drop their opposition and join hands with the Deputy Commissioner in making it a success. I write this letter as I belong to the Ludhiana district and it pains me to see the discussion continue any longer.

Lajpat Rai

1. Letter to the editor published in *The Panjabee* of 6 March 1905.
2. Dewan Tek Chand.

2. To G.K. Gokhale[1]

Lahore
26 July 1906

Dear Mr. Gokhale,

Thanks for your letter which I got by last mail. Evidently you did not consider any of these matters worthy of any action in England. If so, I cheerfully accept your decision. You will be sorry to hear that we in the Punjab are hopelessly divided. Some parties have been at me ever since I returned from England and was received so enthusiastically by the public but the worst has happened since Nundy[2] came here as editor of the *Tribune*. He has simply increased the gulf. He has won the confidence of the Anglo-Indian officials and the Aligarh Mussalmans in the Punjab and that will explain the whole thing. I am afraid the prospects of . . .[3] work in the Punjab are not very cheering. However, the whole country feels proud of you and is very grateful to you for the high example of duty and self-sacrifice that you are holding to them in your own person. This is no flattery as you know I am not given to it.

Hoping you are enjoying sound health.

I remain

Yours very sincerely,
Lajpat Rai

1. G.K. Gokhale Papers (microfilm), N.A.I.
2. Alfred Nundy.
3. Illegible.

3. To G.K. Gokhale[1]

Lahore
18 August 1906

Dear Mr. Gokhale,

The Indian Association[2] have desired me to request you to draw the attention of the Government to the sensational case of oppression that has lately occurred in Jullundhar Cantt., a full account of which has appeared in the *Tribune* of the

1. G.K. Gokhale Papers (microfilm), N.A.I.
2. The Indian Association of Lahore was formed on 26 July 1876 with the same aims and objects

10th March. A copy of the *Tribune* is herewith sent for your reference. We are sending a special man to enquire into the facts but the session is drawing to a close, any delay might mean a total loss of opportunity.

The Indian Association have last night opened a list for subscriptions to meet your expenses to England.

Hoping this finds you in the best of health.

I am

Yours very sincerely,
Lajpat Rai

---

as the Indian Association of Calcutta formed the previous year, namely, (1) the creation of a strong body of public opinion in the country, (2) the unification of the Indian races and peoples on the basis of common political interests and aspirations, (3) the promotion of friendly feelings between Hindus and Mohammadans, and (4) the inclusion of the masses in the great public movement of the day.

4. Need for Vigorous Political Activity in Punjab[1]

It is a matter of very great satisfaction that our Ambala friends should have given us an opportunity of coming together and conferring on certain public questions of the day which so vitally affect the future of our country, including the little province which we call our own. For this our best thanks are due to the organisers of this conference, most prominent of whom are Rai Sahib Murli Dhar, Pandit Madho Ram,[2] Babu Hari Nath Mukerjee[3] and Mr. Alakh Dhari.[4] It may not, however, be altogether out of place to mention here that almost at the same time when our Ambala friends were resolving to organize this conference I had sent a letter to the press proposing a small informal conference of a limited number of friends interested in political questions to consider and discuss some of the matters which are now included in the programme of this

1. Address to Punjab Provincial Conference, Ambala, 30 September 1906. Published in two instalments in *The Panjabee* of 10 and 13 October 1906 respectively.
   The address written in English was, however, delivered in Hindi.
2. A close associate of Lajpat Rai; member of Punjab Provincial Conference; member of Reception Committee of Lahore Congress held in 1909.
3. A prominent Congressman of Ambala.
4. A prominent Congressman of Ambala.

gathering. A proof of that letter was sent for the perusal of Rai Sahib Murli Dhar and Pandit Madho Ram. However, the moment I learnt of the proposal for holding the conference at Ambala, I abandoned the idea of issuing my letter in the hope that the conference might afford the opportunity of gaining the object aimed at by my letter. It is my desire in this paper to review our position in this province in the matter of political work and to make suggestions, for your consideration, in order to improve the existing order of things, if possible. First to begin with the agency for work.

It must be frankly admitted that so far the Punjabees have shown very little aptitude for political work. The Indian Association of Lahore has been in existence for over twenty-five years but if we were to examine its achievements I am afraid we won't find much to congratulate ourselves upon. For some years, in its early history, it did a lot of useful work in carrying on an agitation to prevent the then Punjab University College being incorporated as a purely Oriental University under the scheme put forward and pressed by the late Dr. Leitner.[5] Fortunately for the Punjab the formal legislative incorporation of the University happened to be undertaken in the time of a liberal Viceroy like Lord Ripon with an equally liberal Lieutenant-Governor like Sir Charles Aitchison[6] and the Punjab was saved from what would have been nothing short of a disaster to see educational progress of the province.[7] These were those good old days when the present ill-feeling between the Hindus and the Mohammedans had not been started and when no less a person than Sir Syed Ahmed Khan himself considered it an honour to speak under the auspices of the Indian Association calling the Hindus and Mohamedans the two pupils of his eyes. For a number of years afterwards, thanks to the energy, patriotism and zeal of Babu J.C. Bose,[8] the Association continued to show some activity in the shape of submitting memorials to Government and giving addresses of welcome and farewell to coming and departing Lieutenant-Governors. Its financial burdens were chiefly borne by the late lamented Sardar Dayal Singh whose generosity evidently made the other members free of the duty of paying their subscriptions to the Association. This left the members of the Association to a group of men without any real stake in its affairs and without any inducement

5. (1840-1899); Principal of Punjab University College, Lahore; favoured reviving ancient Oriental learning and promoting vernacular studies.
6. (1832-1896); entered Indian Civil Service in 1856; Foreign Secretary, 1868-78; Chief Commissioner of Burma, 1878-80; Lieutenant-Governor of Punjab, 1882-87; member, Viceroy's Executive Council, 1887-88; President, Public Service Commission, 1887-88.
7. The Punjab University was incorporated in 1882 on the model of the other Indian universities and Leitner's scheme of opening an Oriental university in the province was dropped.
8. Jogendra Chandra Bose; a prominent Congressman of Lahore and member of Lahore Indian Association.

to show real zeal in looking after the same. In the meantime other causes had also sprung up which combined to lessen the influence of the Indian Association. The Association had been taking great interest in matters educational. In fact that was its chief work which appealed to the people. But since the Aligarh party of Mohammedans concentrated their attention and energies on the Aligarh College and the Arya Samaj on the D.A.V. College, the Association was deprived of that important hold on public mind and gradually lost in importance. The educational work of the Arya Samaj, supported by a very large section of the best energy, intellect and public spirit of the province monopolised all public attention for some time until the division of the Samaj into two parties again diverted the attention of the people to matters other than religious, social and educational. The matters were in this pass when Babu Jogendra Chandra Bose and Rai Sahib Murli Dhar, in whose persons alone the political activity of this province was chiefly centred, got a valuable ally in the person of the late lamented Bakshi Jaishi Ram.[9] The success of the last Punjab Congress, the one held in 1893, was chiefly due to these gentlemen. At the time when the Congress was first invited to Lahore the balancesheet of the Indian Association showed a lamentable state of things and the arrears of subscriptions were simply fabulous. The Congress of 1893 was, however, with all its shortcomings an unqualified success, though it was followed by an almost death-like lull. The only matter of political interest for several years was the question of the annual contribution to the British Committee of the Congress which always elicited a lively discussion. This was the period of the growth of the industrial movement which has ever since absorbed the little diversion that was created by the split in the Arya Samaj. The industrial movement opened the eyes of the people to the money-value of the time which they could spare from their official or professional engagements. The leading Arya Samajists had always been known to be averse to political activity of the kind of the Congress though some of them attended the annual meetings now and then, Bakshi Jaishi Ram alone never missing any. The aversion of the leading Arya Samajists to political activity was to a great extent shared by those non-Arya Samajists who took the lead in the industrial movement. It was this double aversion which was to a great extent responsible for the absence of any agitation worth its name, on such retrogressive measures as the Punjab Land Alienation Act[10] and the

9. An eminent Arya Samajist of Lahore; member of D.A.V. College Managing Committee, Lahore; member, Reception Committee, Lahore Congress, 1893; elected Director of Punjab National Bank in 1898; d. 1900.

10. The Punjab Land Alienation Act enacted in October 1900 by the Indian Legislative Council imposed restrictions on the right of landholders to sell or transfer their lands, which created discontent among them. The Act was, however, further amended in February 1907 by the

subsequent separation of the Frontier districts[11] from the Punjab. Both these measures were adopted in the face of the opposition of the then head of the Punjab Government[12] as well as of the opinion of a very influential section of the Punjab Civilians. During this period we have had a meeting of the Congress in the Punjab but beyond this we have hardly shown any interest in political matters. The country at large has, in the meanwhile, thanks to the genius of Lord Curzon, practically undergone a great change and is at the present moment almost in the throes of a revolution (at least so far as Bengal is concerned).

The first question then that I wish to put to the educated community of the Punjab is, if in their opinion the time has not come when we ought to pay greater attention to the political affairs of the country? Are we or are we not fit or ready for any sort of political activity or shall we wait more? I will not attempt to answer these questions for you. But I may be permitted to say this much that an answer in the affirmation implies a further question which to my mind is of still greater importance than the one already stated. What do politics signify for us? Does it simply mean responding to the annual call of the Congress to send delegates or is it for concessions and reforms which the Government is not prepared to concede—not that in their heart of hearts they do not believe in the soundness of the reforms asked for or in the justice of our claims but because they know that the demand for reforms is not backed by any compelling capacity to enforce the same. Are we, then, to continue to move in the old groove, go down on our knees only to be repulsed with contempt or are we prepared to make a departure and try to create real political environments amongst us which may eventually train us for a true political life? If you decide for the first alternative then I do not consider that there is much occasion for regretting our past indifference in matters political. This decision will be tantamount to a confession that we are not yet fit or ready for any political movement in our province. If so, let us understand it clearly and give up all the befooling that has for some time been going on in appeals for political activity in this province. Let us not dictate constitutions to other people who, perhaps, know better what to attempt and what not to attempt. In this case we can either quietly sit at home as before or be peaceful spectators of what others do. If, however, you

---

Punjab Legislative Council, laying down, among other things, that land could not be sold out to non-agriculturists, thereby making it difficult for the zamindars, who were virtually peasant proprietors, to raise money from money-lenders.

11. The North-West Frontier Province was created in 1901 by separating the frontier districts of Hazara, Peshawar, Kohat, Bannu and Dera Ismail Khan from the Punjab.

12. W.M. Young, the then Lieutenant-Governor of Punjab, was opposed to interference with the landowners' rights in respect of alienation of their lands. He was also against the creation of the North-West Frontier Province by Curzon without consulting the Punjab Government.

declare your mind in favour of the second alternative then also I must ask you to clearly realise the responsibility involved therein. Real, earnest political work, pardon me for using a vulgar expression, is no tomfoolery. It is not child's play but a very expensive and risky game. Those who enter the lists must be prepared for all sorts of sacrifices. They should expect no quarters (not to speak of favours) from the Government or its officials, even if they attempt nothing which is either illegal or outrageous. If ever in the past they have been blessed with the smiles of the *Feringhee* or aspired to honours at his hands they should once for all close that chapter of their life before opening the first page of the new. They must be prepared to devote at least a decent fraction of their incomes for the cause. They must not also grudge to set apart some time for the study of various problems that come to the front in the course of the work. In short, they should be as serious about it, if not more, as about the other activities of their life in which at the present moment they find themselves engaged.

A true political movement worth its name cannot be carried on without men nor without funds. If every minute of the time of those people engaged in political work has so much money-value, which they cannot forego in favour of political work, then we must find out other men to work up the movement who have and can afford to give time to it. Moreover, we must also be prepared to find funds for the same. To make a humble start we require at least Rs. 2,400 per annum, that is, Rs. 200 per mensem. If we cannot afford to find Rs. 200 per mensem for political work in this province we may safely conclude that the times are not yet ripe for any political activity here. Just think of a people putting forth claims for liberal political institutions and pleading inability to spend Rs. 200 per mensem for the cause. Then there must also be people who can find time to devote to the study of political literature and to go into the different phases of political questions. There is no use of indulging in generalities, the bearing of which on the questions in hand is at times not understood by the various speakers themselves. The speeches on political questions would not merely be an issue of commonplace platitudes ending with an appeal to the emotions but should throw ample light on the different aspects of the question in hand which cannot be expected of speakers who have had neither time nor inclination to study the literature on the subject. Second-hand quotations or references are often misleading. What I mean is that there should be made an honest, earnest attempt to study, understand and grasp political questions in a practical spirit. There should also be some real thinking, which may be followed by sincere and earnest action. Unfortunately what I understand from politics in this country, as already hinted, is a little bit different from what others think. Generally politics in this country is identified with agitation against Government, the demand of certain concessions by means of certain memorials and resolutions and so on. This may be political work but what is of greater importance still is the raising of the people both intellectually, and morally, awakening them to a consciousness of their importance and their capabilities and last but not the least of identifying our existence with them. I lay great stress upon the last. In order to be the rightful leaders of the people the educated community must strive to serve the latter selflessly and faithfully. The people must come to realise in the course of time that the national leaders care for them to a greater extent than the Government officials do and that in all their troubles and difficulties they can look to them more effectively than to the Government. The task is, no doubt, very difficult, one may say Herculean. The great resources of the Government and the abilities and general integrity of their agents meet you at almost every step but considering that the Government is foreign and in its policy is often guided by the interests of its own countrymen rather than by those of the people of this country and that its superior agents are also foreigners who do not know the sentiments of the people and do not care to win over their affections, the task of the educated leaders may not be so difficult as it looks to be. Where the Government may fail with its millions the educated leaders may succeed with a few thousands. The real key to the situation then lies in selfless service of the people. The country stands in need of a party of patriots whose sole business should be to go about amongst the people to enlighten them, to study their wants, and to try to remove the same. Till such men are found, let us try to make a start in our own humble way. Coming to actual suggestions for a political organisation in this province I would suggest:

(a) That the Indian Association of Lahore should be maintained and strengthened by the addition of new members and that District Associations may, if possible, be established all over the province; (b) that a separate political Council be established to study political questions, collect information and collate the latter before any action is to be recommended to the larger and more representative body, the Indian Association. This Council should have a paid agency at its disposal and should maintain an office. This Council should be composed of a few men only, every one of whom may be required to pay at least Rs. 50 as admission fee and Rs. 100 as annual subscription. If necessary, some (though very few) may be exempted from the operation of this rule and admitted as honorary members. You will pardon me, gentlemen, for saying that if the whole of the Punjab cannot supply twenty men for the membership of this Council then we may better wait for better times and conclude that we are not yet sufficiently earnest about a political organization in this province.

As to the lines of work I think we might with advantage study the situation in Bengal. To me it looks as if our brothers in Bengal (both of the so-called old school and of the new school) have opened an effective chapter in the future political history of this great country. Only a year before, they were the most

Europeanized of all the races that were to be found in India; they did not know what Swadeshi *Vastu* was, their political work chiefly consisted of speeches, resolutions and memorials; and their great ambition was to lead an easy life. They cared neither for organisation nor for constitution. The leaders and the led both were self-contained.

The troubles of the masses moved them only rarely. Famines after famines desolated the country; the earthquake made a great havoc in this province early last year, but the Bengalee leaders hardly moved their little finger to relieve the sufferings of the affected and the distressed. They spent their force in calling upon the Government to do this and to do that and hurled their anathemas against the foreign bureaucracy which monopolized all the good things of the world and did not give share of the same to them. This time last year, however, a movement was started in Bengal which has since then simply changed the face of the country. Our venerable leader, the revered editor of the *Indian Mirror*, is greatly concerned at the spirit of unrest that just now prevails in Bengal as the result of this activity. He is deeply affected by the disturbances caused by strikes and similar other events and utters a sincere cry for peace. His spiritual balance of mind has been upset by the prospects of an assured peace for ever disappearing before his holy vision. His good soul longing for *Nirvana* cannot tolerate these quarrels for higher wages on the part of labouring classes as these disputes have led to some trifling disturbances in his beloved province. Mr. Narendra Nath Sen[13] is a man of deep religious trend of mind. I have known him for long and have always admired him for his sincerity of convictions and simplicity of life. He is sincerely disturbed as his ideals are mostly spiritual and he seems to care little for the affairs of this mundane world. But he forgets that a people politically enslaved can have no peace. Even if the people were inclined to accept a foreign domination for ever there are other earth-grabbers and military adventures with high imperial ambitions (nine hundred and nine) which will not let them have peace under their present rulers even though foreign. What guarantee can there be that the future will produce no Alexanders, Abdul Qasims, Tamerlanes, Chengez Khans, Nadirs, Ahmad Shahs, Dupleixes and Clives. A nation which once loses its political independence can have no rest or peace except, perhaps, under a wholesale *Nirvana*. Unless, therefore, we are prepared for a national *Nirvana* there can be no peace for us. Unless, therefore, we once for all determine to be and to remain for ever the beasts of burden as we just now are there can be no peace in this country. Every step to advance means unrest, some loss of peace, some disturbance of the existing order of things. What is progress if not *Ashanti* (unrest) writ in big, broad,

13. (1847-1911); journalist and lawyer of Bengal; editor of *Indian Mirror*.

unmistakable characters. If, then, my countrymen you are actuated by a desire for progress, be it religious, social or political, you must pass through a hell of *Ashanti*. The road to heaven unfortunately lies through a labyrinth of hells. You must pass through the latter before you can reach the former. The Almighty has ordained so. Mother nature has also said the same. Why, the heavenly in man is also surrounded and hedged in by everything hellish. Incredibly bold and audacious must be the man who aspires to reach the heaven without passing through, crossing or overcoming, the hell. So it is of no use to be afraid of the loss of peace. Danger of loss of peace is no test of the viciousness of a forward movement, nor should it stand in our way. Let us look for other reasons to see if the movement, that has changed the face of Bengal within the last twelve months, that has converted the average self-satisfied self-contained Bengalee into a true patriot, placing the good of his fellow countrymen before that of his own self, that has made the so-called timid Bengalee seek for occasions of risk and danger, that has drawn out of their shell of retirement, retired High Court Judges and eminent lawyers to lay the foundations of a National Seminary for education,[14] that has transformed talkers into actors and boys into martyrs; and last but not the least that has made the hitherto superbly haughty European bureaucrat tremble in his chair of safety, is sound? Let us examine this new movement, which has given so much vitality to Bengal, from points of view other than those of peace or no peace. If the movement is otherwise sound, good and righteous, peace or no peace, we must follow it and consecrate our lives to it. If on examination it is found to be unsound, vicious and unrighteous we may safely keep aloof from it. If it is defective we may remove its defects and adopt it with necessary modifications. Be what it may, one thing is certain that nobody, not even the mighty bureaucracy that rules this country, can ignore the new movement and kill it by ridicule and contempt. It is a legitimate sequel of Lord Curzon's defiant attitude towards the sons of the soil.

The administration of Lord Curzon, his repressive and retrograde legislation, his defiance of public opinion, led the people to conclude that purely paper agitation on the part of a class of Indians who, on account of their education, considered and still consider themselves to be the natural leaders of the people, is utterly futile in influencing the decisions of the Government. They saw that, notwithstanding a continuous paper and lip agitation for the last twenty years, the Government had gradually withdrawn or nullified every privilege that had been granted to them by Government of Lord Ripon.[15] Local self-government has been made a farce by the officializing of the local bodies,

14. The National Council of Education formed in November 1905 founded the Bengal National College which was inaugurated on 4 August 1906.
15. George Fredrick Samuel Robinson, second earl and first marquis of Ripon (1827-1909);

education has been centralized in the hands of the Government Educational Department, competitive examinations for entry into the public service have either been abolished or curtailed, the universities have been placed under official censorship; in fact, the one sole subject of Lord Curzon's policy has been to shut all sources of public activity to the sons of the soil, where the latter could possibly learn lessons of self-help and self-reliance and receive the necessary training for the government of their country by themselves.

Under these circumstances the leaders in Bengal concluded and rightly concluded that it was high time to turn to the people, the real source of all political power. They had hitherto looked to the Government to grant them democratic institutions evidently forgetting that the latter must be made by the democracy itself. Democratic institutions signify a government of the democracy by the democracy itself. Those who want this must give a *fortiori* look to the democracy and not the powers that are interested in keeping the latter down. It was no wonder, then, that the ruling class looked with contempt upon those who could talk glibly but did not evidently understand the alphabet of democratic movements. Their claims to represent the people were consequently scouted and their resolutions thrown into the wastepaper basket. The claims of the educated classes to speak in the name of the masses because the former were the natural leaders of the latter were simply scoffed at because these so-called leaders never cared to approach those whom they professed to lead. Thank God! the mistake, eventually, went home and the Bengal leaders realised the force of the same. Having done so they initiated the policy of passive resistance and for the first time, during British rule, they took the people into their confidence and attempted both to teach and lead them. This attempt has been wonderfully successful and the success of Bengal has shown to the people of other provinces that what has been done and done successfully there, can be and should be done now or hereafter in other parts of India as well. It pains us that at the present moment the leaders in Bengal should be fighting amongst themselves over a matter which does not seem to be of such a great importance as is attached to it. Is it really such a question of life and death that efforts should be made to keep back Mr. Tilak from the Presidentship of the next Congress or that the other party should stake everything on it?[16] I think not. Is then the struggle in the Bengal amongst the leaders meaningless? Again I must

---

Secretary of State for India, 1866; Viceroy of India, 1880-84; Colonial Secretary, 1892-95; Privy Seal, 1905-08.

16. The Extremists of Bengal were in favour of making Tilak President of the forthcoming Calcutta Congress. But the Moderates were opposed to this. The issue was, however, resolved by persuading Dadabhai Naoroji to accept the Presidentship.

answer the question in the negative. The real and vital question at issue seems to be whether the call to democracy, which has been so successfully made during the last twelve months, ought to be continued or given up at the first show of a trivial surrender by the Government. If the old leaders for whom we have the greatest respect really mean to give up the call to democracy and again begin to call on the Government to give them this and to give them that, then I am afraid they are grievously mistaken. Why should they assume that Mr. Morley[17] can do for them what only the democracy can do for itself? Let it be understood once for all by all concerned that democratic institutions are never conceded by governments (not democratic) but won by democracies for themselves. If this conclusion be correct then it is, perhaps, futile to argue whether we want autonomy in a colonial form of government or complete independence. In due course the democracy shall have what it is fit for. The only thing to be insisted upon and never to be lost sight of is that if democratic institutions are desired, the appeal should primarily be made to the democracy. It is the latter which should be principally worked upon and not the government. That is at least what Mr. Morley's writings teach us and if that teaching is right our course is straight and we need not turn from it even if Mr. Morley wishes us to do. The Swadeshi and the boycott in Bengal have raised the people to a consciousness of their power, they have taught them the uses of combination and for once in the history of British India the industrial and the wage-earning classes in this country seem to be realizing that their destiny and their bread is in their own hands and not in the hands of those handful of people who lord it over them. The secret of this new movement is that educated people, well-versed in the methods of democratic agitation, have condescended to throw themselves amongst the people, to enlighten them on their rights and duties and to influence them for good. These last twelve months have actually worked wonders in Bengal. Where 100 years' lip agitation and paper agitation failed these six months, or twelve months' right work has succeeded. Let nobody misunderstand the real situation. It is the state of affairs in Bengal that is influencing Mr. Morley or strengthening his hands to induce the British democracy to make some concessions to the people of India. In my opinion the new movement materially strengthened the hands of Mr. Gokhale in his last mission to England. But for the new movement Mr. Gokhale might not have received as much attention as he is believed to have secured at the hands of the authorities in England. The present political unrest in India is due to this new movement of self-help and self-reliance which bids fair to inaugurate an era of effective passive resistance. I am sorry that the new party, called the party of

17. John Morley (1838-1923); British statesman; Chief Secretary for Ireland, 1886 and 1892-95; Secretary of State for India, 1905-10; created viscount in 1908.

Extremists in Bengal, should have allowed the real truth to be clouded even for a time by the comparatively paltry question of who should be the President of the next Congress or by the occasional use of rather extravagant language which cannot certainly be justified by the existing condition of things in the country. In my humble opinion, the new movement does not require the so-called exposure of the old leaders nor does it require the use of that extravagant language to which objection is being taken by the old leaders. If the old leaders fail to go with the times, their leadership itself may be in danger. If, however, they are prepared to rise equal to the occasion then there would be no occasion for regret. The party of action need neither curse nor bless. Theirs should be the mission to raise the democracy to a sense of their importance and their duty. It matters little who presides at the next Congress so long as the party of action realise their duty and are resolved to continue their work irrespective of the smiles or frowns of both friends and foes. We have a very high opinion of the leaders, be they of the so-called old school or the new. As to the lines of work, it seems that the whole country must be unanimous about the desirability of acting on the lines of self-help and self-reliance. It is habit (which is often second nature) which now and again sways the leaders of the country not to give up the old methods of work altogether and go at a slow pace. I am a believer in evolution and it is my firm conviction that a few disappointments more and everyone will recognise the futility or at least the insufficiency of what is called the begging policy. Even revolutions are the products of the process of evolution. The political upheaval in Bengal has been rather sudden and it is this suddenness which stuns both the friends and foes. So long as the country is led by honest and sincere men I have no doubt that sooner or later all of them will come to realize that liberty was never conceded but won. By themselves are nations made is a truth eternal and for all times and for all people and it cannot be otherwise for us. What we want of our leaders is to set themselves earnestly to the task of preparing the democracy for the coming struggle. I hope I am not betraying any confidence in saying that in Mr. Gokhale's opinion too, 9/10th of our work lies in India and 1/10th in England. If so let us attend to this 9/10 earnestly. The question of continuing the Congress on the old lines or introducing changes in it is only one of time and procedure. The object is one and indivisible, viz. to unite and win our liberty. Some difference of opinion is bound to exist with regard to it. It has been so in all countries. Let us read history with profit and try to avoid magnifying these differences by adopting an acrimonious attitude towards each other. Every one of us has our failings whether he belongs to the old school of thought or the new. The "old" leaders (I use the word "old" only to avoid any misunderstanding) are entitled to our best thanks for all that they did, according to their own light, at a time when, perhaps, nothing else could be attempted. They are naturally loath to give up old methods altogether and want to proceed very cautiously. I do not think anyone need ascribe motives to them for this. So far as we in the Punjab are concerned we feel real and sincere respect both for Mr. Gokhale and Mr. Tilak. We admire the work of both Babu Surenderanath Banerjea as well as that of Babu Bepin Chandra Pal.[18] We are also grateful to Messrs Mehta, Wacha[19] and others for all that they have been doing and are doing in the interests of their country according to their own light. We Indians just now are not in a position to quarrel with each other and start acrimonious controversies. I know that at times the temptation is too great to be avoided even by the soberest and the most moderate of men, to use strong language as well as to indulge in strong criticisms. Even Mr. Naoroji cannot help doing so at times. But as amongst ourselves I would prefer a more harmonious and compromising spirit of co-operation than may, perhaps, be justified by strict adherence to theoretical principles. In my humble opinion it is a question of *modus operandi*. There can be absolutely no harm in having recourse to expediency in *modus operandi*. But then I see no reason why people should be so thick-skinned as to resent the slightest criticism or to convert differences of opinion on matters of principle into personal enmities. I would appeal to my countrymen outside Bengal to avoid taking sides in this controversy. The controversy as to principles is harmless, nay, perhaps desirable. The controversy as to me should, as far as possible, be avoided. Nor do I think is it necessary to lay down any hard and fast rules as to what shall be our attitude towards the Government. That it must be one of *legal* loyalty is granted on all hands. That we should give up praying to the Government for all times to come need not be laid down as a rule. Everything will depend upon the attitude of the authorities to the altered condition of the times. There is only one thing about which we should be very particular, viz. not to discontinue our work in the masses. If we are true to our determination to educate the masses, to win their affection and attachment, in short, if we remain *loyal to our* own people we have nothing to conceal, nothing to be afraid of. For God's sake let us not fritter away our energies in mutual

18. (1858-1932); a Brahmo leader and "Extremist" Congressman of Bengal; took active part in politics after the partition of Bengal; refused to give evidence in the case against Aurobindo Ghose and imprisoned for six months in 1907; resigned from the Congress in 1908; connected with several newspapers and journals, including *The Tribune* and *New India*; started *Swaraj* (fortnightly) in England in 1908; member, Indian Legislative Assembly, 1923-26.
19. D.E. Wacha (1844-1936); journalist, politician and businessman of Bombay; founder-member of the Congress, and its President, 1901, and General Secretary, 1908-13, left the party in 1919; member, Bombay Legislative Council, 1915-16; member, Imperial Legislative Council, 1916-20; Governor, Imperial Bank of India, 1916-20; President, Western India Liberal Association, 1919-27; works include *Rise and Growth of Bombay Municipal Government* (1913) and *Shells from the Sands of Bombay* (1920).

recriminations and in high-sounding words. As to the Presidentship of the next Congress, I for my part see no reason why the old leaders should be so suspicious of Mr. Tilak. Do they really believe him so devoid of commonsense as to turn everything topsy-turvy if he is elected as President. If, on the other hand, his election is not desired by a majority of the Reception Committee why is not the matter put to a vote and set at rest. The decision of the majority should bind all. If it is decided to invite Mr. Naoroji the whole country will receive the decision with acclamation. In any case, whoever is selected by a majority of the Reception Committee should be accepted with good grace by all concerned.

A word more on the relations of Hindus and Mohammedans and I have done. It is my firm conviction that Hindus shall never cease to be Hindus and Mohammedans shall never cease to be Mohammedans. Their religious ideals are so different that it is impossible to expect a complete social union of them in the near future. But that is no reason why they cannot make common cause in political work. Against non-Indians they have common grievances. In the political future of the country both are equally interested. When a foreigner insults an Indian or treats him with contempt he hardly stops to enquire if the object of his attack is a Hindu or a Mohammedan. When the Europeans want a monopoly of certain high offices in the state they make no exceptions in favour of Mohammedans. Why can't we then stand shoulder to shoulder on the political platform? The press and the public men in this country hardly ever make any distinction between Hindus and Mohammedans when ventilating political grievances or when bringing to light individual cases of oppression. It is no business of any political association to enquire if the sufferer is a Hindu or a Mohammedan. Every public man in the country should consider it his duty to expose official injustice, high-handedness and oppression irrespective of the religion of the victim. Let us then take to work honestly, sincerely and earnestly, my brethren, with a faith in God and in the righteousness of our cause and with a determination to win at any cost

4
VISIT TO ENGLAND AND AMERICA
1. General

1. To G.K. Gokhale[1]

Lahore
17 March 1905

Dear Mr. Gokhale,

Yours of the 13th has delighted me. Please accept my thanks for the same. The movement for electing a delegate from the Punjab would receive a great impetus if you could visit Punjab on your return from Calcutta but as that is not possible we shall be very grateful for your visit later on as suggested.[2] I am sure your visit will infuse new life in the Indian Association of Lahore and we shall be able to push on political work in this province with greater vigour and with better chances of success. I shall send to you a formal resolution of the Indian Association inviting you to the Punjab in a day or two. So far as I am concerned, I shall leave nothing undone to make your stay at Lahore agreeable, comfortable and I will feel greatly honoured if you would agree to stay with me. We have so many things to talk to each other that a stay anywhere else will suit neither. I hope you will give me a definite promise on this and accept my humble invitation. Punjab papers will show that the idea of sending a delegate from the Punjab is gaining ground.

Yours sincerely,
Lajpat Rai

1. G.K. Gokhale Papers (microfilm), N.A.I.
2. Lajpat Rai was eventually elected a delegate of the Congress from Punjab to visit, along with Gokhale, England to propagate the cause of India at the time of general elections to be held there.

2. To G.K. Gokhale[1]

Lahore
29 March 1905

Dear Mr. Gokhale,

You will probably be leaving Calcutta tonight or tomorrow and this letter will find you at Poona. The Indian Association have passed a resolution formally inviting you to the Punjab and to give you a public reception. Now will you please let me have a definite date of your arrival? I may inform you at the same time that we are going to have a great gathering in the Easter holidays as the foundation stone of the new building of the D.A.V. College will be laid in those days by H.H. Sir Maharaja Partap Singh.[2] The event will be fixed for the 23rd probably though we have yet to obtain his H.H.'s consent to the exact date. He has agreed to perform the function in Easter. It will, therefore, give us great pleasure to have you amongst us in those days. I will, therefore, suggest that you may reach here on the 20th or the 21st by the latest and may give us the benefit of your company for five days.

Will you please let me know like a good friend what arrangements will you require for your boarding? I mean to enquire, excuse me for these impertinent questions, if you observe orthodoxy and are a vegetarian? Can you ordinarily take food prepared by one who is not a Mahratta Brahmin?

Can you give me any idea as to the probable time of the departure of the Congress deputatioin? Is it possible that it may not go at all? Will you give me some hints as to the dress or dresses I should prepare for England? I am pledged to Swadeshi articles and I will like to have my dresses prepared here of Swadeshi stuff. Is a black coat an absolute necessity in England? You cannot get good Indian stuff of that colour. Did you keep to your dress when you last visited England? This doesn't mean that I am going for certain but I want to have this information to make use of it in case I have to go. Please also let me know what work will be expected of me there and what literature should I study in order to be in a position to discharge my duty properly if not creditably.

1. G.K. Gokhale Papers (microfilm), N.A.I.
2. Ruler of Jodhpur State and a prominent member of Arya Samaj.

I am afraid I am making a great demand on your time and taxing your kindness too much but in the hope that you will excuse an inexperienced brother if he presumes to make up his deficiency by first-class advice.

I remain

Yours very sincerely,
Lajpat Rai

3. On the Object of His Visit to England[1]

In thanking you for the great honour you have done me by electing me as your representative on the Congress deputation going to England and in assembling here to bid me farewell, I think I am bound to make some observations on the political outlook in general and on the prospects of political work in Great Britain in particular. Coming straight as I am from the Kangra valley I cannot help being very sad and dejected just now as I saw a sight there which has touched me to the core, and which has temporarily at least impressed me with the vanity of all human struggles.[2] However optimistic one may be, the present is a time when no one can help being sad and melancholy at the great crisis through which this country is passing. At first sight the near future is anything but bright. Nay, it is positively gloomy. A sense of overwhelming fatality prevails in the country. On all sides he finds that his country and his people are being held fast by adverse circumstances. To his limited vision even the elements seem to have joined hands with men in running down and chasing to death and destruction the ill-fated people of this land, once the land of the *Devas*. On one side a "benevolent" Government proud of its "unparalleled liberality" is doing

1. Speech at a meeting of leading citizens of Lahore held on 8 May 1905 to bid farewell to him before his departure for England as a representative of the Congress. *The Panjabee*, 15 May 1905.

   Lajpat Rai and Gokhale were elected, at the Bombay session of the Congress held in December 1904, members of the Congress deputation to visit England, at the time of the general election to be held there in summer, to represent the case of the Congress before the British electorate. Lajpat Rai's election was later endorsed by the Punjab branch of the Indian Association which also collected funds to defray his expenses. He, however, set sail on 13 May from Bombay, two months before Gokhale.
2. On 4 April 1905, several villages and towns, including Dharamsala, in the Kangra valley (now in Himachal Pradesh), were rocked by a severe earthquake, resulting in a great loss of life and property. For details, see *post*, section 8.

its level best to put back the hand of the clock of progress, on the other, the demons of disease, pestilence, scarcity and famine seem to have taken a fancy for this country of ours. Without showing any sign of mercy, they are every day tightening their grip closer and closer. While on the one side an all-powerful Government is busily and assiduously engaged in devising plans and making rules, which are very likely to close the gates of secondary schools and colleges, against the sons of the poor and the peasant,[3] on the other the rich and the well-to-do are being hustled into eternity by plague and earthquake. At this moment there is hardly a single class of His Majesty King Edward's Indian subjects who is happy and contented. Even the Royal Prince finds that his position, influence and power are gone and that in the land which was probably his for centuries past, acquired by his ancestors and ruled by his forefathers, he is today possessed of as much real power as a common coolie; that the place which his predecessors only a few decades ago occupied that land of his sires, is now virtually occupied by a common agent of that foreign Government which rules supreme over the 30 crores of Indians; that his honour, rank and emoluments (reader, mark the word emoluments for Ruling Chiefs of First Class Native States such as Kashmere) are at the mercy of a foreigner whose pay is charged against his own revenues: yes, while the Prince is smarting under the loss of dignity from which he suffers by the insults heaped upon him by the local embodiment of the Imperial power, the peasant is no less unhappy in his hut. Ground down by the rigid and inflexible revenue system, crushed by continuous famines, bound down by the forest laws, which prevent him from picking up wild fruit for food, bits of fuel for his hearth and the cutting of grass for his sheep, he drags his miserable lot, cursing neither the Government nor his God but his own fate. Coming to the other classes you hear the same cry of woe from the landlord, the moneylender, the trader, the pleader and the Government servant. The latter who was till lately very cheerful and happy is now the loudest and the bitterest in his complaints against his employers, forced to sit till late in the evening often burning oil to perform his daily task, he finds that his prospects are either gone or seriously curtailed. The number of posts carrying gold salaries, which ordinarily fell to the lot of the sons of the soil, is falling; the salaries are going down while the provisions are going up in prices and necessities becoming dearer and rarer every day. But amidst all these scenes of death, disease and distracting darkness, is there no streak of light and sunshine and not a vestige of hope? I am loath to admit that such is the case. Thinking

3. The resolution on education policy passed by the Government of India on 11 March 1904 laid down stringent conditions for the recognition of secondary schools by the Government, thus discouraging private efforts to promote higher education. It also made higher education expensive.

seriously of the situation I am at times inclined to adopt an attitude of thankfulness towards Lord Curzon for his having opened the eyes of the Indians to the huge delusion under which they were living and to the absolute necessity of unity of classes for the common weal, and to the still greater necessity of never forgetting the truth of the saying that "a nation which cannot win its own freedom does not deserve it".[4]

The unanimous protest made by the whole country against Lord Curzon's attack on our national character and the one unbroken wave of indignation which the Universities Validating Act[5] has evoked, the tangible awakening to the necessity of industrial and technical education abroad and the moral conviction that our salvation must after all come from within, are to my mind some of the substantial gains which the country seems to have scored by Lord Curzon's unmasked benevolence and liberalism. In my humble opinion Lord Curzon has done a service to this country by giving it some object lessons in politics and disabusing it of certain deep-rooted wrong impressions. Although Lord Curzon too has played very freely with that fatal gift, viz. the gift of making soft and grandiloquent speeches, still his occasional slips and the results of his policy have given to the people of this country sufficient and tangible evidences of the real trend of his policy. Although we can never be too grateful to those high-minded British statesmen who have now and then advanced the cause of education in this country and honestly striven to further its prosperity and hold the balance of justice even between the claims of the rulers and the ruled, still I think it is a providential dispensation to have now and then a Governor who, by a policy of retrogression, forcibly drives home the necessity of self-reliance and self-help to the minds of the subject race. Lord Curzon's policy has only laid bare the fact which can be abundantly proved by quotations from the history of British rule in India, if any proof is needed, that British rule in India exists primarily for the British and only secondarily for the sons of the soil and, with the exception of a few high-minded and noble-souled Englishmen, the ordinary run of humanity. From the necessities of the situation and from the ready proneness of the people of this country to believe in the benevolent intentions of others, often taking them at their words, it is necessary that something should occasionally happen to open their eyes to the nature of things and to enable them to see things in their real colour. Viewed from this point of

4. The reference was to Curzon's convocation address to the Calcutta University delivered on 11 February 1905 in which he made a sweeping indictment of Indians love of vile flattery and disregard for truth.
5. The Universities Validating Act enacted in February 1905 officialized the Senates and made University education quite expensive. See also the preceding item.

view, I think Lord Curzon's policy, declarations and acts may prove to be of great value to the people of this country.

One of the signs of the time is the coming to light of a greater desire of unity between the Hindus and Mohammedans. The former have always been eager for it and making substantial advances to achieve that end. But till now except in Bombay and Madras the feeling was hardly reciprocated by the Mohammedans. In Upper India, in fact, a contrary policy ruled supreme for some time and gave birth to a policy of retaliation on the part of Hindus. Of late, however, evidences have not been wanting of a better spirit having taken hold of our Mohammedan brethren. Both Hindus and Mohammedans in Upper India seem to be realising, slowly though, that while each of them can honestly try his best for the good of his own coreligionists, both of them can join hands while common interests are in danger, or where they can join hands without the chances of inflicting any loss on their respective communities. Some educated Mohammedans have of late begun to see eye to eye with the great body of educated Hindus on political questions of the day and this is a very healthy and welcome sign of times. Then again the promptness with which Bengal has managed to send ten of its best graduates (amongst them two Mohammedans) for education abroad and the example set by some Native States too is worthy of note. The industrial awakening, though it requires a very careful handling and a very vigilant nursing, is again very hopeful. Under the circumstances, what the country now chiefly stands in need of is a determination to push on education of all sorts at all costs, and though not quite up to what is required, there are some slight indications of the people having formed or being prepared to form such a determination. On the whole, then I think there is no ground for despondency and no occasion for giving way to hopelessness.

At this stage it might be expected of me to explain if there is much good likely to be done by the Congress deputation proceeding to England and spending Rs. 50,000 upon political agitation there. If it is true that the salvation of India depends upon education why not then spend these 50,000 rupees in furthering the cause of education at home, rather than spend the money in a foreign country under the vain hope of extorting political concessions from the "benevolent" British voter.

Now to be frank in the matter, I have never believed in the benevolent intentions of the British elector more than I do in that of any other man of the world. I think he is as good or as bad a man as there are others in this world. Just now Providence has placed him in a position from which he can afford to be benevolent and liberal towards those less favourably situated than he is. While thus using his opportunities for the greatest good of himself, he does not grudge a little show of benevolence and liberality towards others. But to think that he is prepared to lessen his imperial grip upon you or sacrifice his rights, privileges and interests for your sake or for the matter of that for anybody is counting too far, and living in a world of delusion. He is not going to do anything of the sort unless and until he is convinced that his own imperial and national interests require a change in the government of this country or in the principles upon which the government of this country is at present conducted. With me this has been an article of faith for long and I have no reason now to change or alter it in any way. So far as the British elector, therefore, is concerned it will do no good to appeal to him in the name of political philanthropy or ethical justice in matters political. But then there are Englishmen who think that the misgovernment of India is a danger to the supremacy of England in India and to its position as a first-class power in the world. As patriotic Englishmen, it is their duty to avert such a catastrophe. Now if we honestly believe that the best interests of India for some time to come at least are bound up with the supremacy of England in India, and that for us constitutional agitation is the only safe method of ameliorating our condition, then I think it is our duty to strengthen the hands of such patriotic Englishmen and to cultivate relations of trust and friendship with them. There is no doubt that the Congress deputation will achieve this object more effectually than it could otherwise be done.

Secondly, now that steam and electricity have practically demolished all differences of space and time and have brought the whole world together, it is an absolute necessity for the public men of this country to go and study on the spot the political and educational institutions of other countries in the world and to profit by the experience of others. Then, again, the influence which the press and platform now-a-days exercise not only in the countries where they exist and which they directly represent, but practically all the world over, it is to the best interests of India that it should have supporters amongst these powerful classes in the independent and powerful countries of the world.

India and Indian public men can no longer afford to be segregated and enjoy that aloofness which they have maintained so long. If Western institutions are good and worthy of being copied in India, they must be studied on the spot by some of those Indians who have consecrated their lives to the service of their country and who are in a position to form correct opinions about the same. They must study the circumstances under which they have been brought into existence and have thrived there. They must look if those circumstances exist in their country, and if not, whether they can be brought into existence here, or if that be impossible with what changes and modifications they can be adapted to the needs and circumstances of their country. All this they must study on the spot, which they can best do when they go to these foreign countries in a representative capacity, i.e. not for sightseeing but as the accredited agents of their countrymen, because in such a case they go with a sense of national duty and obligation, which every honest public man must feel the greater if he goes at the public expense. Moreover, the respect which he may command and the opportunities which may be open to him as such may be denied to him otherwise.

Such, at any rate, are the reasons which have swayed with me in making me agree to join the Congress deputation as a representative of the Punjab. I do not know how far I may succeed in these aims, but one thing you may be certain of and that is that I will strive to make the best use of my stay abroad, a use which might help me in the performance of those public duties which I have taken upon myself or which I may hereafter be called upon to undertake. I may assure you that no part of the public money collected for the deputation shall be spent on sightseeing or otherwise on objects which are not likely to further the public interests of my people. If I am conscious of the great honour you have done me in selecting me as your representative, I am no less conscious of my shortcomings to fill up that role. I wish an abler and more capable man could be found to represent you with honour and credit to himself as well as to the province, which we all love so deeply. But in the absence of one such, ready to accept the responsibility, I have presumed to do so in the hope that although in no way equal in literary talents, in facility for speech and writing, in impressive eloquence and in position to any of my colleagues on the deputation who represent the other provinces of our country, I yield to none in the depth of my love for my country and in readiness to serve it at any cost. If so, gentlemen, let me hope that you may have no occasion to be least ashamed of your selection.

4

VISIT TO ENGLAND AND AMERICA

II. On Way to England

1. Journey from Bombay to Port Said[1]

I was overwhelmed by the warm send-off you gentlemen gave me at the Lahore railway station. I was constantly assailed by the thought whether it was not a waste of public money to undertake a trip of whose successful outcome I was doubtful from the outset. What I feared most was that it could be a blemish on my fair name and reputation. When the engine whistled and the train started a European gentleman who was sitting in my compartment asked me if I was a member of the delegation that was going to seek audience with His Majesty the King against Lord Curzon. Taken aback by his query, I told him the purpose of my visit. Dwelling on it further, he said that, of all the British Viceroys sent to India so far, Lord Curzon was undoubtedly the most outstanding and it did not behove Indians to launch a movement against him. I replied that Lord Curzon was no doubt an able Viceroy but what really mattered to us was his demeanour and disposition towards us.

On reaching Bombay I met Mr. Raja who explained to me why Mr. Gokhale had decided to postpone his visit to England. He advised me that taking my cue from him, I should also postpone my visit and instead proceed to America.

From Bombay I left for Poona. At the railway station what surprised me was that women worked there as coolies. They appeared strong and sturdy and were neatly dressed. At Poona station Mr. Gokhale himself came to receive me. We got into a car and drove through the city to his residence. On the way he pointed out to me the buildings and places reminiscent of the Maratha Peshwas' historic past. At first sight Poona looked bigger and more prosperous than Lahore. Maharashtrian women do not observe purdah. They themselves serve food to guests. Mr. Gokhale lived in a grand three-storeyed building and occupied the ground floor overlooking a large courtyard. The rest of the building was occupied by the landlord himself, a prominent lawyer of the city. Mr. Gokhale has two children, both girls, the elder one being of about thirteen years of age. His wife has passed away and now his house is managed by a widowed sister. Mr. Devdhar is Mr. Gokhale's secretary who has decided to dedicate his life to politics.

The people of Poona sleep on the floor and one rarely comes across a charpoy in their houses. But Mr. Gokhale does have a charpoy in his house and

1. Despatch sent after reaching Port Said on 27 May 1905 for publication in *The Panjabee*. But since the *Panjabee* report is not available an English translation of its Urdu version published in the book, *Europe, America Ke Safar Ke Halat*, compiled by Lal Chand Falak is printed here.

he insisted that I should sleep on it. He told me that he was in no mood to go to England, but had perforce to abide by the wishes of the [Servants of India] Society and the general public and so might yet make the trip. According to him, training and discipline are essential prerequisites of a successful public life.

The next day I called on Mr. Tilak who brings out the weekly *Kesari*. He was contemplating entrusting the responsibility for publication to a limited company. He leads a simple spartan life almost like that of a Puritan. I did not see any servant in his house from which I inferred that he attended to all the household chores himself. His two sons were also very simply dressed in *kurtas* and *langotis*. He has three daughters, all married.

In the course of the day I met the Principal of Fergusson College and members of the teaching faculty; they were all very nice to me. I was impressed by the way the college hostel was being run. The college is located at a distance of about one mile from the city. Each professor is entitled to fifteen rupees as monthly fare for a hackney carriage. But these noble men travel together in the same carriage and the savings so effected are returned to the college for its benefit. I dined at Mr. Tilak's house; the food had been cooked by the ladies of the house and was very delicious.

Finally I returned to Bombay and boarded the ship for my voyage. People had come to see off their relatives and friends in large numbers and many of them were loaded with flower garlands which reminded me of my departure from Lahore. But here I found myself alone which made me pensive. But not for long as the vast sea which stretched before me soon absorbed me. As the ship sailed on, the land slowly disappeared from sight. Standing on the deck I wistfully gazed at the land which was my native land, my own country. I was leaving it behind in the hope that after a few months I would come back equipped to serve it better. I thought I was duty bound to shun all pleasures and forego all luxuries in order to serve my country in a befitting manner. I prayed to God, "O Mighty One, give me enlightenment, give me strength so that I may devote the remaining years of my inconsequential life to the service of my motherland with greater fervour."

I was sailing in an Italian ship. All its sailors hailed from Italy. The kitchen too was manned by Italians. Only a few who attended to menial jobs were non-Italians. They were Indians, all of them being poor lowly Muslims. My heart almost broke as this realization dawned on me. It pained me the most that in all walks of life only Indians were doing menial jobs. Alas, I also came from a nation which commanded little respect and had almost no standing in the comity of nations. Neither did it have any ship of its own, nor any Indian was a sailor.

The ship in which I was travelling was splendid; it was spacious and provided ample comforts to its passengers in comparison to the fare it charged.

But things like beef, mutton and pork, which were taboo for a Hindu, could hardly give any sustenance to me.

After sailing some distance we saw another ship appearing on the distant horizon. We kept watching till it came near us. For those of us who had never gone on a voyage earlier, it was a fascinating sight. We could even read the name of the ship—*Arcadia*. And it was bound for Bombay. Unknowingly and unconsciously, it was carrying my thoughts back to my country.

My cabin mate was an old missionary who is a professor in a missionary college at Calcutta. He was of the firm view which was based on his vast educational experience that Lord Curzon had started educational reform on the wrong note. An Anglo-Indian was also travelling with us. From his demeanour and bearing I could easily make out that he must have been a high government official in India. He looked askance at my going down and chatting with deck passengers. I learnt that many Hindu passengers were Aroras and Khatris from Sindh and were going to Gibraltar where they did business. They also owned shops in Malta and Port Said. We were approaching Aden. I thought I would post my next letter from Suez or Port Said.

May 22—The harbour of Aden nestles between barren and rugged mountain cliffs. If this is the place which the Christians' God and Islam's Allah had selected for man's habitation and Satan had a hand in banishing man from here he could not have done greater service to man, for there could not be a worse place on earth for man's habitation. There is no sign of greenery on this vast stretch of land. There are no trees, no shrubs, not even patches of grass to be found anywhere around. The whole place is so terribly hot that we cried to heaven for mercy. Since the 15th of the month we had not sighted land and we were mightily pleased when our gaze fell on this landscape even though it held no charm. The passengers had started collecting their baggage before the ship entered the harbour. Those bound for Aden were now ready to disembark. The officers on board hastily took stock of the merchandise which was to be unloaded. The second class passengers—men, women and children—came out and stood against the railings, watching the scene. It was quite a crowd. In the meanwhile a number of boats loaded with miscellaneous items of merchandise came and docked against the ship. The African boys on the boats noisily hawked their goods. There were some Muslim salesmen also who were selling different varieties of picture postcards, ostrich feather fans, ostrich eggs, lion and tiger skins, necklaces of various kinds of beads and suchlike curios. When a bargain was struck the seller placed the thing in a basket attached to a string which the customer lifted up and then lowered it with the money placed in it. I bought some picture postcards. The African boys spoke English with great facility. To start with, they would demand exorbitant prices and ultimately reduced them to reasonable limits. An Englishman threw a four-anna coin into the sea. A boy promptly dived and came up with the coin. Some men on the boats were Punjabis as was evident from their dress. There was a letterbox on the ship in which the passengers dropped their letters for clearance at the next port of call.

The sea along the harbour was quite shallow and when a ship started moving, the water became muddy. I kept watching the moving ship till ten o'clock and then went to sleep. When I woke up in the morning I was told that we were passing through the Suez Canal. On both sides, there were wild shrubs and sand dunes and there was a vast land stretching in front of us. It was a wondrous sight. The canal cut through two vast continents separating the land-masses from each other.

May 23—A high wind kept blowing throughout the day. I saw many ships proceeding towards India. Here the water of the Red Sea was very clear, as if someone had swept the bottom clean with a huge broom and spread a white sheet over it. The sea was full of rocks. So to prevent the ships from floundering several lighthouses were there across the sea. Had I not been travelling by this ship I would not have known that, apart from Englishmen, people of other European nationalities also inhabit India in fairly large numbers. As the ship ploughed through the sea one saw land on both sides and in some places the African land stretched far into the distance creating the impression that it was travelling with the ship. I regretted not having brought enough books with me to utilize my time to good purpose.

For the next two days our ship moved placidly without tossing or shaking, so much so that while eating in the dining room I felt as if I was eating sitting at home. The Europeans—men and women alike—were, generally speaking, of a happy disposition. They sang, laughed, played and read; they knew how to enjoy life when they were not preoccupied with work. As regards urbanity and courtesy, they in no way lagged behind the people of Lucknow or Delhi, whose sophisticated manners are well known. They were sticklers for decorum and knew what good manners were. They did not slurp milk or tea but drank without making any sound and ate with the knife and fork elegantly. They did not stare at women nor pick their noses in public. They removed their caps while entering the dining room and were all courtesy to ladies.

May 24—Again, a strong wind blew all the day and the sea was also rough. At night some European gentlemen and ladies arranged a musical soiree. It was held in the second class dining hall and invitation was extended to all the first and second class passengers. The invitees were served iced drinks and snacks. Liquor flowed freely. It was an Italian ship and liquor produced in Italy was available at subsidized rates. Except for a Protestant missionary and two Englishmen, all others drank down to the dregs. Even the children had a go at it. It was an occasion for merry-making. Only we Indians, of whom there were many, avoided drinks. It was a beautiful dining hall full of gaiety and mirth. We felt completely oblivious of the fathomless sea rolling beneath our feet.

May 25—The sea had turned cold and placid cliffs of various shapes, some of them big enough to look like mountains, greeted our eyes in the course of the day. In the evening when we were about 200 miles away from the Suez Canal we saw an island, with a range of hills about five miles long, rising a mile away to the west of our ship. The coast here was slightly above the sea level and seemed to be jutting out into the sea, presenting a beautiful sight. This place through which we were now passing, as if in a trance, was viewed as very dangerous by the sailors, both for man and man-made ships. Under the surface of the water, unseen rocks make navigation hazardous. There was no sign of habitation anywhere. Even when seen through binoculars, one did not find any trace of greenery even on the mountains. As we sailed past a big lighthouse along the coast, it occurred to me that, like these lighthouses, how nice it would be if we could have more guides among us in the form of great men to illumine the path of life and to save the erring mankind from straying into wrong courses. In the evening the temperature dropped further, and the night became all the more chilly. In the cabin I felt the need for pulling the blanket over my body.

May 26—In the morning the coast was visible on both sides and the sea had become narrower. As I got up I felt that the wind had become very cold. By about eight-thirty the shrillness of wind seemed to have died down and the sea appeared a gigantic pond. Last night I had a long chat with an American missionary who was keen to know my opinion about missionary activities in India. He particularly wanted to know if their work had done any good to Indians in general. Without mincing words I told him with utmost candour that the people were averse to their acts of religious conversion. In fact it did great harm to the people. Apart from the fact that such conversion was contrary to my religious beliefs, a rise in Christian population could have a baneful effect on the Indian populace. Then he wished to know whether the present trends augured well for the country and if so in what direction the country was proceeding. On the social plane, I told him that as things were, I was sanguine that our country was bound to make great progress and it was not long before our country would emerge from the mire of poverty and passive slothfulness. I told him about our college and about the activities of the Arya Samaj. He agreed that a country which had such institutions was bound to make progress. He also probed me about the Hindu philosophy and the allied Hindu literature. I dwelt on the subject quite at length and seemingly to his satisfaction. From the expression on his face it seemed as if he had wandered into a domain hitherto unknown to him.

May 27—It is now about nine and the port of Suez is already within my sight; it is at a short distance. Since my starting from Bombay it is for the first time that I am watching signs of greenery. The Red Sea abruptly ends at the mouth of the Suez Canal. Perhaps it would be more correct to say that the continent of Asia ends here and it is here that the handiwork of man seems to have annihilated distance. By digging a canal by artificial means man has brought the landmasses of Asia and Europe nearer to each other. The man who thought of this device must indeed have been a veritable genius.

The port of Suez is very beautiful. As you enter the canal from Asia you find that the left bank is throughout paved with stones and beautiful houses flank the entire length of the bank. The road has offices of the shipping companies of various maritime nations with their respective flags flying over them. By digging this canal Europe has bound Asia hand and foot. But for this canal Europe would not have been so powerful and lording it over Asia.

Even though our ship was anchored in the Red Sea about a mile away from the Suez Canal, a large number of vendors came by boats to the ship to sell their wares. The items of sale were nicely arrayed on the deck. They included necklaces of colourful beads and artificial corals, picture postcards, fancy goods made in Europe and a plethora of other fancy stuff. A lot of haggling preceded the actual sale.

In some places the canal is at the same level as the land. It is about fifteen feet deep near the bank but is much deeper in the middle so that big ships may pass through it without any difficulty. Only one ship can pass through it at a time. The ships coming from the opposite direction have to wait for their scheduled turn. Dredging of the canal goes on all the time so that the required depth is constantly maintained. The statue of the French engineer who conceived the concept of the canal and built it is a permanent fixture in a prominent market place of Port Said.

2. On His Voyage from Port Said to Naples[1]

On the morning of the 27th, we reached Port Said which is the entrance of Suez Canal from the European side. It is Egyptian territory and a sort of cosmopolitan place where you find men of almost all nationalities. The French are perhaps the largest in number. The Suez Canal was the idea of a French engineer. The Canal was engineered, financed and dug by the French. Hence

1. Second despatch written on 1 June 1905 was published in *The Panjabee* of 3 July 1905.

they were the first Europeans to have the most influence in Egypt and Egyptian waters but eventually they were outdone by the British who are now virtually supreme in Egypt, although an Arab cab driver resented my remark to that effect when I made it in his presence. He, of course, stoutly maintained that the country belonged to and was ruled by the Arabs through their sovereign, the Khedive. The trading and business houses are mostly owned and managed by the French who have got a post office of their own as well as a bank. The nationality which seems to be the next best represented is the Italian, as Italy of all the great European countries is the nearest to Port Said. The administration is, of course, in the hands of Arabs, most of whom are dressed after the Turkish fashion, in European coats and trousers with a Turkish fez.

Here you get the first peep into the dark side of the Western civilization, when at almost every step you are offered obscene photographs not by Arab hawkers only but by apparently respectable European merchants. These photographs represent indescribable and unspeakably revolting scenes.

The French and Italian languages are better understood at this port than the English. It is at places like these that you are most strongly impressed with the superior aptitude of the Asiatics to pick up languages. The Arab traders, guides, cabmen and other similar people speak English, French, Italian and some of them even Hindustani, pretty fluently while most of the Italians on board our steamer do not understand a word of English. We have got a number of trained Missionaries on our steamer who are supposed to know Latin and French very well, but even they have to use signs to make themselves understood by Italian stewards and attendants. It is also evidenced by the fact that an Indian on board our steamer can talk Italian very fluently as well as understand a bit of English while the Italians can neither talk nor understand English.

At Port Said the Government evidently owns all the boats that ply for hire. They charge 3d. for one passenger and the boatman expects only a *bakshish*. The boatmen, however, charge heavy fares from strangers. The Arab town is at a little distance from the port, say, about a mile, but the port settlement continues up to the town itself. The Arab town has got narrow lanes kept as horribly dirty as those in Bombay, but the Arabs, both men and women whom I saw here, are mostly fair complexioned with handsome features and graceful figures. The original Arab dress seems to resemble very much the dress worn by Kashmiri men and women at Srinagar. The Arab veil, however, has got some curious specialities of its own. It is quite unlike the *burqa* we see at Lahore. Part of the face is visible though an attempt is made to conceal the nose. The Western-educated, the cultured and the well-to-do have mostly taken to European dress in various modified forms just as in India. The Turkish fez is very common. Port Said is the terminus of the Egyptian Railway and we went over and saw the railway station and the railway carriages. The 3rd class carriages have got a corridor in the middle with seats on both sides; otherwise they seem to be no better than those on the Indian Railways. The 1st and 2nd class carriages are decidedly inferior to the Indian ones. There is no Intermediate class. The platform tickets are sold by the gatekeeper at the gate, who is always present, and not at the booking office as at Lahore. This is very convenient and ought to be copied by the Indian Railways. The Arab mosques here are quite dissimilar to those in India. You miss the Indian domes. There is only one central minaret on the gate. Provisions seem to be dear though labour cannot be very costly as we paid only 2sh. (i.e. Re. 1-8) for a two-horsed victoria for 2 hours to drive us through the town, and only 6d. to a guide for the whole day.

The Greek church and the offices of the Suez Canal Company are amongst the most remarkable buildings. A brisk trade is carried on in Egyptian tobacco, cigarettes, photographic cards, and Palestine onions. Arabian dates and Turkish sweets are also sold largely. The European settlement is almost choked with a French atmosphere and you are very soon disgusted with it. Coffee is the favourite drink both among the Europeans and the Arabs. Cafes and restaurants are very common in both the European and Arab quarters.

This is the port for changing steamers for the Black Sea, the Adriatic Sea and the Greek isles. Our steamer goes straight to Sicily right through the Mediterranean without calling at Alexandria or at any other port. We were in the harbour the whole day. Shortly before dusk, a party of Italian singers, including a woman and a girl, all playing on guitars and other similar instruments, came near our ship and seated in a boat began to serenade us. The Europeans on board threw them bits of silver pieces for which they held a reversed umbrella. In the evening the harbour looked very pretty and the scene was very beautiful; the lights and lanterns reflected in the sea and the people strolling about or rowing in boats. The lighthouse here adds a great deal to the charms of the place at night. The three streaks of revolving light coming in rotation make the whole situation magnificent.

At about 9 P.M., we weighed anchor, and left the harbour to step into the deep dark blue Mediterranean. We encountered a strong wind and a furious sea. All the next day (28th) the sea continued to be agitated and rough and we felt very uncomfortable on board. The steamer, though not quite rolling, shook terribly, and most of the ladies became sick and several of the gentlemen too. The wind was very cold and chilly and I had to put on heavy clothing. I felt very uneasy and took little food but did not vomit. Sometime in the night, the sea became calm and the shaking of the steamer ceased. The morning of the 29th was nice though pretty cool. We were steaming into the island of Crete on our right. The snow-clad hills of this island are very pretty to look at. Crete is a Greek island and has of late given much trouble to the Government of Turkey to whom it really belongs. The interference of the European powers and the encouragement it gives rise to have made the Christian population very turbulent, and in consequence one hears of so many political disturbances there. As usual, the so-called Turkish brutalities fill page after page of the European press and the European powers get a fresh handle to put pressure upon the Turkish Government which is forced to yield. The island is now practically under European management and Turkish suzerainty is only nominal. It was so cold at this time that I had to put on my *pugree*. I am the only man on board the steamer with an Indian *pugree*. There are some Indian traders (Hindus) as 3rd class passengers but they all use caps.

On the 29th and the 30th we had a furious sea agitated by strong wind followed by a squall and something like a storm. We had rain also. The great waves rising and beating about the steamer appeared as if expressing the anger of the sea at the presumption of our boat in piercing through the heart of the great ocean. It was here that I got a little idea of what the sea must be in stormy weather. It was beautiful weather but awful, good to look at but terrible to be in. Our steamer rolled as if it was reeling under the influence of wine, of which there was plenty on board which was supplied to passengers free of cost at their discretion. The ladies and my companion[2] were very sick; I myself felt unpleasant sensations and at times my head reeled but I was straight all the time. Not once did I vomit. The 30th was the worst of all the days we passed on the steamer. With a stormy sea, rolling ship, chilly weather, disagreeable food we felt as if it was better to stay at home. The morning of the 31st, however, dawned in better mood and on more agreeable scenes. As soon as I was upon the deck, a finger pointed out the white-capped snow-clad Etna on our left. Who could think that the white summit had a seething heart of burning fire? On the right were the hills of Italy with white-washed village buildings and some zig-zag streams pouring their humble quota of waters into the sea. A little later on we had on our left clearly visible piles of buildings, raising their heads in majesty, with beautiful verdant hills at their back and the cool calm sea in the front. The field and opera glasses and binoculars were at once in demand and fingers began to point out the broad neat streets, the spires and towers of lofty buildings, the ramparts of forts, railway bridges and many other things visible from the steamer to eager spectators who were all clustered on the same side. Some of us thought that it was Messina, once the capital of Sicily (no longer a separate kingdom but a part of Italy) and now the most important town of the two Sicilies. But our steamer continued its onward march as if it did not care to call at the port or as if this was not Messina. When we had a run parallel atmost to the end of the city, lo! the ship began to turn round,

2. Lala Diwan Chand Kapur of Lahore, who was going to England on business, accompanied Lajpat Rai during the journey.

and someone told me that we were now going into the harbour. The truth of the matter is that the harbour of Messina is oval-shaped with its entrance on the north, and as we were also going north, our ship had to take a turn to enter it. As soon as we entered, the majestic city was at once in full view. The harbour had a number of steamers riding at anchor with swarms of boats, including a torpedo boat, with people busy in loading, unloading and transhipping cargo. It was one of the most picturesque sights I had ever seen. As soon as we dropped anchor a number of small boats surrounded us, some selling fruits and others containing the friends of people on board come to receive them. We were, however, warned not to have any communication with the shore people or to buy anything until the doctor had come, examined us and declared the steamer free from plague. On enquiry we learnt that the last port we called at (Port Said) had a plague case the very day we left and therefore we were in quarantine again. At about 10 A.M. the doctor came and just then the breakfast bell rang and we all went down to the saloon to take our meal. A short while after when most of us were at the table, the doctor came in and counted us. That was all the medical examination we underwent and *bus*! Immediately after, we came up and wanted to go ashore but no, the doctor had not yet given the word.

Oh, how interesting it was to study the faces of the Italians on board who had reached their sweet beloved country! Their faces were all beaming with that happiness which is only known to and felt by those who come home after a long interval spent in distant places. How impatient they were to go and embrace their dear ones and yet how annoying it looked to detain them in that supreme moment of joy! At first the effect on me was saddening. With the sight of the Italian flag flying on the harbour, the lighthouse and various other places, with the idea that all Italians spoke one language, were under a national Government, could aspire to the highest honours which a patriot could think of; sailing in their own ships and managing their own affairs, I could not help making comparison with the state of things prevailing in my own country. The thoughts gradually led me to remember that only 50 years before Italy was not a political unit, it was divided into many States ruled by different sovereigns who were almost all of foreign origin thrust upon the people by domineering neighbours at the point of the bayonet; its sons all debased and divided amongst themselves, having no aspirations worth the name and with the ambition of traitors to get into the favour of the ruling powers, and that all this had been changed by the devoted labours and self-sacrifices of a handful of Italians who, though very poor in resources, had dedicated their lives to the service and elevation of their country, forswearing all pleasures and felicities which only make existence on earth bearable. All those thoughts naturally reminded me of the great soul, the prince of Italian patriots, the greatest, the noblest and the purest of all nationalists that was ever born in Europe, Giuseppe Mazzini,[3] the apostle of Italian unity, the great teacher and maker of modern Italy. From Mazzini my thoughts went forth to that great soldier of the 19th century, whose military exploits, daring courage, unflinching devotion to the cause of his country and inspiring zeal, eventually liberated Italy from the thraldom of slavery, and united it into one kingdom under a national monarchy, who won kingdoms only to give them over to his sovereign, who conquered the different provinces of Italy by the mere force of his invincible courage and by the equally invincible sacrifice of his companions, only to unite them into one great State.[4] Oh, the thrilling scenes of his Sicilian campaign—depicted by his own pen in his autobiography—led by his "one thousand", the clash of arms wielded by hired assassins on one side and the vindicators of the cause of national liberty on the other, the futile attempts made by foreign usurpers and sensuous tyrants to defeat the efforts of determined patriots, all re-echoed in my ears! I thought as if I was even at that very minute hearing the cries of "Viva La Garibaldi" on his victorious march into the streets of Messina. Just when full of these memories I raised my head to look around, my ears caught the airs of the music of a military band playing the Italian national anthem and lo and behold in front of me was marching an Italian regiment with Italian colours! Of course, I was all eyes and followed the march until the last man was out of sight and I heard a voice close by announcing that the doctor had now been pleased to allow our going ashore. At once I sprang to my feet and sought the company of two Messinians to go. We were all four including my friend Lala Diwan Chand. As soon as we stepped out of the steamer, the curiosity of sightseeing drove out all traces of Italian fight for independence out of my head and a few minutes after landing on the Messina jetty I became a sightseer pure and simple. The Messina

3. (1805-72); Italian patriot and nationalist who worked, mostly while in exile, for the unification of Italy under a republican government; exponent of European federation and internal liberties; imprisoned several times and twice sentenced to death; member of the Triumvirate of the short-lived republic of Rome in 1849; founded several organizations including Young Italy, Young Europe and Young Switzerland and started several journals including *Giovine Italia (Young Italy), L'Italia del Popolo and Pensiero ed Azione*; wrote *Doveri dell'uomo* (1860), an ethical treatise dedicated to the workers of Italy.
4. The reference was to Garibaldi.

   Giuseppe Garibaldi (1807-1882); Italian patriot and soldier who greatly contributed to the unification of Italy; fought in the South American wars from 1836 to 1848; returned to Italy and joined Young Italy, founded by Mazzini, and fought for Sardinia against Austria in 1848 and for the Roman Republic against France in 1849; with 1000 volunteer "Red Shirts" conquered Sicily and Naples in 1860 and made the king of Sardinia, Victor Emmanuel, the king of Italy; attempted in 1862 and 1867 to unite Papal states with the new kingdom; liberated Rome in 1870 which was made the capital of Italy next year; helped France in fighting against Prussia.

harbour is commanded by a long street with well-paved roads and footpaths which run parallel to the sea. Just near the jetty is a fountain and almost in front, the "Municipio". The different parts of this street we found marked as "Carso Vittore Emanuele",[5] the king liberator of Italy. From this broad street the city is entered by small arched gates (without doors) and also by some broad by-lanes and sub-streets. By one of these we passed into a bazaar marked "Viva Garibaldi". This was, we thought, the principal street of the city with fashionable shops on both sides. It is a very long bazaar. Most of the buildings are three storied and very nicely done up. There are several chawks—Piazzas they call them here—one of which I found marked "Piazza Garibaldk". At another place I read "Stida Garibaldi". I was just wondering in my mind if "Mazzini", was equally honoured when my glance fell on a marble slab containing the following inscription: "Viva Vollitte Mazzini".

This aroused a curiosity in my mind to see a statue of Mazzini and I looked around just in front of the street on a wall of which the above slab was displayed, and I found a small municipal garden with several statues on stone pedestals. The garden had very many shady trees with numerous benches for people to sit on. The whole look was so inviting that we all stepped in. You can imagine how gratifying it was to find that the 1st statue that presented itself to my view was of that good man Joseph Mazzini. For a while we rested in that garden and then a further stroll. It being lunch time now my companions began to look for a proper restaurant and in order to get into a respectable place we hired a cab and asked the cabman to lead us to one. He took us to a very good restaurant, very fashionable, neat and at the same time sufficiently cheap. All of us paid 6 francs equal to less than 5 sh.—English money for good lunch. Then we took a drive through the city. We paid 2 francs equal to about 1sh.—8d. to the cabman for 2½ hours. At first, the man grumbled a little but was eventually satisfied and went away. We then had ice cream—3d. for one cup each. All this shows, at least it was so remarked by my companion who has been to England and France, that life was comparatively cheaper here than at any of the northern towns and cities.

The city of Messina is a pretty town as I have already said with a picturesque situation. People well-dressed and neat; streets well-paved and clean; buildings high and well-built. Italy is believed to be the poorest of European countries but it gave no look of poverty. In fact, if it is to be judged by the style of its buildings and the style of living of the Messina population, it must be immensely

5. Victor Emmanuel II (1820-1878); king of Italy; succeeded his father, Charles Albert, as king of Sardinia in 1849; proclaimed king of Italy following its unification under Sardinian auspices in 1861 and ruled till 1878.

better off than India. There is hardly a single-storied house in the whole town. Very few men poorly dressed, and only a few beggars.

On the whole, it made a very pleasant impression on my mind with the conclusion that in the whole of India we had not a single city like that. Only the big street at Karachi and the Fort in Bombay are something like it. Then the population is almost all literate; plenty of art and plenty of music. Yes, I forgot to note that for the first time today, since our departure, we had news of the Russo-Japanese war and how glad was I to hear that the Japs had almost annihilated the Baltic Fleet, the last hope of Russia.[6] Everybody on board seemed to be happy at the result, but a little after they began to discuss the chances of the Yellow Peril. Altogether we passed a very enjoyable day. At 9 P.M. we steamed out of Messina harbour.

The 1st of June opened on a beautiful calm sea with the dark smoking Vesuvius to our right, the Bay of Naples before us and the island of Capri to our left. The scenery in the Bay of Naples and the sights at Naples are said to be the best in the whole world. About Naples the saying is: "See Naples before you die." A peep through the opera glasses opened a panorama before our eyes. We had one of the most magnificent views before us. The whole of the right coast, dividing itself into semi-circles (in some places almost forming the shape of a crescent, at others that of a horse-shoe and so on), is studded with populous towns and villages containing lofty and grand buildings. Slowly and steadily with the majesty of a liner, conscious of having performed a successful trip and having braved the great great sea boldly, our steamer entered the Bay of Naples and we had an almost full view of Napoli, a city which is believed to be one of the most beautiful if not the most beautiful in the world. In fact, the idea is that no city in the world beats it in the grandeur and beauty of its situation, although in grandeur and magnificence it may have to rank second to Paris.

The situation is similar to that of Messina in many points with green hills at the back and the sea in the forefront. From the base of the sea the city rises as if built on terraces. The general look of the whole city may be described as a great and many-storied structure with roads, squares and open places in every storey. It is as if there were so many galleries in the great spacious amphitheatre. At 11 A.M. we reached the harbour where many steamers of many different liners were at anchor, loading and unloading cargo and taking in and discharging passengers. We were, however, not allowed to land until the steamer had been medically examined and declared to be free from plague. One of our fellow passengers was an Italian belonging to one of the suburbs of Naples who had

6. Provoked by Russian penetration into Manchuria and Korea, Japan attacked, in 1904, Port Arthur and destroyed the Russian fleet at Tsushima. The peace settlement arrived at in 1905 reduced Russian role in East Asia.

returned to his home after 18 years. As a boy he had gone abroad to seek his livelihood without any capital at his back. He had chosen India as the field of his labour and was now a successful merchant, doing business in Calcutta. He was now paying a visit to his native place with his wife and two small children aged about 6 and 2 respectively. He had married a girl at Calcutta. His people, amongst them a sister whom he had left while she was only 3, a brother and several other relatives had come to receive him. The meeting between the brother and the sister was very touching. The man on the steamer had to ask which was the sister. On enquiry, I found that one of his brothers is working in Canada and another in Australia and that they had never met each other during the last 18 years since they parted to seek their fortunes in different climes.

How pathetic it was to look at the meeting of the so long-parted ones and how sad it was to reflect that while India could afford asylum and bestow fortunes on the enterprising and energetic of all countries in the world, it could not in its present state afford sufficient scope for the energies and talents of her own sons and even could not feed and clothe satisfactorily at least 50 millions of them! This is what is true cosmopolitanism. Oh, the working of *Karma*! that immutable and unerring law which makes no distinction of caste, creed and colour.

At about 12.15 P.M. the medical inspection commenced. The 3rd class passengers were the first to be gone through and they were examined rather carefully. The 3rd class accommodation in this ship is not so bad as it is often supposed to be. There are a number of six-berthed cabins with cushioned and broader berths than are generally available in the Intermediate class carriages on Indian Railways. There is every protection from cold, rain and sun, when warm. They have a deck reserved to themselves where they can sit and sleep at night or day as they please. Most of the poorer Europeans who were as well dressed as most of our well-to-do middle class countrymen, or in fact better than them, were travelling 3rd class and I do not think they were in any way uncomfortable. I should think that the 3rd class passengers on board the steamer were certainly much better off than the Intermediate class passengers on the Indian Railways. As a rule, they get the same food as the ship's crew does, but those of them that object to take that food on account of religious scruples can cook their own food. In fact, the Sindhi Hindu traders who were travelling in this ship to Malta and Gibraltar cooked their own food.

The 1st and the 2nd class passengers were only counted in their respective saloons and their soiled linen disinfected. It was after 2 P.M. that the steamer was declared free of plague and allowed to have communication with the shore. And then there was a rush in and a rush out. A lot of boats came near the ship, some to carry the passengers, others selling fruits and provisions and some carrying professional singing parties. There were a number of hotel porters canvassing for their respective establishments. As we had determined to go down at Naples and leave the steamer for good, we made enquiries, and settled terms with one of the porters belonging to an English hotel. He asked for 10 liras a day and we agreed. He wanted 8 liras a day for another hotel but as it was not an exclusively English one and as we thought we might be in difficulty if we were to go to a hotel where English was not properly understood, we chose to pay higher tariff and go to an English hotel. An Italian lira is equal to a French franc, 23 francs being equal to an English sovereign. One lira or one franc is divided into 100 cents or centimes as they are called. It seems that everyone in Europe expects a tip or as we call it *bakshish* (*inam*) in India. We, i.e., Lala Diwan Chand and myself paid 5 francs each to the steward and 2sh. to the man who used to give us water for bath. It was very strange to find a hotel porter with the cap of a particular hotel striving hard for another hotel and not trying for the hotel which he professed to represent. Eventually we made a bargain with him and pointed out our baggage to him. Henceforth our way was very clear. He arranged for the clearing of our baggage, for the hiring of a boat, for the removal of our baggage from the boat and for its examination at the Customs House. At the jetty we found a very large crowd of people ready to embark on the different steamers for different places. The jetty shed gave the appearance of a very crowded waiting room, where people were purchasing tickets, getting things examined and, otherwise, waiting for the departure of ships. Police constables in a grand and beautiful uniform with white feathers in their caps were in attendance at the several gates. While in the steamer, the medical staff had fixed red labels on our baggage signifying that they had been examined by the medical authorities. In the Customs House we were asked to declare if we had any dutiable goods. On our saying "no" and expressing our readiness to show our things, the officer passed our packages and one of his subordinates put fresh labels (like stamps) on all packages and marked them with a red chalk. The porter then removed our things and at the gate another police constable marked our things with yellow chalk and allowed us to pass. After all, the ordeal was over and we were in the open, where the different carriages of the various hotels were waiting for their customers as also other carriages for hire. It was my impression that the hotel porter whom we had accompanied from the steamer had saved us a lot of botheration and annoyance. But for him it might have taken us several hours to come out. Here outside there was a telephone office and the porter communicated with his manager who wanted 12 liras for each passenger. Eventually my companion L. Diwan Chand himself communicated and after a little bargaining we settled at 10 liras a day including room, attendance, light, breakfast, lunch and dinner. Upon this the porter put our baggage in the hotel omnibus and begged leave of us, of course claiming and receiving payment from us for boat and portage. We were three and we paid him 6 liras altogether. In the omnibus we drove to the hotel which is situated at a great height from which you get a lovely view of the Bay, the Vesuvius and the city. It is as if we are on the 20th storey from the lowest floor. The hotel waiter showed us 3 rooms on the 3rd floor where we are at present comfortably lodged. Here I close this letter leaving an account of Naples and its sights to my next.

3. Naples[1]

Of the beauty and grandeur of Naples I said something in my last letter. The expectations that were raised by a view on board the steamer were fully realised. The most remarkable building in the bazaar is an arcade called Galeria Umbero. The 1st roof of its kind was seen by me at Messina and the second one at Naples. This building in Naples is designed in the shape of a cross or our Indian *Chaupar*. The roofs are naturally very high and of Gothic style.

The Cathedral of Naples is a very grand building erected on the spot where previously stood the temples of Apollo and Venus. The Cathedral includes the 1st Chapel built by Constantine[2] and is decorated most profusely and artistically. The present building was commenced by Carlo II and the outside decoration has just been finished. It is the finest and the largest-roofed place of worship that I have seen up to this time. It abounds in confessing boxes, each containing a priest who hears the confession of Catholics and grants them full and unreserved *muafi* (absolution). One of the naves is called the Treasure House on account of its containing the gold and silver articles of great value. The pictures and representations and paintings on the roof and the walls are simply superb. The church contains the tombs of many bishops and cardinals. There is another church called that of Santa Chiara which contains the tombs of kings and queens of Italy. It is an equally well-furnished and well-decorated building. One of the statues of a queen placed on her tomb in a position wherein she is represented as reclining on two pillows is simply exquisite. From a distance it seems as if the pillows were of cloth as those in ordinary daily use.

The 3rd church, which I next saw, was the one called Jesus Nuovo. It was an equally splendid building in no way inferior to those I had seen before. There are many more churches in Naples which visitors see and which are

1. Third despatch sent from Naples was published in *The Panjabee* of 10 July 1905.
2. (288-337); Emperor of Rome, 306-37; gave legal recognition to Christianity in 313 and himself became a Christian in 337.

grand and imposing structures, but I was quite satisfied with a look at these three and did not care for the rest.

The next important building in the city which I saw was the one called Castle Nuovo with its fine Aragonese gateway. In this castle the remarkable places shown to visitors are royal chaples and other apartments, all most beautifully and exquisitely painted and richly decorated, containing some of the masterpieces of the best artists of Italy. Underground is the prison of the King of Naples where under the old regimes refractory bishops and revolutionary reformers were shut up and most cruelly treated. In this prison in 3 glass cases I saw the last remains of 3 illustrious prisoners. This castle overlooks the maritime harbours, both commercial as well as naval. In the port were five torpedo-boats and several warships. Outside the port were about 5 warships of the British. Naples is believed to possess the tomb of Virgil, the author of the *Aeneid*, one of the 3 great epic poems of the European world. The road to this tomb lies on a very high hillock whence you get a splendid view of the sea and the lower town. The town extends up to the hillock and in fact higher still, but for the convenience of the public, the Government has, in a convenient place, provided an electric lifter, which carries visitors up and down every six minutes, on payment of 10 centimes (one anna) each way. On the other side of this hill descending many hundreds of feet is the reputed tomb of Virgil.

But the two most interesting places in Naples are the National Museum and the Aquarium. The latter is a most useful place for the study of Natural History. Here in artificial tanks, covered with massive roofs and having walls of solid transparent plates, are accumulated the sea animals of numerous kinds, all found in the Bay of Naples, and also sea plants, shrubs, flowers, &c. This is a most interesting collection and is delightful to look at. For a student of Natural History and Biology the collection is simply invaluable. They charge a fee of one franc each for admission to this Aquarium, except on Sundays when entrance is free. There is a printed guide to this collection of animals sold for one franc, a copy of which I have purchased for the library of the D.A.V. College. The National Museum contains perhaps the largest and the most interesting collection of statues, sculptures and other art productions of Italian masters.

At a distance of 13 miles from Naples is the site of the ancient town of Pompeii which was destroyed by a volcanic eruption in the Vesuvius some 2000 years ago. The ruins of this town have since been excavated and are being excavated and most interesting and valuable evidences of Roman civilisation discovered. Almost all articles of use from the luxuries down to necessities have been found out more or less injured and are now preserved in the museum. Statues, paintings, frescoes, landscapes, fountains, sculptures, coins, gold and silver jewelry, iron, bronze, copper and wood articles, Roman armoury, Roman manuscripts, &c., &c. have been found and are placed in this museum. A complete catalogue of this collection with illustration of the principal statues exists in English, a copy of which I have purchased for the College library for 35 francs. The museum also contains the articles found out of the ruins of another town called Herculaneum, about 6 or 7 miles from Naples on the way to Pompeii. By a careful study of this museum one can fully complete a History of Roman art, of Roman life and of Roman civilisation in general, in pre-Christian times when these towns were burnt down by the streams of volcanic lava that flowed from the Vesuvius for miles and miles causing complete destruction and devastation in its march downwards.

Of course the chief attractions of Naples are these ruins which take one at once to the life of man on this earth at a period of more than 2000 years hence and I could not neglect to pay a visit to them. One whole day was spent in this trip. To the ruins of Pompeii one is carried by railway in one hour and by a cab in 2 hours and a half as the way is full of ascents and descents. These ruins are enclosed and there is only one entrance, with an exit on the other end. For the second time within a month I was looking at the havoc wrought almost in the twinkling of an eye by one of those sudden cataclysms in nature before which human skill, human brain and human foresight are simply vain. The city was buried in 79 AD and the ruins now display an accumulation of public buildings, streets and private houses in the very shape in which they existed at the time of the great catastrophe. The sight is quite unlike that I witnessed at Kangra where the whole town has been simply razed to the ground. This place was evidently buried under the lava and the ashes. The most important of the public edifices of old Pompeii are grouped round the powerful market place or forum of the city from where numerous statues have been discovered and placed in the museums at Pompeii and Naples. The temple of Jupiter has been completely dug out and so have the temples of Apollo and Basilica, and a large edifice for the use of the courts of justice and commercial operations. Two of the principal theatres have been discovered with their stages, galleries and boxes, &c., and so have the buildings identified as the temple of Isis, the gladiators' gymnasium and the amphitheatre in which the gladiators from the gymnasium presented themselves before the public in the games so much delighted in by the Romans. The streets of Pompeii appear to have been very narrow (not fit for carriages, &c.) flanked by causeways, paved with polygonal slabs of pre-historic lava and provided at frequent intervals with high stepping stones. Some of the dwelling houses are found in perfect order with their courtyards containing fountains of various designs and plans, bedrooms, sitting rooms, libraries, kitchens, bathrooms, &c. Traces of high and perfect art, of high tastes and luxurious habits, are visible everywhere. Some of the frescoes and paintings are very fine. The pictures and statues are mostly nude. In one place I found the most obscene and indescribably horrid representations of men and women, in the act of. . . .[3] The numerous wine shops still bear testimony to the loose morals of the ancient Romans. In one house I observed a kitchen in almost working order with pipe connection for water, iron stoves, &c. In the museum attached to the ruins are found the remains of men, women, children and animals which present a most pathetic and heartrending spectacle to the eye. They have been placed in the museum in the same posture in which they were found when excavated. In one place you find the remains of a woman and a girl together. Some of these figures have got complete sets of teeth. Some skulls are in perfect order. Some of the skeletons preserved in glass frames are complete. You have the figures of a dog and a horse. Most of the household utensils and, in some cases, cereals, vegetables and other articles of food are to be found in the original shape (petrified of course). These remains make a great impression upon you and are well worth the trouble and expectation involved in visiting them. Around these ruins is a village of small size mostly containing shops and places of comfort and convenience for visitors and travellers. En route to Naples I paid a visit to the ruins at Herculaneum, another big town similarly destroyed. There is a fairly large-sized town in existence now on the spot where these ruins have been discovered. The ruins were by chance discovered while a well was being sunk. A complete theatre is the principal building with galleries, stage, back doors, pit, &c., &c. There are two statues of ruling Consul and pro-Consul. I think these ruins must be several hundred feet below the level of the modern town. You can simply go by aid of candle light, and when down below, you begin to feel chilly. The walls of lava are enormously thick and seem to be massive mountains close by; at a short distance is an enclosure containing the ruins of houses and buildings. Extensive excavations have been carried on without injuring the existing town and its houses, &c.

I could not go and see the Cave of the Vesuvius as the volcano is just now dangerously active. At night you see the burning streams of lava from miles. It seems as if the mountain is on fire. But even from a distance it is a sight worth seeing. One can never forget it.

The next day I paid a visit to the Casanova Industrial Institute and with the aid of an English-knowing guide, whom we paid 8 francs for half a day, I studied the institution carefully and took notes. I reserve an account of the same for another letter. From the Institute I went over to one of the University buildings where I saw the statues of Bruno,[4] Galileo[5] and other distinguished Professors of Italy, both ancient and modern, but mostly modern. At Naples

3. Omission in source.
4. Giordano Bruno (1548-1600); Italian philosopher who rejected dogmas on the grounds that "knowledge is infinite and final truth cannot be established".
5. Galilei Galileo (1564-1642); famous Italian astronomer and physicist who constructed first astronomical telescope and discovered four brightest satellites of Jupiter.

the chief articles of manufacture are macaroni (an article of food), tiles and corals. The morals of the Nepalitans are said to be very loose and you could observe many evidences of it in your visits to different places, but the people are very polite and obliging. From here we go to Rome, an account of which you might expect in my next.

4. Rome[1]

It was in the afternoon of the 4th that we entered Rome, the holy city of the Christians, the eternal city of the Roman Catholics, the capital of the great Roman Empire and the place of St. Peter. Rome is decidedly the first city on earth inasmuch as it has figured in history most of all and has for centuries been the mistress of the world. From within its walls went forth the mandates of the Roman emperors, Roman Caesars. It was from Rome that, till late after the Christian era began, the whole of Europe, the whole of Northern Africa and the whole of Western Asia up to the Hindukush, was governed. Then again it was the Pontiff of Rome that had for centuries exercised supreme power in Europe, making and unmaking kings and kingdoms and empires and emperors. In short, there is no other city in the world which has wielded so much power and exercised so much influence on the destinies of mankind as Rome.

Again, perhaps there is no other city in the world, unless we are to link the name of Delhi with it, which has seen so many reverses of fortune, been ruined, looted times out of number and which is still at the present moment one of the grandest and most sublime places on earth. But, then, to add, Rome is again the capital of a ruling monarchy, the metropolis of a kingdom with its own flag, its own army and its own navy.

It is impossible to write of the multifarious sentiments and feelings which are evoked by a visit to Rome in the mind of a student of history. In the last 2500 years one hardly finds a single epoch in which Rome has not played a part, and a remarkable part, in the history of the globe. Whether in power or in misfortune it has always attracted people's attention and been present in their thoughts. Why, the very history of its late political struggles is full of so many thrilling incidents as by itself to give it a high place in the studies of an earnest reader of the decline and fall of nations. Was it not within the walls of Rome that in 1848 Joseph Mazzini and Giuseppe Garibaldi declared a republic which

1. Despatch sent from Rome and published in *The Panjabee* of 24 July 1905.

was soon after strangled by French ropes, woven by the strong and treacherous hands of the French Emperor?[2]

Was it not on its walls that Garibaldi, and other patriotic Italians, including the then enthusiastic students of the colleges of Rome, defended the Republic with their lives and made a desperate stand against the cruel attacks of a foreign army that was sent to the help of the Pope, who had for so long been a standing enemy of progress, of Italian unity, nay, of a national Government of Italy be it in any form? Was it not in Rome again that in 1868 the great ruling idea of Mazzini's life was realised and the Italian unity proclaimed under a National Government? In short, a student of history, when he enters the city of Rome for the first time, feels himself as if in a trance, his head full of all that he has read of Rome, and an all-engrossing desire of seeing the various places where so many thrilling scenes in the drama of the world had been played and played with effect.

In about half an hour of the arrival of our train we were comfortably lodged in the room of the Mitchel Hotel, a great American and English hotel having a very large, lofty and commodious house and fitted with all the comforts of modern life, viz., electric light, lift, reading room, etc., etc. I paid 9 francs a day for room, light, service, 3 meals and the use of the sitting and reading rooms, etc. For the bath in the tub you have to pay separately in all European hotels. At Naples I paid one franc a day for a bath and at Rome I had to pay 2 francs a day. Fortunately for us, the 4th of June was the 1st Sunday in June on which day is celebrated the anniversary of the declaration of Italian unity. This day is observed as a national holiday throughout Italy. In all the important towns the day opens with a review of troops and then follow other festivities. At Rome the king himself reviews the troops, all public buildings are decorated and at night illuminated, the festivities ending with a great display of fireworks at 9 P.M. in front of the Royal Palace. In the morning we were at Naples where we saw crowds of people in gay attire and in holiday dresses going to the review and in the afternoon we were at Rome where we saw the whole population out in streets, squares and other places enjoying and observing the festival in various ways. At about 5 P.M. when we were driving we happened to pass the monument of Garibaldi which has been placed on an elevated hill commanding a fine view of the city where we saw a large crowd of people with a number of troops in national uniform. This monument consists of an excellently-executed statue of General Garibaldi on horseback placed on a light pedestal, the work of one of those artists for which Italy is renowned in the world.

On two sides of the base are two representations of "Italian Union" and of

2. Louis Philippe (1773-1850) was the Emperor of France from 1830 to 1848.

"Liberty" with two very graceful and elegant figures. The populace had placed garlands of flowers on all these figures paying greater attention, however, to the representation of Italian unity. The pedestal, which had been besides decorated with Italian flags, was occupied by a number of men, young and old, some of whom were giving speeches by turns. One of these speeches was received with vociferous and repeated cheers; I could only make out this much that it contained many references to Garibaldi. This statue of Garibaldi has been so located as to give it the place of the Guardian Angel of modern Rome. It has deliberately and with consummate skill been so designed as to make the great General look right through the Vatican into the private apartments of the Pope as if threatening vengeance on him and his class for all crimes of commission and omission of which they have been guilty in this city of the mighty Romans. In this drive we had no guide with us and the driver too did not understand English, so we could not make much of it except that we took a general view of the city. At night after dinner we engaged a carriage for 7 francs and went to see the fireworks. In our opinion the fireworks which we saw from a great distance, and at a great disadvantage, were very poor. We came back to our hotel rather disappointed. The whole city, however, was out to see the same and one of the guide books which I had consulted had raised very high expectations of the same. On our return we went up to the reading room and were very much gratified to find that two American ladies who were touring alone expressed a desire to talk to us. These Americans are not so haughty and reserved as the English are said to be. The next morning we decided to make full use of the time and to see as much as possible of the city in the course of the day. In Rome, or rather in Italy throughout, French is very commonly understood but not English. Consequently, as we could do nothing without an English-speaking guide we engaged one for 15 francs for the whole day and a carriage for 12 francs for a day of eight hours. In Italy the Department of Public Instruction holds a special examination for the diploma of a qualified guide, and the holders of these diplomas have free access to all the public places of the town even where visitors are admitted only on payment of a prescribed entrance fee. With this guide we started at 9.30 A.M. and went straight to the Vatican. The Vatican is the name of the Pope's palace. Within the boundaries of this palace the Pope is supreme and owes allegiance to no human being, having sovereign powers of his own, the only remnant of the unlimited temporal power which he formerly possessed. The principal building of the Vatican is the Church of St. Peter, the grandest and the most magnificent church in the whole world. It is 200 yards long, 150 yards wide and about the same high, with numerous columns and galleries, etc. its decorations and paintings are wonderful and past all description.

The site upon which the Church stands is the same as was occupied by the circus of Nero where great many Christians were in the early days of Christianity murdered. St. Peter is buried here. The building is the joint production of the best architects, the best artists, the best painters, the best sculptors, the best engravers, etc. who have been produced by Europe. Every Pope adds to its magnificence and splendour. In the largest of the 3 naves is a bronze statue of St. Peter with the key of heaven in his hand, and all around are placed the statues of the Popes, the Saints, etc., not to speak of the numerous representations of Christ and the Virgin Mary. All these representations, whether on the roofs, on the walls or anywhere else, are in mosaic. The material used in the building is the richest and the most splendid that could be had in the world. The outside of the building too is very majestic. Just in front of the Church in the square are two statues of St. Peter with the key of heaven in his hand and St. Paul with a sword. On the huge bronze gate are the representations of various Christian martyrs, along with the most obscene pictures of the pagan times, reproduced there in order to scandalise, by comparison, the pagan religion. While pointing out this to us our guide, who was an Italian by birth and a Roman Catholic by faith, told us that the state of morality in the Romish Church was no better. In the interior of the church one of the statues at the foot of that of a Pope was represented to be that of a mistress of one Pope and the niece of another. Opposite this latter was that of her daughter, the famous Lucretia, who was said to be the offspring of the amorous connection of the Pope with her mother. The former was an outline of vanity and the latter of passion. It is useless to attempt to describe the church and of all the art treasures which it holds. Suffice it to say, generally, that if anyone wants to see for himself how a masterhand can bestow life on stone, clay, canvas, bronze, copper, etc. and can make them look and appear as living beings, he ought to pay a visit to Rome and see its numerous statues, paintings and pictures. The whole history of the Christian Church with the fables of the Holy Bible and those that have been gathered round it since the time of Christ till now, with the stories of miracles performed by Christ and his Apostles and his followers and with the real or supposed accounts of their martyrdom are reproduced in the Vatican and in other churches in Rome on canvas, paper, stone or clay, and in mosaic. Man has risen to the height of his genius in doing this work and I do not think there is any other place in the world where walls speak so loudly and so expressively. Most of the pictures, paintings, statues and other representations of the pre-Christian period, whether of men, of women, or of gods and goddesses, are nude, exposing in nakedness all the features and muscles of the personality represented including the genital organs and the secret parts. The same may be said of many Christian pictures also. It seems as if the masterminds of Rome in art could only show the excellence, the vigour and the power of their hand and their brain in exposing every part of a human body in its original shape uncovered by cloth, or anything else. Some of the representations are most revolting to our sense of decency though exquisitely perfect and sublime from an artistic point of view.

I have seen numberless European and American ladies, looking at these pictures with admiration, rather with rapture, nay, some of them trying to reproduce them with their own chisel, or on their own canvas. Still, we are told that even a naked foot exposed to the gaze of a European lady offends her decency. Is it not a wonder that art should have served so profusely and slavishly only those religions that are idolatrous in their essence and their practice and depend on mythologies? It is the same story whether in the case of pagan churches of pre-Christian Rome or in the old religion of the Greeks, or in India, or in China, or in the churches of the Catholics. I find hardly any distinction between paganism and the cult of the Roman Catholics. In both, one is required to believe in the most incredible of stories. In both, the practices, rites and ceremonies are the most idolatrous and full of symbolism. In the Catholic churches people prostrate before Christ, the Virgin, Apostles, Saints, Popes, Bishops, etc. as they do in Hindu temples at home. The pulpits, the bells, the offerings are almost the same. The confession, the expiation and the purification are similar as well as the pilgrimages and the splendour and magnificence of temples and gods. But, to proceed, the next best church in Rome is that of St. Paul. In one of these churches there is a representation showing Christ in the arms of his mother, the Holy Ghost fluttering his wings on his head, and father, the God, looking at him from a distance. In one of the churches are preserved the remains of St. Peter and St. Paul, which I am at the same time told have been distributed all over the world. In another church are preserved, in most costly and beautiful caskets of gold, the iron chains with which Peter and Paul were bound in the prison. In another church is preserved a column brought from Jerusalem which is supposed to be the column on which Christ himself was bound and so on. On the last day we were very fortunate in seeing a reception at St. Peter's to which the present Pope came in a procession. The church was almost full. There may have been 20 to 50 thousand men and women. The way was lined by the guards of the Pope, a picked stalwart men in most gorgeous and splendid uniforms and armed with bayonets. First in order came the various crosses which represent the different orders and sects and societies of the Roman Church with the leading bishops, archbishops and cardinals in procession. Each cross had two burning candles, one on each side of it, then came the various flags of the Romish churches, which were followed by the bodyguards of the Pope. After the bodyguards came the Pope himself on a platform borne by Roman Catholic priests. Only his head and face were uncovered, the rest of him being covered by a rich white cloth worked up in sparkling gold with gems and diamonds inlaid. The Pope was seated under a canopy of valuable cloth and on both sides of him were two grand "chowries". He was followed by some cardinals and archbishops and they by other Papal guards. The whole scene reminded me of the procession of the Shankaracharya, the Jagat Guru, on his visit to Lahore. Of course, there could be no comparison between the two so far as splendour and magnificence were concerned. The admission to the church was by tickets which were issued gratis to the people of Rome, many of whom sold the same to strangers and outsiders. At first we were asked to pay 5 francs each but then eventually we obtained two for two francs. No seats were provided for any. All had to stand. The church was gorgeously decorated and the rush was great. There were thousands and thousands fully 2 hours before the time fixed for the procession. And yet there seems to be very little religious life in Rome. In the churches too there are more visitors than worshippers. The number of Christian gods and goddesses, etc. (I mean the objects of worship) too seems to be unlimited. It may very nearly approach the Hindu figure of 33 crores. Their relics are worshipped all over the world and preserved in costly caskets and in gorgeous buildings. Of the other sights of Rome the most remarkable are those relating to ancient Rome. There is the Roman Forum with its columns and palaces discovered only lately. Excavations are in progress even now. There are the remains of the great amphitheatre of Flavius, called Collosseum. This building is unrivalled in the world in its magnitude. It is 170 yards high and about 200 yards wide. Its circumference is 550 yards. It is said that it provided accommodation to 1,00,000 people. There were 5000 wild beasts and many thousand gladiators killed in one day. The Collosseum was connected with the Royal Palace by a secret passage. There was one passage for ingress of gladiators and another for the removal of their bodies when dead. In different storeys of it separate rows were provided for the household of the emperors, the senators, the patricians and the plebians. The buildings stands on columns, which are built in a different style in each storey.

Besides the Collosseum there is the great Pantheon of the Romans now converted into a church. There are the remains of several triumphal churches erected by Romans in honour of victories achieved by different consuls and pro-consuls. There are the remains of many old palaces such as those of Nero, Rienzi, Julius Caesar, etc., etc. Then there are the ruins of the Great Roman baths and the temples of Venus, Apollo and Jupiter, some of these latter having been converted into Christian churches. In many of the Christian churches statues have been made out of the material of the old idols broken by the Christians. Our guide told us that pagan idols were broken and melted in order to convert them into Christian idols. The churches are full of the loot of the temples. In Rome the number of museums of art and picture galleries is legion and except one who has a very fine artistic taste and a capacity to appreciate its excellence and perfections one soon gets tired of these statues and pictures because there are so many that one feels lost in them.

Most of these churches have been repeatedly built after having been repeatedly destroyed, burnt and looted by the various barbarian hordes that attacked Rome on many occasions between the fall of the Empire and the Renaissance. Italy is full of statues and I suppose there is no Italian home without a picture or a statue. The exterior of houses, of big centres of trade, of shops, everywhere, in every city you find statues and portraits and pictures and likenesses of gods and goddesses, of Christian Saints and Popes, of great men and great women or of handsome men and handsome women. On many palaces in Rome you find the coat-of-arms of the Romans, i.e. sucking the she-wolf and the two wolves portrayed in stone or bronze or on canvas. I was very sorry to find that in Rome itself there was no statue of Mazzini though as I was told it was now in contemplation to build a great monument to him very soon. For the modern Romans the most popular god at whose altar they ungrudgingly offer their homage and worship is Garibaldi. Some of the patriots who fought under Garibaldi are still alive and in the festivities of the 4th of June they were marked by their uniforms which they wore in the struggle for independence. Their uniform consists of red caps and red coats which look more like shirts. Some of them had several medals on their breasts conferred on them by a grateful country in recognition of their services. In the new chamber of deputies there is a place which is always kept vacant as the one which was occupied by Garibaldi and in the long list of state museums there is a Garibaldian museum where are preserved a number of articles belonging to Garibaldi and connected with his glorious deeds. It is thus that a grateful country and a liberated nation commemorates the services of its liberators.

Of the chief articles of trade in Rome the most in demand are its mosaic curios, its pictures, paintings and statues. Modern Rome is a great city worthy of its history. Its buildings are lofty, grand and magnificent. Its streets and squares beautifully laid out. Its roads and streets well-paved, neat and tidy. Most of its buildings seem to have been very artistically designed and are good and grand both to look at as well as to live in. Generally the look of the people is happy. There seems to be little sign of poverty. Rome is always full of visitors although winter is said to be the season for visitors. In winter the number is said to exceed 100,000. The hotels are generally full and carry on a brisk business. Businessmen in Italy seem to have no scruples in cheating and telling lies. A man demanding six francs for an article was willing to give it for half a franc and this was by no means a solitary instance. The "tip" is very common. Italians as a rule are very courteous and obliging to strangers.

I do not propose to give a full account of Rome as visited by me, but even this meagre description will be very incomplete without a few lines about the catacombs. The catacombs are the ruins of old temples, houses and chapels dug underground. At the present moment they cover an area of 14 miles and this area is being added to by fresh excavations which are continually carried on. In it the most prominent things shown to visitors are the tombs of Christian martyrs murdered, buried or burnt by the so-called heathens and the ruins of the old chapels destroyed by the same. In these ruins too there are numerous marks of artistic taste, frescoes, paintings and statues and in some places remains of bodies too have been found out. The remains of the woman with her hair were in one place shown to me preserved in a glass receptacle. The most valuable finds have been removed to the museums and churches. The catacombs are in the charge of Romish monks.

Rome is in fact the most suitable place for a study of ancient history and affords a great field for antiquarian research. In these catacombs, museums and galleries you find numerous evidences of the old civilization, the customs and the manners of the people, their modes of living, their laws and their literature. Manuscripts, coins and other articles tell their own tales. The guide who was engaged by us knew the whole history of Rome by heart, giving us dates and other particulars of all the places and the events associated with the same in full.

Generally the people seem to be well-educated. Italy is believed to be very heavily taxed. All the principal buildings except those included in the Vatican are in the charge of the Government and at most of these the visitors have to pay a fee of half to 1 franc each. On Sundays the admission is free. The Italian soldiers and police and custom-house officers wear very beautiful uniforms. Even the uniforms here are designed by artists. The uniform of the Swiss guards at the Vatican is said to have been designed by Michelangelo. Some of the taxes are ludicrously high as, for example, 3 and a half centimes are charged for every box of matches, the selling price of which is 10 centimes equal to an anna in India. But still living is said to be comparatively cheaper than in England. The climate is warm in European language. It is like October and February weather in Upper India, but it is liable to sudden changes. It has been drizzling almost every day since I landed in Italy. Hotels and restaurants are numerous. Wine shops and cafes (i.e. coffee houses) probably occupy ¼ of the area of mercantile quarters, but the wines of Italy are believed to be mostly non-alcoholic and really I found no signs of drunkenness.

5. Journey Through the Continent[1]

Having left Rome at 9.10 P.M. on the 6th, we reached Milan at 9.17 A.M. on the 7th. The 2nd class railway carriage in which we travelled was in no way superior to the same class of carriages in India. The latrine was decidedly worse. In Italy and probably in all Europe, the fares are charged in accordance with the train by which one proposes to travel. There are slow, fast and express trains and for each train the fares are different. Then there are certain trains which carry no 3rd class passengers and others who do not carry even 2nd class. By a careful maneuvering of the railway guides I don't think it would be beyond the reach of a man having plenty of time at his disposal to travel cheap. The country from Naples right up to Milan and further is very fertile. On both sides of the railway you could hardly find an inch of ground vacant which was not covered with crops. Some of the farmer's houses seemed to be single. The villages too seem to have nice buildings and nowhere could I find the traces of the poverty, want, destitution and filth which characterise our villages. All buildings are *pucca*, mostly of stone, there being only a sprinkling of thatched roofs here and there. In fact, this latter class of structures is very rare. I found plenty of bullocks in southern Italy, though in the north, the horse is the most important domestic animal even for the plough. Milan is the capital and centre of the proverbially "fertile plains of Lombardy," now an Italian province, formerly an independent state where the present ruling family of Italy reigned. It was here that Cavour[2] spread his diplomatic nets and secured the unity and independence of Italy. The population of the town has since then risen from 1,32,000 to 5,00,000. The commerce and manufactures of Italy are mostly centred in the north and Milan is the most important commercial and industrial town of Italy. Its principal manufactures are silk, velvet, satin, pained cotton, leather, flannels and carriages. It is also noted for its agricultural produce, specially butter and cheese. Silk and piece-goods and satin are largely exported to India from this place which is very frequently visited by Bombay merchants for the purpose. The Milan railway junction station is the most important in Italy as it is from here that trains start for different parts of the Continent, viz. to Genoa, Venice, Austria, Germany, Switzerland and France. It is a beautiful city with grand and lofty buildings and several monuments of Italy's great men, amongst them being Victor Emmanuel, the King Liberator, Garibaldi and

1. Written after 6 June 1905 and published in *The Panjabee* of 7 August 1905.
2. C.B. Conte di Cavour (1810-1861); Italian statesman and Premier of Sardinia, 1852-59 and 1860-61; sponsored Garibaldi's campaign leading to the unification of Italy under Victor Emmanuel II.

Cavour. The grandest of its structures is the Duomo, a cathedral which the Milanese claim to be the grandest in the world, though to me it did not strike as much as the St. Peter's at Rome. However, the style of architecture is quite different and in my opinion grander and more beautiful than that of St. Peter's.

On the 8th we paid a visit to Como, a great manufacturing town situated on a lake of the same name, a very beautiful and charming place. The lake is not very wide but very long and circles round hills and mountains. On both banks it is studded with buildings and villas and a very large number of Europeans from all parts come here in spring and autumn to enjoy their holidays. This is the chief town where silk goods are manufactured.

On the morning of the 8th at 7.10 A.M. we left Milan for London. On the railway station here the porters and guards go about shouting the exact time of the departure of each train in all waiting rooms, refreshment rooms and buffets attached to the station. They are very polite and courteous. All goods are examined for customs purposes before departure but the examination is very easy and not harassing all. You are required to put your packages on the counter and declare, if there are any dutiable articles in the same. It is very seldom that your word is not believed or you are required to open a package for examination.

From Milan we started in Swiss carriages. These carriages are excellent in design as well as make. They are the finest of all I have yet seen. There is through communication in all the carriages and a man sitting at one end of the train can go about and see another sitting at the other end. Similarly, the guards and railway officers on duty go about the train freely and check and collect tickets. On this railway as well as on French and English railways, the tickets are collected while the train is in motion and almost before the 1st station is reached. Even in 1st class and second class carriages there is only one latrine for the whole carriage and not separate for each compartment as in India. No sleeping accommodation is provided in these carriages unless 50 per cent is paid over and above the 1st class fare. This train passed right through Switzerland, piercing the very heart of the Alps. It is a most wonderful feat of engineering. Right through the mountains bordering on lakes, rivers and streams you have a double line of railway which runs as smoothly as a well-balanced boat without any joltings or shaking worth the name. The train does not go up and down like the Indian hill trains but almost straight passing through numerous tunnels, some of which extend over miles. One of them is over 9 miles long and another just finished in another direction is over 12. En route we passed along most of the Swiss lakes. The scenery all the way is simply lovely and in no way inferior to the best of the Himalayas. The route traversed by this railway lies through a magnificent part of the Alps and all the way you feel as if in raptures. With lakes, rivers, rivulets, waterfalls and almost milky streams, the scenery is simply superb and defies all description. Then, again, human hands have added to the beauty of Nature as if providing variety and inviting competition and comparison by well-designed, well-built and equally well-kept cities, towns, villages, hamlets, houses and gardens. In some places, canals have been cut from the lakes and carried right through the towns. The roads and streets and surroundings all looked so neat, tidy and well-preserved as to give an idea of having been specially swept and prepared for the visit of a very high personage. The people are strong, well built and happy. Switzerland is, perhaps, the only part of Europe which is exceptionally happy under a Republic, which jealously guards its own borders and never concerns itself with affairs of others. The whole population is about 3 millions but every man is a soldier and every woman a lady. Surrounded by some of the most warlike and troublesome of European powers, it elicits the admiration of the world by never allowing its independence to be interfered with or questioned by others. The people elect their President every year. The land knows no poverty or destitution, nor has it ever had to face the difficulty of the unemployed. In short, it is an ideal state.

At 3.15, we reached Basel, an important Swiss town situated on the Rhine, close to French territory on one side and the German on the other. Two miles beyond is Germany. The place is the terminus of the St. Gothard line and here we had to stay for about 4 hours and change trains. We took a drive into the town and found the place very interesting with hardly any evidences of want or destitution. At 11.50 P.M., we left the place in French carriages. Shortly after leaving, our goods were again examined in the train itself by the Customs Officers of the French Government. Henceforth our route lay mostly in a flat but very fertile country. At daybreak we found ourselves passing through the north of France. Reaching the port of Bologne on the English Channel at about 11.30 A.M., our train went into the harbour, and we stepped out of the railway carriage to walk only a few paces to enter the steamer. It was then raining and the sea was rather rough but in about 2 hours we reached the English port of Folkestone and landed there in perfect safety. The upper 2nd class deck on board the steamer was not provided with a shelter or awning but still most of the passengers, men, women, and children, kept to the deck, some with umbrellas on and others in the open (the drizzling rain notwithstanding) in preference to the saloon, thus showing the Englishman's love of adventure. Thus it was in the afternoon of the 10th that we landed in the land of our rulers after spending fully ten days on the Continent and passing through Italy, Switzerland and France, amidst 3 languages and 3 sets of coins, and under the jurisdiction of 3 different Governments. We understood neither Italian, nor French, much less Swiss. But with a knowledge of English and a few words just 4 or 5 of Italian (the equivalents of how much, too much, water, milk &c.) we completed our journey without any inconvenience at all. The English gold money is accepted every where but not silver and copper. The silver and copper coins of these three different countries are similar in weight, appearance and value, though the inscriptions are different and the coins of one country are not generally acceptable in the other. In these countries wine is used almost like water, but there is not much of drunkenness as the wines are mostly non-alcoholic. But in England the case is different. The Italians seem to be thoroughly unscrupulous in demanding prices. But at Basel in Switzerland no cabman accepted less than the legal fare. In the countries you can hardly find one per cent of the passer-by in poor dress. The people are scrupulously clean and well dressed. This will do for the Continent.

4
VISIT TO ENGLAND AND AMERICA
III. In England

1. On Urgency of Gokhale's Visit to England[1]

It may appear that the postponement of Mr. Gokhale's departure has been a great mistake and that Sir William Wedderburn has been quite misunderstood. In fact, the position has become very anomalous. The following facts will throw light on the situation. Some time ago, in May last, Sir William in his capacity as Chairman of the British Committee addressed a circular letter to all the Liberal Associations, the members of Parliament and all the candidates for seats in the next Parliament informing them of the intended visit of the Congress deputation and asking their help in arranging public meetings to hear the delegates. A fairly good number of those to whom these letters were addressed have replied favourably.

Secondly, by the efforts of some members of the Indian Parliamentary Committee the date of the discussion of the Indian Budget has been fixed early this year, viz. the 22nd June and the members of Parliament interested in Indian affairs wanted Mr. Gokhale's help in preparing those speeches, which opportunity is now completely lost. Then again the general Liberal Federation of Great Britain and Ireland holds its annual sitting on the 3rd July 1905 and they have already agreed to give a hearing to the Indian delegates. The British Committee have, therefore, wired Mr. Gokhale to come at once. Mr. Naoroji thinks that Mr. Gokhale and myself can do a lot of useful work in July, because nothing at all can be done in August and September. I have, therefore, under advice from Mr. Naoroji given up my intention of proceeding to America at once. Sir William Wedderburn is not in London but at some distance at his country house. He has invited me to his place through the Secretary of the British Committee but I had addressed a letter to him before I had seen this latter gentleman and am awaiting a reply to the same. I am afraid the British Committee will be put in a false position if Mr. Gokhale does not reach here by the 1st of July and the only alternative left may be to arrange for a speech of mine before the Federation on the 3rd of July.

1. Written after arriving in London on 10 June 1905. *The Panjabee*, 10 July 1905.

2. On Debate in Parliament on Indian Budget[1]

I reached London on the 10th of June, fully one month after my departure from Lahore and have ever since been engaged in doing the work for which I was sent by my people. The first week was passed in making calls on Mr. Naoroji, Mr. Hall,[2] the Secretary of the British Committee and Sir William Wedderburn, the Chairman, who very kindly explained to me in full the circumstances under which Mr. Gokhale was asked to come at once either alone or with another delegate to do preliminary work connected with the programme of the deputation which was to be observed on their arrival in autumn. Sir William has already addressed a rather lengthy letter to the Joint Secretaries of the Indian National Congress on the subject with a request that due publicity may be given to the same in India so that the supporters of the Congress all over the country may be fully informed of the matter. I hope that the said letter has by this time been published in India and do not, therefore, consider it necessary to put down its contents here.

In order, however, to make my narrative continuous and to justify the emphasis which I intend to lay on certain matters connected therewith, I will briefly state the situation in as few words as may be possible to do.

In December last when the Congress was holding its session, the dissolution of Parliament was imminent and Sir William Wedderburn and others considered it very likely that it may occur before spring or thereabout. They consequently urged upon the Congress the desirability of sending their delegates to England to represent the case of the Congress before the British constituencies at the time of the general election so that some interest may thereby be raised and felt on Indian questions. On their return home they found a change in the situation but were still hopeful of a dissolution being forced before summer. With the advance of the spring, however, the hope was destroyed and it became clear that the dissolution was as far this year as it was last year. Moreover, some people considered that the summer was not a favourable time for holding public meetings in this country. All the same, however, Sir W. Wedderburn and his colleagues were of opinion that the summer should not be allowed to pass without some steps being taken to ensure a fuller discussion of the Indian Budget and the laying down of a clear and adequate line of work for the autumn. Consequently, they considered it necessary that Mr. Gokhale should arrive here

1. Written at London after 22 June 1905. *The Panjabee*, 17 July 1905.
2. W. Douglas Hall, secretary of the British Committee of the Indian National Congress, was associated with its official journal *India* also.

about the end of May or in the 1st week of June either alone or in company with another delegate. The work which they proposed for him or them was this: (a) To address formal or informal meetings of the Indian Parliamentary Committee with a view to prepare them fully and to equip them with facts and figures for the debate on the Budget. These facts and figures were no doubt available to the members in blue books or in the records of the proceedings of the supreme Indian legislature but it was considered that the members being very busy men, with very many and multifarious duties, could not reasonably be expected to wade through streams of figures which are not only the most difficult to digest but at times most perplexing and often not very clearly intelligible even to the cleverest of English politicians who has not made a special and laborious study of the same. Then there were certain matters, which required further explanation, discussion and elucidation. The British Committee had, therefore, planned that Mr. Gokhale and his companion, if any, should spend the two months of June and July in England in raising interest in Indian affairs by visiting influential politicians both in and out of Parliament by discussing Indian affairs with them personally, by writing in the press and by addressing such meetings as could conveniently be arranged in these months.

Along with this an effort was made through the friends of India in the House of Commons to obtain an earlier date for the debate on the Indian Budget. Ordinarily the Indian Budget debate used to come on at the end of the session towards the close of July or in the beginning of August. This year, however, a special effort was made to get an earlier date and it was in view of the possibility of this earlier date that Mr. Gokhale and another delegate were desired to reach here early in June. As a matter of fact, this effort resulted in the 22nd of June being fixed for the debate and the British Committee, therefore, wired to Bombay pressing the necessity of Mr. Gokhale's immediate departure for England. Besides this, the following programme of work was arranged for the month of July.

July 3 – London Liberal Federation at the N.L.C.
July 5 – Ryegate Conference of Women's Liberal Association
July 14 – The Fabian Society
July 15 – Young Briton's Society
July 19 – Kidderminster and Council meeting
July 20 – Kettering Garden party
July 30 (or Aug. 17) – Leeds and District Labour Representative Committee
July (any Thursday) – Bealthamston Council meeting
July (any day after July 15) – Hoxton Council meeting

July – Indian Parliamentary Committee, Public breakfast, Mr. Fisher Unwin[3]

July 29 – Skipton Council meeting

July 31-August 5 – International Statistical Institute of 1905

Aug. 7 – Hampden House Aylesbury

Sep. 6 – Council Holborn Liberal Association

But the Bombay Committee evidently did not realise the importance of this work with the result that they declined to send Mr. Gokhale except for the general election. The situation was, therefore, reconsidered in the meeting of the British Committee held on the 21st of this month and it was decided that as Mr. Gokhale could not come in time for the most important of these engagements, there was no use in having him at all in August and September. It was further decided that as there could be no certainty as to when the general elections were to take place and as there was every possibility of a sudden dissolution coming on at any time, a definite date should be fixed for the arrival of the Indian deputation in order to enable the same to raise interest in Indian affairs and to create and educate public opinion. Sir William Wedderburn, as Chairman of the British Committee, had addressed a circular letter to a large number of British organisations seeking their co-operation in the mission of the deputation and asking them to arrange public meetings to hear the delegates. These letters have met with a good response and the number of favourable replies is sufficiently large and encouraging. The Committee have, therefore, decided that the deputation should reach England not later than the 1st week of October in order to enable them to start work before or by the 15th. Sir William Wedderburn then proceeded to arrange an informal meeting of those members of Parliament who were likely to make speeches during the course of the debate on the Budget before the same came on, so that they may get an opportunity of putting questions to me and getting their facts and figures strengthened and supplemented by my local knowledge. But the debate was fixed for the 22nd and the Parliament was just going to open after the Whitsuntide holidays. Then, there had been some misapprehension about the date of the debate as the whip had by a mistake informed the members that the debate was to come on Friday and therefore a good many members had not yet returned. However, we decided to do what was possible and Mr. Herbert Roberts, M.P.,[4] the Secretary to the Indian Parliamentary Committee, arranged an informal conversation in the conference room of the House at 11.30 A.M. on the 22nd. As arranged, therefore, myself and Sir William Wedderburn met some members of the House of

3. Thomas Fisher Unwin (1848-1935); founder of the publishing house, Fisher and Unwin, London.
4. Liberal M.P. who asked questions about the partition of Bengal in the House of Commons.

Commons and had a long and interesting conversation with them on Indian topics. This useful work continued for about 11 hours after which I went over to the India Office to get some figures which were wanted. Precisely at 2.30 P.M. I, in company with Sir William Wedderburn entered the premises of the House of Commons.

I would not here stay to dilate upon the feelings raised in me at the moment, but proceed to relate what I actually witnessed. Fortunately and by the kindness of one of our friends (Mr. Samuel Smith, M.P.)[5] I got a seat just behind the last bench of the members under the gallery from where I could hear and see better than from the gallery itself.

The South African stores scandal was the subject just then being discussed in the House and I saw a scene which I shall never forget. There was on one side Mr. Balfour[6] (the Prime Minister), full of resources and conscious of his power and the strength of his majority and there was on the other side the leader of the Opposition fully cognizant of the support of public opinion in the matter of principle for which he was fighting.[7] On the side of Government, Mr. Balfour was the sole speaker whose voice was often drowned either in a chorus of applause or in a blast of ridicule and denunciation. Intense was the excitement and keen the desire to humble the Government. Many strong and cutting passages at arms passed between the two sides. At times the scene gave the look of a squabble where the great words were the instruments used in place of weapons.

In February last, I had witnessed the proceedings of the Indian Legislative Council at the sitting when the Universities Validating Bill was passed into law and the scene I saw in the House of Commons this day involuntarily led me back to the memories of the former.

But what a contrast!!! I could not at the moment make up my mind whether to give preference to that cut-and-dried affair at the Indian Council meeting with its almost death-like regularity and the overbearing attitude of its President or to this seemingly bazaar scramble and the look of a real tough fight between the two parties here who stand on equal rights, equal privileges and equal footing and one of whom considered themselves to be as much entitled to rule the empire and wield the supreme sceptre of authority as the other wielded at the time.

5. (1836-1906); Liberal M.P., 1886-1906.
6. Arthur James Balfour, first earl (1848-1930); British Conservative leader; Prime Minister, 1902-05; as Foreign Secretary drew up Balfour Declaration in 1917 giving assurance of British protection for Jewish settlement of Palestine after its capture by British forces.
7. The Opposition had alleged that certain irregularities had been committed in defence purchases.

Sometimes I was inclined to consider the scene in the House as unbecoming the dignity of a Parliament but then on mature thought I concluded that the best interests of the empire required this keen interest and almost maddening zeal which had the look of a scramble but beneath which was covered the best guarantee of successful administration in England. None of the speakers there was under any delusion of convincing anybody by his arguments and reasonings but all the same every speaker was conscious of the necessity of displaying himself to the best advantage as he knew that he was not speaking for the audience before him but for the millions of well-read people behind him who were as if listening to him with great attention.

After all, the turn came of the Indian Budget and lo! at once we witnessed a transformation of the House. The first to clear away were the ministers leaving the Secretary of State for India[8] as the sole occupant of the Front Treasury Bench. Their example was soon followed by the Opposition who left the lead of affairs, if any lead be needed at all, to Sir Henry Fowler.[9] Most of the members left abruptly and started away as the hour began to grow late. At times the audience was reduced to hardly more than a dozen on each side.

Without any attempt at rhetoric Mr. Brodrick spoke or read his speech with vigour and force as if conscious that there was not much fear of criticism or opposition.[10] He, however, studiously refrained from mentioning the name of Lord Curzon often and did not indulge in very many boasts of unrivalled peace or unparalleled administration. He was followed by Sir Henry Fowler who fully agreed with the Secretary of State for India in everything that he had said pertaining to the administration of Indian affairs so far as they affected the Indian people or the taxes levied from them or the methods of rule followed there. His chief interest lay in pointing out that the present fiscal policy of the Government of Great Britain was not approved by the Government of India and that the Government of that country which had the largest volume of trade with England did not share the views of Mr. Chamberlain.[11] He tried to utilise the views of the Government of India on this question as well as the differences

8. Sir John Brodrick; Secretary of State for India, 1903-05.
9. Liberal M.P. who had been Secretary of State for India in 1894-95.
10. Brodrick moved a surplus budget claiming that despite the visitations of plague and earthquake and scarcity of foodgrains in certain districts owing to the partial failure of monsoon and severe frost the revenue collected during the year had been the "largest ever gathered in India, the trade showed the largest return, and the expenditure by the poorer classes was on the most satisfactory scale." He added that the trade of India with the United Kingdom tended continually to increase.
11. Joseph Chamberlain (1836-1914); British Liberal leader; President of Board of Trade, 1880-85; resigned from Gladstone's cabinet over Irish home rule policy in 1886; Secretary of State for Colonies, 1893-1903; championed imperial preference tariffs.

between Lord Kitchener[12] and the Military Member of the Indian Council for party purposes.[13] From an Indian point of view his speech was perfectly useless, nay, mischievous. He was followed by Lord George Hamilton[14] who well-nigh followed the track of Sir Henry Fowler and for the first time that night used superlative terms for their superb rule in India; but the worst was yet in store and we had not to wait for it long as Lord George was followed by a Liberal member, whom dame rumour assigns the high place of Lord Chancellor[15] in the next Liberal cabinet, who raised Lord Curzon and his Indian administration to the highest sky and displayed an utter want of those Judicial parts which ought to characterise a would-be Lord Chancellor. This man began by harping on the old topic of the diversity of races and creeds in India and went out of his way in assuring the Government that not a single member of the House (on either side) desired to associate himself with any of the attacks which had been made on Lord Curzon. This learned lawyer did not speak for himself only but for every section of the House and it does not bode well for the 'Judicial' and 'Legal' representation of England if the same has in future to be maintained by a man of such a trend of mind.

Eventually, the time came for the friends of India to speak and they had a rather tough work to do. None of them had received any payment for their services to India! Nor did they ever expect to receive any. Naturally enough, they had no reason to be so enthusiastic over the so-called infallibility and immutability of the Indian Government and their ways of administration. They could not forget that they were Englishmen and as such shared the pride of the nation on their rule in India. This rule, whether good or bad, often and deservedly evokes the admiration of the third party. How could they be expected to condemn it outright and thereby wound the susceptibilities of their countrymen at large? But while acknowledging the good intentions of the Government and the general success of British rule in India, they could not be blind to its shortcomings, and to the many pitfalls into which it is liable to fall if it is not checked by proper and effective control and hedged in by a circumstance of its stability and future success. Slowly, gradually, haltingly but with a noble broad-mindedness they unfolded the tale of Indian disabilities and tried to raise a discordant note in the midst of the chorus of self-praise which had been just sung and sung so valiantly

12. Horatio Herbert Kitchener, first earl (1850-1916); British Field-Marshal; Commander-in-Chief of India, 1902-09; Secretary of State for War, 1914-16.
13. Kitchener wanted to take over the work of the Military Member of the Governor-General's Council and also of the Military Secretary. But Curzon differed with this and held that it would "set up a military autocracy in the person of the Commander-in-Chief".
14. (1845-1927); Secretary of State for India, 1895-1903; laid down a moderate frontier policy.
15. Earl of Crewe.

by the Secretary of State in office and the two ex-Secretaries of State and a would-be Chancellor. The best and the longest speech on this side was that of Mr. Samuel Smith who advocated a greater extension of education and exposed the so-called surpluses which had been secured by an artificial and false currency. Valiantly did he fight for the poor agriculturist. The Government was not, however, to go undefended and in the absence of better and more qualified speakers the defence of the Government and Lord Curzon was undertaken by a retired Anglo-Indian officer who uttered a great deal of unadulterated nonsense and represented that rampant school of militarism in India who think that the British India Government is the most perfect Government that India could have and that nobody should at all intervene between the Government and the people of India.[16] The interest on the Conservative side had so far dwindled that this gallant member had often nobody to cheer and applaud but the Right Honorable the Secretary of State himself and a lone Sir M. Bhownagree,[17] who made a most telling and forcible speech on the question of the disabilities of British Indians in South Africa; but he cut a sorry figure when he sarcastically characterised the Indian grievances as "so-called grievances" and deprecated a Parliamentary enquiry. But the most vigorous speech of the evening came from Sir Charles Dilke[18] who exposed the singular inconsistency of Sir M. Bhownagree's complaint about the disabilities of British Indians in South Africa with his sarcastic reference to the "so-called grievances of Indians." Sir Charles Dilke very forcibly pointed out that a country which suffered so much from famine and plague, both of which were the natural consequences of poverty, could not be said to be prosperous. But the greater part of his speech was taken up by the fiscal problem and the decision of the Government in the matter of differences that had arisen between Lord Kitchener and the Military Member of the Viceroy's Council. Mr. Herbert Roberts made a gallant stand for Parliamentary enquiry and Sir James Fergusson[19] repeated the superlative adjectives of Major Evans-Gordon[20] in reply.

At last the Secretary of State replied. His reply was principally concerned with the party moves of Sir Henry Fowler and Sir Charles Dilke. To other matters he made practically no answer, not because the arguments on the other

16. This sentence was, however, published later in *The Panjabee* of 28 August 1905, with the editor apologising for its having been "unaccountably omitted" from the text of the speech published earlier.
17. Sir M.M. Bhownagree (1851-1933); Conservative M. P., 1895-1906.
18. (1843-1911); British politician and author; M.P., 1868-1911; Under-Secretary to Foreign Office, 1880-82; President, Local Government Board, 1882-85.
19. (1832-1906); Governor of Bombay, 1880-1885; Conservative M.P., 1885-1906.
20. (1857-1913); joined British army in 1876, retired as Major in 1896; Conservative M.P., 1900-1907.

side needed no reply but because he was sure that nobody attached any importance to the same. After all, the clock struck 12 when a Chamberlainite was explaining that Indian prosperity was chiefly due to the countervailing duties on cotton piece goods and sugar. It was about quarter past eleven when the division on the motion was taken and suddenly the House began to fill. Members who had evidently taken no part whatsoever in the debate and who had heard none of the speeches were ready there to vote against the motion. Both Conservatives and Liberals vied with each other in voting against the motion. Sir Henry Fowler was, during the course of debate, observed giving tips to the Secretary of State for India. The results of the division showed 65 for the motion and 116 against it. So long as the debate lasted, at no stage could I count more than 50 or 60 members on the benches on both sides. Thus ended the debate on the Indian Budget and such is the interest displayed by British people in Indian affairs. To me, the whole thing seemed to be a farce though I don't know how to style it, comical or tragical. All the same it cannot be denied that these gentlemen who spoke for India and who take interest in Indian affairs deserve the greatest credit for the same. They do so against great odds and under great difficulties. With the people of Great Britain so indifferent about Indian affairs, with the Government in England so callous about the same with the chances of being dubbed as faddists, little Englanders, misguided philanthropists and so on, by the authorities in power and the people in general, their position is extremely involved. The people in India cannot possibly realise the difficulties under which these gentlemen raise their voice in support of Indian claims, and still the work is as thankless as any could be. I think these members deserve the best gratitude of the Congress people for their noble advocacy of the rights of the people of India and for the support which they accord to the Congress by their sympathetic attitude towards the same. The speeches delivered on the occasion will be fully reported in *India* and can be read therein. I intend to send you my impressions about the British Committee of the Indian National Congress and *India* in my next letter.

3. Interest of English Ladies in Indian Problems[1]

It is now about 4 weeks since I reached London, and with the exception of 2 days that I was at Meredith, I have been all the time here. Although I have had very busy time of it all the while, the last two weeks I had almost overworked

1. London, 7 July 1905. *The Panjabee*, 31 July 1905.

myself, so much so that it began to tell upon my health, and I thought I might better do things at ease rather than at this breakneck speed. But then there are so many things to be seen, studied and noted that one cannot afford, at least does not like, to leave many things unobserved. However, it is impossible to see or study London in the course of one or two months, and I have, therefore, decided not to worry myself about what cannot be helped. I have, by this time, seen a number of schools, elementary, higher elementary and secondary, both of boys and girls and also a number of polytechnics. I am collecting information about the latter more particularly, and hope to be in possession of some valuable material to enable my people to decide if they can in any way use the same to their benefit.

I have up to this time delivered 3 speeches. Two of these occasions were principally Indian functions and the 3rd an almost exclusively English one. The 1st was an after-dinner speech on the occasion of a farewell dinner given on the eve of the departure of some seven Indian students for home to India on finishing their studies here, to which I was invited by the kindness of the organisers and where I had the pleasure of meeting and forming the acquaintance of a number of my countrymen staying here, mostly for study, a few for pleasure, and a fewer still for business. The second was on the occasion of the opening of Mr. Shyamji Krishna Varma's[2] India House. On this occasion were present several Englishmen and ladies. Amongst the former were Mr. Hyndman,[3] the well-known Socialist leader. Mr. Swinney, the President of the Positivist Society of London, and Mr. Quelch, the editor of *Justice*. Mr. Shyamji is probably sending a report of the proceedings of this meeting to India by today's mail and you might read it in some papers.

The 3rd meeting was very remarkable. It was a unique meeting of its kind, at least to me. I daresay you must have heard of an agitation in favour of women's suffrage. The women of this country have organised themselves into a number of Associations in order to get the franchise for their sex. Most of these Associations are, of course, Liberal. They have got a central organisation called the Women's Liberal Federation. Under it there are a number of Local Associations and Unions. There was a Council meeting of the Kent, Surrey and Sussex unions of Women's Liberal Association at Reigate (a town about

2. (1857-1930); educated at Bombay and Oxford; advocate, Bombay High Court; Diwan in Ratlam state, 1885; Counsellor in Udaipur state, 1886-7; supported "extremist" school of politicians; left for England in 1895; founded India House and started *Indian Sociologist* in London in 1905; left for Paris in 1907 and later settled in Geneva.
3. H.M. Hyndman (1842-1921); British socialist leader who took keen interest in Indian affairs and supported the nationalist movement; condemned the demand of Muslims for separate representation in Legislative Councils; criticized the British Government for the Jallianwala Bagh tragedy; works include *The Truth about India* (1921).

25 or 30 miles from London) on the 5th, to which myself and Sheikh Abdul Qadir,[4] B.A., of Lahore, were invited. This union claims about 15,000 members and this was a yearly meeting of their Council at which about 300 representative women of these Associations were present. The chair was occupied by a lady of a remarkable firmness of character, of great abilities and of advanced political views. Somehow or other it was arranged to devote this meeting principally to the consideration of Indian affairs and so we were invited to speak. They had of themselves fixed the subjects, viz. taxation, Frontier warfare, famine, plague and irrigation. As a delegate of the Indian National Congress, I was required to speak on the two first named and Sheikh Abdul Qadir on the other three. From London we went over to Reigate in the company of a lady, Miss Annie A. Smith, who is the London correspondent of *Amrita Bazar Patrika* and who has worked with the late Mr. W. Digby.[5] She is a very well-informed lady and takes great interest in Indian affairs. Mr. Dhanraj Sawhny, son of my friend Dr. Bhagat Ram Sawhny of Jammu, also accompanied me at my request and similarly Sheikh Abdul Qadir was accompanied by two Mohammedan young friends. We started from London at 10.55 A.M. and reached Reigate at about 12. We had been invited to lunch by the Chairman elect of the meeting at a certain hotel and we, therefore, proceeded to that hotel, where the Chairman designate and the Secretary joined us very soon after. They had both come from a long distance on a motor car belonging to the former. The lady remarked she was not at all fond of motors, that in fact she did not like the same but then it was so convenient and saved so much time that she kept one and used it on occasions. This lady is of advanced age, say between 50 and 60, and is held in great respect in Liberal circles. She is said to be a great and influential worker in the Liberal cause. The Union has 3 Secretaries. We had the pleasure of meeting two of them. One of them, Mrs. Heron Maxwell, seems to be a woman of very strong character and of very advanced views. She does not seem to care a bit for fashion or conventionalities in dress. In fact, amongst the 200 ladies present that evening, she was a unique and remarkable sight. She dressed, except in the matter of her having a loose gown in place of trousers, just like men. Her hair was cut and dressed like men, she wore a gentleman's straw hat and I should say a gentleman's short coat with collar and necktie. She had no holes in her ear, which seem to be very common here also. But for her gown she looked just a man. Nature too has been rather kind to her in this respect and her face looks more like that of a man than of a woman. The other Secretary is a

4. Editor of *The Observer* published from Lahore.

5. William Digby (1849-1904); editor of the *Madras Times*, 1877-79; founder-director of Indian Political Agency in London, 1887-92; editor of *India* (London) 1890-92; works include *Prosperous British India –A Revelation*.

young lady who too seems to have given up most of the conventionalities of the English dress. In England, the one thing of which every man and woman seems to be very fond of in talking is weather. No conversation can begin without a remark about the weather, specially when it is a fair day. It was rather a warm day we passed at Reigate. But don't you imagine that it was anything approaching to even a mid-April day at Lahore. We were dressed in full warm clothing and I had my *pugree* on but for the matter of that we did not feel very uncomfortable. Some of the ladies here put on very thin bodices as thin as muslin or silk. The upper garments are often very fantastic. I don't think that Lucknow ladies of fashion could have ever devised more ingenious ways of displaying the different limbs of their bodies to the best advantage. However, to revert to the subject in hand, we were very hospitably entertained at lunch, and from there we proceeded in a body to the place of the meeting. The meeting was held in a very nice garden attached to the residence of a leading Liberal lady of the town, Mrs. Powell. The town itself is very lively but the house and the garden are simply charming. The ladies sat under the shade of a cluster of trees but most of them were in the open sun. Some of them had their umbrellas on but there were others who had no umbrellas. The hostess was a very intelligent woman, of fairly advanced age. She had a son at Cambridge who was present that afternoon and helped in the arrangements of the meeting. The meeting was fixed for 2.30 P.M., but the proceedings, which could not commence before 2.45 P.M., were opened by a speech from the chair in which she welcomed the delegates and the visitors, commented upon the work done by the different Associations and announced the programme for that afternoon. Our names were very kindly received with cheers. The principal business was to hear speeches on India and to discuss Indian matters. The President's opening speech, which was delivered with grace and fluency, was a very remarkable one and I was delighted to hear a lady talking of high politics in a most masterly and statesmanlike way. As the first item of the programme, she called upon me to address the meeting. The time allowed was half an hour. I had taken notes of my speech but as usual I could not even refer to them once and went on at random. I am sending you the notes of the speech and you might use them as you like. You will probably find a brief reference to it in today's *India*, and I think a report of the proceedings is likely to appear in the English papers as well, cuttings from which I may send you next week. I was followed by Sheikh Abdul Qadir, who read a very well-written paper on famine, plague and irrigation. His paper will, I am sure, be read with great interest in India. The speeches were heard with rapt attention and great interest and applauded rather enthusiastically. You could see from the faces of your audience that you were talking to a very intelligent set of women who followed you very closely both in your facts as well as in your reasoning. After the speeches were over, another speech on India was delivered by a lady of the name of Miss Martin. Her speech was very sympathetic in tone and liberal in sentiments and she spoke remarkably well. After the speech was over, the Chairman invited discussion and asked the audience to avail of our presence in getting information on such Indian matters as interested them. A number of questions were then put. The very nature of the questions will show you the interest aroused. One lady asked us if it was not true that much of the poverty of the country was due to extravagant and expensive child marriages and to the exactions of the money-lenders. Another asked if it was not true that a large number of Indians held offices of trust and they had votes in the management of the affairs of their country and so on. The replies and explanations seem to have been satisfactory. A number of ladies spoke and spoke so well that I was astonished to hear them. In the programme they had allowed 1½ hours to the discussion of Indian affairs including our speeches but I am sure more than 2 hours were spent without any signs of slackness of interest. Many ladies desired to speak but the Chairman had eventually to close with a firm stand.

The next item on the programme was a speech of Mr. Thomson, the Organising Secretary of the Liberal Federation, on Registration reform. He explained to the audience many points concerning the registers of votes, the anomalies of the existing law, the advantages which the Tories had under it, how could it be worked to the advantage of the Liberal party and in what matters and how it needed reform. The speech was both an exposition as well as a criticism of the existing law of Registration. The question which most interested the women is their right to vote for the election of members of Parliament and their right to sit in Parliament. As the matter now stands, the women in England have a right to vote for, as well as sit in, county councils and various other local bodies. The Tories are, of course, very vehemently opposed to such a measure. A large number of Radicals support the scheme, but Mr. Labouchere,[6] the Editor of *Truth*, is opposed to the idea and his name was received with sneers and hisses. In England, women play a great part in elections. The idea is to use that influence only in favour of members who pledge themselves to women's suffrage. The discussion that followed Mr. Thomson's speech was the most interesting that I have heard in my life. The proceedings were more dignified than what I had seen in the House of Commons. The knowledge of the subject, the keen legal acumen, the clearness of reasoning, the political sagacity and a full and comprehensive knowledge of party tactics displayed by the lady speakers were not only remarkable but at

6. Henry Dupre Labouchere (1831-1912); British politician and publicist who was popularly known as "Lobby"; Liberal M.P., 1864-68 and Radical M.P. for Northampton, 1880-1906; founded *Truth* in 1877 and edited it for several years.

times showed glimpses of masterly intelligence. The discussion was followed by some resolutions proposed, seconded and supported by leading delegates from different Associations. I am enclosing a copy of the resolutions relating to India with the original letter of the Secretary forwarding the same. Most of these ladies spoke without any notes and some with notes. One of them said she did not like Rudyard Kipling[7] but was quoting him simply for the pleasure of contradicting him. Then she quoted that well-known verse of Kipling that "East is East and West is West" and so on and said that this meeting furnished a refutation of Mr. Kipling's idea. She had promised to write out her speech for me and I am expecting it every moment. I may send it to you by next mail. The proceedings were eventually brought to a close by an exceedingly nice speech from the chair wherein she thanked us and expounded the duties of Englishmen and Englishwomen towards India. She pledged her Union to greater attention of Indian affairs and exhorted her audience to use their influence in favour of Indians. I was asked to respond to the resolution thanking us and which I did warmly acknowledging their kindness and hospitality. Before the meeting broke for tea, a local photographer photographed the assembly. Tea was provided by the lady of the house with any amount of cake and fruits. All were kind to us and took great care to make us comfortable. While sitting at tea, we carried on conversation on Indian affairs and the ladies showed great interest.

In fact, I was twice asked to change my circle of talk and enlighten the different circles of ladies on India by turns. One lady asked me about Lord Curzon and the Durbar.[8] Another asked me about the chances of the success of representative institutions in face of the differences between various sects and creeds and so on. Sheikh Abdul Qadir was also similarly entertained and questioned. We showed the photographs of the scenes at Kangra after the earthquake and also the photos of the famine orphans in which the ladies felt greatly interested. One lady promised to raise subscriptions for Kangra relief. After tea we were again photographed with a small group of officers and leading delegates. Altogether we passed a most delightful afternoon and I saw a sight (the first of its kind in my life) which I can never forget. Blessed is a country which has women like these. With mothers like these it is no wonder that Englishmen are the rulers of the world.

At 7.30 P.M. was fixed a public meeting in the Town Hall of a place some

7. Joseph Rudyard Kipling (1865-1936); British poet, short story writer and journalist; worked on the staff of the *Civil and Military Gazette* (Lahore) in 1882; awarded Nobel Prize for literature in 1907; works include *Plain Tales from the Hills* (1888), *Jungle Book* (1894), *Kim* (1901) and *Reward and Fairies* (1910).
8. The Durbar held on the occasion of the coronation of King Edward VII in 1903 was presided over by Curzon.

miles distant from Reigate. Tickets for reserved seats had been sent to us. It was a Liberal party meeting and Doctor Macnamara, a well-known M.P., was expected to address it. So leaving Reigate we proceeded to Redhill, the place of the meeting, by train and saw another sight. As the day was a very pleasant one, the children of Redhill had gone to an outing some miles off. It was just their returning time when we entered Redhill and we saw that the streets and roads were crowded with men and women come to receive the children and see them returning. However, we proceeded to the Town Hall and were comfortably seated. The regular proceedings were preceded by the singing of some Liberal songs, a copy of which I am sending you, sung most enthusiastically by men and women in chorus. The meeting was again presided over by the same lady who had presided over the meeting of the women that afternoon. She opened the proceedings with a nice little speech and then called upon the M.P. to speak. He met with a warm reception and he hit the Government hard. You are struck with the amount of freedom and liberty people enjoy here in criticising the Government. They don't spare anyone and speak most openly and fearlessly. A Lord and several ladies also spoke and so did the Liberal candidate of the place. Our train was to leave at 9.47 P.M., so at 9.30 P.M. we left the Hall and reached London by 11 P.M.

Thus ended my first effort to address an English audience. At first I would not accept the invitation, being afraid of my making mistakes in a meeting of ladies. I felt very shy and timorous and had to be pressed before I agreed to speak. However, all went on very well and I had the satisfaction of feeling that the honour of starting this year's Indian campaign in England was reserved for the Punjab. Then it added much to my satisfaction to have my friend Sheikh Abdul Qadir on the same platform with me. He has expressed his satisfaction on this incident in his speech which I am sure will be read with great interest all over India.

I am afraid I have no time left to give you an account of my impressions in other respects. In fact, it seems to be impossible to do so even if I had time today which I have not. The country, its life in all its shades and conditions, its institutions, its manners and customs are so different from ours that one requires a large amount of leisure to put them in black and white. You will be astonished, perhaps, that during my 4 weeks stay in London I have not been to a theatre even once nor have I seen the most celebrated public buildings of the place. Between the schools, the charitable institutions, the correspondence and the calls, I get no time for recreation and sightseeing. Next Monday I propose to go into the interior of the country. The distances in the town here are so large that half your time is spent on the tram cars and the omnibus. In addition to the members of Parliament, to whom I was introduced in the House of Commons,

I called on Lord Reay,[9] Lord Ripon, the editor of the *Contemporary Review*, and the President of the Education Department of the London County Council, all of whom were very kind to me.

More in my next.

9. Donald James Mackay, eleventh baron Reay (1839-1921); Governor of Bombay, 1885-90; Under-Secretary of State for India, 1894-95, who believed in "divide and rule".

4. The Haileybury College[1]

Lord Reay very kindly gave me a note of introduction to the Headmaster of the Haileybury College, which I sent to the latter along with a request for permission to see his institution. Mr. E. Lyttleton, the Headmaster, who has been selected for the Headmastership of the Eton School and is going there in September, very kindly invited me to luncheon on Tuesday last at 1.30 P.M. The Haileybury College is situated at a distance of 3 miles from the Broxbourne station on the S.E. Railway, Broxbourne itself being only 17 miles from Liverpool Street station, London. The return 3rd class ticket costs only 2½ shillings but the cab fare from the station to the college is 4 shillings going and 3 shillings coming. The situation is lovely, the surroundings most interesting and the scenery charming. The buildings are rather old fashioned but the grounds are extensive. The look of the buildings is, however, grand. The main block is quadrangular, with a very extensive grassy courtyard. The buildings consist of classrooms, examination hall, residential houses, the library, the kitchen, the dining hall, the chapel and the houses of the masters. The residential houses for students are called after the names of distinguished Indian civilians who had received their education within the walls of the building. One of the houses is called "Lawrence House". They are just like barracks, almost similar in design to what we once built in our College Boarding House for the use of school-boarders and which were subsequently converted into college rooms. These dormitories are divided by partitions into so many seats. Each boy is provided with a bed, a cupboard, a curtain and a stand for miscellaneous things. He is not supposed to do any reading or writing there. Then, there are common baths, dressing-rooms and drawing-rooms. Each house is in the charge of a master who does not sleep actually in the boys' dormitory but outside, though very close to it.

1. Written at London on 12 July 1905. *The Panjabee*, 7 August 1905.

The college has got a very splendid swimming bath, a good gymnasium and 3 workshops for carpentry, smithy and mechanical engineering. They have got a rather small laboratory. The workshops are a recent addition. The swimming bath is in charge of two keepers who are present all the time the boys bathe. Each class comes by turns. The hours for each class are fixed by the master and put on the noticeboard. Each boy has to put mark after his name indicating that he has had a bath, though it is not compulsory to do so. The discipline in the dormitories is maintained by a number of monitor boys and the House Master. The dormitories are very large and contain from 48 to 100 boys. They provide 3 servants for each dormitory to keep it neat and clean. All boys dine together at fixed hours. The kitchen is a very interesting place and the lady cook in charge is very proud of the same. The kitchen, the larder and everything connected therewith was scrupulously clean and well arranged.

Each House has got its own colours for caps, exercise clothing and so on. The exercise clothing and other articles required for play are sold at a shop maintained in the college. The ages of the boys range from 12 to 21.

No boys over 14 are generally admitted but of course there are exceptions. The college or the school, as it should be called, takes up boys who have finished their elementary education elsewhere and come here for secondary education. The classics are a specialty of all English Public Schools, but science, modern languages and other similar subjects are now gradually making their way. The number of boys is over 400 and below 500 for whom about 31 masters are provided. Of all the important Public Schools of England, Haileybury is probably the cheapest. The Headmaster told me that, everything included, a boy could be educated there for £100 a year. £80 are the college fees and £20 extras. The masters are allowed to take backward students on their own terms, i.e., to teach them beyond college hours on extra payment. The teaching period consists of about 6½ hours and 4½ hours respectively every alternate day. Riding, dancing and workshops form the special feature of this school. The Headmaster believes in the government of boys by boys and is proud of his system. The riding master provides his own horses and charges so much per boy. The Headmaster was very bitter against translation, notes and keys. He has promised to send me a copy of the Prospectus, Rules and Regulations &c. The College has got very many Indian Associations about it. It was originally built with Indian money by the East India Company as an institution where Indian civil servants were trained. After the East India Company ceased to exist, it was purchased from them by a local committee and converted into the existing school.

In the chapel is a tablet containing the names of all those Haileybury students who died in the Indian Mutiny. Similar tablets have been put up to commemorate the memory of those who fell in the Afghan, the China, the Zulu and the Boer wars. Outside the college just in front of the entrance, they have erected a beautiful monumental column in memory of those who died in the South African War. In the library are to be seen the statues and portraits of some of the most eminent writers and scholars of England.

The Headmaster is a man of great repute, learning and character. The very fact that he has been appointed the Headmaster of the Eton School, the most important and the greatest of the public schools of England, is significant of his position as a teacher of boys. He and his wife were very kind to me. The wife told me with a certain amount of pride that the last Indian who sat at their table was Sir Pratap Singh of Jodhpore. She said that Sir Pratap had been kind to one of the Haileybury boys in India and so Haileybury paid homage to him and gave him a splendid send-off on his visit to this place. She was very much gratified to learn that Sir Pratap had only recently laid the foundation stone of our College. She spoke of Sir Pratap in very high terms and asked me to convey her kindest regards to him on my return to India, which I promised to do. There was another lady sitting by me who had been born in India. In the course of conversation she told me how the railways in India were, so to say, taking the very interest out of travelling. The Headmaster related to me some anecdotes of Lawrence[2] and Lord Salisbury.[3] He said Lawrence was one of the rowdiest boys at Haileybury and it caused quite a surprise to the then Headmaster to learn of his great work in the Punjab. It was quite in a state of wonder that he asked one of his colleagues what had become of all his good boys. It is thus you see that the rowdiest boy of a free country gets the opportunities of making name, fame and fortune for himself and, what is the most valuable of all, of rendering signal services to his country. He related to me several interesting stories of the failing memory of Lord Salisbury in his old age. It was very interesting to know from him how Lord Salisbury, one of the greatest statesmen of this country, once mistook a son-in-law of his for Lord Roberts and talked with him of military affairs under the same impression.

It was altogether a delightful afternoon that I passed at Haileybury for which my warmest and sincerest thanks are due to Mr. and Mrs. Lyttleton.

2. Sir John Lawrence (1811-1879); joined East India Company's service in 1830; Chief Commissioner of Punjab, 1853-58, and Lieutenant-Governor, 1859; member, Secretary of State's Council, 1859-62; Viceroy of India, 1864-69; created baron in 1869.
3. Robert Arthur Talbot Gascoyne-Cecil, third marquis of Salisbury (1830-1903); Secretary of State for India, 1866-67; Prime Minister, 1885, 1886-92, and 1895-1902.

5. Manchester[1]

I left London on the afternoon of the 12th for Manchester. The view that met my eyes, when we approached the suburbs of Cottonpolis, was something which I could not have even conceived. There were towns after towns with a ghastly black outlook. The houses, the factories, the pavements are all black and on both the sides of the railroad you could see only mountains of coal dust and ashes. The number of chimneys was countless. Here is a place which has drawn the wealth of the world in exchange for her pretty goods. When I reached Manchester, I found it busy preparing for the reception of the King[2] and the Queen who were expected the next day to open the new Docks. The 13th was a great day for Manchester, the whole city was *en fete*. Lakhs of people had gathered to see the King and the Queen and to welcome and cheer them. Here was an expression of loyalty that came from the hearts of a free people who are all the same very fond of Royalty. It was not a reception or an expression of loyalty wrung from an unhappy starving people by promises, threats and fears. The whole thing was spontaneous and on a very grand scale. The people felt very happy and gay. The English people like their holidays very much and enjoy them right royally. The poor also liked it as it gave them an opportunity to make some money in various ways. The traders, of course, had a great day. People must have spent thousands of pounds on this reception but still not a sovereign went out of the country. How different is the case in India where lakhs and lakhs spent on similar occasions mostly go out of the country and impoverish it and its starving millions! The King is very popular. He was not accompanied by any of his ministers as they were all busy in fighting their battles in Parliament.

1. Written at Manchester on 14 July 1905. *The Panjabee*, 7 August 1905.
2. Edward VII (1841-1910); King of Great Britain and Ireland, 1901-10.

6. To H. Birtwell[1]

17 July 1905

Dear Mr. Birtwell,[2]

I cannot tell you what a great pleasure it was to me to see you and to talk to you of the state of affairs in India. It goes without saying that your expression of sympathy, and your promises of help, were very gratifying to me, and when they are known to my people in India, I am sure they will give great satisfaction to them.

I would, however, prefer to have a brief record of your views in your own words, for communicating the same to my countrymen. Your opinion as to the real mischief lying in the humility of the Indians, and in their failure to assert themselves and make a stand against undue assumption of authority and airs on the part of Europeans, struck me very much, and I am particularly desirous of conveying that part of your opinion at least to my people in your own words.[3]

There seems to be a strong impression in India that British manufacturers generally, and Lancashire merchants in particular, are so jealous of Indians that they do not allow them opportunities of learning their industries and trades, and refuse them admittance to their factories and workshops. Since my visit to this country, however, I see that the impression is not quite right, at any rate, not to that extent to which it prevails in India.[4] I have by this time paid visits to a number of polytechnics in London, and seen your School of Technology here. I must say that I have everywhere met with uniform courtesy, and have found absolutely no ground for thinking that Indian students, desirous of studying in these institutions, will meet with a different treatment than is accorded to English boys. I have made particular enquiries from the heads of these schools, and they told me that Indian students were as welcome as any others.

1. *The Panjabee*, 28 August 1905.
2. A leading merchant of Manchester.
3. In his reply of 24 July, Birtwell wrote: "I regard every Indian as a comrade of the Empire, entitled to all rights and privileges. . . . The bedrock of all true friendship is mutual respect and toleration—how can a native, then, expect that friendship while by his quiet acquiescence he meekly consents to be treated like a dog!"
4. In the same letter Birtwell wrote: "I cannot agree that we are in an undue degree jealous of the Indians learning our processes and methods. . . . Given the necessary capital any or almost any industry now worked here could be transferred to India. . . . I don't know of any industry, however, that it would be impossible to carry on satisfactorily in India provided the right people were behind the venture."

Then the question remains of practical training in factories and workshops. So far as my enquiries go, the difficulties of getting admission thereto have been rather overstated. If English industries and British factories and workshops are open to Japanese, who are the rivals of the British in trade and industries, there seems to be no reason why the same should be closed against Indians who form, so to say, the clientele of the British manufacturer and trader. Therefore, when the Japanese and Americans are quite ready to impart all knowledge to Indians, there seems to be absolutely no reason why the British should act otherwise. I think the interests of the British manufacturers also require that Indians should be well-grounded in technical and industrial knowledge, so that they may be in a position to manufacture those things at home which are imported from Germany and the Continental countries. It is no interest of England that India should get all cheap and coarse goods from Germany, Japan or other places and not manufacture them at home. I should, therefore, think that there is no reason why the British manufacturer should hesitate at all to impart that technical knowledge, and give that practical training, to Indian students, which might enable them to supervise and carry on the manufacture of those goods which they get from the Continent and Japan. I shall be very happy to know your views on the matter, so that the wrong impression that is prevailing in India might be removed, and better feelings restored.

Thanking you in anticipation,

Yours etc.,
Lajpat Rai

7. Need for Better Relations between Lancashire and India[1]

Mr. Birtwell, Ladies and Gentlemen,

Let me first thank you for the opportunity you have given me of placing my views before you regarding the relations of Lancashire with India. A strange and inscrutable Providence has brought these countries so near each other that, notwithstanding a distance of thousands of miles intervening, the fortunes of one are closely allied with those of the other. While Lancashire is represented in almost every homestead in India by the goods manufactured by its people, few of the latter can go to bed without having had, in the course of the day, an occasion to think of India, either as a purchaser of their finished produce or as

1. Speech at a meeting of Englishmen held in the Stockport Labour Church at Lancashire on 27 July 1905. *The Panjabee*, 21 August 1905.

a supplier of the material without which a great number of Lancashire operatives might go without work.

Under the circumstances, I am convinced that a better understanding on the part of Lancashire of the state of political conditions prevailing in India is sure to be useful to both. It is to be greatly regretted, Gentlemen, that India which plays such an important part in the fortunes of England should receive so little attention at the hands of its politicians and statesmen. To one who even by a few days' residence in this country cannot help remarking how shrewd, generally well-informed and keen businessmen the English are, it seems quite inexplicable that there should be so much ignorance and indifference about the affairs of India which is admittedly the brightest jewel in the crown of Great Britain. In fact, so extensive and so culpable is this ignorance that very often foreign diplomatists have been heard to be chuckling over the same in their criticisms of England and English affairs.

The late Mr. Henry Fawcett,[2] quoting a distinguished German diplomatist and statesman, remarked upon the strangeness of the fact that while the possession of India was looked upon as the greatest distinction which England had obtained and that the loss of India through misgovernment would be the greatest blow to the reputation of England and fatal to its prestige, yet so little did Englishmen at home realise the vast responsibility of the trust they had assumed that he found that there was not so much attention given to Indian affairs and that there was not so much known of the subject in England as in Germany. Not to talk of the interest of Englishmen in general, even the Parliament is so neglectful of Indian affairs that hardly any importance is attached to the discussion of the same. Ministers and members both join hands in putting the debate on the Indian Budget to the fag end of the session and when that inevitable date does come, both vie with each other in flying from the House. Who can doubt the truth of the remark once made by Mr. Henry Fawcett that "India, having no representative of its own in the House of Commons and little public opinion in her support out of doors, had to bear the disadvantages of party government without any of its advantages. India may be neglected, her money may be wasted, her affairs may be mismanaged, it will not affect the interests of party, it will scarcely raise a ripple on the surface of politics." If so, Gentlemen, I may congratulate you upon the trouble you have taken tonight of arranging this meeting and of coming over to hear the views of an Indian regarding the government of his country by the English.

I do not know if it will be of any use discussing generally whether British

2. (1838-1884); professor of political economy at Cambridge, 1863-84 and a great sympathiser of India; M.P., 1865-80; moved a resolution in the House of Commons in 1868 for holding the Civil Service examination simultaneously in India and England.

rule in India has been an unmixed blessing or an unmitigated evil. You know that even on this question, as on every other in the world, there are two parties. One of them is led by that vainglorious school of British politicians whose chief credit lies in singing the praises of their countrymen abroad, nay, often in reciting their own glories, who maintain that British rule in India has resulted in the unparalleled prosperity and the unheard of happiness of the people of India. They hold it to be a marvel of success and the greatest boon which the people of India could hope for from a merciful Providence. They are not prepared to admit any mistakes nor do they acknowledge any shortcomings or failures. I wish these gentlemen, at least for the sake of experiment, had occasion to live under a similar regime. Then there is another party who argue that the rule of the British in India has been nothing short of a curse of God and a visitation of Providence in one of its fearful aspects. They contend that the British in India have reduced the country and its people to a state of want and destitution never before known, even in that land of fluctuating seasons and changing fortunes, and that never before in the memory of man, as strengthened and supplemented by the records of history, has India witnessed such widespread misery and universal poverty. Probably both these statements have some truth in them. Those who talk of the success of England in India base their judgment on the outward glitter of western institutions transplanted into India by the English. They look to the railways, the telegraph, the schools, the universities, the harbours and so on. Having been under the impression that never before was India in closer touch with the outside world, they think that in opening out that land of mysteries to the civilised world they have conferred the greatest boon on the people of the country.

Well, so far may be admitted and admitted gratefully that the English have to a certain extent helped the Indians to come out of that shell of superstition and ignorance in which they were at the time when the country passed into the hands of the British. They have certainly afforded us opportunities to come into touch with the other civilised parts of the globe and thus given us facilities to assimilate their civilisation and culture as far as our circumstances permitted of the same being done with profit. But then they forget that civilisation, without the means of enjoying the fruit of the same, is surely not worth much. Nay, it is positively injurious. A starving man cannot appreciate or bless your civilisation. A little bit of education in exchange for all the commodities of the world which make life enjoyable and bearable on earth is hardly a precious possession. Indians have, therefore, no reason to be thankful to the British for having civilised them (even if that be conceded) in exchange for all the other good things of the world of which they have been deprived by the unnatural rule of the foreigner and his extremely unsound financial and economic policy. But let us stop and examine your claims regarding having civilised us. Now that the labours of your own savants and scholars have opened out the closed pages of ancient Indian history to the great delight and benefit of the whole world, they have removed the justification for that boast even. The period of Indian history which enabled the British to assume the sovereignty of that great peninsula, was the darkest in the annals of that land and the British cannot reasonably base their exaggerated estimate of their good work in India on that foundation. It is true they have provided some schools and colleges for educating the sons of the soil but even these latter, if you look closely into the state of things, afford no ground for that display of self-glorification into which Anglo-Indians are apt to indulge. Firstly, the principles of liberal educational policy laid down by a succession of broadminded wise statesmen like Macaulay,[3] Canning[4] and Ripon are being deliberately undermined and just now a policy of reaction is in the ascendant; secondly, what comparison can India stand in matters of education even with the least civilised countries of the West? The institutions for imparting education are very few, the percentage of those who can read and write is extremely low and one of which every British politician ought to be ashamed.

I wonder how can the Englishmen talk with any pride of their work of spreading education in India when after a century and a quarter of their rule in some parts of India we find that more than 90 per cent of the population of those parts is still entirely illiterate and unable to either read or write. The expenditure on public education in India stands at a figure of which no civilised Government can ever make a mention without a blush, viz. about 3d. per head per annum. Then the methods of education are old and rotten, antiquated and superseded, abandoned and changed by all progressive peoples in the West. Under these circumstances, it is hardly justifiable for Englishmen to boast of the great results achieved by them in the way of civilising India. But Indians are a nation of people who are easily satisfied and they make no secret of it that they are grateful to their rulers even for such small mercies. All this gratefulness, however, vanishes away when they look around them and observe the evidences of that universal poverty which at this moment prevails in India and which on the first failure of rains reduces the whole mass of people to the verge of

3. T.B. Macaulay (1800-1859); British politician, orator, administrator, essayist and historian; entered Parliament in 1830; Secretary of the Board of Control which supervised the administration of India by the East India Company; served on the Supreme Council of India, 1834-38; introduced, along with William Bentinck, Western-oriented system of education in India in 1835; as President of the Commission on Indian Jurisprudence drafted a penal code that later became the basis of Indian Criminal Penal Code; works include *Laws of Ancient Rome, Critical and Historical Essays* (1843) and *History of England*.
4. Charles John, earl of Canning (1812-1862); M.P for Warwick, 1836-56; Under-Secretary of State for Foreign Affairs, 1841-46; Postmaster-General, 1853-55; Governor-General of India, 1856-62.

starvation. It is no wonder, then, that they are not prepared to admit that British rule in India has been quite a blessing. Thus you see, Ladies and Gentlemen, as I have already remarked that this question of British rule in India having been a blessing or not is a very long and disputed one. It has its two sides and a great deal can be said on both sides with some show of reason. The truth, however, is that a foreign rule, however well-intentioned it may be, can never be a blessing, much less when it is conducted on despotic lines by autocrats invested with powers larger than even the angels could be safely trusted with. The Government of India, as at present constituted, is a Government of irresponsible foreigners, whose principal aim is the exploitation of the country and its people and who are allowed to have their own way in ruling the country without any reasonable amount of control from the great nation in whose name they rule and whom they profess to represent. It is true that by the declarations of the Sovereign, the British have pledged themselves to treat Indians as fellow subjects. It is equally true that now and then we happen to meet a statesman who tries to be loyal to these declarations and who strives to vindicate the honour of his Sovereign and redeem the pledges given by him, but then the odds against him are so many and the difficulties in his way so tremendous that at the end he finds all his efforts ending in smoke and all his good intentions resulting in nothing. In fact, sometimes you see that the policy inaugurated by a well-intentioned statesman does more harm than good inasmuch as it leaves very bitter memories behind and with a bureaucracy at the helm of affairs determined to take their revenge and not only reverse all that he had done, but to carry it to the other extremity.

Viceroys might come and Viceroys might go but the political conditions in India must remain hopeless of reform unless and until the system of Government is so changed as to reduce the vast, unlimited and unhampered powers which the bureaucracy wields without any sense of their responsibility to the people of the country and unless and until something substantial is done to act up to the declarations of the Sovereign and make the Indians realise that they are the free citizens of a great empire and not the subjects of a foreign people. So long as there exists in India a ruling class separate and distinct from the ruled, it is futile to hope for any improvement in the condition of things in India. Man is after all man, be he of any nationality or creed or colour. That man must be an angel and something of the divine who can rise above the ordinary animal limitations of man and decline to take advantage of the superior position in which his good luck has placed him. It is not much use, therefore, to discourse on the iniquities of the despotic autocrats who in the name of the British people carry on the government of India in a bureaucratic spirit and exact the full pound of flesh to which they think they are entitled by virtue of their domination over that country. As it is no wonder that after a century and a quarter of British rule in some parts of India, the people of those parts find that the treatment which they meet at the hands of their rulers is anything but just and fair and far from what was likely to make them forget the humiliations incidental to the conditions of a subject race.

The distinctions of race and colour observed in the bestowal of Government patronage, the disqualifications from which the sons of the soil suffer in the struggle of life, the indignities that are often hurled at them simply by reason of their colour not being white, the persistent refusal to give them a substantial or even a reasonable share in the administration of the affairs of their own country and the patronising tone so often assumed by Anglo-Indian administrators cannot but remind them at every step of their life that Englishmen in India are not prepared to treat them as citizens of the Empire and that they have yet to win their position as such. In my opinion it is rather unfortunate for England as well as for India that the educated Indians all over the country should be imbued with the spirit of a fight but the circumstances under which they live and the antiquated methods by which they are governed by a despotic bureaucracy leave them no other option. The inequalities from which they suffer, the humiliations to which they are subjected, the disadvantages under which they labour, the misery of the bulk of the population, the state of destitution and poverty from which the great mass of the people suffer, the increasing insolence and impertinence of the ruling classes and the offensive intolerant bigotry and greed of the powerful bureaucracy at the helm of affairs leave them no other alternative. The only redeeming feature of the situation is that they have not yet lost all faith in the fairness of the great British nation. The great bulk of the people in India still believe that the *Feringee* at home, as the ordinary Indian rustic calls an Englishman, is more just and open to reason than his arrogant and puffed up brother in India. Whether rightly or wrongly (it is for you gentlemen to say and to show by your deeds) every educated Indian who has read English history believes that, in addition to his sound business instincts, John Bull is generally a kindly disposed person and a lover of liberty and it is not likely that he will ignore the lessons of history—of those blood-written pages of English and European history, in the writing of which he has played such a prominent part. Gentlemen, it is idle to shut your eyes and close your ears to the dictum of history—that infallible recorder of the wisdom and folly of mankind and that never-failing guide of those who have eyes to see and hearts to feel. It is not likely that Indians who have drunk deep of the fountain of the history, including that of modern Europe, will not benefit from the lessons imparted therein. Then, again, you will have to destroy all your telegraphic and railway lines to keep any people on the face of the globe ignorant of what so often happens in the Near East and of what has now been happening in Russia and in the Far East. Under the circumstances, Indians hope that the British at home may be expected to take a better, a truer and a sounder view of the relations of India and England than their representatives in India take or are likely to take. Being at such a distance from the contaminating atmosphere of a subject country, breathing the air of independence and freedom, being free from those absurd notions of false prestige and insolent dignity which so often guide or misguide the average Anglo-Indian and drive him so far away from the paths of justice and fair play, the average Briton staying at home is believed to be more likely to take a more businesslike view of the duties which Englishmen owe to India. But if that is expected of an average Englishman at home much more is expected of Lancashire and its people. The interests, the well-being and the prosperity of the latter are so much linked with India that they at least should not see the growing discontent and poverty in India with indifference. Whatever may be said of the ethics of the policy which has resulted in the crushing and dislocation of Indian industries, it cannot be denied that at this moment India is the greatest and the most paying customer of Lancashire.

Great Britain claims more than 70 per cent of the total import trade of India and more than 30 per cent of its exports, of which Lancashire can be credited with the best and greatest slice. The growing poverty of the Indians means so much decrease in their purchasing power. The growing disaffection of the Indians means the transference of that affection to countries other than the British. I am, therefore, inclined to maintain, Gentlemen, that the prosperity and good government of India are of paramount importance to Lancashire and all classes of its great trading community, be they manufacturers, shippers or working men. You know, perhaps, better than I do how these recurring famines, chronic and long-staying pestilences and constant frontier wars affect and dislocate trade. Scarcity in India means calamity to Lancashire. It means a contracted supply of cotton and other raw materials and a still more contracted demand for manufactured goods, a state of things which tells heavily on both the manufacturer and the workman. Why, the problem of the British unemployed might be solved very considerably if things could be so arranged as to increase the purchasing power of the Indian masses. A bumper harvest in India means a bumper season for Lancashire. But, as at present circumstanced, the average value of an Indians' trade with England is only represented by the small figure of 4s. 8d. per annum which, according to the calculation of the late Mr. Digby than whom a greater authority on questions like these could not be quoted, falls to under a half penny per head per annum in the case of 171 millions of them. If so, Gentlemen, may I ask if as sound businessmen it is not your duty to see that the purchasing power of every Indian increases and that he has more to invest in the good things of this world? The Indian National Congress, that great organisation of educated Indians, points out the way how to bring about that result. It pleads for a cheaper and more representative system of government.

It urges for a sounder and lighter system of taxation. It asks for extended facility and more practical methods of education. All these reforms, if effected, lead to one result, viz., the prosperity and the contentment of the people of India. "The great concern of the people of India", said James Mill,[5] who could hardly be accused of any partiality towards Indians, "is that the business of Government should be well and cheaply performed". Well, the Indian National Congress points out how this can be achieved, viz., by a larger employment of the Indian agency in the transaction of Government affairs and the reduction of military expenditure. Many years ago the late Mr. Henry Fawcett, while speaking from his place in the House of Commons, deplored the great increase in the military expenditure of the country. With that mastery over facts and figures which he commanded, he showed how India, with a much smaller revenue than England, maintained an army more costly than that of this country. But be it noted that the expenditure on the army at that time, to which he objected so vehemently, was 10 millions while in the blessed year of 1905 it has been raised to the portentous figure of 23 millions. He had also sounded a warning to the effect that if increase of taxation was a pretty serious affair in England, it was a hundred times more serious in India. But look at what has happened. Since then taxes after taxes have been piled and the finances of the country have been brought into a muddle. You have of late become familiar with "prosperity" budgets but I do not know if you are aware of the artificial methods by which, notwithstanding years of pestilence, plague and famine, the Government has been able to put on a face of prosperity. Prosperity indeed, when millions die of diseases which are directly due to underfeeding, underclothing and unwholesome housing! I am afraid I will tire you out by details, otherwise I could conclusively establish to your satisfaction the utter unreliability of these prosperity Budgets and the utter unsoundness of the system of Government accounts as prevails in India. Many of the evils pointed out by Mr. Henry Fawcett exist in their entirety up to the present moment and account for these fictitious prosperity Budgets. The Indian National Congress pleads for an economical and cheap system of government which means more money to be left with the people for being spent in the country. Then, in the matter of the employment of Indian agency in the business of government, there too the reform is sure to lead to the efficiency of the administration and prosperity of the people. It means a partial control of that economic drain which is just now telling so disastrously on India. India pays heavily for civil servants, judges and administrators who do not know the vernaculars of the country and are absolutely ignorant of the customs and manners of the people. So much so that

5. (1773-1836); British philosopher; an associate of Bentham and advocate of utilitarianism; wrote *History of India* in 1817.

some judges, highly paid civilians and barristers display a ridiculous want of knowledge of the language of the country when failing to understand the evidence of a witness speaking his own tongue, they mistake the names of animals and articles for names of human beings. What will you think of a Judge who, not knowing the vernacular equivalent of a buffalo or a donkey, will insist upon the latter being produced to give evidence? Oh! We are sick of these anomalies and I am sure you would be sick of them if you were to know of even one-tenth of them. But it is difficult to remedy the existing evils unless you all wake up and take a greater and more intelligent interest in the affairs of India. You know, Gentlemen, how difficult it is to deal with vested rights. There are certain classes in this country who think they have vested rights in India. You know to your cost how difficult it is to deal with such classes, and so long as India is a convenient place to find comfortable and paying berths for the dull, indolent, luxury-loving and otherwise good-for-nothing scions of these classes, one cannot expect any appreciable reform in the system of government in India or in the treatment of Indians by Englishmen. Do you know, Gentlemen, that the dullards of whom I have spoken above, when they fail to pass the Indian Civil Service examination by open competition, get commissions in the Indian army and from there are transferred to the Civil Service. Thus we find that in the Punjab and some other provinces a system of hereditary succession to high government offices from father to son and from son to grandson prevails. These men, who are worthless otherwise and often incapable of following the commonest law point argued before them are possessed of a very thick crust which is difficult to penetrate through even with a clear statement of your case as they are often found working as Judges and administering law. It is this class of Anglo-Indians who are most anxious to maintain the existing *status quo* and keep out the sons of the soil from a proper share in the administration of their own country.

If your aristocrats, Ladies and Gentlemen, care precious little for the middle classes and the working men of this country, much less are they likely to care for Indians so long as the system of government there suits their purposes and meets their ends. But what may be difficult for us to achieve alone may be considerably altered by your help. It is to you, therefore, that we appeal for co-operation and support. You may excuse me for pointing out to you that the misgovernment of India might be productive of more serious harm than at present you can conceive of. You know a starving man cannot properly discriminate. It will be no fault of his if he is disposed to lay the blame upon the whole British community and in a moment of despair think of desperate measures. Thank God that as yet the matters have not come to that pass but the things are so rapidly going from bad to worse that any day might arouse you from your sleep. There are some people in India who argue and argue loudly that the best way to bring home to Lancashire and manufacturing England the state of things in India is to boycott English-made goods, not necessarily in favour of Indian goods but in favour of any goods not English. Gentlemen, it will be worth your while to study who amongst the Indian population are the largest consumers of English-made goods. A little careful observation will show that as yet most of the costly goods produced by Lancashire are consumed by the English-speaking Indians. If so, am I wrong in asking you to extend your sympathy to these English-speaking Indians and help them in their constitutional fight for political rights against the bureaucratic government of India? Assisted by you they might succeed in obtaining a better system of government for their country by which, in the words of James Mill, means of accumulation may be afforded to your Indian fellow subjects and under which they may have chances of growing rich as cultivators, merchants and manufacturers.

A few observations more, Gentlemen, and I have done. I cannot let this opportunity go without saying a word as to another impression gaining ground amongst Indians which it may be worth your while to remove. There is an impression in India that Lancashire is very jealous of Indian manufactures and is interested in keeping down Indian industries. Well, Ladies and Gentlemen, I have no doubt that the impression must be wrong because I cannot bring my mind to believe that shrewd, highly intelligent, and well-read in history and politics as Lancashire merchants are, they can believe in that old, rotten, antiquated fallacy of the secrets of trade. Now when the doors of knowledge have been thrown open everywhere in the world no one can, arbitrarily or out of jealousy, be kept out of that knowledge which is a *sine qua non* of industrial pursuits and manufacturing capacity. This knowledge and the facilities to acquire it are accessible to anyone who has the means to pay for them in the wide, wide world, in Germany, in America, and last but not least in Japan. I cannot believe that the highly gifted class of Lancashire merchants do not realise and cannot see this. It is an insult to their intelligence and broad-mindedness to think otherwise. My own idea is that it will be to the interest of both India and Lancashire to understand each other better. India can gain nothing by substituting Germany, America, or any other country for Lancashire either for the purposes of import or export, because it must be long before India can supply its own needs. For a long, long time to come India must continue to import finished and costly goods from outside and there is no reason why it should purchase those goods from anyone but England. On the other hand, it will do no harm to Lancashire if the latter were to take Indians into their confidence and qualify them to manufacture those cheap and coarse goods which it is at present importing from Germany and other countries. Such a sympathy from Lancashire will, I am sure, meet with a reciprocal goodwill on the part of India in the matter of supplying raw materials. Remember, Gentlemen, that it lies in the power of India to make you to a great extent independent of America in the matter of the supply of cotton.

It is, therefore, my humble conviction that a better understanding and reciprocal good feeling between Lancashire and India will be to the good of both. The more prosperous, wealthier, happier, the better educated and skilled India is, the better for Lancashire. Let Lancashire then exert for the good government of India and for the removal of those anomalies and disqualifications from which Indians suffer and India will, I am sure, amply repay the kindness of Lancashire.

May we hope that on the occasion of the next general election you will make it a point to take certain pledges from your candidates to the effect that they will take greater interest in Indian affairs and vote in favour of reform measures?

In the end, I thank you for the patience with which you have heard me.

8. On Arya Samaj[1]

J.C. Oman[2]: Is the Arya Samaj an exclusively Hindu sect?

Lajpat Rai: A Muslim was admitted by Swami Dayanand[3] himself, but was never able to secure a social footing amongst the Hindus, though he was allowed to be present at the ceremonies and festivals of the Arya Samaj. He is still living, and is recognised as an Arya, having renounced Islam. The Arya Samaj, Gujranwala, have admitted a Muslim graduate to the Samaj, and freely eat and drink with him. A few other Muhammadans have been admitted elsewhere. Mazhbi Sikhs have also been received into the Samaj, and they freely eat with others. Many families of Christians and Muhammadans (converts from Hinduism) have been admitted into the Samaj. The intermarriage of these with the other Aryas has not been yet satisfactorily arranged.

1. Interview to Prof. J.C. Oman, London, July 1905. Home Department (Political-B), Nos. 55-58, July 1911, N.A.I.
2. Author of *Indian Life—Religious and Social*, published in 1889 and reprinted in 1908 under the title *Cults, Customs and Superstitions of India*.
3. (1824-1883); founder of Arya Samaj and religious and social reformer; established the first Arya Samaj in Bombay in 1875 and Lahore Arya Samaj in 1877; works include *Satyarth Prakash* and *Commentary on the Rigveda*.

J.C. Oman: Is there any formal ceremony of initiation into the Arya Samaj? If so, what are the details of such a ceremony?

Lajpat Rai: With Hindus mere signing the declaration of faith is sufficient. In the case of non-Hindus a *Shuddhi* (purification) ceremony of a simple kind is obligatory, though not necessarily carried out by a Brahmin. Yet, of course, such Pundits are usually employed. After feasting, bathing, shaving and changing his clothes, and after the *Hom* ceremony has been performed, he accepts the *Gayatri*.

Those who were originally (as Hindus) entitled to wear the sacred thread are again invested with it. In the case of men who are not Hindus by origin the thread has also been conferred, and this has, as might have been expected, given rise to some objection and opposition.

J.C. Oman: Are the ordinary rules of the Hindu caste system set aside in the Samaj? Do Arya Samajists intermarry or even eat with one another irrespective of caste?

Lajpat Rai: In the Punjab eating in common is usual; but hardly yet in the United Provinces. As regards marriage, the position is very delicate and quite experimental. Marriages between members of sub-castes have occasionally been carried out, and it is the policy of the Samaj to encourage such marriages, leaving the castes to be dealt with later on. In theory the Samaj does not recognise hereditary castes. In the case of marriages of orphan girls adopted by the Samaj, the usual caste rules have been set aside and such marriages have come to be accepted, or, at any rate, have not been objected to.

J.C. Oman: Idolatry, I know, is condemned by the Aryas; but do they repudiate the Hindu Gods, Vishnu and Siva, and deny them worship?

Lajpat Rai: These names, Vishnu and Siva, are accepted as names of one God; but the reputed consorts of Vishnu and Siva—Durga, Kali, Devi, etc.—are not regarded as divinities.

J.C. Oman: Do the Aryas conduct their birth, marriage and funeral ceremonies without the help of Brahmins?

Lajpat Rai: Generally Brahmins are employed, but qualified persons who are not Brahmins often officiate in the performance, particularly of birth and funeral ceremonies.

Cremation is practised, but no post-funeral rites are carried out, beyond the purification of the house where the dead body lay by the performance of the *Hom* with all the prescribed mantras.

J.C. Oman: I am aware that the Aryas profess belief in the transmigration of souls and that they venerate the cow; but are their ideas of a future life and hell and heaven those of the orthodox Hindu?

Lajpat Rai: Yes, the doctrine of reincarnation is believed in, and the cow is venerated by the Aryas. Heaven and hell, in the Hindu or usual sense, are not believed in the Arya Samaj.

The Arya Samaj holds with Swami Dayanand that there are three entities, the Supreme Soul, the Soul of Man and Matter.

J.C. Oman: The Samaj is said to be aggressively anti-Christian. Is this so?

Lajpat Rai: Certainly, [it is] on the defensive.

J.C. Oman: The teaching of Swami Dayanand in regard to *Niyog* is, I understand, taken by all his followers as an essential part of the Master's doctrines. Am I right?

Lajpat Rai: The Samaj does not consider *Niyog* an essential doctrine.

J.C. Oman: After the murder of Pandit Lekh Ram,[4] there was, I know, an attempt to bring about a reconciliation between the two sections of the Samaj. What was the result?

Lajpat Rai: The division still exists. The Mahatma Samaj[5] made good progress, but is now suffering from internal strife.

J.C. Oman: Have there been any other schisms in the Arya Samaj since 1893?

Lajpat Rai: No.

J.C. Oman: Some time back it was given out that Swami Bhaskarananda Saraswati had established a branch of the Arya Samaj in Philadelphia, United States of America. is this true?

Lajpat Rai: Not credited by those who knew him best.

J. C. Oman: What are the political aims of the Society?

Lajpat Rai: None at all.

4. (1858-1897); hailed from the Frontier side; a staunch Arya Samajist and a great devotee of Swami Dayanand; joined police service but resigned in 1884 to serve the Arya Samaj; edited *Arya Gazette* from 1887 to 1890; assassinated by a convert Muslim at Lahore in March 1897, which led to a temporary reunion of the two parties of the Arya Samaj; works include *Takzib-i-Burahin-i-Ahmadiyah* and *Risala-i-Jihad yani Din-i-Muhammadi Ki Bunyad* (1892).
5. In the Arya Samaj conflict during 1892-93, the party led by Master Durga Prashad and Lala Munshi Ram (Swami Shraddhanand) was named as Mahatma Samaj by the rival party led by Lala Hans Raj who was supported by Lajpat Rai.

9. To Ganga Prasad Verma[1]

London
3 August 1905

My dear Babu Sahib,

I am sorry I could not write to you earlier but then I wanted some time to mature opinions and confirm impressions. I have now been about two months in this country and have seen members of almost all sections of the Liberal Party. Permit me therefore to communicate my opinions to you as you are the man to whom the whole credit of my visit to England is due if there is any credit in the same.

1. Regarding the chances of Mr. Dadabhai Naoroji's candidature. Mr. Naoroji told me that he was opposed by another Liberal and a Conservative and that in case Liberal retired he had good chances of success which meant that otherwise he had no chance of success. Mr. Shyamji K. Varma and Mr. F.H. Oddonnel, President, National Democratic League, of which Mr. Dadabhai Naoroji is a Vice-President, are of opinion that Mr. Naoroji has not the remotest chance of success. The latter told me that the official liberal candidate who opposes him would rather see the Conservative is returned than retire in favour of Mr. Naoroji. Shyamji is very bitter against Naoroji and openly tells everybody that this man has been wasting the money of the country so long and that he does it simply as a profession. He has told me that Mr. Naoroji is completely in the hands of his election agent who spends money like anything. Mr. Naoroji's previous Secretary was Mr. Mukerjee, a Bengalee, who has married an English woman and has a child from her is now Secretary of Mr. Shyamji's Indian Home Rule Society and seems to be in Mr. Shyamji's confidence. My own opinion is that whatever truth there may be in Shyamji's statement about the sources of Mr. Naoroji's income, Mr. Shyamji is jealous of Naoroji and wants to pull him down in the estimation of Indians. Shyamji is an extremist of that class who is not agreeable to anybody's advice and who wants to rule supreme. So far I think his fellowships too are not likely to be a very great success as his conditions are very onerous and his attitude very exacting. So far his India House too is not attractive. Out of the five fellowships granted by him the two granted to the Hindus have not been availed of. But that is a digression. It must be, however, admitted that Mr. Naoroji does not seem to possess much influence or any influence at all in official Liberal circles. For election too he depends almost exclusively on the working men.[2]

1. G. K. Gokhale Papers (microfilm), N.A.I.
2. Dadabhai Naoroji, however, lost the election.

2. *India*—So far as England is concerned, *India* commands no reading circle and almost no influence but it cannot be denied that for India it is very useful. My own impression is that the paper should be edited by an Indian young man of ability. If you want the Indian political mission in this country to gain any ground or to make any impression, you ought to have a number of well-connected young Indians here devoted to the work, able, energetic and pushing. A whole-time Indian for the editorship of *India* will be a great gain. He would be able to make the paper more interesting for Indians and at the same time devote the whole of his spare time to push on our mission. He could find time to call on the editors of English dailies, write to them without any recommendation and generally exert to influence British politicians. But the difficulty is that Sir Henry Cotton wants the job for his son. In fact, I would go a step further and say that the post of the Secretary of the British Committee should be filled by an Indian but that seems to be rather difficult of achievement as the present incumbent has held office for so many years and knows ins and outs of the same so thoroughly well.

3. England is a money-ridden country and here almost everyone wants to be paid for the services that he renders to anyone. There is not much of philanthropy here except such as is displayed in maintaining some national charitable institutions. The press here will do nothing unless it is paid for the same and the same may be said of politicians. I am of opinion that English press is regularly subsidised by foreign governments and those people who expect to be served by the same. The Japanese maintain a special office for the purpose here. Under the circumstances, it is perfectly impolitic for us to expect to achieve anything here unless we have enormous sums at our disposal to spend. The official Liberal Party and the official Liberal press care little for India or Indian interests. Their party purposes are not served by the same. The only section in the House of Commons that is favourable to India is the Democratic and the Irish Party. The Socialists, the Democrats and the Labour people are coming to the front every day and I am of opinion that your only chance lies with them. But here again they will not attend much to your needs unless you are prepared to subsidise their movements by funds. The Democrats, the Socialists and the working men are prepared to support you provided you make it worth their while to do so. I leave it to you to judge how far we are all in a position to do so.

4. Most probably the general election will come off in October or November. The delegates, therefore, if coming at all might be here by the end of September.

5. I want to make a suggestion about the next Congress. Is it possible for you to bring about a gathering of at least a lakh of men on that occasion from

the different parts of India?[3] The place selected is just the place suited to carry out such an idea. I am of opinion that we should not erect a *Pandal* nor should we in the Congress Committee arrange for the accommodation of delegates or visitors. At any rate, we should fix one day for monster meeting—a great demonstration of at least a lakh of people on the bank of the Ganges in the open air to protest against the policy of Lord Curzon. From the Ganges the whole assembly should return to the city in a procession singing national songs. Some speeches may also be delivered in vernacular from different platforms. After this you can have your ordinary Congress for two days consisting of not more than 200 delegates. I think a demonstration of a 100,000 people thus collected as a protest against the policy of Lord Curzon will carry more weight and will impress the people in England more than any number of your Congressmen. I am of opinion that if properly organized and worked the movement is bound to be a great success. People are just now fairly well excited and you should not fail to take advantage of this. Unless you are prepared to change the nature of your movement in this direction you are not likely to make any progress towards political freedom at all and I am sure that if the Congress will not take the initiative in this matter some other movement may have to be set up to do the same and then the Congress will dwindle into insignificance. Do kindly give your best thought to the matter and take counsel amongst your friends. This letter, at any rate, the first four paras are strictly confidential. The contents of the 5th para if approved of by yourself can be made public. Please do pass on this letter to Mr. Gokhale as I have no time to write two long letters by one mail. I am writing some educational articles for the *Arya Gazette*.[4] Do please read the same.

Yours very sincerely,
Lajpat Rai

3. In 1906 the Congress session was held at Calcutta.
4. The *Arya Gazette*, an Urdu weekly, published from Lahore, which served as the organ of the College section of the Arya Samaj, was edited by Lajpat Rai, in collaboration with Lala Hans Raj, for nearly two years.

10. To G.K. Gokhale[1]

London
3 August 1905

Dear Mr. Gokhale,

I owe you an apology for not having written to you earlier and for the publication of certain matters in the *Panjabee* which you might perhaps be disposed to consider as breach of confidence. But I may explain to you that my first letter published in the *Panjabee* was addressed to a friend with certain passages marked to be struck out before the letter was sent to the press. But it looks that through oversight the letter was sent to the press without this being done. I have this day addressed a long letter to Mr. Ganga Prasad Varma and asked him to send it to you for perusal.[2] I am afraid the situation here is anything but cheerful. There is nothing to prevent Sir Henry Fowler becoming the Secretary of State for India even if the Liberals come to power. Please do let me know if you are coming and, if so, when? I may be out in America when you reach here but I will be returning by the time you commence your work.[3] So far my way has been rather smooth though I do not think that I have done really much for India or could do better. I think you have lost a capital opportunity in not coming earlier. July was the best month for meetings like these for the simple reason that all these political associations and clubs &c. hold their anniversaries and it costs them nothing to give you a hearing.

Hoping to hear from you soon,
I remain

Yours very sincerely,
Lajpat Rai

1. G.K. Gokhale Papers (microfilm), N.A.I.
2. See *ante*, item 9.
3. Lajpat Rai left for America in mid-September and returned to England early in October.

11. Need for Reform in the System of Government of India[1]

Mr. Channing,[2] Ladies and Gentlemen,

This being my first visit to this part of England, I cannot say even the few words that I intend to speak this afternoon without first paying a sincere homage to the memory of that great and good man who for several years so successfully represented your neighbours in Parliament, and over and above that manfully fought the battles of the unrepresented millions of India. If ever any Englishman won the hearts of the people of India by his fearless and disinterested championship of the rights and interests of the downtrodden millions that inhabit that land and fully established a claim to be called "the Member for India" it was the late lamented Charles Bradlaugh.[3] Perhaps in no other part of India was his premature death felt so keenly and mourned so truly and deeply as in the Punjab where we, the Punjabis, raised a memorial to the sacred memory of that good friend of ours. In November 1900 the Reception Committee of the second Lahore Congress built a permanent public hall at Lahore at a cost of more than £2,000 and named it after Charles Bradlaugh to remind the coming generations of the Punjab of the substantial services rendered to their country by that noble Englishman. It is very unfortunate that by the carelessness of a tenant the Hall should have been lately damaged by fire, but we hope we shall soon restore it to its original state. Our successive misfortunes, the recurring famines, the plague and the poverty of the people have, till now, prevented us from doing the needful.

Now, ladies and gentlemen, with your permission I shall proceed to make a few remarks on the system and methods of government that rule supreme in India. As you are accustomed to see the bright side of English rule, which is so frequently and profusely painted before you by that band of Anglo-Indians who can never see its shortcomings, I beg your pardon for confining my remarks to the dark side of that rule. It is always an unpleasant task to find fault with the doings of men in whom one's audience is interested, and who in a way derive their power and authority from the latter. But then that is the only tribunal to which aggrieved people like ourselves can appeal and from which they can

1. Speech at an open-air meeting of Liberal and Radical Associations of England held at Kettering on 10 August 1905. *The Panjabee*, 4 September 1905.
2. F.A. Channing.
3. (1833-1891); member of Parliamentary Reforms League, 1866; elected to Parliament in 1880; supported the Ilbert Bill which was passed in 1884 removing judicial disqualifications based on racial distinctions in India; drafted in 1889 the Bill for the reform of the Legislative Council which was passed in 1891; attended Calcutta Congress in 1890.

demand that justice which is withheld from them by those in immediate authority over them in their own country. The class that holds the reins of power in India owes that power to you. It is from you that they derive their authority and it is therefore to you that we look for redress. We do not care to be personal, because we know that however perfect and benevolently inclined persons may be, they are men after all. Unlimited powers given to any man without any check or control from within the country and much of supervision from without are liable to be misused. It is the system we attack and it is the system to which we trace our misfortunes and the failings and shortcomings of British rule in India. We do attack individuals also now and then but it is very rare, and then we never claim redress of them. What we press for is such a change in the system and methods of government in India which may remove the existing anomalies and which may tend to strengthen the ties of fellow-feeling and brotherhood between Indians and Englishmen. We ask for this because we are convinced that the good of England also requires the same. No foreign rule can ever be very safe and secure, at least for any great length of time, unless it is based upon the affection of the people and unless the latter are so well treated as to be justified in identifying themselves with the former. This cannot be achieved until the ruling class are prepared to merge themselves in the people, give up the special and anomalous privileges which they enjoy and put an end to all class distinctions as such, and unless they treat the people as fellow subjects of a common Sovereign Power and as fellow citizens of a common empire. So long as there is a ruling class in India distinct from, and quite independent of, the people so long the Englishmen in India must be considered as aliens and their rule as unnatural and tyrannical. That this is the opinion of those who at present constitute the Government of India, and that this is the conviction of the ruling bureaucracy here as well is quite clear from the several acts and declarations of the members of the Government in India as well as in England. The very fact that in the matter of the larger employment of the Indian agency in the administration of the affairs of the country, the absolute necessity of maintaining the existing undiminishable minimum as they say of European strength is considered necessary, coupled with the recent anxiety of Lord Curzon to increase that strength, shows that the Government is alive to and conscious of the fact that the people of India are not sufficiently contented to be relied upon. You would not require either Lord Kitchener's extraordinary scheme for converting the country into a military canton[4] or Lord Robert's 500,000 Britons identified with to defend India against any possible foreign attack if the Government of India believed that Indians were so thoroughly identified with

4. Lord Kitchener reorganised the army with a view to meeting the threat of external aggression instead of internal rebellion.

the Government as to defend it at any cost against any attack from without. There is no lack of fighting men in India. Races who have always maintained their own against the best soldiers of the world would not surely be found deficient when they have to defend their own country and their own hearths and homes if they were inspired with the idea that they were required to do so by the highest dictates of patriotism and not the niggardly salaries allowed to them by an unsympathetic, all-absorbing foreign Government. The Sikhs, the Gurkhas, the Rajputs, the Pathans and the Afridis have always elicited the highest praises of every officer under whom they have ever been required to serve; but these praises alone are not likely to inspire them with the highest devotion and the noblest of self-denials as long as they find that there is such a great difference between the treatment which they receive and the treatment Tommy Atkins receives from the Government, and so long as you continue to deny them positions of trust and confidence in the Army. If that is true of the military classes, it is more so of the civil population who are at almost every step reminded that they are a subject race living as if by sufferance and for the benefit of the ruling classes. Whether on the hills, on holiday and health resorts, in courts of justice, on railways, in markets or in municipal corporations, everywhere a native of India meets with evidences of an Englishman's arrogance and racial pride. It is no wonder, gentlemen, that under the circumstances Indians are very much dissatisfied with the Government of India and that there is a great deal of discontent. We, Congressmen, are often charged by interested Anglo-Indians with exaggerating the situation and misrepresenting the ruling classes. But let me challenge our opponents to come forward and prove that there is a single class of Indian population which has not got grave charges to advance against the ruling bureaucracy. Is it not a fact that just now every Indian who has a grain of self-respect in him, from the Ruling Chief down to the lowest ryot, is unhappy and miserable? Princes of Royal blood whose ancestors have enjoyed sovereign powers for centuries and centuries past and who can trace their authority to a period of history when the English had not yet stepped into civilisation are at this minute made to feel the humility of their present position by the insolent behaviors of petty British Agents and the assumption of a haughty and overbearing attitude on the part of Viceroys and Governors. Treaties entered into at a time when upon the friendship and goodwill of these houses depended the continuance of British rule in India are being tampered with, changed, altered and disregarded to the utter disadvantage of the native States. That man must be under a strange delusion and one who can have no idea of what human nature is who believes that these people can be happy and that they do not smart under the insults which are heaped upon them by a Government whose agents presume they are too powerful to care for the feelings or sufferings of those scions of old, ancient and noble houses. Descend a step lower and have a glance at the landed aristocracy of the land and you will find them in no better state of mind. Descend a step still lower and you will find the peasant and the trader and the artisan bemoaning their lot as British subjects. With their occupations gone, their means of making a decent livelihood narrowed and cut down, taxes and cesses constantly multiplying and the prices of the necessaries of life gone high, it is no wonder that they are in a sullen mood and do not find their lives worth living. Look to the great and ever-increasing mortality from famine, plague and fever. All these result from want of good and sufficient nourishment and want of well-lighted and well-ventilated habitations. Plague germs find a congenial place to grow and multiply in darkness and in insanitary conditions. Why? You may inoculate the whole Indian population but the plague will not disappear unless you take steps to change the conditions of life under which the great mass of people live. Then, last but not the least, look to the educated classes who are loud with their complaints and whose sentiments find expression in the writings of the Indian press. Even the Government of India has to admit that the educated classes are discontented. It makes no difference whether they are Government servants, lawyers or doctors or what. They all feel the injustice of the situation and express it sufficiently loudly not. But has any one ever taken the trouble to enquire why these intelligent classes of His Majesty's subjects are so dissatisfied with British rule? Surely, they are not mad, nor were they so discontented always. Why this change for the worse? Have a thorough and independent enquiry conducted by people in whom the educated classes have confidence, and you should at once find that the complaints of the Indian press and the grievances which are voiced by the Indian National Congress are based on truth, and in the interests of both England and India they require to be looked into. Gentlemen, excuse me for saying that however powerful and strong a Government may be, it shall not pay it to continue to act in entire disregard and in utter defiance of the public opinion of the country. Look to your legislation. It is not occasionally, but of late rather frequently, that you have made laws which were vehemently opposed by the people.

Look at the recent enactments that have been passed by the Government of Lord Curzon. There is that Official Secrets Act, enacted in defiance of the public opinion of the country, both Indian and Anglo-Indian.[5] There is that Universities Act, and its corollary the University Validating Act, which have

5. The Official Secrets Act enacted in 1903 made it an offence to give any information regarding civil matters or reveal any military secrets or make any comments in newspapers that was "likely to bring the Government or constituted authority into suspicion or contempt". The burden of proof, according to the Act, lay on the accused, so the freedom of newspapers to give information was greatly curbed by the Act.

been put on the Statute Book in the teeth of the opposition of all classes of Indians—Hindus, Mohammedans, Christians, Parsis, and Buddhists.[6] The last named piece of legislation was carried through in defiance of all principles of good government, whereby a dangerous precedent has been laid down of the legislature stepping in to validate a matter the validity of which at that very minute was under discussion in the highest judicial tribunal of the land. The partition of Bengal has been ordered in opposition to the unanimously declared opinion of all classes of His Majesty's subjects in that Presidency.[7] The Indian National Congress has for the last twenty years been crying over the evil which results from the continued combination of Judicial with Executive functions. The highest authorities in India and in England have accepted the justness of the complaint. The reform has been approved all through, yet the Government always pleads want of means to carry out the reform. While this declared paucity of funds is represented to be the cause of the evil which allows the combination of the functions of a Judge and a Prosecutor in the same person resulting in numerous judicial murders almost everyday, finances are of no consideration in creating new Provinces requiring an additional outlay of millions on new and separate administrations. The N.W. Frontier Province was separated from the Punjab notwithstanding the strong protest of the then head of the Punjab Government and the unanimous dissent of the Punjab Civil Service and of the people.[8] Bengal is now undergoing a similar operation against the strongly-expressed opinion of the whole nation. This is surely despotism with vengeance, and you cannot expect the people who are so slighted and insulted at every step to have any but feelings of disgust and distrust for your Government. It is not strange then that in all these cases your legislative and administrative measures cannot be attributed to the best of motives. And surely you do not add to the contentment of the people when you do not legislate for them but in spite of them. Under the circumstances, it is no wonder if, relying still upon constitutional methods, the people of India should have commenced talking of boycotting Government service and boycotting English-made goods. You are, gentlemen, just now very much exercised over the military stores scandal in connection with the South African war. But do you know that in India these things are very common and still it is rare that they can see the light of day. Have you ever taken the trouble to enquire to what do a good many of the retired Anglo-Indian Commissariat Officers, or retired Indian Political Agents, owe their palaces, saloons and other luxuries of life which they find at their disposal on their return to this country. They get princely salaries there in India

6. For details see *post*, section 6, item 10, fn. 2.

7. The partition of Bengal was effected in 1905. See also *ante*, section 2.

8. The North-West Frontier Province was created by partitioning Punjab in 1901.

no doubt, but these salaries could hardly account for the great fortunes which some at least of the retired Anglo-Indian Commissariat Officers and Political Agents are known to possess. We know how in our country fortunes are made often in a ridiculously short time, say in one border expedition, by contractors who were known to be comparatively poor before. Don't you think, gentlemen, then, that this state of affairs requires a looking after, and that the sooner you do so the better? I have already taxed your patience too much and will not tire you out by further details. I thank you for the patient hearing you have given me. It is only natural for us Indians to expect that the liberty-loving Radical and Liberal voters of Charles Bradlaugh will be friendly to us and will throw the weight of their votes in favour of reform in the system and methods of government in India. But there is one thing, which I will like to make clear before I sit down, viz., that in demanding reforms in the system of government in India, we are not asking for anything which as patriotic Englishmen you could not entertain. In fact, we base our claims on the solid rock of the mutual good of both countries. We know that it will not do to beg for favours, which you could not grant without being false to your own people. What we urge is that the present methods of administering the affairs of India are undermining the stability of your Government there. As patriotic Indians we are interested in seeing that our country continues to enjoy that peace which it was the privilege of the English to establish and that it is also happy and prosperous at the same time. It is the desire of the Indians to enjoy the same amount of political freedom which the other parts of this self-governing empire do and in asking for that we know we are making a demand the granting of which will redound to the credit and glory of England and which is sure to benefit all parties concerned.

12. Characteristics of Englishmen[1]

There is, however, one thing which is pre-eminently characteristic; unpaid labour or paid service is never false to the country. In every sphere of life, be it in the school or in the factory, in the workshop or on the stream, an Englishman or an

1. Extracts from a letter written by Lajpat Rai published in *The Panjabee* of 14 August 1905 with the following note by the editor: "We have no communication from Lala Lajpat Rai for publication this week. However, we cull the following passages from a private letter of his received by the last English mail, which we trust will be found of general and absorbing interest."

English child never forgets his country. If there is anything which is most prominent and patent on the face of every institution it is an Englishman's love for his country and its political institutions. I have seen books taught in the Primary schools which aim at impressing on English boys how precious liberty is and what struggles they have passed through in bringing down the rights and privileges of monarchy. At every step they are impressed with the magnitude and greatness of their empire and their duty to derive the fullest benefit out of it. The other day I was reading a question paper set up for the final examination of an Elementary Girls' School and was struck with a question which enquired in what way Canada, Australia and other colonies named therein were useful to England. The system of life and the system of education in the country are bound to produce patriots.

Englishmen and women generally indulge in a colossal ignorance about India. At every step they are simply surprised at our knowledge of the English language and at the fluency with which we speak it. Other foreigners who come here can never imitate the English accent nor can the English very well imitate the accent of other nations but Indians can do it very well. Oh! they are simply unsurpassable in imitation!!! What is there that they cannot imitate except that they cannot adopt that strength of character, that stamina, that backbone, those habits of self-reliance and self-respect that characterise other nations.

The little Jap is just now the hero of the hour. He is literally worshipped, and with him his art and his habits too are receiving a great deal of attention. Here at Manchester they show a mock fight (an imitation of *Mukden*) twice every week with fireworks. At the end the portraits of Oyama, Nogi and Kuroki are exhibited in fireworks and every time the Japs are lustily cheered. It reminds you of the truth of the adage that nothing succeeds like success. At times people stare at us and say we are Japanese.

13. To G. K. Gokhale[1]

Oxford
Monday
[August 1905]

Dear Mr. Gokhale,

On Thursday and Friday the watching business about which I wrote to you reached its climax. On Friday I was shadowed by the same man who followed me on Thursday for full four hours, as I went from Hamporto to 84, 85 Palace Chambers, from there to George's Hospital and thence to Mr. Mackarness,[2] M.P.'s house where I was to lunch. He disappeared before I could point him out to Mr. Mackarness. I was so much worried that I left London for Oxford that very afternoon. I was going to return by this afternoon's Express in order to be in time for your meeting when I received a letter from my son informing me that more than one man watched my house at one and the same time and twice an effort was made to decoy me out after dark under the pretence of meeting an Indian near the Hamporto Health station. This has roused my suspicion and it is possible that it may be more than merely watching my movements. Possibly the *Daily Express* people are laying a trap for me. Under these circumstances I decided to forego the pleasure of hearing you this evening and not to return home after dark.

I hope you will excuse my absence and if possible arrange to be at the club between two and three where I intend to see you.

I am dictating this letter because I have put atropine in my eyes and cannot read and write.

Sincerely yours,
Lajpat Rai

1. G.K. Gokhale Papers (microfilm), N.A.I.
2. A friend of Lajpat Rai who asked questions in the House of Commons about his arrest and deportation without trial in May 1907.

14. To Duni Chand[1]

Dear Mr. Duni Chand,[2]

I had not written to you again as there was hardly anything special to be written. Everything worth knowing appeared in *India* and other Indian papers.

On the 30th of August on my return from Paris and the Continent where I had gone for a fortnight,[3] I wrote to Sir W. Wedderburn to let me know his wishes as to how I could make myself useful to my country, in September. In reply, I had received a letter, which I beg to enclose, a perusal of which will show to you that I am going to America on duty. I have been really doing the work of Sappers and Miners here and I am required to do the same work in America. I would gladly do any work that is likely to be of any use to my country, however rough or troublesome it may be. There is such a great rush of passengers just now to America that I have not been able to secure a good passage. Moreover, I found a *Madrassi* graduate stranded here. He had left home for studying in America and on his way found he had not sufficient [money] according to the laws of America to be allowed to land there. Thus he came to London and sought the shelter of the Home for Destitute Indians. He sought the help of Mr. Shyamji Krishna Varma whose terms, however, are not acceptable to him. He is a young graduate and I am taking him with me to put him in some college there. It is impossible to refuse help to an Indian under such circumstances, and I hope you will agree with me in that I am only doing an act of duty. I propose to return from America in the 1st week of October and join Mr. Gokhale in the campaign. I hope my work in England has met with your approval and trust that my work in America also may bear some fruit.

If you have no objection, you may just hand over these letters or copies of the same to the *Tribune* and *The Panjabee.*

Sincerely yours,
Lajpat Rai

P.S.—Did you hear that at one of the Paris hotels my purse containing gold worth £ 20 and my return passage to India were stolen from my bedroom? That means a dead loss of Rs. 500. I may, however, get a duplicate ticket but it is doubtful.

1. Written after 30 August 1905 and published in *The Panjabee* of 2 October 1905.
2. (1870-1945); a Congressman of Ambala; practised law at Lahore; member of Lahore Municipal Committee; participated in agrarian movement in Punjab in 1907; active member of Indian Association; went to jail several times during the freedom movement.
3. For his impressions of Paris and the Continent see item 6 in section 5.

15. India's Expectations from England[1]

Mr. Lajpat Rai, who was most cordially received, addressed himself to the disadvantage under which the Indian people laboured under the present system of government, and to the necessity of measures being taken to render them happy, prosperous and contented. Broadly and briefly put, their demand was: "India for the Indians, under the guidance and control of Britain". When he said that, he did not say it on his own authority, but on the highest authority within these realms. He based the claim on the Proclamation of the Queen-Empress when she took over the government of India from the East India Company in 1858, and upon the declarations of British statesmen. The Proclamation pledged the British Government to throw open the offices of the Government of India to all Her Majesty's subjects, irrespective of nationality, caste or creed in India. It was 46 years or more; since that Magna Carta of India was promulgated. It was renewed in that great assemblage of Indian princes, nobles, gentry and people, when the Queen was proclaimed Empress of India.[2] But the obligations which Her Majesty had declared should be faithfully and conscientiously observed had not been carried out, excepting in a very limited degree and in a grudging manner, by those who had been entrusted with the administration of British rule in India. And Indians wanted to know why the government of India was not conducted on the principles thus proclaimed. The reason was not far to seek. Vested interests had grown up in connection with the official classes, who resented any measures which interfered with their predominance by giving increased opportunities to the Indian people to share in the government of their own country. Englishmen knew well the doctrine, and insisted on it in their own government, that there should be no taxation without representation. They recognised that in countries where the people were taxed without having a voice in the expenditure of the money taken from them, the system of government was unsound. There might be countries where the state of civilisation was such, where there was no education, where these principles could not always be applied. But in India, where there had been in the past a high state of civilisation, the people had proved in almost every sphere of life, in the universities, on political platforms, in the administration of justice, that they were capable of taking a part in the government of the country, to the advantage of the people and of the state. He contended that the

1. Report of a speech delivered at a meeting held in the Union Church, Putney, on 9 October 1905. *The Panjabee*, 6 November 1905.

The meeting was presided over by Mr. Garatt who had lived in India for five years.

2. In 1858.

taxes should be raised with the consent of the people, and that they should be expended according to their wishes. The prosperity and the good of England, as well as of India depended largely on the prosperity and contentment of the people of India. If the people of India were poor, unhappy, starving, discontented, it could redound neither to the credit nor to the good of England. The strength of British rule lay in the prosperity, loyalty, and contentment of India. They had to consider whether the condition of the people of India was better and more prosperous than since they had been under the British Government. Even if it were no worse it was a reflection on British rule, for they would all agree with him that there ought to be improvement and progress in the course of time. The late Lord Macaulay, in advocating gradual measures of education and self-government over seventy years ago, had declared it would be a proud day for England when India, in the main, could govern herself. But the liberal policy foreshadowed by Lord Macaulay and other great statesmen of his time, had not been carried out, and the result was not for the good of India. The financial policy of the British Government had failed to encourage the industries of the people or to make the people wealthier or happier. The form of Indian government was despotic, for it had no element of representation in it. There was not a single Indian on either of the Executive Councils. Then even the decision of the Viceroy made, it might be, in the interests of India—so unsound was the principle on which India was governed—could be upset by the authorities in this country if it were considered to clash with British interests. Where policy was determined by the pressures of British officials on the Secretary of State's Council in British interests, surely some heed should be paid to the views of those most intimately affected, namely, the people of India themselves. The fiscal policy of the Government had practically ruined Indian industries and thrown out of employment millions of people who lived by those industries. The East India Company had destroyed them by the imposition of heavy duties and by encouraging the import of foreign goods free of duty. This had compelled the people to fall back on agriculture, had lessened the prosperity and wealth of the people, and rendered them an easy prey to famine and plague. India was a land of vast resources as well as of vast populations; the government should be so directed as to develop these resources for the benefit of those vast populations—but India was sacrificed to British interests. The land tax had been oppressive, against the judgment of statesmen like William Pitt,[3] and had told against the prosperity of the agricultural population. He cited the Tibet expedition as an illustration of the way in which courses were taken for British interests, and then the poor people of India, to whom it was of no interest, were

3. (1759-1806); Prime Minister of Britain, 1783-1801 and 1804-06.

called upon to pay.[4] Seventeen and a half millions of rupees were raised from the land tax, and the Indian army expenditure had been run up to 23 millions. Why should such a great army be maintained in India? If the people were prosperous and contented there would be no need for it. And as for the Russian bogey, that surely had been laid. What he said was that India was loyal, and, on their account, there was no need for such armaments; and why then should they be called upon to bear such oppressive burdens? They were loyal, but not much contented or happy; yet it was neither their desire nor object to overthrow allegiance to England. What they asked was that England should do them justice, in the promotion of education, in the granting of measures of self-government, by which the people could have a voice in the government of their own country, and in the encouragement of industries, to increase the prosperity and happiness of the country.

4. In 1903, Curzon, being keen to establish direct contact with Tibet without any interference by China, had, under flimsy pretexts, marched troops to the border which advanced to Gyantse and Lhasa and compelled Tibet to sign a convention in September 1904 opening trade routes to India. It also agreed, under the convention, to pay an indemnity to the Government of India.

16. Responsibility of British Electors to India[1]

Mr. Lajpat Rai said the Congress he represented was a political institution started twenty years ago by educated Indians with the aid of distinguished Anglo-Indians, who had come to the conclusion that a representative body of educated Indians was required to give expression to the needs of the Indian people. The Congress had generally dealt with subjects upon which all classes of Indians were unanimous, and had reported its proceedings to the Government, but had received scant attention. He criticised British rule in India in the past, and said that whilst so many millions of people died of starvation and disease, the administration could not be said to be efficient. Millions of tons of grain were exported even in the years when famine was going on, but the natives could not keep it within their own country because they were unable to earn sufficient money to purchase it with. As for the plague, which annually claimed

1. Address to a meeting of Liberal "800" at Derby on 27 October 1905. Reproduced in *India* of 3 November 1905 from the *Derby Daily Telegraph*.

thousands of victims, it was only likely to flourish in a country where the people were starving, and where the condition of many of their houses was most insanitary. How was it that after more than a century of British rule affairs in India were so bad that the rate of mortality, instead of decreasing, was increasing? The reply of the National Congress was that British rule in India had been extremely ruinous in its economic results, the fiscal policy not having been in the interests of the Indians, but in the interests of other people. The system of government was bad; the wishes of the people had no place in the Councils of the country. The people were not consulted, and if they expressed their opinions those opinions were not regarded as important. A handful of officials, appointed by England, knowing the history of the country very indifferently, who were given to assuming high airs of superiority in official chairs, ruled India on a system of red tape, instead of on a system of sympathy and interest in the people.

He discussed various legislative measures in force in India, and described the partition of Bengal as the crowning folly of the last decade of British rule in India. He said it was objected to by all classes of the population, but their objections were unheeded, and the chief effect of it would be to stir up religious bitterness and strife. Lord Curzon's rule was unpopular, and the measures which he had enforced were extremely distasteful to the people, who were not likely to forget either that he had called them from his Viceregal throne a nation of liars.

The purpose, he said, of his visit to England was to rouse the British elector to his responsibility in regard to India, for it was the electors of Great Britain, if they would only realise the fact, who could ensure the Indian people the reforms that were needed. Let them have a system of gradual self-government, and with a loyal and contented people India might more truthfully be called the brightest jewel in the British crown.

17. British Misrule in India[1]

The lecturer, in the course of a very clear and well-reasoned address, said as the Chairman[2] had stated, India was the brightest jewel in the Crown of England. It contained 300 millions of people; it was 1,900 miles long, and 1,900 miles

1. Address to a gathering in Gladstone Hall of National Liberal Club, Windsor, 27 October 1905. *The Panjabee*, 4 December 1905.
2. Alderman E. Bampfylde.

broad. The country had had a very brilliant past, and boasted of a civilization long before many other countries could claim it. The question was, then, how it was that Indian affairs received so little attention from England. The answer was, because its Government was left in the hands of a few officials, and because there is a spirit of indifference in England to the affairs of India. It was therefore his object, as a delegate of the Indian National Congress, to ask them as British voters to take a little more interest in the affairs of that country, and influence the Government by their opinions. At present the people of India had very little voice in the management of their own affairs. There was no Indian on the Council of the Government of India, and there was most inadequate representation on the Legislative Councils. A great drawback was that the Secretary of State for India[3] had never been to India, and was not conversant with the affairs of the country; he did not understand the language, and he did not know the manners and customs of the people who lived there. Another thing that was wrong was that an Indian student had to come to London if he competed with an English student for a position out there, whereas examinations should be held in both countries. Then Indian affairs were relegated to the background in the House of Commons. Only one or two nights a year were devoted to India, and the consequence was that they had a government of despotism out there. It was a government of officials by officials, and it was not a healthy government. No government that was not controlled by popular opinion could be trusted to do justice to the people. The Government in India carried out measures against popular opinion. It hardly differed from that of a despotic monarchy. If they read the history of British rule in India they could not show any record of which a liberal Englishman would be proud. If they judged it by results they would probably say that it had been disastrous. The English rule had not done any great good for India. It had advanced it in some ways, but in others there had been retrograde movements, and they could not help but condemn the rule. When Lord Cromer[4] was Finance Minister of India it was estimated that the number of people who went to bed every night without a second meal was fifty millions, and another estimate of those who were only able to satisfy their hunger once a day was seventy millions. Then let them look at the death rate in India. During the last 20 years it had gone up from 24 per year per 1000 to 34 per year per 1000. This was so notwithstanding the fact that the death rate in other civilised states in the world had gone down. In England it had decreased from 20 per cent to 16.8 per cent. In India they had

3. Sir John Brodrick.
4. Evelyn Baring Cromer (1841-1917); British administrator and diplomat; Private Secretary to Viceroy Northbrook, 1872-77; Finance Member in Viceroy's Executive Council, 1880-83; works include *Modern Egypt* (two volumes) (1909) and *Abbas II* (1915).

practically six famines in ten years, which had carried away several millions of people. Some authorities had estimated it as much as forty millions. The majority had died of starvation. Many of the natives only earned £2 in a year, and out of this 10d. was taken from them for taxes. If after a century or more of British rule they found the country in such a state of abject poverty, destitution and starvation, they could not well say that British rule in India had been successful. England had certainly given them a better system of education, but they could not change education for food. What was the economic reason for this state of things? It was simple enough. The government of India was originally run by East India Company's merchants, who looked after their own interests. They suppressed Indian industries until they were ruined. Europeans settled there and sucked the moisture from the land. Proceeding, the lecturer said that the social and economic problems received little attention from the Government, which was bound up by red tape, and was carried out on Russian lines. Lord Ripon, when Viceroy, tried to get some small measure of self-government for the Indian people, and his name was still greatly cherished in India. Lord Curzon had, however, created a vast amount of discontent. The speaker contended that the Government of India did not depend upon the strength of the army there; the country was not won by the British army, but by the rank and file of the people, who were led to believe in the pledges made to them by the English authorities. They were told that they were going to have an enlightened Government in India, whereas they had one based on Russian models. For the last ten years the situation had been bad, and at the present time India was in the throes of a crisis. Never was India in such a state as she is now. The country was discontented and dissatisfied. There was not one single class at the present moment that was very well satisfied with the British Government.

The lecturer then went on to condemn the Official Secrets Act, which was opposed by the whole of the press of India. The cutting up of Bengal into two portions was also alluded to, which would, he said, injure the solidity of the Bengalees and belittle their importance. He emphasized the assertion that the pledges held out to India by men in exalted positions had not been fulfilled, and claimed that the Government should repose confidence in the natives and not shrink from raising them to the higher posts. They demanded real, not nominal, equality, a voice in the government and a career in the public service. Lord Ripon was the most benevolent and popular Viceroy that India had ever seen, and his wish was that the people should be trained to a sense of self-help and self-reliance. The lecturer referred to the administration of justice as an instance of the bad state of things existing in India. The man who instituted the prosecutions afterwards sat in judgment upon the accused. This was an evil which had shaken the people's belief in justice. This reform was greatly urged. India wanted judges who were independent of the executive. Referring to the

Indian Budget, the lecturer said there were vast sums spent on the army, the amount going up from six millions to twenty-three millions a year. This money was taken out of the country without any return for it and the country was consequently growing poorer every year. There was a continual drainage of taxes going on, and yet they had no voice in the government of the country. It was a system which savoured more of Russia than of the freedom-loving British. The people of India wanted the people of England to keep their pledges, and to carry them into effect. They also wanted the people here to take more interest in the affairs of India. They wanted more members for India, and they wanted to hear more of India in the House of Commons. Millions of people were dying of starvation in India not because there was no food there—they exported vast quantities of food to England—but because they had no money to purchase it. There poor people were in the land of plenty and yet they were starved. As voters they must impress upon the members they returned to the next Parliament to see that the people of India were no longer neglected but fairly dealt with. They wanted some measure of self-government, and the spirit of friendly relationship and cordial co-operation would automatically come. The spirit of indifference and officialdom was crushing the people of India, and the sooner it was remedied the better it would be for the people of both countries.

18. To G.K. Gokhale[1]

National Liberal Club
White Hall Place, SW
1 November 1905

Dear Mr. Gokhale,

Enclosed please find a letter to Messrs Jeremiah Lyon & Co., 4 Lawboard Court, E.C.[2]

Any order given by you will be duly looked to. I owe a small amount not exceeding two or three shillings, I think, thanks to Mr. Hall, Secretary of the British Committee. As I could not see him today I have not paid it. Would you

1. G.K. Gokhale Papers (microfilm), N.A.I.
2. See the following item.

kindly pay it to him on my behalf? I will pay it to you at Benares. Excuse this liberty.

With my sincere best wishes for your success and safe return.

I remain

Yours sincerely,
Lajpat Rai

P.S.—Please excuse if I have ever been disrespectful to you even in joke.

L.R.

19. To Messrs Jeremiah Lyon & Co.[1]

National Liberal Club
White Hall Place, SW
1 November 1905

Book Deptt.
Messrs Jeremiah Lyon & Co.

Gentlemen,

Please do treat any order for books given by Mr. G.K. Gokhale as mine and ship the books as desired by him. He will pay for the books but if not please send me the invoices and I stand responsible for the same or send the bill of lading subject to payment by Bombay. He will assure payment there.

Yours truly,
L. Rai

1. G.K. Gokhale Papers (microfilm), N.A.I.

4

VISIT TO ENGLAND AND AMERICA

IV. In the U.S.A.

1. England Responsible for Poverty and Backwardness of India[1]

India today is the poorest country on the face of the globe. It was once known as the richest. India today is ruled by the British merchants. The Government is rotten with antiquity. It has all the rotten laws of past ages and all the disadvantages of modern government.

In the famine of 1900 more than 1,00,000 died of starvation. Sometimes for several months of the year the victims of the bubonic plague reach from 30,000 to 50,000. This fact alone is enough to condemn the administration of the English Government.

Lord Curzon's administration has been very unpopular on account of certain reactionary legislative measures, educational and otherwise. However, in his controversy with Lord Kitchener, he held the right position, defending the right of the civil authority to have the final say in all matters, military and otherwise.

The 300 millions of India have suffered much economically by the partial decay of native industries, and the encouragement, by the English policy, of British merchants and manufacturers, rather than the natives. They are also heavily taxed and a great burden of military cost is laid on them to guard against a suspected invasion of the British territories by Russia. That danger may now be dismissed from consideration for some years to come, and the military expenses can be much reduced. Little is now done for education by the Imperial Government, and consequently three-quarters of the people are illiterate. The present British policy is one of suspicion of the native inhabitants; this mistake has increased under Lord Curzon. Many thousands have died in recent years from famines, the bubonic plague and the maladies that accompany a famine; and nearly all the people are wretchedly poor. They have to sell their crops early to pay their land tax, and are at the mercy of moneylenders, while they are to some extent deprived of justice in the courts. The approved Indian remedy is to admit more native Indians into the administration and the legislative bodies of India, and to encourage self-reliance and make the industry of the people of India a greater factor than it now is in the buying and selling of the country.

Famines and other woes of India are the direct consequence of the British policy of exploiting India as a market. There is food enough raised, but no money with which to buy it, among the people. The British have been for a

1. Speech in the Parker Memorial Hall at Boston on 17 September 1905. Printed in *India* of 6 and 13 October 1905 and in *The Panjabee* of 30 October 1905; originally published in *Post*, *Republican* and *Transcript* of Boston on 18 September 1905.

Lajpat Rai, who went from England to the U.S.A., reached Boston on 16 September.

century deliberately ruining the old native industries and exports, in order that British goods and commerce may have the field there to themselves.

2. Need for Gradual Extension of Self-Government to India[1]

I am a delegate of the Indian National Congress to England, my duty being to represent the grievances of the people of India to the British electors. I have just reached this country, and will endeavour while here to enlighten public opinion as to the sufferings and prevailing conditions there in the hope that it will influence British opinion in our favour.

We are not a revolutionary body, but are organized to propagate our views in the hope of securing redress of grievances and effect the gradual extension of self-government to India.

The present system of government there is very unsatisfactory, as it practically gives no voice to the people in the administration of affairs and has resulted in bringing about an extreme condition of poverty which causes great mortality on occasions of famine and pestilence. You are probably unaware that $10 a year is the average earning of one of our natives, and out of that goes $ 2.50 (10 shillings) as taxes to the Government.

The famine of 1900 resulted in the death of more than 1,00,000 persons, starvation being the principal cause.

At the present time the bubonic plague is rampant and a total of 50,000 deaths in one week has resulted.

The present fiscal policy has ruined all Indian manufacturers, and there is no way out of the difficulty unless the Government adopts some favourable attitude. This policy is bound to bring in great suffering.

The great burden on India is the tremendous military expenditure which has been increased by Lord Kitchener to $ 23,000,000 this year, giving India practically a military form of government.

As to the controversy between Lord Curzon and Kitchener, the former was acting in the interests of our people but his administration has been unpopular and his policy has been extremely unfavourable to India.

We felt that with such a strong power as Japan in the East, England would

1. Interview given to a representative of *Globe* in Oxford Hotel at Boston before 20 September 1905. *The Panjabee*, 30 October 1905; first published in *Globe* and reprinted in *India* of 6 October 1905.

be content, fearing no encroachment from Russia, but such is not the case as the enormous increase in the military budget shows.

3. On His Visit to Educational Institutions and Other Activities in Boston[1]

I reached here on the morning of the 16th and took a room at the Oxford Hotel which is close to the Back Bay railway station where I got down from the train. Boston is one of the most important towns in the United States, the capital of Massachussets and one of the earliest cities founded by Europeans in the new world. It is a great centre of missionary activity and is well known for its public spirit. It is also a great centre of educational activity. Its School of Technology is believed to be one of the best in the world and one of the two best in the United States. It has about 5 universities in a radius of about 20 miles, the most important and the celebrated of which is the Harvard University founded in 1636 A.D., only 6 years after the settlement of Europeans in the locality. This University is one of the greatest in the world. It has 1,000 students on its rolls and possesses a set of the finest and most magnificent buildings in Massachussets. Its special feature is a great number of museums such as are not to be found attached to any university in Great Britain, and its great Stadium. This last building is a sort of amphitheatre built after the fashion and on the model of the Roman Colloseum. In the centre is the football ground and the place for athletes and around are rows of seats which will, when completed, accommodate no less than 30,000 people. It is built of solid granite and has cost 1,25,00,000 dollars, the gift of one man. The system of education followed in this University, to a great extent, varies from that followed in England. Here more attention is paid to teaching which is being done more on the methods of a school. The University does not insist on residence, although it provides dormitories for those who choose to live. Students make their own messing arrangements while the University allows them the use of its halls for dining purposes. Rich students form their own clubs where they dine and live in great style. The minimum cost of boarding is believed to be 250 dollars (Rs. 750) a year. The museums attached are extensive and well equipped. The University is said to possess property of the value of 1,200 to 1,400 millions of dollars and gets munificent donations from its old alumni as well as other charitably-inclined

1. Written at Boston on 20 September 1905 and published in *The Panjabee* of 6 November 1905.

people very frequently. It exercises hardly any control over the moral character of its students, although it takes harsh measures, if any serious defect is ever brought to its notice. Failure to attend lectures or to do well in house examinations is at once noticed. The dormitories are controlled by post-graduate students. It has a great post-graduate school attached to it for research purposes. It charges a uniform fee of 250 dollars a year from each student. A student can live fairly decently in 500 to 600 dollars a year (i.e. Rs. 1,500 to Rs. 1,800). It gives degrees in all faculties (Arts, Law, Medicine, Divinity, Modern Languages and so on). Descending downwards all other education is free in Boston. At the lowest ladder you have well-furnished kindergarten schools, which send pupils to Primary Schools.

Above the Primary Schools you have got Grammar Schools and then the High Schools. The courses of studies in these schools extend to about 14 years or in some cases 12 years. The subjects taught in the High Schools are elective and education is thorough and being given on the most approved and modern lines. Books, paper, pen, ink, i.e. everything necessary for school life, is supplied free of cost to every pupil up to and in the High School. The benches and tables are of the most improved style. Each one can be fitted to the pupil, i.e. according to his length and size. Schools are generally mixed, i.e. classes contain pupils of both sexes. The relations between the pupils and teachers in the High Schools are most friendly and cordial. Complete and extraordinary arrangements exist for the ventilating, heating and cooling of the rooms. Every 11 minutes the air in the rooms gets renewed. In case of excessive heat or excessive cold the apparatus gets automatically cleansed and adjusts the temperature. A big artificial ventilating fan is worked by steam power which introduces fresh air into the buildings while the vitiated air gets out in another direction. Elaborate arrangements exist for supplying warm air.

In fact, the furniture, the apparatus and the ventilating arrangements that I saw here are much superior to anything I saw in England. Lectures on the Civil Government of the United States form an important part of the studies in the Grammar Schools. This is calculated to instil patriotism and love of liberty with a knowledge of the institutions of the country at an early age. American national flags (stars and stripes) decorate almost every room in the highest as well as the lowest school. Up to the Grammar Schools the teachers are mostly women but in the High Schools also I saw a number of lady teachers teaching advanced subjects. Every classroom has got a clock which strikes automatically just at the same time when the clock in the headmaster's room strikes. The science apparatus is most complete and up to date and the students and teachers prepare their own photographic slides for the purposes of illustration. Some rooms are fitted up with magic lanterns which are freely used in teaching all subjects. Every room is connected with the office by telephone. Pupils in these schools enjoy more freedom than in any of the European states. The education, as I have said, is entirely free. It is compulsory up to the age of 11; over and above that a vast number of scholarships are awarded to bright students. In the university the scholarships are of very high value, e.g. of 1,000 dollars a year. Poor students can easily work their way by giving private tuition which is generally well paid for or by serving at the table or doing other work after the college hours. The teaching is believed to be of a very high order.

On the 16th, I delivered a lecture on the religion of the Vedas at the Parker Memorial Hall and on the 17th I delivered a lecture on the political condition of India at the same place. This second lecture was given under the presidency of a very distinguished literary man, a friend of the celebrated American writer Emerson.[2] Both days a number of questions were put to me by various ladies and gentlemen in the audience. The most interesting of these questions are relating to the supposed spiritual powers which Indians are believed to possess in an extraordinary degree. A lady and a gentleman asked me if there was a school of prophets in India. Another asked me if a Yogi could live without food and water for a number of days. Another asked me if one could leave his body and live in astral state. With reference to political condition, the general question is how and why 300 millions of people tolerate such political oppression and so on.

There are two Ceylonese gentlemen just now in America who give discourses on religious topics. They are both learned men and their addresses are well spoken of. One of them is a Theosophist and another perhaps a Vedantist. There is a good preacher called Baba Bharati who is not so well spoken of. Ladies are mostly interested in religion and in matters spiritual.

Ladies interested in the Hindu religion complain very bitterly of the misrepresentations and the exaggerations which Christian missionaries generally present here in this country in order to get funds for mission work in India. A lady reminded me of the revealing statements made by Ramabai[3] in this country when commenting on Hindu morality. She is believed to have said somewhere here that no young girl was safe in a Hindu family and so on. Many a false story is set afloat to win the sympathies of the rich people and get funds from them.

The other day there was held a conference of missionaries in which

2. R.W. Emerson (1803-82); American philosopher, writer and poet; became minister in Old North Church (unitarian) in 1829 but left the church in 1832 because of his radical views about religion; author of several books including *Nature* (1836).

3. (1858-1922); scholar of Sanskrit, educationist and social reformer; honoured with titles of Pandit and Saraswati; married Bipin Bihari Das, a *Shudra* by caste; embraced Christianity in 1883; founded several organisations, including Arya Mahila Samaj and Sharada Sadan, for uplift of women and relief of widows; works include *Stree Dharma Neeti* and *Balodyan*.

President Copen is said to have advocated the extension of mission work for the benefit of the American trade. I cull the following report from the *Boston Advertiser*: "Save the world to save America" was the theme of the annual address of President Copen. He said in part we need to develop foreign missions to save our nation commercially . . . it is only as "we develop missions that we shall have a market in the Orient which will demand our manufactured articles in sufficient quantities to match our increased facilities. The Christian man is our customer. The heathen has, as a rule, few wants. It is only when man is changed that there comes this desire for the manifold articles that belonged to the Christian man and the Christian home. The missionary is everywhere and always the pioneer of trade."

The Indian admirers and friends of Christian missions ought to note this commercial ideal of the American missionary. The missionary is not "the pioneer of trade" only but also the pioneer of the political supremacy of the Boston people in the East. I think that the frank statement of a leading Christian ought to open the eyes of all who see no danger in the work of the Christian missions in the East. Four of the most important dailies of Boston have been sending their representatives for interviews. All of them have published sympathetic paragraphs. Here and there they have erred in reporting the interviews and my speech but the mistakes are very unimportant. So far I have no reason to be dissatisfied with my work at Boston. Our thanks are principally due to Mr. Ewing Winslaw, Secretary of the Anti-Imperialist League, for the help he has given. He has in fact arranged everything and done all what he could. One of the ladies interested in India told me that lately an Englishman had been going round making speeches and giving "talk" to the effect that British rule in India was very perfect and steady and that there was no hope or chance of Indians ever trying to gain their independence. She also related to me how one of the Indian preachers said once (only recently) that the Indian people did not care who policed the country so long as they enjoyed religious liberty and could devote themselves to spiritual exercises. How mischievous is the effect of statements like these you cannot imagine. Swami Ram Tirath[4] is generally admired and held in regard by those who know him and so is Swami Vivekananda.[5] You will be surprised to learn that one of the newspaper reporters

4. (1873-1906); originally named Tirtha Ram Goswami, he called himself Ram Tirtha after becoming sannyasi in 1901; professor of Mathematics in Forman Christian College, Lahore, 1896; retired to Himạlayas in 1900; founded Advaitamritavarshini Sabha at Lahore; started Urdu periodical *Aliph* to propagate *Vedantic* thoughts; visited Japan and America and presented a copy of his *Appeal to the Americans on behalf of India* to President Roosevelt in 1903; presided over First World Unity League at St. Louis Church in America in 1904.
5. Swami Vivekananda (Narendranath Datta) (1863-1902); a spiritual leader and social and religious reformer; disciple of Ramakrishna Paramhansa; attended the Parliament of Religions

who called for an interview was a blind man. He had a machine by which he did his shorthand writing. He said he will read all what he had written and will then write it in type with the aid of a typewriter. He asked me very interestingly if the Government of India maintained schools to educate people who had no eyes.

The most wonderful thing to be seen at the museum of the Harvard University are the glass flowers. Almost all kinds of flowers known in the world are made of glass and preserved in glass cases. These are so fine and look so natural that one is struck at the extraordinary skill of the artist. The only two persons in the world who are believed to possess the knowledge of how to make these are a father and son who have entered into an arrangement with the Harvard University not to make these flowers for anyone else but the University. They are not prepared to teach their art to anybody.

You will excuse me for an absence of arrangement in my letter. The fact is that I have been writing from memory. Now to give you an idea of the Peace Society and the speeches made therein. The meeting was presided over and opened by a lady who seemed to be possessed of a great emotional nature and who seemed to be a worshipper of Emerson and his cult. A gentleman speaker pointed out that universal peace and an abiding peace could not be obtained on the basis of love unless love was synonymous with justice also. The speakers seemed to have a great faith in the efficacy of the kindergarten system of education in establishing a reign of peace on earth. The Chairman hailed me as a brother from a land which was pre-eminently known for its peace and love. In the few remarks that I made I took particular care to say that it was my wish we had less of that desire for peace which has been spoken of in such high terms by the Chairman, as, in the opinion of some persons competent to form an opinion on the subject, our peaccable nature and our love of peace have been our ruin. I said it was impossible to hope for international peace so long as the different ruling nations were not prepared to give up their aggressive attitude towards others and so long as they were not prepared to respect the boundaries allotted to each nation by nature.

On the evening of the 20th I was invited to a select party at the house of Mr. Ralph Albertson, a leading reformer (the Secretary of the City School movement and a writer) where an interesting conversation was carried on for two hours. Numerous questions were put to me and some of the answers startled the audience as they had never before heard such plain speaking on the part of an Indian. Professor Parsons, an author of some renown in that part of America

---

at Chicago in 1893 and spent over a year in America and travelled widely in Europe, lecturing on *Vedanta*; founded Ramakrishna Mission in 1897.

and a writer on economics, took great interest and has promised to write on Indian problems if the necessary materials were supplied to him. I will be failing in my duty if I were to close this letter without mentioning that the person who takes the greatest interest in questions affecting India in Boston is Mrs. All Bull, the widow of a great Norwegian reformer. Her grasp of Indian questions seems to be marvellous and she is quite up-to-date in all the ins and outs of the same. She is a great admirer of Sister Nivedita[6] and has lived in India for some time. She is a wonderful woman and extremely sympathetic. Besides, she is a woman of great influence here and is held in great esteem and regard in all respectable and learned circles. You will be glad to know that there are about 20 Indians in different parts of America studying in various branches of technology. A Bengalee doctor here is said to possess an extensive practice and the other day I met a Sindhi gentleman who was coming from Cuba where he keeps shop. You will thus see that the situation is hopeful and there is no reason for despondency.

6. Sister Nivedita (Margaret Elizabeth Noble) (1867-1911); an Irish lady who came under the influence of Swami Vivekananda when he visited England in 1896; came to India in 1898 and worked for the relief of plague victims in Bengal in 1899; participated in Swadeshi movement during 1905-06; edited *Karmayogin* for some time.

4. From Boston to New York[1]

The last I wrote to you was from Boston. I left Boston on the evening of the 21st for the Niagara Falls by railroad. This was practically my 1st journey on an American railway, with the exception of a 3 hours' trip I had from Providence to Boston. I daresay it will interest your readers to know something about American railways.

American railways are owned by corporate companies who make enormous profits by the same and are very powerful. There is a good deal of competition on the surface as one and the same place can be reached by several routes traversed by different railways owned by different companies. But really there

1. This account of his trip from Boston to New York written after starting from Boston on 21 September and before reaching England in the first week of October 1905 was published in three instalments in the issues of 13, 20 and 27 November 1905 of *The Panjabee*.

is no competition as the railroad companies have practically entered into a combine and have a secret understanding as to rates. The longer the route, the lesser the fare. That the United States railway companies control American politics is a common article of faith in this country. The fact is that the politics here are said to be governed by the mighty dollar and the power of the purse carries the day here as anywhere else on the surface of the globe. The officials in this country, except the high servants and the Judges of the Federal Government, are believed to be generally corrupt and dishonest. Municipal Government, they say, is rotten to the core. Bribery and corruption is said to be the rule. The principal commercial interests in the country rule as they like. They can purchase votes as well as officials. The railroad companies, being in the class of the richest commercial concerns, of course, play their own part very well and mostly do things as it suits them best.

Ordinarily, there is only one rate for all passengers. Everyone is supposed to travel first class. The rate is 2 cents or one anna per mile. But there is a provision for the richer classes to travel in special carriages by the payment of extras.

The ordinary passenger car is generally a long saloon with only two doors one on each side (breadth-wise). Velvet-cushioned benches are provided with two seats each. The carriage is divided into two rows, space being left in the middle for people to go about:

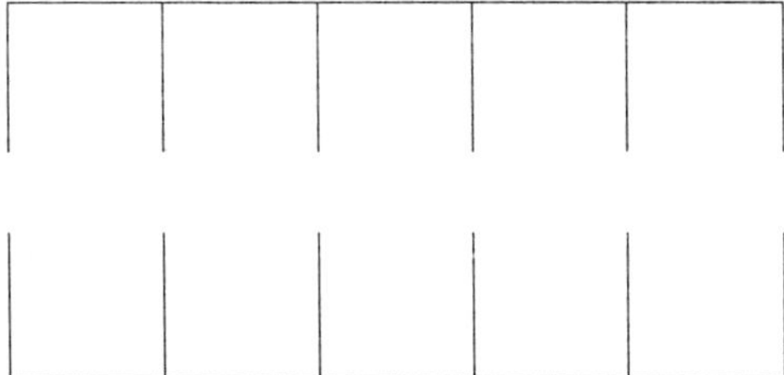

One can walk from one end of the train to the other while the train is in motion. At each end are provided latrines with toilet cabins. In the toilet cabin are provided soap, one common towel and a washbasin. There is separate provision for men and women. Similarly, drinking water is provided in tanks one attached to each end of the carriage. One glass is also provided with each tank. These carriages afford no sleeping accommodation, nor is there much room for baggage. In fact, I have never seen any heavy baggage in these cars. Only handbags or what are called dressbags are carried. There is a porter on the train who keeps the carriage clean. At every station the porter and the guard announce the name of the station and the next succeeding one, in each carriage. The special carriages mentioned above are called Pullman cars. They are owned by a separate company which seems to have the monopoly of their supply. These cars are splendid. They are small wooden palaces. They have smoking, sitting and observation parlours, and some even drawing rooms. On these cars sleeping accommodation is provided on payment of at least 2 dollars (Rs. 6) per night or more according to the distance one chooses to travel therein. The sleeping berth or the sleeper, as it is called, is fitted up with bedding cushions, blankets and curtains. In fact, it makes a sort of a small room securing the strictest privacy to the occupiers. One can dress or undress as he pleases. Every traveller is provided with new sheets and new covers for cushions and new towels. Towels he can use as many as he likes. There are separate parlours for gentlemen and ladies, though sitting and sleeping accommodation is provided in the same saloon. Every car has a servant of its own who fits your bedding, cleans your boots and brushes your clothes and helps people in getting down or entering the carriage. Each seat is numbered. Some trains consist of these cars only. In the United States tickets are examined, checked and collected in the train and provision is also made for newspapers, magazines, books, servants, sandwiches, etc. There is, besides, the dining car which is generally attached at meal times. In towns and cities, the crossings are not, as a rule, provided with bridges, nor is there much fencing on both sides. The trains run at tremendous speed. Ordinary fast trains run at the rate of 40 to 60 miles per hour. There are some express trains, however, which run faster.

We reached the Niagara Falls at about 9 A.M. in the morning. The river consists of the volume of water that flows from Erie lake and then empties itself into lake Ontario. Coming out of the Erie lake it divides itself into two currents, one passing the territory of the United States and the other that of British Canada. On the spot where these currents adopt different courses the water precipitates with great rush into a lower level. These currents are hence, on this spot, called the American and the Canadian rapids till they fall into the valley, at one place 167 feet lower and at another 158 feet. These are called Falls. There are two principal Falls on the Canadian side and two on the American side. The scenery here is magnificent, grand, and awe-inspiring. Here you see Nature in its naked majesty and are at once struck with its grandeur and beauty. But here, again, at the same time you are forcibly reminded of the equally great powers of man. Here is this tiny animal—man—possessed of a small body, which compared with some other animals is very contemptible in its size and dimensions, who holds a very uncertain and precarious tenure of life, liable to be cut down and shortened by the bite of even some of the smallest of the reptiles, controlling everything on the globe from the mightiest and grandest of nature's material works to the lowest and highest of its animal kingdom. Here one sees the subtle mind of man controlling this great and wonderful phenomenon of Nature and commanding its service for his or her own uses; because as you know they are generating vast volumes of electrical power out of these Falls. Then these Falls, i.e. just underneath below the Falls, they have excavated and built subterranean passages where people go and see the back of the Falls. These places are reached by elevators (or lifts as they are called in England) in place of stairs. The Canadian Government as well as the contractors of the American Government are supposed to be making a large amount of money by these Falls in various ways. Below the Falls the river forms itself into whirlpools where in some places a few feet higher or lower the water is believed to be 250 feet deep. One Captain Webb, an Englishman, once tried to swim one of these whirlpools and plunged himself into the water from a height of over 150 feet but lost his life in the attempt. The place is now a flourishing town of fairly good size where a brisk trade is carried on in the views of the Niagara Falls and Indian (Red) curiosities, because this is the place which was formerly occupied by hosts of Red Indians whom the white population has now driven into mountain fastnesses, etc. The neighbourhood is full of Indian Associations and the fact that a great many Indian curiosities are sold here makes me suppose that probably there are some villages occupied by Indians within easy reach of the place. We passed a great day here and enjoyed it very much.

We left Niagara Falls in the night at 11 P.M. and reached Chicago city the next day at about 9 A.M. There is a difference of full one hour between Chicago time and Boston time, i.e. when it is 9 A.M. at Boston it is 8 A.M. at Chicago. We paid 18 dollars as railway fare each of us and 6 dollars for sleepers, i.e. 24 dollars equal to Rs. 72 each. Chicago is one of the greatest cities in the United States, one that has risen to importance and its present size within the last 25 years. It extends to about 20 or 30 miles in length and several miles in breadth and is served by several railways, surface trollies, i.e. electric tramcars, elevators and railways (electric cars that run on rails laid down by rooting the roads and streets.) It is a very important commercial centre. But I have not, in the course of my trip, seen a more filthy and dirty city either in Europe or in America. Its population is increasing every day and its size and dimensions are growing. It has huge iron, stone, and brick buildings consisting of 10 to 30 stories. These buildings are served by electric elevators or lifts which run 24 hours, i.e. day and night. Each building consists of thousands of rooms, every one of which is numbered and carries a high rent. On the ground floor you find a directory of all tenants put on boards on the walls. You have to tell the elevator man the number of the floor you want to go to and he will leave you there and then bring you back when you have done your business. Here I stayed for 3 days, one of which was Sunday. Most of my time was spent in making calls, seeing people and inspecting 3 schools. A theosophist lady for whom Swami Rama had given me a letter of introduction almost compelled me to stay with her and I enjoyed her hospitality. At her house we had talks with different people about Hindu religion, Hindu philosophy and Indian politics. Some huge buildings are made of iron only with bricks and stone used in giving the corners, or in the foundations.

At this place I formed the acquaintance of a highly-gifted lady, Miss Anne Adams, who holds a great position in the city. She is a member of the School Board and Chairman of the School Management Sub-Committee. She takes a great interest in school and political work and is a centre of great social activity. She invited me to lunch and I enjoyed her conversation a great deal. With one of her Assistants I paid a visit to 2 or 3 of the filthiest and dirtiest quarters of the city inhabited by poor Italians and Jews where she and her co-workers carry on their social service work. Now, here I must tell you something of this work which has grown out of and is the direct result of the social as well as the political condition of the West. As matters now stand, the poor classes in Europe are growing every day poorer and poorer. With the high standard of life prevailing, which is perhaps necessary under the climatic conditions of the countries comprised therein, and with the high prices of necessities of life, life in Europe is becoming pretty hard for the poorest of European population. The introduction of machinery and the latest improvements effected therein, which save both time and labour, have resulted in vast numbers of men being thrown out of employment. Wages are high and the natives of Europe are rolling in wealth in their corporate and national capacity but that does not necessarily bring prosperity and happiness to the masses. I am sometimes led to think that the imperialistic tendencies and conquering proclivities of Europe are perhaps the direct and natural result of the economic conditions existing there. Just take the case of England. Without its dependencies and possessions a vast number of its population would simply starve as most of its people will have to go without employment. As matters stand, even now the cry of the unemployed for work and food is growing both in volume and intensity every day. With the advance of science and improvements in mechanical processes it is sure to increase. Then, besides these economic causes those populations in Europe which are unjustly treated by their respective Governments, for instance, the Jews and Finns of Russia and the Irish of Ireland are forced by circumstance to find an asylum abroad in order to find more congenial conditions of life. America is a new world and the Europeans having thrown in the background or even in some places extirpated the original inhabitants of the people there is ample field there for hardworking, for industrious white men and women. Consequently, you find that hundreds and thousands of Europeans from Ireland, France, Germany, Russia, Italy, Scandinavia and other countries every year migrate to the United States. The worst of it is that these immigrants mostly settle in the cities or in their neighbourhood. The cities thus get a vast addition to their population every year and are almost incredibly growing in size and dimensions. They have always a great number of unsettled population. Besides, the fact that this population is composed of diverse nationalities, speaking different languages, professing different religions, following and observing different customs and manners, adds a great deal to the difficulties of the City Government in the United States. Then, we should not forget that it is mostly the lowest strata of European population that migrate to America in search of opportunities to earn their bread and butter. Consequently, you find that the quarters of Chicago which are inhabited by these moving and houseless communities are in an extremely filthy and dirty condition. I went through the quarter occupied by the Italians, the Jews and the Scandinavians and found the conditions of life extremely nauseating and demoralising. The authorities are doing everything in their power to extend the facilities of education to the children of these communities, and the charitable and social societies and associations of the country do a great deal to help them to settle, get work and make their surroundings healthy. Great public schemes have been organised where education on the best modern lines is imparted free. All school materials and necessaries are supplied free of all cost. Every child under 16 must attend school. If a parent neglects to send a child to school, without sufficient reason, he is punished and if after enquiries it is found that the absence of a child from school is due to no fault or negligence of the parents or the guardians, then the State takes charge of that child and educates and feeds him free. These schools are, I think, called Penitentiary Schools. There are a number of gentlemen called guardians of juveniles whose duty it is to look after the juveniles, and then there are others who possess summary powers to punish juveniles. These form juvenile courts. One of these gentlemen engaged in the work took me round the streets and explained to me how he interested himself in the juveniles and helped them. Then there are a number of settlement workers. These workers with their families settle in these slums and watch the population around them. They try to cheer them up, provide good society for them, help them in getting work, find facilities for improving their conditions, and in cases of need get extraneous help for them. Notwithstanding all this, the sight I saw in these streets was very repulsive.

I visited two schools at Chicago, a public school in Langley Avenue and a Normal School with a big Practice School attached to it in Cork Square. All these schools are mixed schools, i.e. both boys and girls read there together. They are mostly staffed by ladies. The teachers of these Grammar Schools (corresponding to our Primary and Middle Schools combined) draw from 500 dollars to 1,100 dollars a year. A dollar is equal to 3 rupees. The Principal gets 1,500 a year. They have got the most improved and approved appliances. Almost every school provides for manual education. Every school has got heating arrangements by which the air of every room is changed every 10 or 11 minutes, and fresh hot or cold air is supplied as wanted. The playgrounds provided are large and extensive. In the Normal School the lady Principal took me round and showed me everything with great interest. In the Normal School there are 400 to 500 girls as against 15 to 20 boys. On being asked the reason for this the Principal explained that the office of a teacher was not sufficiently paying for men. In this country an ordinary unskilled but efficient day-labourer gets 1½ dollars a day. They exact very hard work but they pay very well. You can get a clerk or a teacher on lesser salary than a labourer. Still, the number of those who cannot get continuous work is pretty large. This school has been recently built. It is a four-storied fireproof building possessing two halls about 200 feet long and at least 50 feet wide. It has a Manual Department also where book-binding and other work is done. In every American school great attention is paid to singing, drawing and drill. The Model School attached to it, called the Practice School, is an equally great building fully equipped and largely staffed by ladies. The Principal, however, is a male. In all these schools separate rooms are provided for cloaks and hats, for meals, for toilet and for other necessary purposes. It is a pleasure to see these schools. Much more must it be to be educated therein. This is not the place to write about the American ideas on and methods of education.

I was told by Miss Adams and another highly cultivated lady at her house that dogmatic Christianity or for the matter of that doctrinal Christianity was fast losing ground. Not only the congregations have no faith in doctrines, but even the Ministers seem to possess none. The result is that in matters of religion the highly educated classes of Americans are very liberal. The undenominational places of worship and the liberal churches are crowded. I attended one of them at Chicago where the attendance was very large and where not even once in the whole service was the name of Christ uttered. In churches here they make collections of money after service. Baskets are sent round and the congregations drop coins therein. Large donations are announced in the course of the service.

The next place to be visited was Washington, the seat of the Federal Government and the capital of the Republic. Washington is situated in the District of Columbia and does not from part of any of the states in the Union. It is directly administered by the Federal Government. It is the prettiest and the neatest of all the American towns I visited. It was a pleasure to see it and still more to pay a visit of pilgrimage to the home and tomb of that great man whose name is enshrined in the heart of every American and whose statue adorns almost every American city—George Washington. He is worshipped as the founder of the Republic and the father of his country. The city takes its name after him. On the banks of the Potomac river stands a huge stone column 550 feet in height as a memorial to Washington. Different parts of the structure are adorned by different memorial stones and plates donated by different American cities in honour of the great hero. People are taken up and brought down by an electric elevator for which no charge is made. Besides this there are two other monuments. One just opposite the Capitol where the Congress and the Senate hold their sittings. This statue bears the following inscription divided into 3 parts and inscribed on 3 marble slabs located on 3 sides of the statue—"First in war", "First in peace", and "First in the hearts of his countrymen". In this representation Washington is dressed as a Roman of old. The other is in Washington Circle where he is dressed as a General at the battle of Remilton June 3rd, 1777.

The Capitol is the finest of buildings of all kinds in the whole United States. From an elevated site on Capitol Hill 97 feet above the level of the river it overlooks the amphitheatre of the Potomac and is a conspicuous feature of the landscape for miles on every side. The cornerstone of the main building was laid by Washington himself in 1793. This is the building where the Congress and the Senate meet and where the Supreme Court of Justice sits. The crowning glory of the Capitol is the central dome called the Rotunda springing from a peristyle of fluted Corinthian columns and terminating in a lantern which is surmounted by the statue of Freedom towering 397½ feet above the Esplanade. It is of iron and weighs enormously. It is so constructed as to expand or contract according to temperature "like the folding and unfolding of the lily". The statue represents freedom with a crest of eagle's beak and plumes, a sheathed sword in hand and a shield, and supporting the globe with its legend *E Muritious Union*. On the tympanum of the Rotunda portico is an allegorical group of the genius of America. In the centre stands America with the eagle at her feet. Her shield with its legend U.S.A. rests upon an altar inscribed with the significant date July 4, 1776. She is listening to the inspiration of Hope and indicating her reliance on Justice, whose scroll of Constitution bears the date of the adoption of that instrument, September 17, 1787. Besides this there are two other colossal groups on the portico, one represents Columbus[2] and an Indian (Red) girl; the other represents the settlement of America—a pioneer in desperate conflict with a savage. On either side of the doorway are representations of War and Peace. Over the doorway is a composition of Peace and Fame placing a wreath of laurel upon the brow of Washington. The fortunes of the American Indians furnish a theme which is pathetic indeed and which constantly recurs in the decorations of the Capitol. The subject is the American development and the decadence of the Indian race. In the centre stands America in the effulgence of the rising sun bestowing honour upon General Washington. On the right are Commerce, Education, Mechanics and Agriculture; on the left the Pioneer, the

2. Christopher Columbus (1451-1506); Italian navigator who discovered America.

Hewer, a dejected chieftain and an Indian (Red) mother with her babe mourning beside a grave. This picture tells volumes of history—Oh, what a pathos! and what a fact!

In the Rotunda are placed some of the magnificent paintings representing events of great national importance, for example,

1. The landing of Columbus on San Salvador 12th October 1492
2. Discovery of the Mississippi
3. Embarkation of the pilgrims from Delft Haven 1620
4. The Declaration of Independence 1776
5. The Surrender of Bargoyne by the British 1777
6. The Surrender of Cornwallis 1781 and
7. The Resignation of Washington at the close of the War of Independence 1783.

The Capitol is full of paintings which tell on canvas in colour the history of the pioneers of this wonderful country, and recall great incidents in the life of the nation. There are many statues of distinguished statesmen and other great Americans in the building. Some of the representations are grand both in conception and in finish. In one place Washington declines to accept overtures from Lord Cornwallis.[3] In the other at the battle of Lake Erie Commodore Perry gains a decisive naval victory over the British. For an Englishman the Capitol is full of humiliating themes, and the Americans up to now do not seem to have much regard for the feelings of the English. We were a party of about 25 to 30 visitors, ladies and gentlemen, that were being conducted and shown over the building by an authorised American guide. There were probably some Englishmen in the party. At one place the guide drew the attention of the party to the floor which was paved by beautiful tiles imported from England. While pointing out that that was the only English material used in the building of the Capitol, he said that it was a matter of great satisfaction that the only English material used for the building of this national edifice was one which was always underfoot. The remark was cheered by other Americans. Now, what a tale does this remark tell!

Almost opposite the Capitol, stands the magnificent building of the Congressional Library, the biggest library in the world. The building is the finest in the world as a library and cost over 6 million dollars. It has three stories and a dome; and is in area 470 ft. x 340 ft., covering nearly 3½ acres of ground with four larger inner courts, 150 x 75 to 100 ft. and nearly 2,000 windows. The whole building is lighted by electricity and the scene in artificial

3. Charles Cornwallis, first marquis (1738-1805); British general; during the War of American Independence his surrender at Yorktown marked the end of fighting in 1781; Governor-General of India, 1786-93 and 1805.

light after sunset is something superb and past description. On the floor is a great reading-room where one can find a selection of the newspapers and magazines of the world. It is a great hall most magnificently furnished and open to everybody. The other reading hall is connected with the wings of the library and is 100 ft. in diameter and 125 ft. in height. Of the paintings and decorations, representations of the muses of History, Biography, Literature, Religion, Poetry, Labour, Commerce, Tragedy, Comedy, &c., it is impossible to speak too highly. In every direction, in almost every corner, you come across statues and paintings of great writers with appropriate quotations from their writings. In one hall you find the manuscripts of great statesmen and writers of America. The most prominent features of American cities are the statues of Freedom and Peace which you find placed in numerous places. Beautiful works of art and very noble representations they are of these divine virtues.

We also paid flying visits to the Treasury Building and the Bureau of Pension with its great hall seating 40,000 people and the White House (the official residence of the President), and also to the National Museum. But the place which interested us the most after the Capitol and the Library was the home of Washington where are buried the remains of that great man. This place is 16 miles south of Washington and is reached both by river as well as by electric cars. This is the place where Washington lived before and after the War of Independence. It was originally built in 1745 by Lawrence, half-brother of Washington, and was improved by him in 1759. Here he lived and conducted his farm until called to the field; to this place he retired after his term of office as President had expired and lived till his death in 1799. The estate consists of a house of wood, kitchens, stables, gardens and extensive grounds. Here is his grave, the simplest of all the buildings I saw in America, an ordinary grave with a roof and a door. When in 1855 a descendant of Washington, without the means to maintain the estate, offered it for sale, a committee of patriotic Americans, headed by a lady, resolved to save it as a permanent shrine of patriotism. Before the end of 1859 the required sum was forthcoming and the estate was purchased and made over to the nation as a place of national pilgrimage to be preserved for the generations to come. The following epigram is well worth copying here. "No gilded dome swells from the lowly roof to catch the morning or evening beam; but the love and gratitude of United America settle upon it in one eternal sunshine. From beneath that humble roof went forth the unselfish warrior, the Magistrate, who knew no glory but his country's good; to that he returned happiest when his work was done. There he lived in noble simplicity, there he died in glory and peace. While it stands, the latest generations of the grateful children of America will make their pilgrimage to it as a shrine; and when it shall fall, if fall it must, the memory and the name of Washington shall shed an eternal glory on the spot."

In the main hall are preserved the key of the French Bastille sent by Lafayette[4] to Washington after the capture of the prison. With it came the model of Bastille preserved in the banquet hall. Originally a fortress of Paris, the Bastille was converted into a state prison and was hated by the people as an institution of despotism. One of the first events of the French Revolution was the storming of this prison-house by the French mob, July 14, 1789. Lafayette wrote with the gift: "Give me leave my dear General to present you with a picture of the Bastille just as it looked a few days after I ordered its demolition, with the main key of the fortress of despotism. It is a gift which I owe as a son to my adopted father, as an aide-de-camp to my General, as a missionary of liberty to its patriarch."

Lafayette served in the American War of Independence and his name is much honoured in America. He was a Frenchman. In this hall are preserved three of Washington's swords with the following clause of his will. "To each of my nephews. . . I give one of the swords or *cutlasses* of which I die possessed and they are to choose in the order named." The swords are accompanied with an injunction not to unsheath them for the purpose of shedding blood, except in self-defence or in defence of their country and its rights, and in the latter case to keep them unsheathed and prefer falling with them in their hands, to the relinquishment thereof.

Many other relics of this great man are preserved in this house. His plate, cutlery, his dessert, set photographs, etc. His library is also preserved intact. But one's courage begins to fail when he approaches the room in which the great General died. Involuntarily he removes his hat and stands there in, front of the hall gazing upon the coach on which he slept last and on the simple furniture of the room. With a respect, characteristic of the American, is preserved the Lafayette room which the great Frenchman occupied as a guest of General Washington.

The kitchen is no longer used although the crate still hangs in the fireplace and the brick oven is well preserved. What a world of difference between a modern Western kitchen and this old-fashioned place where Washington's food was cooked!

The visit saddened me much but I came back with an elevated soul, resolved to read lessons of simplicity and patriotism in the noble life of the great man.

Reader! Can I tell you what thoughts arose in my mind in the course of my itinerary through Washington and what feelings and sentiments were born and

4. Marie Joseph Paul Lafayette (1757-1834); French soldier who went to America in 1777 and fought for the Colonies in the American War of Independence; elected to French National Assembly in 1789 and commanded the French National Guard for three years, but having antagonised the Jacobins by his moderate views fled the country; imprisoned by Austrians but released by Napoleon; led moderates in the July Revolution of 1830.

stifled in the course of two brief days I stayed in this city. No! I cannot! I dare not. Bonded slave as I am, how can I give utterance to thoughts which though noble in themselves cannot be uttered with freedom and impunity in the land of the mighty Aryans—in the land of Pratap and Shivaji—in the land which is mine by birth and by the birth of my forefathers but where I now live only by the sufferance of the foreigner. Oh! how sad not to be allowed to utter noble thoughts in your own country. On! how crushingly sad to be forced to keep silence or to utter words of hypocrisy in the land which you love so intensely and so sincerely. But such was not always and let us hope by the grace of God such may not be always. Still better days may dawn on us when the existing laws may be withdrawn and nobler and juster laws enacted instead.

At Washington I went over to the Bureau of Education and had a long interview with the Commissioner of Education who seemed to be very much interested in Devanagari characters and Sanskrit. I wanted to talk of education and he wanted to know something of our alphabet, our language and our religion. Thank God, I could satisfactorily answer all his questions, for you know I cannot claim much knowledge of Sanskrit. He has given me a complete set of the reports of the Bureau, very valuable publications on education, for the college, which I am bringing with me. I have given him a complete set of the D.A.V. College reports which he accepted with great interest.

We left Washington at 7 A.M. on the 29th and reached New York about 1 P.M. In the train we met an Indian Muslim of Surat who is doing business here for the last 2 or 3 years. He speaks remarkably good English, in fact much better than a large majority of Americans themselves. He told me that he made an income of 8 to 10 dollars a week and had worked his way from Calcutta to New York. The train in which we travelled stops at New Jersey and the passengers have then to cross the river by boat. On the New York side of the river we met Mr. M. Barkat Ullah,[5] the President of the newly established Hindustani Progressive Association of New York. This gentleman does literary work, writes for the newspapers and magazines here, mostly on subjects relating to Asia and makes a decent living. At the house of an American friend of the Indians, Mr. Edmund Russell, he had arranged a reception in my honour where I had the pleasure of meeting a number of my countrymen engaged in various occupations in New York and also about a hundred American ladies and gentlemen interested in India and its religion. Mr. Russell has been to India and knows many of that country's noblemen and gentry. The room where the

5. Maulvi Barkatullah; hailed from Bhopal; president of Hindustani Progressive Association of New York; strong advocate of anti-British pan-Islamism; appointed professor at Tokyo School of Foreign Languages in 1909 where he started a journal, *The Islamic Fraternity*, but dismissed from the post because of his anti-British views; arrived at San Francisco in 1914 and started propaganda work for Ghadar Party.

reception was held was furnished almost exclusively with Indian and Oriental furniture. Here Mr. Barkat Ullah on behalf of the Hindustani Association and Mr. Russell on behalf of the Americans gave me a cordial welcome to which I responded at some length. Here I had the pleasure of shaking hands with a descendant of the Washingtons and made the acquaintance of many estimable ladies and gentlemen interested in India. The number of Indian gentlemen was quite large and I was rather surprised to see so many of them. Two of them, Mr. Iyangar, a Madrasi young man, who is the Secretary of the Association and seems to be quite a bright young man, the other a Parsi gentleman, are engaged in learning electrical engineering, and most of the others are in business. Among them was a Panjabi Hindu of Khushab (Shahpur). We passed a very pleasant evening here and Mr. Russell served refreshments and was very kind and attentive throughout. Two full days were spent in making calls, giving interviews to the representatives of the press, seeing the editors of leading papers and making acquaintances. The leading daily, the organ of the thoughtful and the politician, the *Evening Post* came out with a leader devoting a full large column to the substance of the interview. The account published contains some minor errors but none of very great importance. Several other papers came out with paras. It was a very busy time I had at New York with hardly any rest or occasion for sightseeing. It was a great relief, therefore, to come aboard and resume my return journey to England.

Kaiser William the Great is the name of the steamer in which I sailed from New York and in the saloon of which I am writing this account of my trip. It is a twin screw mail steamship and over 14,000 tons in weight with 28,000 horse power of engines. In the last 22 hours it made a distance of 400 nautical miles. It is one of the last steamers of the North German Loyd, quite a huge palace with all the comforts and luxuries of modern life. It is fitted with wireless telegraphy and submarine signalling apparatus and is one of the fastest boats that run between Europe and America.

America is a very busy country. It has quite a heterogeneous mass of population consisting of almost all the nationalities of the *world* (mind, not of Europe only). In fact, I do not know if there is a single nationality in the world (unless they be the savages of some unknown parts of the globe) that are not to be found in the United States, not as travellers on temporary business purposes but as citizens permanently settled. Of course, the white Europeans form the vast majority. There are great numbers of freed Negroes who have, in several States, in the eyes of the law, quite equal rights with others. However, the whites have a great prejudice against what are here known as the coloured people. The Negro problem is assuming rather formidable proportions as they are multiplying much more rapidly than the whites do. Besides these there are Filipinos, Cubans, Indians (both Red and East), Arabs, Syrians, Chinese,

Japanese and so on. Almost every nationality in fairly good strength publishes its own organs. Thus you see a good number of dailies published in Hebrew, Chinese, Arabic and so on. Of course, there are very influential papers published in German, Italian, Swedish, Polish, French, etc. The dailies here are sold by lakhs and millions. Some of the Sunday papers are of very big size, illustrated with very good pictures and cartoons of 40 to 60 pages in size and discussing, almost every topic that is conceivable, politics, law, police, trade, commerce housewifery, dress, fashion, railways, cooking and so on. The price is 5 cents (2½ annas). The price of the dailies ranges from 1 cent (½ anna) to 3 cents (1½ annas). *The Evening Post* is sold for 3 cents. Everyone reads newspapers. Some of the best papers are regularly subscribed by wealthy millionaires and large trade associations, etc. The offices and the printing presses of these papers are huge buildings. They issue several editions every day. Some are morning papers, some evening. The morning papers continue to be published every two hours from 4 A.M. to 12 noon and so do the evening papers up to 9 or 10 P.M. Some are both morning and evening either under the same name or with two different names. The editorial staff is large. There is one managing editor who writes nothing. Then there are morning and evening editors, foreign and city editors, literary and political, and so on. There is a horde of reporters attached to each, everyone vies with the other in giving sensational headings. There are no leaders, mostly paragraphs.

I have not seen so much multiplicity of communications anywhere as I have seen in America. Firstly, there are steam railways, secondly, there are electric train cars running on the surface, thirdly there are electric railways running in the subways i.e., subterranean roads consisting of tunnels underneath the surface roads, &c. Some of these have been carried under the beds of rivers also. Then there are elevated railways running on the roofs of roads and streets. In the subways and on the elevated roads there are generally 3 or 4 tracks, one or two each way and reserved for local or express trains. Sometimes there are railways and elevated trains even above the elevated cars. Thus some of the roads are quite dark. Cabs and carriages are comparatively few and fares exorbitant. One dollar, i.e. Rs. 3 is lowest fare for a cab. We had to pay 3 dollars, i.e. Rs. 9 to reach the steamer. Baggage is generally sent by express baggage carts which charge from 25 cents (12 annas) to a dollar (Rs. 3) per package. The train and elevator fare is 5 cents (2½ annas) for any distances and for any number of changes.

There is no language that is not spoken in the U.S. All immigrants speak their own language and can at the best pick up a few words of English. Their children born in the U.S. speak better English and often these immigrant parents are at the mercy of these children to make themselves intelligible to others.

The number of those who can speak or write good English or pronounce it well is very limited. No wonder people marvel at our command of English. They do not know how much it costs us to learn and how we are often tortured to learn it well.

Schools and colleges are of course numerous. There are more than 50 universities in the U.S. Some cities have several. Educational facilities are endless and there is no counting of schools and colleges run for profit or on commercial lines. There is no attempt on the part of the state to control these institutions and there is no talk of underselling education or of education for the sake of knowledge.

Crime is enormous, well organised and cleverly planned. Infant mortality (the offshoot of sin and immorality) is indescribable. Lately a syndicate was discovered which ran the business of burning illegitimate children on regular commercial lines. Similarly, a professional nurse was arrested and her house searched with the discovery that burnt bodies of children and bones were found in large quantities. She was, of course, sent to jail, but her jail life was (thanks to her patrons and patronesses who, for fear of unpleasant disclosures, supplied her with money) believed to be anything but unpleasant. Then theft, robbery and burglary too are rampant and seem to be very well organised. Fire by dynamite is very common. Accidents on railways and trains, to carriages and automobiles, are countless. In the streets and on roads you have often to run for your life. Life is a constant struggle and movements are incredibly fast and rapid. Business is done on huge scales, cheating and corruption and fraud are very commonly resorted to. Failures and disasters are frequent.

Living is very costly. Food is comparatively cheaper than in England, but only what is produced in America as gage, dairy produce, and some kinds of meat. Fruit is abundant but not cheap. Rents are very high, clothing exceptionally dear. Travelling very costly. Books are dear. Wages of domestic servants or others high. In most places you pay 10 cents (5 annas) for blacking of boots. Things and articles made in America are dearer in the country than in England because in America there is no fear of outside competition. High duties protect the home industries, and most of the manufacturers combine to stifle competition, and economise labour.

Religion is mostly a matter of show, but a large number of people are inclined towards mysticism, and amongst ladies you find a great many earnest students of religions and seekers after truth. The ordinary intelligence of an American educated young man is higher than in Europe and the amount of work taken, exacted or expected is also larger.

Buildings are huge, grand and very high. Some of the buildings are 20 to 30 stories high occupying not more than 4 to 5 yards of ground in width. America is the land of wooden cottages built from top to bottom of wood. The residences of the middle classes mostly in smaller towns and villages are of wood. For miles and miles along the railway you see nothing but these "log cabins" as they are sometimes called. There are some big buildings too (as, for example, school rooms) made entirely of wood and removable at will. Huge buildings are constructed mostly of iron and wood with a few layers of bricks or stones used in joining corners or in laying the foundations. Except the buildings of the rich and wealthy, ordinary business buildings give an ugly look. Millionaires generally live in separate streets and have their own clubs where no one who is not a millionaire is admitted. Fortunes are easily made and lost. The Americans are generally intensely patriotic, gentle and hospitable. Ideas of patriotism are cultivated from the very cradle as there is nothing else which an American child is taught to love and respect as the American Flag. In the nursery, on the dining table, in the drawing room, in the library, in the bed, in the office, everywhere one finds a miniature flag (stars and stripes) decorating the room and being permanently exhibited. Some Americans pin it to their coats and at most of the places where people go for sightseeing and enjoyment these flags made of different substances are sold and purchased eagerly as souvenirs. In schools, every room is decorated with the national flags placed in different positions. In theatres and playhouses the exhibition of the flag is vociferously cheered. As to hospitality, why, even the slightest acquaintance elicits an invitation to dinner or lunch. Sometimes these invitations extend to your staying at their houses as guests. You can ordinarily expect nothing like this in England. There hospitality like this is an exception while in America it is the rule. On the whole, it is a great country with still greater possibilities of further development and rise in the comity of nations. Indians can learn a great deal. How and what may be discussed separately.

5. The Lesson that India should Learn from the United States[1]

The object of my visit to the United States was to study your educational institutions. One lesson that India should learn from this country is the spirit of unity and nationality that obtains here among a mixed population composed of all nations of the earth.

The object of the Indian National Congress is to present to the Government the defects of its administration. Our chief aim is to get, by gradual concessions, a system of representative government, by which the natives of India may get a voice in the imposition of taxes, and in the administration of affairs. On my

1. Interview to *Evening Post* before leaving New York on 29 September 1905. Reproduced in *India* of 13 October from *Evening Post* of 2 October 1905.

arrival in England our deputation will tour the country and address the people at public meetings, hoping so to excite their sympathy, and asking them to demand from their members at the next election pledges to reform the conditions of Indian government.

The poverty of the country is directly due to the fact that the economic policy of the Government has ruined Indian industries and reduced the country to depending for support entirely on agriculture. Originally India was a manufacturing country, and had a large export trade. This has been suppressed by high duties, and importation has been encouraged. For example, cotton goods manufactured in India are so heavily taxed for home consumption that they have no advantage of prices over the cotton goods for Lancashire. Agriculturists are reduced to poverty on account of the high land tax and the rigorous land policy. The land tax is uncertain, liable to revision now and then, and the Government professes a right to 50 per cent of the economic rent, and sometimes to more in the shape of land cesses. The poverty of the country may be judged by the official estimate that the average income of a man in India is ten dollars a year, and that 40,000,000 of the population go to bed every night without a second meal. Thus there exists throughout India a normal condition of famine. Lately a representative body of Anglo-Indians asked a special enquiry into these conditions. The Government refused to grant it.

Unfortunately, England is now under an Imperial wave, and the attitude it maintains towards its subjects is not of trust, but of suspicion. The Indian Congress thinks that there would be greater contentment throughout India if there were some local government, and that there would accordingly be no need of so large an army.

Lord Curzon was a very unpopular Governor-General among the Indians, but Lord Kitchener is already still more unpopular. Lord Curzon's policy was one of interference and distrust. He interfered with the liberty of the press, and his educational policy was reactionary, for his aim was to officialise the educational system, even when the funds were furnished by private means. Thus he left no independence to private educational enterprises. Moreover, he carried out the partition of Bengal and Punjab against the unanimous feeling of India. He created high-paid posts for Europeans, and increased the military expenditure. But, unfortunately, his resignation resulted from a point on which he was right, and on which he had the support of the Indian public.[2] Thus he presents the curious instance of an unpopular Viceroy turned out while supporting a popular cause. But while Lord Curzon was unpopular in regard to his civil administration, Lord Kitchener is still more unpopular on account of the military rule which he is establishing.

2. Curzon resigned in 1905 as he held that the civil authority should prevail over the military authority while Kitchener held a contrary view. See also *ante*, sub-section 3, item 2, fn. 13.

4
VISIT TO ENGLAND AND AMERICA
V. Miscellaneous

1. To Editor of *The Panjabee*[1]

Sir, Permit me to convey my thanks to all those friends who have been pleased to congratulate me on my safe return.[2] It is almost impossible for me to acknowledge all letters and telegrams individually. The cordiality of the welcome accorded to me has touched me deeply and I pray that although I have not in the past done anything to deserve it, I may yet live to become worthy of it though only partially.

Yours sincerely,
Lajpat Rai

1. *The Panjabee*, 4 December 1905.
2. Among these friends were Madho Lal of the Benares City Congress Committee and Madan Mohan Malaviya.

2. Acknowledgement of Congratulatory Letters and Telegrams[1]

Sir, The number of congratulatory letters and telegrams received by me since my return from Europe is so large that I cannot possibly thank the writers and senders thereof individually. I have therefore to ask your permission to use your columns for conveying my deep gratitude to all such gentlemen. The appreciation shown of my humble services has exceeded all expectations and I can only ascribe it to the goodness and broad-mindedness of my people rather than to any merits of mine.

Besides, I have been receiving a vast number of enquiries with regard to the means and facilities of education abroad. It is again impossible for me to reply to the same at once. If my friends will only allow me a little resting time, I hope to be able to meet their wishes satisfactorily and in a short time. The pressure of work within the last two weeks has affected my health a little, and I do not feel in a position to deal with my correspondence also. I beg of my friends and countrymen to excuse delay which is not in the least due to any want of inclination on my part to do all I can to help them.

Yours &c,
Lajpat Rai

1. Letter to the editor published in *The Tribune* of 9 December 1905.

5
REFLECTIONS ON HIS VISIT ABROAD

1. Politics and Begging[1]

Everywhere I went in the West, the one common and invariable question that was put to me was, "How is it possible that 30 crores of living souls submit to all this tyranny and oppression from a handful of people?" It was a difficult question. But I thought if we solved it therein lay our salvation. The Britishers are such that they won't be satisfied by mere words, speeches or memorials, but they want systematic efforts on the part of the criers to make their position felt. Of course, when we weep before them and lay our grievances before them, outwardly they pity us and sympathise with us but inwardly they only laugh at us. At best they pass resolutions in our favour but really they don't meant to do anything for us. I do not believe in "political begging". For me there is no such term and I cannot see any relation whatever between politics and begging. But as I was selected by my province, I went to England and did not wish to turn my back on my work. At least, I tried my best to impress upon the people of England that it was in the interests of Britain herself to rule India justly.

Lord Curzon did really a great service to India. We want lashes and whips to rouse us from our *Kumbhakaranic* sleep, and but for Lord Curzon the present wave of "love for country goods" would not have been there.

Oppression and tyranny teach much. This unification of all the provinces, if accomplished, will be due to Lord Curzon. Before, the Bengalees laughed at the idea of Swadeshism when put before them by the Panjabees but now Lord Curzon's past six months' policy has taught us that this movement is superior to all others for therein lies the salvation of India. The only thing now required is "firmness and determination", and if we achieve that we will surely win. Boycott has affected the people in England and if it continues it is sure to rouse them as it touches their pockets directly and considerably.

I believe that the Swadeshi movement is an inspiration from the above. It is sure to succeed if we are but firm. Swadeshism took its birth in Bombay and was adopted by the Punjab and now it has been adopted by Bengal, as the Punjab, being too poor, cannot continue it for long. Other countries guard their industries by protective tariffs which are in some cases as high as 60 per cent. But India cannot do anything in her own interest as its administrators here are only subservient to the will of the British elector, who can never allow his own

1. Speech at a public meeting held under the auspices of Swadeshi Vastu Pracharini Sabha, Bombay, 18 November 1905. *The Panjabee*, 27 November 1905.

   Lajpat Rai had returned from England to Bombay on 17 November. For details about his foreign tour see the preceding section.

industries to die out for the sake of India. We have to exert ourselves and rely upon our own strength. In this respect the Swadeshi Vastu Pracharini Sabha is doing commendable work. I would advise you to establish national universities and not hanker after Government degrees. Philosophy won't do now. We have had enough of it. We should take education in our own hands and impart it in our way.

2. Need for People to Take Initiative[1]

In order to gain any rights we must convince our rulers that we are in dead earnest. I do not believe that a nation whose best intellects are engaged in serving aliens can rise. In order to improve our industries, we should ourselves levy protective duties in order to check the tremendous inflow of foreign goods. The Government won't do it, and cannot, even if it desired to.

The Congress so far has done tremendous good to the country. It has spread political knowledge throughout the length and breadth of the country. It has also done much in the direction of unification of the provinces. Now the Bengalees, the Mahrattas, the Punjabees and Madrasees do not feel themselves so much divided from each other as they felt before the Congress came into existence. It has thus spread the idea of common nationality.

There are very few educated persons in India but the Congress can only be successful when the masses join it. In order to achieve this desirable consummation the Congress should work amongst the masses, and I am sure the masses will join the Congress and co-operate with it, when they come to know its real purpose.

1. Speech at a public meeting held in the compound of Victoria School, Agra, 21 November 1905. *The Panjabee*, 27 November 1905.

Lajpat Rai, who left Bombay on 19 November for Lahore, halted at Agra for a day.

3. Need for a Substantial Change in Methods of Agitation[1]

No patriotic Indian can return to his country after a trip to England, including a visit, however short, to other countries in Europe, without being forcibly struck by the intense desire for political liberty and freedom that fills the European atmosphere and that distinguishes the West from the East. He finds that in Europe people are always agitated about their political rights and are extremely jealous of interference with or suppression of popular rights and privileges. Life in England or in Europe is a great struggle—constant, unending struggle—for right and liberty. Freedom from limitations and restrictions, removal of disqualifications and trammels, be they of any nature, perfect freedom from bondage of every kind, is the ever-increasing and ever-recurring cry of modern Europe. Democratic spirit is the keynote of Western civilization in all its branches and departments, but in politics it rules almost supreme. The government of the people, by the people and for the people is the ideal all over, whether in democratic England, monarchical Germany, autocratic Russia or republican France. The press, the pulpit and the platform are all ringing with the cries of "away with the tyrants and autocrats who stand in the way of democracy and who desire to check or stop the wheel of progress onwards or who have the audacity of trifling with the wishes of the people". One should be here in Europe to realize the truth of the above remarks on occasions when anything is done or attempted to be done by the various Governments in power, which is opposed to the democratic spirit of the times or by which a popular demand is thrown out or anything else is done which is opposed to the wishes of the people or which does not tend to further their interests. In July last the rejection of the London Tramways Bill by the House of Lords afforded such an occasion. The city of London, as our readers know, is situated on the banks of the Thames. The river divides the city into two main divisions, one on each side of the river; the tramways end on each side and are not allowed to run across the bridges. This results in great inconvenience to the people as they have to leave the tramway at one end of the river, cross the bridge on foot and then take another tramway at the other end. For busy London people, men and women, boys and girls, who come to the city every day from miles for business and then return to their homes after business hours, this means a great waste of time and money. The London County Council, therefore, proposed to take their tramways across the bridges and thus add to the comfort and the convenience of that great mass of people who cannot afford to engage cabs and hansoms.

1. *The Hindustan Review*, October-November 1905, pp. 349-56.

The Bill passed in the House of Commons was rejected in the House of Lords on the ground that its acceptance involved the destruction of the spectacular effect of the bridges and would make them look ugly. The days and nights that followed the rejection of this Bill presented a spectacle in London which required to be seen in order to be fully realized and which is past all description. People were mad with rage and frenzy and on all sides and from all quarters you heard the cry "down with the Lords", "down with these hereditary robbers and thieves". In clubs, in theatres, in political meetings, on the tramcars, on the buses, in trains, everywhere in fact, the audacity of the House of Lords was the one absorbing topic of discussion and comment, and the proposal for abolishing the House of Lords was being freely and seriously discussed. It found loud expression in the columns of the democratic press, was re-echoed in society papers and was exhibited on the stage. Angry resolutions were passed at the meetings of the London County Council and at other public meetings whether convened for that special purpose or not. For a few days the atmosphere was surcharged with revolutionary ideas. The semi-official liberal and radical press joined in the cry and demanded the abolition of the House of Lords as the only remedy. The Tory press could not but disapprove of the action of the Lords and was either discreetly silent or printed indifferent paragraphs. No serious attempt was made to defend the action of the Lords by anybody.

In short, the whole city seemed to be in a state of ferment and the public mind was intensely agitated. Even the *Daily News*, the organ of the Whigs, demanded the abolition of the House of Lords. The country resounded with the cries of "end it or mend it". Almost immediately following this, came the defeat of the Government on Irish supplies and the statement of the Premier that he intended neither to resign nor to dissolve the Parliament. On this question, of course, the country was divided and the Whigs and the Tories sided with their respective parties. But even the Tory papers acknowledged that a crisis had come and in a suppressed tone. The *Times* also admitted that a great constitutional issue had been raised.

One of the Radical extremists wrote: "It is no less than Revolution! The King is dead. Mr. Balfour has established an autocracy to supplant the monarchy. As defiant of the nation as the Tsar and his bureaucracy, he laughs at public opinions and governs by paper constitutions. He has only to propose a measure prolonging the life of the Government indefinitely and the cowardly criminals at his back aided by the land thieves in the hereditary chamber will pass it. Defeated in the House of Commons, he ignores a hostile vote and continues the government of incompetence and corruption. This is Revolution."

Another paper, after lamenting that the real government of the country was not in the hands of the electorate but in those of the rich, wrote as follows: "Let us rejoice, then, that we have been reminded before the election, and not after it, of the Permanent Tory Opposition which will confront us after the battle is won. Now that we have the issue raised again, in sheer wantonness, by the old and new nobility, let us not suffer it to be dropped. We will come into power in 1906, not only with a mandate upon the fiscal question and education and the publicans and Chinese slavery and labour legislation, but upon that monstrous survival of the bad old times which we call the House of Lords."

At about the same time occurred another incident which showed the ascendancy of the democratic spirit in this country. The Government announced what was practically a dropping of the Unemployed Bill and said there was no chance of the Bill being passed into law this session. This announcement met with a chorus of disapproval from the public, and at once a number of monster demonstrations of the unemployed were organised. Thousands of the unemployed assembled in different places and protested. In some cases thousands marched to London to prove to the Government the intensity of feeling on the subject.

At a meeting of the unemployed at Manchester a regular march to London was proposed. In discussing the proposed measure one of the speakers said: "They had no hesitation in declaring that such a march would be a menace to the towns they passed through, but if the Government wanted to prevent it, they must give the legislation asked for." Another speaker said that if, in the opinion of the authorities, "Human life was not worth any consideration they, the unemployed, would say that they were not prepared to consider property. They would take immediate steps to see to it that they had that which was necessary for their sustenance and they would not be particular where they got it." The demonstrations of the unemployed men are supplemented by similar demonstrations of the unemployed women, and the wives of the unemployed in London who eventually sent a deputation to the House of Commons to meet the Premier. The result was that all parties had to give in and the "Unemployed Bill" was taken up and passed into law.

Then there is another question that has been agitating a section of the British public for several years past, viz. the Education Act. This Act forces Non-Conformists to pay rates which they consider iniquitous. The Bill was passed in the teeth of a great and vigorous opposition and the Non-Conformists have not yet been reconciled to it. A great number of them every year refuse to pay taxes voluntarily and the same is realized by the seizure and distraint of their property. This has been going on for the last three years and still continues. The methods of agitation followed by the Irish nationalists are too significant and well known to need special mention. In the House of Commons they obstinately obstruct business and at times make the transaction of it almost impossible. Their policy in this respect is open and avowed. In the country itself they throw as many difficulties in the way of the Government as they can.

Their success in these methods is well known and, as a result thereof, they have extorted many valuable concessions from unwilling and hostile Parliaments. In other parts of Europe they go a step further and in the demand for political liberty have recourse to anarchist methods, which at times culminate in murders, assassinations and crime. This is wicked no doubt, but it shows how intense is the desire for political liberty and at what risk and under what conditions people are striving to get it, in their own way and according to their own means. Now, on seeing and studying all this, one cannot help contrasting the same with the political conditions that prevail in India. Not that I necessarily wish that all of these methods may be adopted by my countrymen but I keenly feel by contrast the apathy, the indifference, the want of earnestness, the absence of a spirit of sacrifice for the cause and for the principle, the colossal timidity and the consequent failure of those who carry on political agitation in India. There are neither leaders nor followers who fully realize what political freedom is and what stupendous efforts and sacrifices are required of them in order to get to even the fringe of the same. One is apt to feel that a set of wordly-wise (or perhaps unwise), greedy and cowardly people as we are, we do not deserve a better treatment at the hands of our rulers than what they accord to us. Why? What sacrifices do we undergo to deserve what we want? Anything more than the trouble of attending the annual session of the Congress and enjoying a holiday? Yes, a few do more than that. They write articles and deliver speeches. A few do even more than that, they subscribe small sums of money for the political propaganda. But what proportion does that bear to their incomes or to their expenditures on luxuries and holidays, &c., you should not ask. Because in answer to that question even the greatest and the loudest of Indian patriots will have to hide his head in shame. But why be so hard on them? Have they not big families, sons, grandsons, daughters, wives, mothers, and, last but not least, their great selves to provide for? Why, have they not to have estates, build palaces and otherwise provide for the dim uncertain future? Yes, they have to do all that, and we have no quarrel with them for doing so. Only we object to their assuming that they are patriots. In our humble opinion no one is entitled to call himself a patriot who holds anything (excepting his religion, of course) dearer than his country. But this is a very high and almost unapproachable ideal, you will say. Very well, let us in any case try to do something better and more tangible than we have been doing heretofore. Let us, at the close of each year, feel certain of some progress. Let us take stock and say if we are, to be sure, making substantial progress. Looked at from this point of view even, I am afraid we cannot hold out a cheerful and promising record. Our past record shows that, in truth, the struggle for freedom has not even yet commenced, we have done absolutely nothing to inaugurate it. The country is as yet wanting in those conditions which must precede the dawn of an era of real, earnest struggle.

Where are the political thinkers of the country, whose sole thought by day or by night, sleeping or waking, should be, how to initiate and carry on the struggle for freedom? Where are the political sannyasis whose sole work in life should be the preaching of the gospel of freedom, who should, even at the point of the bayonet, say with Galelio, "there they are, I see them moving"? Where are the *Vaishyas* of the movement who will only earn and make money for the struggle and who will finance it; who will live poorly and modestly and save every pie for the sacred cause in order not to let it suffer for want of the sinews of war? And, last but not least, where are the people who will quietly, ungrudgingly, without complaint or murmur, suffer for the cause and in their persons prove the truth of the saying that "the blood of the martyrs is the seed of the church"? In short, where are the people who will raise agitation for political rights and liberty to the dignity of a church and live and die for the same?

Let us look round and find out if there are men in the country who are fit to properly initiate and inaugurate the struggle for freedom. Bengal is renowned for its writers and speakers. Let some of its best sons consecrate their lives to the cause. Their only business in life should be to write books, tracts, pamphlets, articles and notes, also to give speeches all over the country expounding what liberty is, how it was won by other peoples and how it can be won by us. Let them seek no payment for their labours but what is sufficient for their sustenance. Let them build no houses, create no estates and have simple frugal lives. If possible, let them be celibates. Maharashtra has justly earned a name for statesmanship and powers of organisation. Let some of its best sons consecrate their lives to the work of organising political movements in India. Our revered friend, Mr. Bal Gangadhar Tilak, is one of the fittest persons to undertake the work, if the Government, which has been persecuting him so long, is inclined to let him alone, which is not likely, he having roused its worst suspicions. Well, in that case, the best thing for him is to bid goodbye to his motherland, be a voluntary exile and take his residence somewhere abroad. He should devote himself to the task of influencing English and foreign public opinion in favour of political reforms in India. The other leader who is fitted to do this work is Mr. Gokhale. I may be pardoned for hazarding an opinion to the effect that the Supreme or any other Legislative Council chamber is not the place for him. He has shown the way to others, he has proved to the world sufficiently that even poor Indians can hold their own against clever autocratic bureaucrats of the class of Lord Curzon, and that is enough. Let the non-official members of the Bombay Legislative Council find another representative champion for the

Supreme Council and leave Mr. Gokhale alone to be the whole-time Secretary of the Congress, to organise a central office, to go about, and guide the Provincial Congress Committees. The other provinces also should, if possible, prevail upon one or two capable persons in each centre to renounce their professions and take to the work of carrying on political agitation and spreading political propaganda.

If there are any provinces which cannot fix upon their own leaders, let them follow the lead of the better situated and more lucky ones and assist in bringing about one compact political organization determined to carry on the struggle for political rights.

As to actual work, we think the time has come for more vigorous measures and for a substantial change in the methods of our agitation.

Bengal has just shown the way in agitating against the partition of Bengal.[2] What Bengal has done should be done by every province in ventilating its grievances. Besides occasional provincial demonstrations like those recently held in Bengal, we ought to improve upon the general annual demonstration at the Congress session by arranging to bring about a greater and a bigger meeting every year attended by no less than a hundred thousand persons from all parts of India. The educational and political value of such gatherings cannot be overestimated. Let the next session of the Congress at Benares set the example. Actual deliberative work should be done by a smaller conference attended by not more than a hundred of the best men of the country. Two whole days may be reserved for this work and one day, the opening day, for popular demonstration, at which speeches may be delivered to the assembled masses from different platforms by different men in their own vernaculars. The executive and administrative work of guiding the movement all round the year should be done by a still smaller standing committee of 20 to 30 men. This committee ought to meet at least twice or three times a year, and if Sir Pherozeshah Mehta cannot spare time to attend its sittings at some central place, let us unanimously agree to fix Bombay as the headquarters and meet only there. Or, if that be not acceptable to our Bengal friends who are equally indispensable, let Bombay and Calcutta have the honour of being the meeting place every alternate year. For the sake of unanimity and for the sake of our motherland let us all agree to this even though it may be inconvenient and expensive to Madrasis and Punjabis to do so.

Then the next thing which the whole country ought to do simultaneously with the above is the adopting of and giving effect to the Bengal resolutions regarding the boycotting of English goods. This in my opinion is the most effective way of bringing the Government to its senses and will be most telling

2. Bengal was partitioned in October 1905. For details see *ante*, section 2.

on England. Even if we cannot do without foreign goods, let us import them from Japan and China first, and from Germany, France or the United States next. Let us try to gain the sympathy and goodwill of the Indian retail-sellers, and there cannot be the least doubt that we can carry on an effective political propaganda. There is another thing which I would do, viz. to spread a knowledge of English laws and regulations by broadcast. Let the people realize the full significance of the laws under which they live and demand the full pound of flesh given to them by the same. If all these measures carried out for a number of years fail to make an impression upon the Government, though I am sure they will, then there will be time to think of more effective methods of constitutional agitation to bring about the desired reforms in the government of the country.

I have my own ideas about carrying on the Indian political campaign in England which I reserve for another occasion.

4. India and English Party Politics[1]

I am of the opinion that those who talk of identifying the Congress with the Liberal Party in England presume too much. Firstly, they assume without justification and, perhaps, against all experience that the Liberal Party, as a party, are prepared to open their arms to them. My experience tells me just the otherwise. It is true that the response to the circular letter of the Chairman of the British Committee of the Indian National Congress, asking for platforms for Indian delegates, came mostly from the Liberal and Radical associations of England, including trade unions, Labour and Socialist circles. It is equally true that what little hearing we received in England was given to us by the Liberals, but then we cannot shut our eyes to the fact that the Liberal leaders and the Liberal executive kept themselves as much aloof as the Conservatives. The Liberals are in substantial agreement with the Conservatives in keeping Indian affairs out of party politics. At the discussion of the last Budget in June there was only one influential Liberal, Sir Charles Dilke, who spoke in favour of Mr. Herbert Robert's motion for a Parliamentary enquiry. The other leading Liberals went in a body against it. You have only to be a few days in England to come to the conclusion that the Liberal executive is as indifferent to the

1. V.C. Joshi (ed.), *Lala Lajpat Rai—Writings and Speeches*, Vol. 1 (Delhi, 1966), pp. 87-89; originally published in *Indian Review* of November 1905 and reproduced in *The Panjabee* of 11 December 1905.

Indian affairs as the Conservative and that as a party the Liberals are not prepared to receive our advances. For the time being some of them may utilise you for party purposes in those matters in which they differ from their rivals, the Tories, but beyond that they will not go. As such, it is futile to discuss the wisdom or the non-wisdom of identifying the Congress with the Liberals as a party. The question is, at present, outside the range of party politics. If it were possible to do so, I would rather have the Indian affairs fought and discussed on party lines. So far I am quite in agreement with Sir Pherozeshah Mehta. Anyone even slightly acquainted with political life in England will tell you that, as a rule, English politicians are not prepared to devote any time and attention to any matter which does not further party interests. Matters outside party politics receive hardly any consideration. Nobody cares for the same. People do not feel sufficiently interested to spare any time or attention for matters which do not seem to concern them in any way. The press cannot afford to spare space for them for it does not pay them. The man in the street is absorbed in his own affairs. The ordinary citizen or voter argues that a matter upon which both parties agree and hold the same views must be well looked after and needed no care on his part. To be just and fair to English Liberals, I must say that those who could be approached were found to be very sympathetic and for the time being at least appeared to have been touched by the tale of woe narrated before them. Some of them passed resolutions of sympathy and so on, but beyond that I don't believe they will take any further trouble of pressing it either on their representatives in the House of Commons or on their party leaders as such. So far the greatest sympathy has been expressed by the Labour and Democratic and Socialist circles. The working men in England are now awake and they are as much disgusted with the present system of class government as we are. They are pushing forward their own candidates and they hope to return a solid body of Labour members in the next general election.[2] The Democratic and Socialist sections are in favour of Home Rule for India and so, of course, are the Irish. These are the people upon whose active sympathy Indians can safely rely and who might help Indians if they are sufficiently strong to make themselves heard. But they are poor, and poverty in England is, perhaps, a greater curse and calamity than anywhere else in the world. They generally denounce the Liberals as well as the Conservatives, though their members in Parliament seem to have a certain sort of alliance with the Liberals. They are perfecting their organisations and are advancing steadily. The Socialists and the Democrats are allied with them. I was much impressed with their sincerity

2. In the general election of 1905 the Labour Representation Committee (LRC), a combination of the Independent Labour Party, the Fabian Society and some trade unions, secured 29 seats in the House of Commons, while in 1900 it had won only 2 seats.

of purpose and genuineness of sympathy, and am of opinion that it is this class only with which at present an alliance is possible, if any. It is no doubt true that in high Whig circles this class is not looked upon with favour and very reasonably too. They aim at their overthrow and claim a share of the power of which the former have been enjoying an exclusive monopoly so far. The fact that of all countries in the European world, England is the most conservative and very slow to adopt new ideas makes it probable that the Labour and Democratic influence will take a long time to develop and to attain the power which they aim at. But all the same it is hopeless to expect anything at the hands of the Liberals for India. When in power they might send a sympathetic Viceroy but that they cannot and will not follow systematic, persistent policy of advance in applying democratic principles of government to India is as certain as that the sun will set this evening and rise tomorrow morning.

There are some good Liberals who sincerely desire to rule India on sound liberal principles, but at present they are in a hopeless minority, their voices do not count for much and there is little chance of their gaining any prominence or coming to the front Benches in the near future.

Under the circumstances, the only advice I can offer to my countrymen is as follows:

1. That they should mainly look to themselves and their own exertions for political progress. The English voter, whether Liberal or Conservative, is a sympathetic creature no doubt, but then he is absorbed in his own troubles and affairs and to care for us has neither the time nor the inclination to attend to anything which does not directly concern him or which is likely to affect his pocket injuriously.
2. That if there is any class in England which deserves our confidence and upon whose votes we can place any reliance at all it is the Labour Party, including the Democrats and the Socialists and the Irish, of course.

5. Religion in the East and West[1]

When a person like myself who has lived all his life in the East and studied its customs and manners goes for the first time to the West, he is astonished at all that meets his gaze there. My belief is that the exalted manners and customs of

1. Speech at a meeting held under the auspices of Young Men's Samaj at Lahore on 9 February 1906. *The Panjabee*, 14 Februry 1906.

a nation are an index of its greatness, if not wholly so to a greater degree at least, and vice versa. One finds two opposite currents running in the two sets of countries. Whereas in the East he finds त्याग (renunciation) and बैराग (asceticism) obtaining on all sides, in the West भोग (enjoyment) and सुख (material comfort) prevail everywhere and have taken possession of the people's mind. In the East we have Bhartrihari[2] and Maulana Rumi[3] clearly voicing the ideals of the people; in the West Rousseau[4] and Voltaire[5] are followed unquestioningly. The East claims for its ideal the life of a hermit in a lonely forest, the West wants a Vatican palace for its Pope or St. Peter for its Church. These are the typical differences which distinguish the East from the West in the matter of religion. There are opposite scenes too in both the countries but they are exceptions rather than the rule, for instance, Comte's religion of humanity in the West and Islam in the East.

This evening I shall confine myself to a few observations which I was able to make during my travels. There is nothing like spiritual purity in the West. But in social efficiency they, the Westerners, are incomparable and their work and zeal are simply beyond praise. Equally is the case with their political side. But they lack and lack deplorably in spirituality. Gambling, drinking and flirting are the order of the day. Members of all ranks, high and low, even leaders of public opinion, politicians, statesmen, ministers of religion and demagogues do not dislike these things. They indulge in all three everywhere, be they in the club, the restaurant, the railway train or the steamer's deck. They consider no sin in it. I do not say that you don't find these things in the East, but here we look upon them as vicious and hate them as such. But in the case of religious leaders they are simply intolerable. I had on board my ship some clergymen, a majority of whom freely indulged in gambling and drinking. In long journeys they constantly play cards with high money stakes. Even Western kings and emperors participate in the vice of gambling in the form of lotteries and betting on horse races.

I should now come to the religious systems of the West.

2. A famous poet of the seventh century who composed a number of short poems on love, worldly wisdom, etc., and author of the famous grammatical work called *Vakyapadiya*.
3. Jalal-ud-Din Rumi (1207-1273); a great Persian mystical poet who devoted himself to the pursuit of Sufi philosophy and founded the Mevlevi order of dervishes.
4. Jean Jacques Rousseau (1712-1778); French philosopher who considered property and the state causes of inequality; works include *Contract Social* (1762), *Emile* (1762) and *Confessions* (autobiography).
5. (1694-1778); French philosopher and writer whose ideas influenced the movement which culminated in the French Revolution in 1789; works include *Zaire* (1732), *Letters Concerning the English Nation* (1733) and *Candide* (1759).

(1) Roman Catholicism—You think that the Roman Catholic religion is extinct from the world. No, it is not the case. It claims a surging humanity as its followers. Of course, the real spirit of religion is gone but the form, the outer covering, remains and is still there. I saw big Roman Catholic churches at different places which must have cost an immense amount of money. Outside the St. Peter's Church at Rome, I saw two statues, one of St. Peter with the key of Paradise in hand and the other of St. Paul with his right hand grasping the hilt of a sword.

The significance of these two statues is clear enough. 'Take from me the key of Paradise,' exclaims St. Peter, or St. Paul is ready for you with his sword. I cannot understand how can Christianity criticise Mohammadanism for spreading itself by the sword; but that is a digression and I must leave it aside and proceed with my subject. I saw in these churches crosses of gold and various other paraphernalia which in themselves must come up to a pretty big figure. There can be no better illustration of idol worship than in these churches; and the mockery of it all lies in the fact that these churches and idols were built after destroying the heathen temples and gods of worship because idol worship was preached therein. You still find prevailing in these Roman Catholic churches the crudest form of worship of confessing one's sins and getting pardon for them. Some years back we Lahories wondered very much at the torches which we saw burning in the daytime before the Jagat Guru, but that was the only occasion I saw such a thing in my life, while in Europe it is a scene to be witnessed every day and everywhere in Roman Catholic countries—any number of lamps burning in daytime. There is not only one idol before which they kneel and bow and touch their foreheads. They do it before many. In the churches there are statues and portraits of different Popes and along with them of some females whom the guides call their (the Popes') mistresses; all these have been canonised and now are worshipped as saints or demi-gods.

(2) Protestantism—Turning to Protestantism or the reformed church as it is described, we find that there is no नैवेद्य (food-offering) to be found in their churches. There are no idols too excepting those of Mary and Jesus; but I saw nobody bowing before them.

On Sunday, or the sacred Sabbath as they love to call it, all business is closed. In the afternoon confectioners and restaurant keepers open their shops, and along with them you find billiard saloons and bars opened also; but the rest of the business is closed. In London a whole population does not go to Church, a very small minority do go however. In order to see how they do pass their Sunday you have simply to go to the various parks and gardens and see what they do there. Even in Edinburgh, where the old Presbyterian sentiment of the Covenanters is still predominant, all the people do not go to Church. The majority prefer to go to the seaside and to parks, and a lot of business is carried on in these places. You find Christian preachers in the parks and gardens holding religious discourses, but few listen to them. The predominating characteristics are the same everywhere—gambling, drinking and flirting, and along with these the passion to make wealth rapidly and be merry during the rest of one's life. It is a strange fact that Asia which possesses a sun which shines clearly and brightly all the year round has only paleness and gloominess for its children while Europe, where the luminary is never seen for months together, possesses liveliness and brightness. The Westerners have made excellent arrangements for bringing up children who are prematurely born or are forsaken by parents for one reason or other. Perhaps the promiscuous sexual intercourse which is raging in the West requires these institutions. One finds on deeper investigation all these social and philanthropic institutions to be the necessary results of the social structure.

In America, too, spirituality is at a great discount and is confined to a very limited few. The omnipotent dollar is supreme in America, they say, and it is actually the case. But Americans like the mysticism which is so much associated with Eastern religions. In Europe they feel very keenly this want of spirituality or godliness. They want to fill in the gap. Only the covering is left, the binding force is gone. Even their greatest minds are seriously thinking about it.

The reason of all this discontent in the West is that where सुख and भोग are made the end and aim of life, there is no concern for the means, foul or fair, whatever they be; and a man like myself is at a loss to understand how can these people pass their lives comfortably and preserve 'Peace of Mind'.

On the other hand, we have made our ideal: To renounce the world, to keep naked and pass life in forests. The question is how can we give up our gloominess and lifelessness, safeguarding at the same time our godliness and spiritual purity; and with all our त्याग and बैराग can we preserve cheerfulness and brightness of mind? Is it proper for us to give up this sacred heritage and adopt Western civilization?

My belief is that the only answer to these questions is that we should keep both. If we adopt one, destruction is at our doors. We should lay spiritual purity in the foundation and raise a structure on it, which structure may contain in it materialism of the whole world, broad-mindedness and all worldly comforts and pleasures, but at the same time consistent with the path we want to lead. Our country is in a transitory state. We should preserve our own essence. Let us garb Western civilization with Eastern spiritualism and the path is clear.

6. Paris[1]

Paris, the capital of France, is regarded as the most beautiful city of the world. To the people of Europe it is heaven on earth. It is every Englishman's cherished wish to visit it at least once in his lifetime and see for himself its picturesque splendour. There must indeed be some unfortunate few, whether hailing from America or from within Europe, who have not been to Paris even once in their lives. Some people are so enamoured of the city that on the least pretext they make a trip to it. Paris is said to be the epitome of modern civilization and the soul of liberty.

Most of the political revolutions of Europe were nurtured in the lap of France and most of the contours of Europe were drawn by the people whose main source of inspiration was the French literature. Perhaps it would be no exaggeration to say that the modern concept of freedom had its genesis in France. The maxim of the equality of man was first propounded in France from where it spread to other countries. Several centuries later the concept of democracy was also first conceived in France. In fact, France is the real birthplace of democracy and on its soil were born many renowned political thinkers. Voltaire was born and educated here. It was here that he placed his thoughts on the high pedestal of political philosophy for the enlightenment of people. This is the region where Thomas Paine[2] preached the sermon of the people's political and religious rights, calling them the bible of freedom and sang unremittingly about them. This was the place where the people raised the flag of revolt against despotic rule and religious suzerainty. It was here that one of the most outstanding military generals of the modern times was nurtured whose very name struck terror in the hearts of royalty, for it was he who brought the most powerful kings to heel. That is why the powerful European rulers conspired against him to weaken his hold on them.

The reader must have readily understood whom I am referring to. The general is none other than Napoleon Bonarparte whose ashes are interred in this city in a grave with a golden dome, which is a specimen of architectural splendour and which is visited by the people of all parts of the world in a spirit of pilgrimage. As you enter the building you are reminded of Humayun's tomb

1. Article published in *Zamana* (Urdu monthly) of February 1906 (translated from Urdu).
   While in England, Lajpat Rai paid a short visit to Paris in the last week of August 1905, returning to London on 30 August.
2. (1737-1809); American writer who stood for independence of American colonies and supported the French Revolution; accused of treason in England, fled to France in 1792; works include *Common Sense, The American Crisis* and *The Rights of Man.*

and the Taj Mahal. The Taj Mahal is incomparable, but Napoleon's dome bears a close resemblance to Humayun's tomb though the inner layout is entirely different. The former is laid out with beautiful costly marble. As you enter you see tombs of Napoleon's era, many of them of his own dynasty, flanking both sides of his grave which is resting right under the golden dome. They have made a magnificent plinth over which Napoleon's coffin rests surrounded by beautifully-carved slabs of costly stones. The plinth has been built inside a circle resembling the sun. There is another circle within that circle on which are carved the landmarks in Napoleon's life, and outside it fly the replicas of flags representing the countries which Napoleon had conquered.

On both sides of the Dome are the graves of Napoleon's valiant generals who had made a name for themselves in various battles. Facing one of the graves is a sketch of Britain steeped in gloom. Next to the Dome there is a plinth on which is installed a statue of Christ along with a cross. Behind it is an iron door on which Napoleon's last Will is inscribed. The text of the Will written in French reads: "My ashes be buried in the soil of France on the bank of river Seine with which I have been deeply in love." On either side of the cross are idols of Angels. Then comes a big church on whose walls hang numerous flags of various countries which Napoleon had vanquished in battles. In one part of the building are arrayed the cannons Napoleon wrested from his enemies, and in another part are kept a wide range of meticulously preserved articles of his personal use. Every day people flock to the Dome in large numbers from France itself as well as from other countries. In the courtyard is installed a huge statue of Napoleon which keeps alive the memory of the emperor in the hearts of his countrymen. On various walls of the building are inscribed the sketches of various battles which Napoleon fought. These sketches remind one of the glorious period of France.

In world history France is known for its political revolutions. In the course of the past two centuries the country passed intermittently through an autocratic rule and a democratic form of government. In its history hardly fifty years passed without the people rising in revolt and bringing about some significant change in the form of government. At present France has a democratic form of government headed by a president.

There was a time when France ranked among the leading powers of Europe and its naval power was unrivalled. But after Napoleon's defeat decline of the country set in. It was overrun by Germany twice. Once it had to pay a huge compensation and also cede a part of its territory to Germany in order to arrive at a truce with it. However, even today France's naval power is rated next only to that of Great Britain. As history bears out, France and England were constantly at war with each other for ages. England's first supreme ruler, William the First, had in fact migrated from France. In the war between Russia and Japan,

England sided with Japan and France with Russia. But now for certain reasons France and England are veering towards each other. Recently when the President of France visited England he was given a royal reception. Again, recently when a British naval fleet made a formal visit to France it was received with great fanfare. Later on, when a French fleet made a similar visit to England it was received by the British king himself at Port Esmouth. Evidently, both the countries are striving hard to live in amity with each other. This is being interpreted in political circles as a move against Germany. Some time back the Czar and the German emperor called on each other and political observers believe that the friendship struck up between England and France is a subtle move to forestall the designs of Germany.

I have mentioned all this by way of an interlude and would like to revert to what I personally observed in Paris. On a prominent thoroughfare they have installed a female statue which symbolically represents the French republic. It overlooks three other statues, comparatively smaller in size, which stand for (1) Liberty (2) Equality and (3) Fraternity. The French flag is a composite representation of these three concepts and stands mainly for freedom. It propounds that all men are brothers, having equal rights, and the French republic upholds these principles.

At another place they have installed a statue of Napoleon on a high pedestal. The statue is standing on one leg and represents Napoleon's hypersensitive nature. It also symbolizes the place where there was a prison before the advent of the Revolution. It was ransacked and demolished in the course of the Revolution. The part of the city where the palatial residence of the President is situated is surrounded by beautiful gardens, and nearby there is a hugé public square where there are several statues and also a long pillar commemorating Napoleon's conquests. On that pillar are also etched the icons of ancient Egyptian kings. Along the right side of the pillar runs a boulevard flanked by gardens on both sides. Between the gardens and the boulevard are laid out grassy lawns with chairs and benches laid on them which are used by the people free of charge. The boulevard ends in a wide road the like of which even London cannot boast of. Along the entire length of the road there are footpaths for pedestrians. The road ends in a magnificent archway which was constructed in memory of Napoleon Bonaparte. There is another road leading from the archway and terminating near a big park where the elite of the city come for the evening walk. The elegantly dressed ladies are quite a sight to behold. The park has many small lakes and ponds.

One of the roads resembles Delhi's Chandni Chowk, the only difference being that the footpaths flanking the road in Chandni Chowk are not wide enough and not as clean as the Paris road which is a matter of great regret.

The river Seine flows through the middle of the city, greatly enhancing its beauty. On both sides of the river there are beautiful dykes and there are many bridges over it which are studded with beautiful statues. There are also public baths at different places and recreation centres. Boats and steamboats ply on the river. They serve the purpose of railways and tramways for the people to go about the city. There are small islands also in the midst of the river having beautiful buildings. One of the islands is so big that there are many roads criss-crossing it.

There is a big building in the city which contains tombs of many illustrious personages. It is a place akin to London's Westminster Abbey, perhaps a notch more beautiful than the Abbey but quite different to it in architecture. The people of Paris call it the building Pantheon. It has a plaque fixed near the entrance describing the purpose for which the house was built. The interior of the building has been beautifully decorated, and its beauty is further enhanced by the artistic statues kept inside it.

Paris's beautiful church Notre Dame is a uniquely splendid building in all respects. There is a roll of the Popes and exalted ecclesiastical dignitaries displayed at the main portal of the church. Inside there are also numerous statues and portraits of Mary, Jesus Christ and other holy persons and angels which command reverential respect of the visitors.

Paris's world famous museum, the Louvre, was originally a huge cluster of royal palaces. In this museum you will find assembled the country's most beautiful and world-renowned paintings. It also takes pride in having a collection of exquisitely carved statues. Inside, there are beautiful courtyards, quite artistic themselves, which have also fountains spraying water round the clock for the visitors' recreation. In the midst of the fountains there is a beautiful granite arch reminiscent of the glories of ancient times.

The museum is a multi-storeyed structure built on a gigantic scale with gilded ceilings having beautiful carvings. It is the biggest museum of the country full of unique artistic pieces comparable to the very best in the world. The halls are so big that, in the limited time at my disposal, I could go round only two halls and that too in a great hurry. The first floor mainly displays paintings and statues in a wide range, depicting the fullness of art, in a way the last word in artistic beauty. There are war paintings so lifelike as if a battle is really being fought. In the same way religious episodes, literary pieces, legends depicted on cloth, paper, clay, stone and metal invest the whole place with an authentic touch. There are also paintings and statues of men and women in various moods conveying expressions of joy and sorrow with artistic finesse. One just marvels to look at them. Paintings of women are mostly in the nude and are marked by anatomical perfection, exhibiting every muscle of the body. Many paintings show couples indulging in loveplay. What surpasses all is the sublime treatment of maternal love full of tender empathy, which effaces the difference between art and reality. In one painting Adam is shown accepting the apple, the forbidden fruit, from Eve's hand. French, Italian, German and English paintings are superb having no parallel in the history of art. The other museums also are full of such paintings acquired from different places at fabulous prices. Here and there, tapestries, embroidery and needlework—unique examples of art—lend variety to the collection. In the various palaces of Paris and in its environs there are paintings highlighting the lives of Napoleon and Louis XIV[3] and their queens and female companions. These paintings cater to all sorts of tastes, serious and amorous, and provide ample material for the art historian. Some of the paintings are quite big in size. For the religious-minded there are paintings tracing the history of Christianity. Various martyrs have also been given due importance and justice has been done to their lives, so much so that the onlookers' eyes are filled with tears. Equally interesting are the paintings depicting political tyranny and also portraying the patriots who fought for the cause of freedom. In short, the themes of these paintings, statues and portraits are so splendid and magnificent that the pen cannot do full justice to them.

On seeing the decorations and magnificence of these palaces the people subscribing to modern political views might think that if all the wealth and money squandered on such ostentatious style of living had been put to good use, specially for alleviating the condition of the poor, then the world would have been a much better place to live in. But in that case these unique marvels of art which we are seeing now would have remained locked in the man's mind. It seems there are two facets to every phenomenon and it is up to man to choose one of them. In the underground cellar of the museum are preserved some of the mummies of ancient Egypt which are singing the dirge of man's political and moral degeneration and his propensity to loot. These museums of Europe are full of things plundered from Africa and Asia. The victorious nations of Europe had no qualms in lifting precious things for which they took a fancy from these continents in order to embellish and decorate their own palaces, so much so that they even ransacked graves, underground cellars, resting places of ancestors, palaces of princesses and ancient sacred pilgrim centres. It is supposed that a vanquished nation and the oppressed people have no rights. A man who cannot safeguard his legitimate possessions has no right to own them. The mummies of ancient Egyptian kings now lying in European museums bear testimony to the cowardice and worthlessness of their descendants. A conquering nation does not stop short of looting a country's wealth. It does not spare even mosques, temples and mausoleums. It has no regard for the vanquished country's honour and dignity, nor for its women's chastity. This has been happening since time immemorial. The Christian historians who

3. (1638-1715); King of France, 1643-1715.

upbraid the Muslims for their excesses should first search their own hearts, as the Christians have perhaps outdone the Muslims in this respect in many ways.

You would, of course, remember that in the French republic all men are regarded as equal. But did France not overrun other countries? Did France treat the vanquished in the same manner as it treated its own citizens? Did France not exploit the resources of vanquished countries for its own gain? There is no need to seek a reply to these questions. The museums of France and the old issues of French newspapers readily provide answers to these questions. As the proverb goes, an elephant has one set of teeth to eat and another set to show off.

It is not fair to judge the national traits and way of life of the people of a country on the basis of a few days' stay. Even so, a comparison between France and England may be worthwhile. The English people are serious and reserved by nature. The French are jovial and open-minded. In the matter of dress the English people prefer to wear sober and sophisticated clothes and the same is the case with the French women. The vehicles in England move on the left side while those in France on the right side. The women of England have full liberty to meet anyone they want before marriage which even their parents cannot question. They choose their husbands themselves and marry on their own. Months before marriage, even years sometimes, they go around with men in order to make up their minds about marriage. Of course, after marriage they entrust themselves fully to their husbands and submit themselves to their will. It is presumed that character-wise English women are far less wayward than the women of other European countries. In France girls live under personal constraints before marriage and they have little freedom to move around with men. Of course, after marriage they make ample amends for this deficiency and are free to act according to their lights. Not unoften the husband has liaison with another woman and the wife with another man.

Usually when English people eat outside they eat in silence. While eating in a party they behave in a sober manner and talk in low tone. In contrast, the French become boisterous, laugh and talk loudly. The English people are generally genial and staid while the French are whimsical and capricious. The English people are more religious-minded than the French. Both drink as a matter of habit and drink hard. But the only difference is that while the Englishman gets fully drunk the French man knows how to carry himself even after consuming liquor as he generally drinks wine and not hard intoxicants. In Europe people do not drink water with meals. Instead, they drink wine. In Europe there is only a small percentage of people who drink two or three glasses of water per day, their main drink being hard liquor or wine.

The majority of Englishmen belong to the merchant or service class. As compared to the people of Europe, they are more honest and forthright.

In England a woman cannot openly adopt prostitution as her profession whereas in France there is no such restriction. In France women openly go out in search of clients and strike bargains in public parks and gardens sitting on benches. In London this kind of business is confined to some specified areas. It may be noted that French theatres and amusement carnivals are known for their gaiety and grandeur.

In France men and women cohabit together but often do not marry. Marriage in France is considered out of fashion. Many marriages take place on the explicit understanding that no children will be born. This tendency has reached such proportions that the Government is getting worried about the country's diminishing population. Now it has started spending huge amounts of money in propagating the idea lying behind the marriage, and rightly so. It is their own Government which keeps an eye on what is in the best interest of the country. Alas, we are so unfortunate that our Government is more interested in keeping us as slaves rather than in promoting our health.

You will be surprised to know that though France leads in fashion and French women are regarded as innovators in the realm of fashion and the entire Europe and the whole of America follow its lead, the French people themselves take the utmost liberty in the matter of dress. For instance, when an Englishman wears a frock coat, it becomes incumbent upon him to wear a particular type of top hat. otherwise he is called a yokel. But in France there are no such constraints or taboos. There a man is free to wear any kind of dress he likes, any kind of coat with any kind of cap, and nobody would point a finger at him for this kind of incongruity. In England, particularly in London, one has to be very particular about the colour combination of one's dress. But in France nobody bothers about it. In England one has to wear a particular type of evening dress to visit a theatre or a recreation club. But it is not so in France. In England I have never seen people eating in gardens or in outer verandas. But in France people eat in the open without the least hesitation. They eat at tables laid alongside a highway or a boulevard and in verandas and parks. There wine is so cheap that it is served full bottle with a two-franc meal. But one has to shell out ten francs extra for lemonade soda or fruit juice.

In the field of advertisement and publicity also France is far ahead of other countries of Europe. I have not seen any place in London, Belgium, Italy or Switzerland using a 'biograph' for advertising. In Paris they have 'biographs' outside commercial stores where people flock to see films with advertisements at regular intervals.

In London all shops remain closed on Sundays, but the pubs, hotels and restaurants open in the afternoon to serve food and liquor to their clients. In Paris there is no such hard and fast rule. Many shops remain open on Sundays. In London the pubs close at midnight and in Paris all shops close at nine but there is no such restriction for wine shops and eateries.

France is more advanced than England in science and technology. The French language is understood in almost all countries of Europe. Perhaps it would not be wrong to say that France is more liberal and open-minded as regards new ideas, techniques and methods than England. England believes in following the beaten track. Englishmen do not take easily to innovations of any kind, conservatism being their national trait. They generally suffer from dental trouble. Their teeth are uneven and mostly dirty. Most of them use artificial teeth. It is just the reverse in the case of the French people; their teeth are clean, even and strong. The reason for this eludes me.

For some reason this article has become long and I must stop here.

6
EDUCATION

1. Memorial to Bakhshi Gokal Chand[1]

Sir, The Managing Committee of the D.A.V. College has resolved to perpetuate the memory of the late Bakhshi Gokal Chand[2] in connection with the College either by a scholarship or scholarships or by erecting a suitable building after his name. The Committee proposes to collect Rs. 3,000 at least for the purpose although it is hoped that considering the invaluable services of the deceased and his vast popularity the sum actually raised would be much higher. It should not be at all difficult for his friends to collect a sum of Rs. 10,000 at least. The actual form of the memorial will depend upon the amount of money received for the purpose within the next 3 months. Let me hope that his friends will exert their utmost and pay the last debt of gratitude which they owe to the unique patriot and philanthropist who has just left us in bewilderment and whose place we do not know how to fill up. The Punjab is not likely to give birth to another Gokal Chand for a long time to come.

It will not be out of place to mention here that the good people of Abbottabad have already raised about 700 rupees for the provincial memorial in addition to the local memorial which they are going to build there. Hissar too has raised about the same and promises of about Rs. 800 have been made at Lahore. Then there is no time to be lost. The memorial movement ought not to linger long. Whatever is to be done ought to be accomplished at once.

Yours & c.,
Lajpat Rai

1. Letter to the editor. *The Tribune*, 14 November 1901.
2. Philanthropist and eminent Arya Samajist of Peshawar; associated with D.A.V. College movement; member, Managing Committee of D.A.V. College; supported the "cultural" section of the Lahore Arya Samaj; d. 1901.

2. On Objects and Performance of Punjab University[1]

The special objects for which the Punjab University was incorporated are given on page 35 of the last Calender (Statutes).[2] Taking them categorically, little or nothing worth speaking of has been done to achieve the first object up till now. Very few good books (whether educational or general) have been translated, prepared, or published by or at the cost of the University, and practically no encouragement has been extended to those who were inclined, as well as qualified, to do this work. Towards these objects the University spent only Rs. 570 in the year 1899-1900 out of its general funds, Rs. 5,388-4-0 having been spent in the same period under the head "Endowed Readerships and Translatorships". The University claims savings to the extent of Rs. 1,36,423 under the head "Current Account". At least Rs. 25,000 out of this amount should be devoted for the improvement and extension of vernacular literature, and an annual grant of Rs. 10,000 should be provided in the budget for at least ten years to come. These grants must be equally distributed between the 3 vernaculars of this province, viz, Urdu, Hindi and Gurmukhi, and it should be made worth the while of literary men to produce good and substantial books (both educational and general) in these vernaculars. Competent and efficient committees, composed of members who are qualified both by taste as well as by the amount of leisure which they can command, should be appointed to recommend (a) books for translation or reproduction, (b) subjects for compilation, (c) books for approval, (d) arrangements for their publication. The annual report of the University should make a special mention of the work done and results achieved by the University under this head of its duties.

The regulations for the grant of Endowed Readerships and Translatorships should be so altered as to ensure the selection of such graduates only as pledge themselves to a life of literature or teachership. The candidates, as at present selected, use their Readerships or Translatorships as stepping-stones for entering Government service or the profession of law. The period also for which these Readerships and Translatorships are tenable should be extended to 5 years at the least.

1. Memorandum submitted to the Indian Universities Commission at Lahore. *The Tribune*, 1 and 3 May 1902.

   The Indian Universities Commission headed by Thomas Raleigh, the Vice-Chancellor of Calcutta University, was appointed by Curzon to lay down rules for giving recognition to colleges and making recommendations for raising the standard of higher education in the country. However, the Universities Act enacted in 1904 resulted in making higher education expensive and officializing the administration of universities.
2. The Punjab University was incorporated in 1882.

The third object of this university is said to be to promote the "enlightened study of the Eastern classical languages and literature". The Oriental College is apparently maintained to achieve this object as well as No.5. That the Oriental College has till now substantially failed in attaining object 5 will not, I suppose, be seriously contested. In fact, it could not have been otherwise. The fact that in the last 20 years not even one student has taken his M.O.L. degree in any subject other than Sanskrit and Arabic carries its own condemnation. In Sanskrit also only one student has taken his M.O.L. all other students having taken Arabic. As for the other examinations, it sounds ridiculous to prepare students for the Arts examinations through the medium of vernaculars. The idea is not ignoble but the state of the vernaculars renders its successful realization impossible. A glance at the list of the subjects prescribed for these examinations will show the truth of this observation. To successfully deliver lectures on such subjects as higher mathematics, history, political economy, European philosophy and natural science, you require specialists of a very high order, experts in their own branches of learning, competent to express themselves in vernaculars. That it is impossible for the Oriental College to secure the services of such men at the low salaries that are now paid for the same, even if such men be available from amongst the Indian graduates, is a truth which no one is likely to deny. Not to speak of the Oriental College, even the Arts Colleges in this province have not (except in one or two instances) been able to attract specialists of the 1st and 2nd class. Under the circumstances, there is naturally a strong consensus of intelligent public opinion to the effect that this attempt has proved futile and ought to be discontinued. The growth of our vernaculars is a question of time, and unless that time arrives it seems to be a sheer waste of money to attempt to attain the impossible. The savings thus effected would be well spent towards the accomplishment of the 1st and 2nd objects, viz, the improvement and extension of the vernaculars. The first object would also be better served by the Readers and the Translators in natural science, & c., being required to deliver a number of specially prepared lectures on popular scientific subjects to popular audience in different cities of the province. These lectures might well, in the course of time, take the place of "University Extension Lectures" delivered under the auspices of English universities. As to object No. 3, I think the Oriental College has not been altogether without use, although radical changes are required if an effective realization of the object is aimed at in this branch of its work. I can only speak with regard to the teaching of Sanskrit in the Oriental College. The College has, in my opinion, supplied a class of fairly intelligent Sanskrit teachers to the schools of the province, although the system under which these gentlemen are instructed in Sanskrit is so radically defective that, the efforts of last 30 years notwithstanding, the enlightened and systematic study and knowledge of Sanskrit has not made any appreciable advance in this province. Even now, whenever a specialist is required in any of the different branches of Sanskrit philosophy, in *Vyakarana* (Grammar) or in the *Vedic* literature, you have to look to other provinces to supply the want.

One of the special objects of the D.A.V. College is to encourage and enforce the study of "classical Sanskrit". In the year 1901 it had 4 Sanskrit professors on its staff in the College Department. The senior of them was a Bengali Pundit, a distinguished scholar of the Sanskrit College, Calcutta, and a noble type of specialist in the *darshana* philosophy of India. The other two, claiming scholarly attainments in the two *Mimansas*, received their higher education at Benares. The 4th was an M.A. of the Punjab University employed to help the students in getting up their text-books for university examinations. The D.A.V. College authorities have had very frequently to advertise for specialists in Sanskrit grammar and in the recitation of *Vedic mantras*, and, almost invariably, the applicants whose claims were favourably considered were *Pundits* of other provinces who owed nothing to the Oriental College. If the Oriental College is really intended to promote an enlightened study of the classical Sanskrit, it must undergo radical changes, both in its staff of teachers as well as in the course of reading, in the quality of the former and in the system of the latter, It must have renowned Sanskrit scholars, specialists in the different branches of Sanskrit learning, on its staff, must pay them well in order to induce them to stay, and must adopt a scheme of studies which is calculated to impart sound and substantial knowledge of the Sanskrit language and literature, of its philosophy and its science, of Hindu religion and ethics, of Hindu laws and Hindu sociology. If the financial state of the University renders the realization of the scheme impossible or impracticable, then the best course would be to utilise the funds at present applied to the teaching of Eastern classics to the making of liberal grants to unaided private institutions which at present exist or which may hereafter be opened for imparting an intelligent knowledge of the same, because it should always be remembered that the principal endowments of the University having been received for these objects, they cannot be utilised for other purposes without laying the authorities open to a charge of breach of faith.

With the courses of reading prescribed for the various examinations in Sanskrit language and literature, whether on the Oriental or on the Arts side, I will deal hereafter. The treatment which the University has till now accorded to the teaching of the *Ayurvedic* system of medicine is also hardly in keeping with the importance given to the same in the original scheme of the Oriental College.

Another, rather objectionable, feature of the Oriental College is the teaching of Hindu scriptures on the system of the Oriental scholars of the West, such as Ludwig, Roth, etc. One cannot reasonably expect non-Hindu professors to follow, and regard with respect, the traditional meanings that are attached to *Vedic* texts and formulas in the commentaries of pious Hindu commentators. It is useless moreover to expect a rational understanding of the Vedas by students who have neither studied *Vedic Vyakarana* nor *Nirukta*, *Jyotish*, *Chhands*, & c., which are called the *Vedantas*, and without a knowledge of which no one can approach a proper study of the Vedas. The result is that neither professor nor student can do justice to the most holy and most revered of the Hindu scriptures. The system is open to serious objection on religious grounds. It shakes the faith of the Hindu students in their scriptures and tends to demoralise them by forcing them to learn meanings in which they do not believe, and to answer questions accordingly. In no case should Vedas form part of the courses.

On the Arts side, it is not practicable to convert the Punjab University into a teaching body, unless it is proposed to convert the Government College into a University College for preparing M.A. students preparing for science degrees. Even in that case the personnel of the Government College will have to be materially changed, and the salaries and prospects of the staff will have to be appreciably raised to induce competent scholars (both of European and Indian reputation) to accept the different chairs of literature and science. As things stand at present, the only practicable steps that can be taken immediately are:

(a) The strengthening of the Science Department of the Government College by the addition of some more chairs. There should be at least two professors of physics, two of chemistry, one of botany, one of zoology, one of geology, and one of physiology. The Government College time-table of the science classes will show that at present the science professor can only spare three periods a week to lecture on physics to the M.A. class and so on.

(b) The throwing open of the lectures of these professors to the students of all the affiliated colleges.

It is neither necessary nor expedient to adopt the system of inter-collegiate lectures. The differences in the abilities and the capacities of the professors and lecturers at present employed in different colleges of this province are not so marked as to render the system of inter-collegiate lectures of much practical use. In fact, the number of students that receive their education in the 5 principal Arts Colleges of Lahore is so large, as compared with the number of professors who are engaged to lecture to them, that at present the idea does not seem to be worth even a trial. Besides, in the Punjab there is only one non-denominational college. All others are denominational, each having a religious mission of its own. It will not, therefore, be free from objection to adopt a system of inter-collegiate lectures in these colleges. It is not right to assume that all European professors are superior to all native professors, and when I say that, I do not make an exception even in the case of teaching English.

In the Lahore colleges the system of teaching English seems to me to be very defective. It mainly consists in giving notes and in teaching by paraphrases. One of the most popular professors of English in Lahore, a European, has made a reputation for giving an equivalent expression for almost every word that occurs in a text-book. He solves every difficulty for the students, and enjoys a popularity in coaching up students for that subject. On the other hand, I know, as a matter of fact, that students enjoying the privilege of learning English at the feet of European professors have often been anxious to get hold of the copy-books of the students of the D.A.V. College containing notes given by the Indian professors of English employed in that College.

In my humble opinion a professor of language and literature can effectively teach only a limited number of students. The Punjab graduate is generally deficient in the knowledge of English, the main causes of which are the following:

(a) The foundations are very slender. A Punjabi boy reading in a Government Primary School has to study three foreign languages—Urdu, Persian and English. To this may be added Arabic or Sanskrit if he belongs to a Mahomedan or Hindu denominational school respectively. He has thus to keep four languages up to the Entrance.

(b) The service of the Education Department is not sufficiently paying to attract graduates of high standing.

(c) The number of students with each teacher in the schools is generally too large to allow of a language being efficiently taught.

(d) The strain to which a student is put in learning history and geography by rote is too heavy to allow him a margin to devote time and thought to the cultivation of a taste for accurate writing and speaking.

(e) The teaching in the colleges also is not as sound as it should be.

(f) The number of text-books that a student has to get up, and upon which a professor has to lecture is too large to allow of the professor and the student devoting sufficient attention to the art of accurate writing and speaking.

(g) The text-books in the School Department admit of improvements.

The teaching of Sanskrit in the Punjab is even more defective than that of English. Neither the Department nor the University seems to have yet realized that nobody can acquire even ordinarily correct knowledge of the Sanskrit language without having a good knowledge of grammar as the basis of his studies in Sanskrit. In this matter the Punjab is at a great disadvantage as compared with the other provinces, where a good knowledge of the real vernacular of the province and its grammar precedes the study of Sanskrit. A knowledge of the Bengali, Marathi, Gujarati or Hindi grammar makes the task of a student of Sanskrit easier, while a knowledge of Urdu grammar makes it still more difficult and arduous, if nothing else.

In the Punjab University an effort is made to teach *Rigveda* to students who have not studied *Laghu Kaumudi*, not to speak of Panini, *Nirukta*, and the *Mahabhashya*.

For the Punjab University Arts examinations a student of Sanskrit proceeds to read modern Sanskrit drama and poetry on the slender basis of Dr. Bhandarkar's[3] 1st and 2nd books of grammar prescribed for Entrance examination.

In the text-books on Sanskrit prescribed for the F.A. and B.A. one finds no trace of grammar, although there is a mention of grammar in the subjects of examination where grammar occupies only a subsidiary part of the paper on poetry, the whole paper carrying 75 marks out of 150. The same is the case with the examination for the degree of B.A. From modern prose and poetry in Sanskrit a student at once proceeds to the Vedas, overleaping the *Sutra*, the *Epic* and the *Brahmana* periods of Sanskrit literature. It is no wonder then that the Punjab graduate's knowledge of Sanskrit is most shabby and hollow, and does not even enable him to understand the ordinary book of Sanskrit beyond the text-books read by him for the examination. The case is different with Arabic. The rule prescribes standard books in Arabic grammar both in the Entrance and the F.A. and there is no attempt to force a student to take a leap from modern Arabic to ancient and archaic, covering a distance of several centuries, possibly several thousands of years. The same can be said of Persian. Why should there be an exception in the case of Sanskrit alone is beyond comprehension, especially when Sanskrit is admittedly one of the most, if not the most difficult, the most complex and the most grammatical of all the languages, and still more so when the Sanskrit of different epochs is governed by different formulae and rules of grammar, and when the transition of the language from the archaic to the modern form covers an almost unimaginable distance of time and embraces a vast literature marked by the special peculiarities of each period in the history of its development.

In my opinion a book on Sanskrit grammar should be prescribed for each of the Arts examinations, and substantial proportion of marks should be assigned to this branch of the subject.

The hymns of the Vedas should be omitted from the degree courses and a graduated course of instruction in Sanskrit philosophy and Sanskrit laws should be introduced, or special courses of study, consisting of selections on the model of the Arabic course for the B.A., should be prepared. It may be noted that no portion of the Quran forms part of the selections prescribed for the B.A. examination.

3. D.R. Bhandarkar (1875-1950); famous Indologist and author of several books on ancient Indian history and culture; served in the Archaeological Department of Government of India in 1911; co-editor of *Indian Antiquity*, 1911; taught Indian history and culture at Calcutta University from 1917 to 1936; Fellow of Bhandarkar Oriental Institute, Poona.

The 3rd subject, which is the most neglected in the Arts examination, is "history and political economy". The way in which the candidates are examined in this subject is most faulty. Every Indian graduate should know at least the history of his own country thoroughly. 1stly, the teaching of the subject should be more intelligent in the school, although I am opposed to any paper being set in history and geography in the Entrance examination. This will to a great extent lighten the strain that is now put on the memory of the students, who will have more time for acquiring real proficiency in the languages. 2ndly, in the higher university examinations it should be included in the list of compulsory subjects. So far as the First Arts is concerned the subjects should be divided as follows.

(a) Histories of India and England;

(b) General outlines of the Histories of Ancient Greece and Rome; and

(c) Elementary Political Economy.

In the degree examination one should expect a very thorough and critical knowledge of the periods that may be prescribed. I have a little experience of the teaching of history of India, and I can say that at present, with the prescribed text books on history, the students resent rather than appreciate good and critical lectures based on information other than that given in text-books. Such lectures are more an infliction to them than a treat. Experience tells me that they generally pass by committing to memory ordinary school books, including catechism, & c.

Examinations

(1) (a) I would abolish the Middle School examination altogether.

(b) I would retain the Matriculation for the general body of students, but I think partial trial should be given to the system of allowing affiliated colleges to admit non-matriculate students to their classes by holding an examination of their own, as is now done by the Civil Engineering College, Roorkee.

(2) I would confine the Matriculation to the following compulsory subjects.

(a) English—In the Arts examinations of the London University, English, History and Geography form one subject with English,

(b) An Eastern classical language,

(c) Mathematics (Arithmetic and two books of *Euclid*, Algebra up to simple equations), and

(d) Vernacular.

(3) I would retain the F.A. with the following subjects as compulsory.

(a) English,

(b) An Eastern classical language,

(c) History and Political Economy, and

(d) One of the following: Mathematics, Philosophy and Science.

(4) After the F.A. I would allow the students to specialize and select only one subject for the B.A.

(5) In this case only may the Degree examination be divided into a Pass course and an Honours course; otherwise not.

(6) I am opposed to the appointment of Moderators except in the case of the Entrance examination.

(7) I am of opinion that a student who passes in all subjects but one, and in this latter fails by 5 marks only, should be passed without re-examination, or should be allowed to appear next year in that one subject only.

(8) The examiners should be selected from the professors and teachers of the affiliated colleges of other universities.

(9) If more subjects than one are to form the course for the B.A. degree, then students should be allowed to pass their examinations by instalments in one subject at a time.

(10) All affiliated colleges, specially the colleges teaching up to the B.A., should be well represented on committees that select examiners. At present the private colleges are not represented at all on the committee that selects examiners on the Arts side.

(11) The dates of the medical examinations are very objectionable, and have been fixed with an utter disregard of the interests of students.

In the Punjab the appointment of Fellows has probably been much more anomalous than anywhere else. A number of persons have from time to time found seats on the Senate who could hardly be called educated. A good deal of patronage is exercised in the appointments to seats on the Senate. The Principal of the D.A.V. College, numerically the largest College in the matter of education, had till only recently no seat on the Senate.

The College was recognized in 1889, and the B.A. classes were opened in 1893. Since then the College had been showing excellent results in all the university examinations, including M.A. in Sanskrit, but still the Principal was not taken on the Senate until towards the end of 1899; the matter had to be represented to the authorities, and the Vice-Chancellor and the Chancellor were pleased to give a favourable consideration to this representation. Some of the senior professors of the D.A.V. College have been successfully preparing students for the Degree examinations for the last ten years, but they hold no seats on the Senate, while an examination will show that American and English professors of the Government and Mission Colleges have generally been appointed fellows after only a year or two's service in India. Some of the members of the Punjab Commission (Covenanted) are appointed as Fellows who hardly take any interest in the University or its affairs.

The number of covenanted members of the Punjab Commission who are Fellows ex-officio is abnormally and unnecessarily large. I do not think in the Punjab any difficulty has been experienced on the ground of the Senate being unwieldy. The number of members of the Senate should be about 125 or 150. The Principals of all colleges affiliated up to the B.A. and all professors and lecturers of more than 5 years standing should be ex-officio Fellows of the University. The governing bodies of all aided and unaided colleges should be represented on the Senate according to the size and importance of the respective institutions. The number of representatives allotted to each to be fixed by the Senate every third year. The election of the representatives to be made by the governing bodies subject to the approval of the Senate. Graduates to have the right of electing a fixed percentage of the whole strength of the Senate. All M.A.s and B.A.s of ten years standing to have the right of voting in these elections. All others to be nominated by Government, by virtue of their reputation of office, subject to the condition that only men of literary attainments and those actively interested in the course of education, or likely to take active interest in the same, are appointed. Due regard should be paid to the inclinations and tastes of the persons selected and to the leisure at their command to enable them to render effective service. Fellowships should not be terminable except in the case of elected ones, but liable to be vacated by continued absence from meetings for more than a prescribed period.

The present representation of the Arts colleges at Lahore on the Senate stands thus:

Government College—6 out of a total strength of 8
Forman Christian College—5 out of a total strength of 12
D.A.V. College—1 out of a total strength of 12
Islamia College—1 out of a total strength of 8

Principals of all the 1st grade Arts colleges at Lahore should be ex-officio members of the Syndicate, as well as Principals of the Medical and the Law Colleges (if the latter is to be retained in its present form).

Besides these, the Director of Public Instruction, the Vice-Chancellor, and the Registrar shall be ex-officio members, and so may be the Deans of Faculties if they are not already members of the Syndicate in some other capacity. The rest may be elected by the Faculties as at present. The total number not to exceed 25 and not to fall short of 20. The principal Arts colleges at Lahore are just now represented on the Syndicate as follows:

Government College	–	3
Forman College	–	3
D.A.V. College	–	1
Islamia College	–	0

In my opinion it is neither advisable nor expedient to provide for a school of theology in connection with the Indian universities, nor is it desirable to found a chair of Comparative Religion in connection with each University. The promotion of a study of Comparative Religion must be left to private colleges.

On the Arts and Oriental sides the number of Faculties should coincide with the number of subjects for the teaching of which provision is made in the several colleges constituting the University. For instance, there should be a separate Faculty for each of the following.

(1) English,
(2) Mathematics,
(3) History, Geography and Political Economy,
(4) Philosophy,
(5) Physical Science,
(6) Sanskrit,
(7) Arabic, and
(8) Persian.

Under the present arrangement it often happens that specialists in some branch of knowledge are controlled by others not interested in, or not possessing information on, that subject. Faculties should certainly be strengthened by the addition of recognized teachers and distinguished graduates in the special subjects of the Faculty.

Boards of studies as at present constituted do not seem to be of much use. The present rules of the University as to who are to be allowed to join its examinations are sufficient and adequate; no alterations are needed.

Every college should be required to make adequate provisions for the physical welfare of its students.

As for their moral welfare, the boarding-house system should be extended, and except in the case of students having guardians in the city, all should be required to live in boarding-houses. I am not favourably disposed towards the system of licensed lodgings. This would lead to laxity of supervision and discipline, and encourage a tendency to evade the rules of residence in boarding-houses.

As for the fostering of a genuine university life, I would make the following suggestions.

(a) Inter-collegiate debates and meetings, plays and dinners, should be encouraged.
(b) The University should provide:
    (1) A common playground,
    (2) A good and substantial library and reading-room, and
    (3) A Scientific museum.

They should be open to students of all the affiliated colleges.

(c) The Sports Committee should be better organised and the colleges should be self-represented in fair proportion to the number of students in each.

There should certainly be some rules of affiliation but

(a) There should be no restriction to fees.

(b) Stress should not be laid on the recognition of professors and teachers by the University.

(c) There should not be any interference in the rules of management and internal discipline.

3. Education—the Core Issue[1]

Having been a constant reader of Indian journals, and an active sympathiser with the so-called Indian political party for the last twenty years, since the beginning of my university career, I have come to the conclusion that the Indian political party has accepted the expression "politics" to be synonymous with "agitation". Agitation, constant, unending agitation for political rights, may be one of the means to be adopted by a nation to obtain them; but agitation alone cannot express what is summed up in the word "politics". Agitation only deals with the present and is based on current events. The weight that is to be attached to it must be derived from the facts and figures supplied by the present or by its immediate past. But politics concerns itself with the building up of the nation with a view to its future. It calls to its aid the past and the present, imagines and designs the future, and then proceeds to find materials for the construction of the latter. As such, it is a religion, and a science, much higher, both in its conception and in its sphere, than mere political agitation. The true politician, as I understand the word, has a creed or faith; the agitator has none. The latter has "instincts, passions, often genuine in their origin, but easily deviated, or corrupted by disappointments or the seductions of power, as soon as years have cooled his enthusiasm and his youthful blood". The politician is one "to whom observation has shown the existence of a grave social grievance or immorality, to whom intelligence has shown a remedy, and to whom the voice of conscience, enlightened by a religious conception of the human mission, has revealed the inexorable duty of devoting himself to the application of the

1. V.C. Joshi (ed.), *Lala Lajpat Rai—Writings and Speeches*, Vol. 1 (Delhi, 1966), pp. 26-30; first published in *East and West* (Simla) of August 1902.

remedy and extirpation of the evil". The agitator, or the reactionist, as the writer whom I am quoting calls him, is "one urged by a sentiment of rebellion against injustice innate in mind gifted with any power and very often by the pain and irritation consequent on being unable to assume his true place in the social order, to seek to better his own condition with the help of all who suffer under similar distress". The true politician "will pursue his forward march, whatever his individual position be, so long as the evil endures. The agitator will probably stop short as soon as the overthrow of the power attacked shall have satisfied his self-love and mitigated the sense of rebellion within him." The aim of the one is always to found, that of the other is to destroy. The first is a man of progress, the second of opposition. "With the first it is a question of principle, while the second glories in details. The first has a constructive program, while the second resorts to that analysis which only decomposes and dissolves. The true politician may fail to achieve his aim; but if he succeeds once, his success is permanent, while the victories of a mere agitator, though sometimes brilliant, are not sure to be durable. The former invokes rights first and then duty. The acts of the former are influenced by a strong religious leaning, even when, through an intellectual contradiction, he professes the reverse, while the latter is irreligious and materialist, even when he professes the name of God; with him, i.e. the latter, the present always tops the future, and material interest takes precedence of moral progress. The men of the first class, accustomed to willing sacrifice, labour less for the generation that lives around them than for the generations to come; the triumph of the ideas they cast upon the world is slow, but infallible and decisive; the men of the second class often win victories for their contemporaries, but their children enjoy none of the fruits. The first are the prophets of humanity, the second are the mere agitators of mankind." An agitation can always be met with a counter agitation, and thereby rendered powerless, but principles are irresistible, and none can demolish them, if true. The future of India requires the services of politicians, and not those of mere agitators. The future of the nation requires solidity of principles and purity of methods as its basis, and not mere diplomatic make-shifts or doubtful tactics. India wants men who, whether in good fortune or in bad fortune, nor minding temporary reverses or difficulties, will lead her right through the goal, who will neither feel buoyant through the flush of preliminary success, nor feel daunted by temporary failures. Such are the men that are wanted to found and lead the Indian political party; not men of power, not men of riches, not men of titles, but men of conscience, men of energy, men of will, men who do not know how to give way to temptation or allurements, or how to be cowed down by threats and dangers, and last, but not least, men who do not know how to acknowledge a defeat. Let them chalk out a faith, a programme, and their countrymen, many of whom are ardent in their love for their country, will kiss their feet and follow them right through, in good luck or in bad luck. The first thing that a politician has thus to do is to consult the future of his nation, so far as his vision can reach, and then to devise the means by which future, as imagined by him, can be reached. The second thing which a politician has to do is to choose his creed and promulgate it. Let him first determine whether he is an absolute monarchist, a democrat or one for constitutional monarchy; because it is only then that he can, if at all, think of the proper methods which are to lead the nation to the desired end and because, in any case, the nation has to fit itself for its destiny. As the aim is, so must the means be. The political vision of the Indians, just now, only sees constitutional monarchy within its horizon, and from the very nature of things they cannot, for a long time to come, extend their horizon further. Before them is the spectacle of a nation ruled by a constitutional monarchy, happy, prosperous and politically great. This nation rules over them, and although itself subject to constitutional monarchy, it rules India in the spirit of an absolute despotic monarchy. The only difference is that here in India this despotism does not rest in one individual, but in a class. The first duty of an Indian politician, therefore, even if he is a democrat, is to prepare the nation to be fit to ask for a constitution, and to do so with reason. The first necessary step is not to go in for this demand, or to settle the form of the demand, but to create those forces, the operation of which will justify the nation in advancing its claims. In my humble opinion, the first axiom which every Indian politician ought to take to heart, is that no nation is worthy of any political status if it cannot distinguish between begging such rights and claiming them. A beggar can be turned out of doors without redress, but one who has to be respected as a creditor cannot. No debtor can honestly and effectively ignore a creditor, but every charitably-inclined man can ignore a beggar whom he does not like, or whom he does not consider deserving. No one can deny that, just now, ours is a position of beggars. We live on the charity of our rulers. They not only rule over us, but it is they who think for us, who manufacture for us, who preach to us, and who provide for us.

In a self-governed country, or in a healthy body politic, the Government and its subjects are one and interchangeable. They have their respective and correlative duties by foreigners, the rulers and the subjects are not one. But the aim of all true politicians ought to be to bring about this unity. The great gulf between the subjects and their rulers can only be bridged by bringing the former up to the level of the latter in intelligence, in culture, in moral calibre, in capacity for self-sacrifice and in subordination to high ideals. The nearer the mass of subjects approach their rulers in these qualities, the easier the solution of the political problem. The nearer you reach them, the smaller the number of those duties which really belong to the subjects; but which, in the present state of society, have to be performed by the State. In a perfect commonwealth the real sovereignty rests with the people. The State exists for them and rules in their name, and thus has a smaller and more limited volume of rights than those vested in these so-called subjects. Hence, real political progress consists in befitting the nation to take up those duties which, though at present performed by the ruling class, ought, in a state of political health, to be discharged by the people themselves. The position thus analysed resolves itself into an educational problem. View it from whatever point you choose, religious, moral, intellectual, social, or industrial, the question of India's progress is a question of education. This is, so to say, the question of questions upon the right solution of which hang the destinies of the nation, viz. how to educate the people so as to befit them for the performance of those duties, a proper discharge of which alone can secure for them their position in the commonwealth.

But let my countrymen remember that this momentous question of the day is not one which can be solved by speeches and resolutions only. We must be prepared to undergo great sacrifices, if we are really earnest about the future of the country, and should put our united shoulders to the wheel, to drag the car of progress to its destination, cost what it may.

The car is a heavy one, and those who care to join in carrying it must be men of strong convictions, indomitable will, irresistible energy and untiring perseverance; they must be men of action and men of honour. Let us resolve to spare all we can by living simple lives, for furthering the cause of true education in this country, as it is only useful, solid and all-covering education upon which the nation can build a character and establish a claim to be the arbiter of its own fortunes. No amount of sacrifice ought to be too great to attain this end and the sooner we realise this, the better for ourselves as well as for the nation at large.

4. Progress of D.A.V. College not Satisfactory[1]

We do not think it will be improper in the least to draw the attention of the supporters of the D.A.V. College to the great financial progress of the Mohammedan Anglo-Oriental College at Aligarh[2] and also that of the Central

1. Reproduced from *The Indian Social Reformer* of 30 August 1903.
2. The Mohammedan Anglo-Oriental College founded by Syed Ahmed Khan at Aligarh in 1875 later became Aligarh Muslim University.

Hindu College, Benares.[3] The former is a standing monument of the religious and national zeal of the Mohammedans. With the support of their ruling princes, and with the best, the noblest and the richest of Mohammedan nobility and gentry at the back of the College, the Mohammedans are, at the present time, in the possession of an educational institution, of which they may well be proud. Its financial position is the best and the most secure of all the native institutions in the country. Its buildings are the most splendid of all. Sympathy with it is wide and extensive and workers for the College many, capable and self-sacrificing. With the growing attachment of the Mohammedans for this national institution of theirs, it is almost impossible for any other native institution in the country to achieve that financial position which the Aligarh College has already secured for itself, not to speak of leaving it behind, in that respect. Still, it is a matter of satisfaction that the Central Hindu College, Benares, should have established its position so well that there seems to be no doubt, now, about its financial prosperity. With the eloquence of Mrs. Besant[4] at its command, with the sympathies and patronage of some of the Ruling Chiefs of the community already at its service, with the support of the growing community of Theosophists which already counts upon its list many a man of lead, light, influence, affluence, position and wealth, there need be no misgivings at all about its future.

The Hindus have no reason to be dissatisfied if the Central Hindu College can, in the course of the next few years, come out as financially the second best institution of its kind in India. The so-called bigger donations of May 1903 alone amounted to over Rs. 30,000, including various large sums from places so distantly situated as Madras, Bombay and Cambay. We may at once point out that this brilliant success of the Hindu College, Benares, fills our heart with joy because we think we may reasonably consider it as a tangible sign of a growing sense of religious nationality amongst the Hindus all over India. But this is not the only feeling which the good luck of the Aligarh and the Benares Colleges arouses in us and we shall be suppressing the truth if we were to say so. The successes of these Colleges naturally make us think of our own and on

3. The Central Hindu College of Benares founded in 1898 by the efforts of Annie Besant and cooperation of the Maharaja of Benares and others later became the Benares Hindu University.
4. Annie Besant (1847-1933); British theosophist who came to India in 1893 and worked for the cause of Indian women and education; founded Central Hindu College, Banaras, in 1898 and a girls' school in 1904; president, Theosophical Society, 1907-33; founded *Commonweal* (weekly) and *New India* (daily) in 1914; founded Home Rule League for India in 1916; interned in 1917; President, Indian National Congress, Calcutta, 1917; left Congress in 1921; works include *Religious Problem of India* (1909), *How India Wrought for Freedom* (1915), *Wake up India –A Plea for Social Reform* (1918) and *India, Bond or Free – A World Problem* (1926).

a close examination of our heart, the feeling that we find uppermost in our heart is not one of jealousy (God forbid that we be jealous of the good luck of others and more particularly when one of them is so near and dear to us) but one of keen disappointment at the littleness of success that has met our efforts, extending over a period of about seventeen years. Looking at the vast amount of energy put forth by the promoters and the supporters of the College, at the unique sacrifice of its devoted Principal,[5] at the great privations willingly and cheerfully undergone for its sake by some of its noblest workers, we are simply amazed at the insignificant response of those for whom the institution has, during the last seventeen years, proved nothing short of a blessing. Fanatics may say what they please, enthusiasts may fall foul for its having failed to bring about the revival of *Vedic* life by this time, interested people may well laugh at its having only added to the misery of the country by lowering the price of the graduate and the lawyer and the critic might well point out its shortcomings, but the fact remains uncontroverted that, but for the existence of the D.A.V. College in Lahore, numerous Hindu students would have been deprived of that education and of the position that follows it, which fell to the lot of their predecessors and which is now being largely claimed by the Mohammedan young men of this province.

5. Hans Raj (1864-1938); educated at Mission School and Punjab University College; came under the influence of Swami Dayanand in college days; honorary Headmaster, D.A.V. School, 1886-89, later its Principal when it became College, 1889-1911; leader of the College section in the Arya Samaj split, 1892-93; President, Arya Pratinidhi Sabha, 1891; President, D.A.V. College Managing Committee, 1912-19; actively associated with the famine relief work; took leading part in the *Shuddhi* movement.

5. Scheme for Education of Indians Abroad[1]

All interested in my scheme for education of Indians abroad please note that it is at present impossible for me to reply to the numerous letters and enquiries that are being addressed to me. As soon as my current work allows I intend to draw up my scheme and to include in it all information required by gentlemen interested in the question or by intending scholars themselves. This shall be printed and it shall be open to the public to apply for copies of it. At present I may be pardoned for not attending to individual enquiries as I am very busy with urgent work in hand.

I may, however, inform all concerned that according to American laws of immigration, no 3rd class (steerage) passenger is allowed to land unless (a) he

1. Statement to the press, *The Panjabee* of 11 December 1905.

has at the time of landing at least 50 dollars (equal to Rs. 150) in his possession (b) he possesses a certificate of having been vaccinated or submits to vaccination in the steamer, and (c) is otherwise quite healthy. Every 3rd class passenger is as a rule subjected to a strict medical examination and men having diseased eyes or bald heads have very little chance of being passed as fit for landing.

Young men intending to proceed to America should not venture to do so without getting the fullest particulars about the laws of immigration in force there. These restrictions do not, as a rule, apply to 1st and 2nd class passenger. Other Punjab papers are requested to notice this letter in the interests of young men desirous of proceeding to America for education.

6. Education in America[1]

Sir, Some time ago I promised to publish all the information I possessed on the above subject for the use of intending students and guardians in the columns of the *Panjabee*. I am sorry I should have been prevented from doing so by more pressing engagements which could not be deferred. Moreover, I had been expecting some books from America in order to be able to give as complete information as possible. Unfortunately, these books were delayed, and I received only some of them by the last two mails. I have now made over all these books to a young and earnest friend of mine to compile all the necessary information in a pamphlet form. It is hoped that this pamphlet will be ready before long, and when ready it will be available for sale. In the meantime some selections from the different Calendars are being published in the *Panjabee*. These Calendars will eventually be placed in the office of the Managing Committee of the D.A.V. College where they will be available for reference and inspection on such conditions as the said Committee might fix.

Hoping this arrangement will prove satisfactory.

I remain

Yours &c.,
Lajpat Rai

1. Letter to the editor dated 2 February 1906 published in *The Panjabee* of 7 February 1906.

7. Education of Poor Indian Students in America[1]

As my stay in the United States[2] was very short and I had little time to make thorough enquiries myself, I have considered it fit to put myself in communication with certain American friends asking their advice on the subject of sending poor Indian students for education to America who may look forward to work for their support during the period of their study there. I have received two replies by the last mail, both of which are rather discouraging. I, however, consider it fair to give publicity to them for the information of all concerned.[3] As I am collecting all the necessary information on the subject I will advise intending students to wait further replies from the friends whom I have addressed.

There should be no hurry in the matter.

1. Letter the editor dated 6 February 1906 published in *The Panjabee* of 7 February 1906.
2. Lajpat Rai visited the U.S.A. in September 1905. See also *ante*, section 4, sub-section 4.
3. See the following item.

8. Problems Faced by Indian Students in America[1]

Dear Sir,

I am glad to be in a position to give a few excerpts from two letters that I have received since I wrote to you last on this subject. One of these letters is written by a very sincere and devoted friend of India who has been to America and knows the country well. She writes:

> Dear Mr. Lajpat Rai,
>
> . . . has written to me regarding the problem of the Panjabee boys who wish to go to America for education. I am in deep sympathy with your scheme, but at the same time can quite understand the nervousness which it raises in the mind of . . . who feels neither so young nor so strong as formerly! She writes to me: "To send students over, with enough to pass the customs and be admitted ($50), is nothing, as you will know, in this

1. Letter to the editor published in *The Panjabee* of 21 February 1906.

country, for untrained unserviceable lads . It is true that the Japanese have earned their way, but by making themselves the most competent servants, and doing menial service. They give all their time in service, as cooks, butlers, valets, for 6 months or more, out of a year. Then study the next six. But as they command fancy wages—$50, $60, or $70 a month, this is possible. They have done the same in the Navy."

I do not think you should be altogether sorry that . . . does not feel justified in promising to mother the boys. For to my mind an Indian student, if he has the right stuff in him at all, gains more by being thrown entirely on his resources than by having a powerful friend.

Personally, I would even think it better to make the boys scatter on landing, to hew out each his own path, as an individual than to keep them in a flock. Anything to make them brave, resourceful, enterprising, that is the first power. Social cohesiveness for cooperation ought to come, I think, second.

I am sure that the boys you choose will have special qualities of physical and mental fitness for the task before them.

In any case, their best friend in America would be one who was poor like themselves, helping them as a friend and brother, not as rich lady (the latter help, in America, is apt in my opinion, to do infinitely more harm than good!). And so I send you the last letter I received from a student in whom I am myself deeply interested, who has been working since the beginning of 1903, first in Japan, and then in America, entirely on his own resources, and who has prolonged his stay, primarily for the sake of aiding and placing boys who go from India to the United States for practical education. He has 'roughed it' in all possible ways and knows the ins and outs of every experience, and besides this, he has the strong national feeling and burning desire to help others, which are the necessary moral safeguards in the West.

Please write to him direct, dear Mr. Lajpat Rai . . . and if he advises you to send the boys to the Pacific coast *via* China and Japan instead of the other way round, do not fail to be guided by him. He is a very high caste Brahmin by birth . . . but he went to Japan as a deck passenger. . . and Swami Sadananda, who tried the same experience later, says it is perfectly easy, taking one's own supplies of food, to do this I imagine, moreover, that this mode of travel is made easier if 2 or 3 go together, and I fancy that it gives one more chance of mixing with foreigners than any other. Of course, between Japan and California, something less exposed would probably be necessary.

If you should decide to do this, however, I should strongly advise you to give the boys a little money to spend in seeing something of

China and Japan, *en route*. There are Indian traders at most places, I fancy, if only one could find them out, who might help in this.

Very sincerely and faithfully yours,
"x x"

I cull the following from the letter of the Indian student referred to in the above letter.

Dear,

I do not remember whether I did reply to your last note. However, having been very busy during the vacation I had very little time.

Truly, a man cannot learn all his time in schools especially struggling for his existence and bearing all expenses. I do fully realize it but what I want is to be resourceful on general subjects of scientific knowledge so that I may turn to use whatever I lay my hands on. I think this is absolutely necessary to start with any work in India. Of course, I am very anxious to launch myself into some practical field of activity at this momentous occasion in our life in India but I have to control myself and prepare for some useful purpose. The hard struggle gives, no doubt, a man power of great value, yet it is very saddening to see how much time it takes up from an aspiring and advancing man. I do not see yet whether these losses are to be fully compensated. Now, as regards my own position, I need yet full one year of 12 months at least to satisfy myself but in order to have the full advantage of a year's study I have to wait for another more year simply to get my money means. In this way, my days are being prolonged to such indefinite time but it can't be helped in my present situation.

From the above address, you will see that I am back to California. In Oregon I did collect 6 students there; all of them are in some useful industrial line. They are catching the national ideas very nicely. At present there are about 75 students all over the United States. I have been corresponding with each of them and trying to bring all under an organization. In a few weeks something will be definitely settled.

However, Mrs. . . . has been very kind to me and asked me to go over to Boston since last year but as yet I have not been able to do so. The reasons are that I intend to finish those studies that I have undertaken and for which this Pacific coast has best opportunities. Besides, my idea of leaving some boys all along this coast having succeeded to a certain extent,

> I had to postpone my going to Boston. Moreover, I am always afraid to take anybody's help for my personal living and cause. I can have claim to ask only when I will be directly connected with India's work. I hope you would kindly write to her explaining my position so that she may not misunderstand me.

No comments are needed as I am publishing all this for the information of those concerned.

Yours &c.,
Lajpat Rai

9. Punjabi Students and Higher Studies in America[1]

Since I wrote to you last I have received two more letters from which I quote below. The first is from an Indian Mohammedan who has been residing in New York for several years past and lives by journalism. He writes as follows:

> I should not advise any young man to come over here from India, unless he knows English well and is prepared to do manual work and thus obtain his living and also learn some profession. Young Japanese come to America, become domestic servants, learn the language, save money and then join some of the Universities. It is not uncommon here that American medical students become waiters in the summer at fashionable resorts and thus earn their college fees when they join them in winter.

The second letter is from the Director of the Lewis Institute, Chicago, who writes as below:

> I should say that it is impracticable, if not impossible, for a young foreigner to support himself in Chicago and get a systematic education at the same time. As may be seen from the enclosed circular, the night classes at the Lewis Institute are designed to be of assistance to young men and women who work in the daytime. Those who are working along mechanical lines by day are able to supplement their practice with some theory at night.

1. Letter to the editor published in *The Panjabee* of 3 March 1906.

Those profit most by night instruction whose ability and general education have enabled them to secure positions where more education leads to further advancement.

I think the time has come when we can draw our own conclusions from the correspondence that has heretofore been published on the subject. The net result seems to be that while all Indians at present residing or studying in America are anxious to see their number increased, the general tone of all the letters received from American friends may fairly be said to be discouraging. On my own part, I am inclined to attach more value to the opinion of Indians who speak from personal experience and who have worked their own way. It must, however, be said that it is not an easy job to labour for one's own education in a foreign country. I am of opinion that an experiment should be tried by selecting a few able-bodied, fairly well-educated Panjabees to proceed to America *via* the Pacific. They should be provided with Rs. 1,000 each. Rs. 300 ought to suffice for travelling expenses to take them to the western States of the U.S. of America. With the help of their countrymen, now studying in different parts of these districts, I hope they will be able to get work to enable them to devote certain parts of the year to educating themselves. This will, necessarily, result in a longer stay in the United States than would otherwise be necessary if they were free to devote the whole of their time to study, living at their own expense, that is, getting money for their support and education from people at home (India). But everyone, who chooses this course, must be prepared to face trials and privations and no one, not in possession of robust health and strong physique and a will to overcome all difficulties, should make the attempt.

10. State of Education in India[1]

High Education

It has now more than abundantly been established that the efficiency of a nation depends upon the amount and nature of brain power which it can put forth in the affairs of life. In an address delivered some two years ago, Sir John Lockyier, the illustrious President of the British Association, traced conclusively and

1. Published in three instalments in *The Panjabee* of 7, 21 and 25 July 1906.

convincingly the intimate relation that exists between the provision made by a nation for the higher education of its people and the position taken by that nation in the ceaseless competition between the great countries of the world. Relying upon facts and figures, he compared the educational facilities and the intellectual output of Great Britain and Ireland with those of its rivals, Germany and the United States, and came to the conclusion that the latter were much in advance of the former. Nay, he went a step further and held out young Japan as an example to be followed with profit in the matter of intellectual efforts. Those who are in touch with the current literature of the West must have been struck by the extreme importance which all the civilized nations of the world have, by experience, begun to attach to education as the foundation of all national greatness both in point of wealth as well as of intellect. If then in the struggle of life, education and educational efforts are matters of supreme importance to advanced, independent and self-governing nations like the English, the German and the American, it only stands to reason that they are of still greater importance to a country like India where ignorance and superstition reign supreme, where penury and poverty are the order of the day, where want and starvation are generally prominent, where independence of thought and action is almost unknown, and where the destinies of the nation are completely in the hands and at the mercy of a handful of foreigners who, in spite of all the generosity of mind and benevolence of intentions that they can put forth in the government of this country, are loath to admit the sons of the soil to any decent share in the management of the affairs of their own land. In a country where the economic circumstances brought about by an alien rule force the people to look to other countries for even the necessities of life, where the unlimited resources provided by a bountiful Providence are closed to the sons of the soil and are only accessible to clever, energetic, and enterprising foreigners, where the wealth of the country is being daily drained out of the country and where a fairly intelligent population are for want of education and opportunities being reduced to the position of drawers of water and hewers of wood, education, I say, is a question of life and death. Our future principally depends upon the amount and the sort of education we shall receive.

Having once put the educational machinery into motion our rulers have of late been showing signs of great dissatisfaction with the results. The history of English education in this country shows that originally the framers of government educational policy were actuated partly by selfish and partly by philanthropic and high motives. To quote the words of the Government of India resolution of 1904:

> They regarded it as a sacred duty to confer upon the natives of India those vast moral and material blessings which flow from the general diffusion

> of useful knowledge. They hoped by means of education to extend the influence which the government was exerting for the suppression of demoralizing practices, by enlisting in its favour the general sympathy of the native mind. *They also sought to create a supply of public servants to whose probity, offices of trust might with increased confidence be committed*, and to promote the material interests of the country by stimulating its inhabitants to develop its vast resources.

The italics are mine. This policy appears to have been faithfully carried out up to 1882, by which time the outturn of the educational activity in the land had come to be immensely in excess of the requirements of the administration merely. To quote the resolution again:

> The growth of schools and colleges proceeded most rapidly between 1871 and 1882, and was further augmented by the development of the Municipal system, and by the Acts which were passed from 1865 onwards providing for the imposition of local cesses which might be applied to the establishment of schools. By the year 1882, there were more than two million and a quarter of pupils under instruction in public institutions. The Commission of 1882-83 furnished a most copious and valuable report upon the state of education as then existing, made a careful inquiry into the measures which had been taken in pursuance of the Despatch of 1854, and submitted further detailed proposals for carrying out the principles of that Despatch. *They advised increased reliance upon, and systematic encouragement of, private effort* and their recommendations were approved by the Government of India.

The italics are again mine. This was the first step towards reaction. The Anglo-Indian bureaucracy raised a cry against high education and bitterly complained that the Government was entirely wrong in spending large sums out of their resources on high education. It was thus laid down as a principle of policy to gradually withdraw from the work of secondary and high education and confine the energies of the State to the task of extending primary education. In pursuance of this policy some Government colleges were abolished, a few transferred to private management, and the fees in all Government and aided colleges were greatly raised. To the great misfortune of those provinces which had only recently come under the British rule and where education had only very recently been introduced, as the Punjab, the policy formulated by the Government of India in 1882 affected them most injuriously and was very effectual in retarding high education therein.

As a natural result of this policy, however, the people of the country began to look up for themselves, and systematic efforts were made by them to provide against the loss likely to follow from the partial withdrawal of Government from the field. This withdrawal of Government, or the contraction of Government expenditure on high education, and the raising of fees, have had different effects on different provinces, but so far it has had only a most disastrous effect on the Punjab.

The truth of this remark will appear from a glance at the following table in which the 5 large provinces range themselves according to fee incidence:

Punjab	5.4
Bengal	3.9
Madras	3.5
Bombay	3.0
United Provinces	3.0

The following figures show that of all the 5 important provinces into which British India proper is divided, the Punjab is only next to the most backward of them in the matter of university education.

The following table gives the number of boys of school-going age of whom one was in an Arts College in the 5 university provinces of India.

Bengal	711
Madras	755
Bombay	1,029
Punjab	1,319
U.P.	2,502

The following table shows the increase in all British India in the total number of collegiate students in the 3 quinquennium that have elapsed since 1882.

1887-88 to 1891-92	4,364
1891-92 to 1896-97	1,509
1896-97 to 1901-02	3,215

Thus it took full 10 years for the private colleges to develop in order to reduce the decrease that was so marked and startling in the 2nd quinquennium of this reactionary period.

During the last quinquennium while Bengal gained 1,700 pupils (collegiates), Bombay gained 877 and Madras 239.

Punjab with the N.W.F.P. only gained 160 while the U.P. fared still worse and only gained 44. In 1896-97 the number of scholars receiving education in

Arts College in the Punjab was 1,101. In 1899-1900 it rose to 1,180 and in 1900-01 it was only 1,152.

The following figures show that but for the private colleges, the collegiate education in India would have fared disastrously, as in 1901-02 there were only 4,000 students in Government colleges and 12,000 in privately managed colleges, 54 per cent of the latter only being in aided institutions, the unaided colleges of Bengal alone educating no less than 4,541 of them. The figures of increase in the number of students in different classes of institutions show to what an extent, during the last quinquennium alone, private enterprise in education has come to the rescue of high education in this country. This increase is divided as follows.

Government colleges	448
Aided colleges	998
Unaided colleges	1,005

With the exception of Bengal where the average annual cost of educating a college student is the lowest because of the very large numbers receiving education in cheap private colleges, the cost is the lowest in the Punjab, as shown by the following table.

U.P.	278
Madras	195
Bombay	188
Punjab	136
Bengal	97

While the total expenditure on collegiate education stands thus:

Bengal	8¼ lacs.
Madras	6¼ lacs.
U.P.	4¼ lacs.
Bombay	3¼ lacs.
Punjab	1¼ lacs.

Of these 25½ lacs, only 8,96,000 are furnished by provincial revenues while fees contribute 9¼ lacs, i.e. 80,000 over and above the contribution of Government.

During the last quinquennium the expenditure from public revenues has actually diminished by Rs. 67,000 while that from fees has increased by Rs. 2,31,000.

Compare with the above the amount of money contributed by the

Government of Great Britain and Ireland on university education alone, viz. £1,55,600.

The University of London alone gets a grant of £8,000 (see *Contemporary Review* of December 1903, p. 838); the University of Berlin gets a grant of £ 1,68,780 from its Government and the University of Tokyo (in 1895) £ 1,30,000.

Secondary Education

Descending a step lower and looking at secondary education we shall find that altogether a sum of Rs. 1,26,84,000 is spent on secondary schools, of which only Rs. 32,76,000 are contributed by public funds (Imperial and Provincial Revenues, Local and Municipal Funds altogether) and Rs. 60,76,640 by fees only, the balance being made up from private sources.

In the Punjab the fees ratio of expenditure is shown in the following quotation from the *Review of H.H. the Lieutenant-Governor on the Education Report for 1900-01*.

> It is interesting to notice that on the average native parents are called upon to pay Rs. 1-3-0 per annum for the education of a son in a Primary school; Rs. 11-8-6 in a Secondary school; and over Rs. 80 in an Arts college. These figures, however, do not take into account assistance given in the form of scholarships.

In the *Nineteenth Century* for October 1903 appeared an article on "London Education" from the pen of the Hon'ble Mr. Sydney, L.C.C., in which the writer has noticed the work of the London County Council in providing improved educational facilities for London boys and suggested desirable reforms and changes. Commenting upon the facilities which exist in London for secondary education the writer remarks that

> Every year about *eight hundred* of the ablest boys and girls in the public elementary or lower secondary schools, between eleven and thirteen years of age, are picked by competitive examination for two to five years of higher education. *The two thousand scholarships provide for the cleverest children of the London wage-earners a more genuinely accessible ladder than is open to the corresponding class in any American, French or German city.* In addition to these maintenance scholarships there are *free places at most of the London secondary schools*, from St. Paul's downwards which are utilized as is found to be the case with all provision of merely gratuitous secondary education, by the lower middle and professional classes. *Above*

these opportunities stand the intermediate and senior county scholarships, and others provided by various trust funds, probably altogether about two hundred in each year, for candidates between fifteen and nineteen years of age. These serve partly to carry on the best of the junior scholars; partly to admit to the highest secondary schools the ablest children of parents ineligible for the lowest rung of the ladder, and partly to take the very pick of London's young people to the technical college and the university.

The scholarship scheme has now necessarily to be revised to bring it into accord with the changes lately made in the school-leaving age and the pupil-teacher system. Practically all children now stay at school until fourteen, and it is no longer necessary for any substantial payment towards the maintenance of the scholarship to begin before that age. On the other hand, there is a consensus of opinion that, when a child passes from an elementary to a secondary school, it should do so before the age of twelve, and should remain for not less than four years. It looks as if the limit of age for the normal junior scholarship should be reduced from thirteen to twelve, and its duration extended from two to four years, whilst the annual maintenance allowance up to the age of fourteen might be reduced to 51, rising to 10% and 15% in the last two years. And if the need for pupil-teachers causes the number of scholarships to rise to 2,000 a year, it would perhaps be possible to effect the further desirable reform of beginning the routine process by a preliminary examination, conducted by the head-teachers themselves, in their own schools, of all the children who had attained the fifth standard before the age of twelve; and of undertaking to award the scholarships, not to any fixed number of winners but to all who, in the subsequent centralised competitive examination, reached a certain percentage of marks. Such a reform would organically connect the scholarship system with all the public elementary schools, instead of, as at present, only about a third of them; and would bring London's 'capacity-catching machine' to bear on every promising child.

There must, however, be an adequate supply of efficient secondary schools for these picked scholars to attend, not to mention the needs of those who can afford to keep their boys and girls at school until seventeen or nineteen. There is a common impression that the public secondary schools of London are few and inefficient. Yet including only Foundations of which the management is essentially public in character, *London has today certainly not less than 25,000 boys and girls between seven and nineteen in its secondary schools, actually a larger number of either Paris or Berlin. In the background, and not included in the calculation, stands the horde of private advantage 'commercial academics' and 'colleges for young ladies' of the general suburbs.* The publicly managed schools number about ninety, well dispersed over the whole country, ranging from those like Parmitter's School (Bethnal Green) and Addey's School (Deptford), where the leaving age is sixteen or seventeen, through the dozen admirable institutions of the essentially public Girls Public Day School Company, up to such thoroughly efficient 'first grade' schools as the North London Collegiate for girls (St. Pancras) and Dulwich College (Camberwell) and St. Paul's (Hammersmith) for boys. Yet so dense is London that with one or two exceptions, the very existence of these schools is forgotten by the ordinary citizen, and is often ignored by the legislator or administrator. Many a middle class family, which could well afford to send its boys and girls to secondary schools, is unfamiliar with those which exist within a mile of its home. Even to the best informed educational administrators the real state and quality of the London secondary schools taken as a whole, are far less accurately known than those of the elementary. All the information points to the conclusion that the efficiency varies immensely from school to school; that nearly all of them have good buildings, mostly well provided with science laboratories and suitable equipment; and that, where any school falls below the mark, the weak point is the staffing. *In at least a third of the London secondary schools the income from fees and endowment is insufficient to provide more than one good salary which goes to the head-teacher whilst the assistants, who ought to be University graduates, are paid, for the most part, less than is earned by an ordinary certificated teacher in a board school.* Yet even recognising all the shortcomings of these schools, the department of secondary education is not one which will give the London County Council any serious trouble. About forty of the publicly managed schools are sufficiently well off to be independent of its aid, and these, nearly always charging high fees, and providing an education of high grade, may be left to themselves. The other fifty, including practically all those in need of help, have already shown by their cordial co-operation with the Technical Education Board their willingness to fall into line. It would, of course, be unnecessary to disturb the present governing bodies on which the local authorities are already well represented, *it would be unwise for the Council to interfere in the details of administration. In no department is it so important to maintain variety and independent experiment as in the secondary schools.*

But construct what scholarship ladder we will, the secondary schools can be used only by a small fraction of the population. For the secondary education of the masses there has been organised by the School Board on the one hand, and the Technical Education Board on the other, an extensive assortment of evening classes; providing instruction in various subjects of literature, science, art and technology. The classes of the School Board, which enroll over 1,20,000 students for the winter session and have an average attendance of half that number, are conducted in 400 of its day-school buildings, mainly by the younger and energetic of its staff of day-teachers. The work of the Technical Education Board, dealing usually with a more advanced stage and older scholars, is concentrated in the forty polytechnics, art schools and technical institutes under its management or control, which have in the aggregate about 50,000 students. Here the lecturers and teachers are specialists in their respective subjects, teaching in institutions specially equipped for their work. At six of the polytechnics, the highest classes have been included in the faculties of the recognized London University. These two schemes of evening instruction have now to be coordinated, differentiated and developed. There can be no question of stopping either one or the other, on the contrary, both sides of the work will have to be increased. *It ought not to be too much to ask that every boy and girl who leaves school at fourteen or fifteen should, up to twenty-one, be at any rate enrolled at some evening class institution, even attendance is confined to an hour per week.* Yet there are in London over 6,00,000 young people between fourteen and twenty-one, and not a third of these are at present members of any sort of institution, recreational or educational. Out of 84,000 boys and girls between fifteen and sixteen, only 21,000 are on the rolls. What is happening to the others? We cannot, as yet, compel them to come in, as the Bishop of Hereford proposes, though this is done in various parts of Germany and Switzerland. But we might try the experiment of using the school attendance officers to look after those who have not joined an evening school, using the method of persuasion just as they look after the younger defaulters from the day-school. Meanwhile we could bring the whole of the evening instruction in each borough into a single harmonious organisation; we could allocate the work in such a way as to provide appropriately for each age each grade, and avoid overlapping; we could take care that each subject is taught under the most effective conditions, and properly co-ordinated with more advanced instruction elsewhere; and we could arrange for the progression of the students from stage to stage, until they reach the highest classes of the nearest polytechnic, or the technical college itself.

The italics are everywhere mine and adopted to enable the reader to compare the existing state of things in India with the existing state of things in London or with what in the opinion of the writer in the *Nineteenth Century* should be the state of things there.

It will thus appear that while the London authorities are anxious to see that every boy and girl, whether rich or poor is in receipt of *some sort of secondary education* up to the age of 21, the authorities in India have ruled that the classes in the rural schools be so formed as to exclude the possibilities of scholars reading in them joining the ordinary secondary schools in towns.

The statement that in at least a third of the London secondary schools *the income from fees and endowment* taken together is insufficient to provide more than one good salary which goes to the head-teacher whilst the assistants who ought to be university graduates are paid for the most part less than is earned by an ordinary certificated teacher in a Board School is significant and may with profit be pondered over by the educational authorities in the Punjab who are so strict towards the private schools and are at times inclined to exact higher standards of efficiency than even those observed by some of the Board and mission schools in the province. If even London tolerates the existence of inefficient secondary schools wherein the income from fees and endowment together is not meagre, surely there can hardly be a case against similar schools in India which is educationally so backward.

Primary Education

Coming down to the Primary schools we find the state of things still gloomier. The total expenditure on Primary education is Rs. 1,00,15,000 to which the Public funds (revenues, local and municipal) all contribute only Rs. 60,50,000 while from fees are realised Rs. 31,15,211. The Provincial and Imperial revenues contributed only 13¼ lacs. As compared with the magnificent figure of 13½ lacs of rupees spent by the British Government on Primary education in India, the Parliament of Great Britain and Ireland voted £12,17,368 for elementary education in those islands in 1901 alone. The extent and enormity of the evil have been recognized by the Government of India in their resolution of 1904 in Paras 14, 15 and 16.

How, then, do matters stand in respect of the extension among the masses of primary eduction? The population of British India is over two hundred and forty millions. It is commonly reckoned that fifteen per cent of the population are of school-going age. According to this standard there are more than 18 millions of boys who ought now to be at school, but of these only a little more than ¼ are actually receiving primary education. If the statistics are arranged by provinces, that out of a hundred boys of an age to go to school, the number attending primary schools of some kind ranges from between eight and nine in the Punjab and the United Provinces to twenty-two and twenty-three in Bombay and Bengal. In the census of 1901 it was found that only one in ten of the male population and only seven in a thousand of the female population were literate. These figures exhibit the vast dimensions of the problem, and show how much remains to be done before the proportion of the population receiving elementary instruction can approach the standard recognized as indispensable in more advanced countries. While the need for education grows with the growth of population the progress towards supplying it is not now so rapid as it was in former years. In1870-71 there were 16,473 schools with 60,73,210 scholars; in 1881-82 there were 82,916 with 20,61,541 scholars. But in 1891-92 these had only increased to 97,109 schools with 28,37,607 scholars, and the figures of 1901-02 (98,588 schools with 32,68,726 scholars) suggest that the initial force of expansion is somewhat on the decline, indeed, the last year of the century showed a slight decrease as compared with the previous year.

On a general view of the question the Government of India cannot avoid the conclusion that the primary education has hitherto had insufficient attention and an inadequate share of the public funds. They consider that it possesses a strong claim upon the sympathy both of the supreme Government and of the Local Governments and should be made a leading charge upon provincial revenues; and that in those provinces where it is in a backward condition, its encouragement should be a primary obligation.

It may be remarked that these obligations were also admitted in 1882-83, but little was done to fulfil them, as will be clear from a perusal of the following facts and figures which we cull from Vol. II of the Government of India's reports on the progress of education between 1897-98 to 1901-02.

Number of Primary Schools for Boys

1886	1891-92	1896-97	1901-02
84,673	91,881	97,881	92,226

which means an actual decrease of 5,655 in the last 5 years. The Punjab showed this decrease to the extent of 42, i.e. in 1901-02 there were 42 Primary schools less in the Punjab and N.W. Frontier Province combined. In 1896-97 there was one school for a group of 5.8 towns and villages. In 1901-02 there was one for a group of 6.2. In the Central Provinces there is one Primary school for 23.4 towns and villages, in the United Provinces of Agra and Oudh one for 15.6 and in the Punjab one for 14.5. In the Central Provinces the mean average distance in miles between each boys' Primary school is 8.2 miles and in the Punjab 7.1. This does not mean that schools are equally distributed over the whole area. The fact is that in some districts there is no school for many tens of miles.

During the last 5 years, while the number of schools fell by 5,655 the average strength per school rose only by 2 (i.e. from 31 to 33 per school). The following figures will show the progress made by primary education in the number of scholars receiving education. In 1896-97, 30 lacs and 26 thousand boys received instruction in Primary schools for boys but in 1901-02 the number fell to 30 lacs and 9 thousand (a fall of 17,000). In the Primary schools attached to Secondary schools the numbers in 1896-97 were 31 lacs and 83 thousand and in 1901-02 the numbers were 31 lacs and 84 thousand, i.e. an increase of 1,000. Total loss—16,000. In the Punjab and N.W.F. Province (combined) the numbers in the former schools were 10 lacs and 8 thousand in 1896-97 and the same in 1901 and 1902, but in the latter class of schools it rose slightly, i.e. by 4,000.

In the Census Returns of 1901-02 only 13 million males in British India have been entered as able to read and write out of a total male population of 117½ millions which means that 104 ½ million cannot read and write at all. In 1901-02 only174 out of a 1,000 boys of school-going age were receiving instruction i.e. 826 went without any education at all. But in the Punjab 914 out of a 1,000 went without any instruction at all. Thus in the matter of primary education, the Punjab, that nursery of the Indian soldier, land of the brave and the loyal Sikh, is the most backward of all the provinces, even Assam, Burma and Central Provinces showing much better figure, i.e. 197, 167, 137 per thousand respectively against 86 of the Punjab.

Now to judge of the quality of education imparted in these schools we have only to examine the figures relating to the average cost of a school and the average annual cost per pupil, the former being less than Rs.10 a month and the latter being Rs. 3.7 (per year). The following figures show that there has been practically no improvement in this direction within the last 10 years.

Average annual cost of a boy's Primary school

1891-92	1896-97	1901-02
94	101	114

The improvement can be valued at less than one rupee per month.

Coming nearer home we find that in the Punjab the progress has been in the other direction. In 1891-92 the annual cost of a boys' Primary school in the Punjab was Rs. 222, in 1896-97 it fell to Rs. 195 and in 1901-02 it could only slightly rise to Rs. 202. The net result is that as compared with 1891-92 there is a falling off of 20 per year. The increase in the average cost of educating a boy may be judged from the following figures.

	1891-92	1896-97	1901-02
General average cost	3.2	3.2	3.7
Punjab	4.4	4.4	4.9

Now let us examine the so-called "unparalleled liberality" of the British Government paying the teachers employed in these schools.

The following table shows the average of monthly pay of primary school teachers.

		Government School	Boarding School
Madras	Head Master,	Rs. 3 to Rs. 20	Rs. 8 to Rs. 15
	Assistant Master	Rs. 3 to Rs. 10	Rs. 5 to Rs. 12
Bengal	Teacher	Rs. 3 to Rs. 8 approximately	
Punjab	do	Rs. 8 to Rs. 55	Rs. 4 to Rs. 40
Central Provinces	do	Rs. 6 to Rs. 20 in general	
Bombay	do	Rs. 7 to Rs. 60	Rs. 7 to Rs. 60 Rs. 7 to Rs. 65
U.P. of Agra and Oudh	do	Rs. 2 to Rs. 17	Aided Rs. 2 to Rs. 25 Unaided Rs. 2 to Rs. 25

I do not know how to characterise the conduct of a Government who expect teachers who get the royal salary of Rs. 2 to 5 a month to spread and strengthen the sentiment of loyalty amongst their pupils. In these days even an ordinary illiterate day-labourer gets 6 annas per diem. The prosperity of this country under British rule may better be judged by these scales of pay which we have given above. Any further comments are not needed.

Compare with this the following figures giving the annual cost per child in the Primary stage in Great Britain and Ireland.

	Board Schools	Private Schools
England and Wales	£ 3-0-9d, i.e. Rs. 45-9	£2.6s. 4d., i.e. Rs. 34-12
Scotland	£ 2-17-4, i.e. Rs. 43	£2-15s-6d, i.e. Rs. 37
Ireland	£ 2-10-1, i.e. Rs. 38	

The average pay of a teacher of a Primary school in Great Britain and

Ireland is £ 129 sterling per annum, i.e. Rs. 1,935 or, say, more than Rs. 150 per month.

So long as the cost of general administration remains what it is, and no reduction is effected by the larger employment of native agency for the high-paid and costly European agency, and so long as the military is maintained on that ruinous scale as at present, there is little prospect of increased expenditure being incurred on education from Provincial and Imperial revenues. Every sensible man will agree with the Government that the wider extension of education in India is chiefly a matter of increased expenditure; and any material improvement of its quality is largely dependent upon the same condition. A Government which could heretofore afford to spend only a crore and 4 lacs upon the education of more than 24 crores of people in its charge is not in a position to assume that supreme position in matters educational which it has, by its recent policy, decreed to itself. While the Government in India cannot afford to give more than 1 crore and 4 lacs for the education of more than 24 crores of its people compared with about 19 crores spent by the Parliament of Great Britain for the same object, the former aims at officialising, supervising and controlling every educational agency in the land. In the name of sound education they decry those institutions which, if not up to date in the supply of appliances and apparatus, if not quite up to the mark in the efficiency and competency of their teachers, if not located in beautiful buildings, if not possessed of grand and inspiring surroundings, are at least helping the cause of education and literacy in the land. A Government which pays teachers at the munificent rate of from 5 to 10 or 20 rupees a month in Government and District and Municipal Board Primary schools, and at the lowest rate of 4 and 5 rupees a month to teachers in the Secondary schools is surely not in a position to vote the Private schools out of existence even if the managers of the latter cannot treat their teachers better than or so well as the Government does. In a country where the number of male literates per 1,000 of the male population ranges from 54 to 378 with an average of 102 for the whole of India; where the number of boys in the primary stage per 1,000 of male population of school-going age ranges from 63 in the N.W.F.P., and 86 in the Punjab to 232 in Bengal with an average of 174 for the whole of British India, where the Government can only spare 13¼ lacs of rupees upon elementary education for a population of more than 24 crores in a country where in some parts of it, only one out of 278 is in the secondary stage of an English school and one in 1,032 in the same stage of a vernacular school; in a country where on the average only one out of 1,079 of a population of school-going age is in an Arts college, the Government can hardly be justified in assuming that aggressive and dictatorial attitude towards private enterprise in education which it has lately done.

Conclusion

Even in advanced countries where a very large part of Government revenues is spent upon education; where education is considered as a national asset; where the number of literates in the population is over 90 per cent; where education is compulsory; even in such countries the government is not so hard or does not require high and rigid and almost impossible standards of efficiency from private schools and colleges as the Government has lately been laying down for the same class of institutions here in India.[2] We wonder why the government of Lord Curzon should have forgotten that the systems of education now prevalent in England, the United States and Germany, which he has taken as his models, are the growths of more than a century at least if not of centuries; that all those countries are self-governing countries, where the interests of the rulers and the ruled are identical and where the former only exist for the benefit and protection of the latter. To apply the systems, standards and principles in force in those countries to India is more absurd than even the putting of the cart before the horse. But even in England the voluntary and denominational schools were the pioneers of education and till lately enjoyed—nay, to a great extent even now enjoy—the freedom which the Government of India by their recent policy refuse to the private schools and colleges of this country.

It is not strange then that the people of India should be suspicious of the intentions and the motives of the Government, and that the recent policy of the Government in matters of education should have raised a storm of indignation in the land. We say why should the Government prescribe a tuition fee for the private school and the private college in this land where dense ignorance prevails, where more than 90 per cent of the population is illiterate, and where the Government of the country cannot spend more than 1½ annas per head on education. Again, we say why should the Government, if it is honest and actuated by the best and the highest of motives, in a country like this throw obstacles in the way of private enterprise in education; why should it try to prevent the same from competing with the Government institutions; why should it frame such rules and regulations as to take away all liberty of action and freedom of initiative from them and compel them to submit to dictation and supervision from Government and its officers. If under the circumstances the Government is misunderstood and its motives and intentions misconstrued, it has only to thank itself for these misunderstandings and misinterpretations.

Under the new regulations the Government has almost made it impossible

2. Stringent conditions had been laid down for the recognition of secondary schools by the Government of India Resolution on Education Policy of 11 March 1904.

for a new private educational institution to come into existence and to thrive. No private school or college can, under the present rules, dare to make a humble beginning. Large funds, high-class buildings, official goodwill and a very high state of efficiency in all respects are the conditions precedent even for a start. Under the present rules, institutions like the great Metropolitan of Calcutta, the Fergusson College of Poona, the D.A.V. College at Lahore would not have come into existence. Similar attempts are, as a matter of fact, impossible under the new policy. The conclusion, which the people then are irresistibly led to, under the above circumstances, is that the Government of this country is neither willing to spend its own revenues on education, nor will it tolerate the doing of it by the people for themselves unless the latter are prepared to place their funds and efforts under the control of the former.

11. Resolution regarding Right of Free Elementary Education[1]

That in the opinion of this Conference it is the right of every boy and girl to receive free elementary education and asks the Government to arrange for it at once.

1. *The Tribune*, 9 October 1906.
   This resolution moved at the Fourth Punjab Provincial Conference held at Ambala on 30 September 1906 was passed unanimously.

12. Exhortation to People to Start National Schools[1]

In the course of his address, Mr. Lajpat Rai strongly condemned the present educational policy of the Indian Government, which aimed at creating only law-abiding, peace-loving and loyal citizens, and not self-respecting, self-asserting and fearless citizens. The system which did not equip men with powers to fight the battle of life was doomed in all self-governing countries where the interests of rulers and ruled did not collide, while in countries under foreign domination it was not necessarily so. Mr. Lajpat Rai therefore exhorted the people to put their shoulders to the wheel, and start national schools and colleges with not a penny of grant from the Government. In conclusion, Mr. Lajpat Rai said it was for the younger generation to play the part of educational missionaries in real earnest, and carry the gospel of national education from hamlet to hamlet.

1. Address to Congress Standing Committee, Bombay, 17 November 1906. *India*, 14 December 1906.
 The meeting was presided over by G.K. Gokhale.

13. Patriotism towards the Empire— A Hypocrisy Harmful to Boys and Girls[1]

In May last (1906) the Director of Public Instruction of the Punjab issued a circular order to all the headmasters and managers of government-aided and unaided schools in the province requiring them to celebrate the empire day in a certain way. One of the items of the programme laid down by him for observance was "the recitation of Urdu poems on loyalty to the Crown of England and patriotism towards the empire". We do not know if the head of the Punjab Education Department was responsible for the wording of the above clause. The document seemed to bear on it abundant marks of that jingo statesmanship which has for a number of years been in ascendancy in the councils of the British empire. One thing, however, is clear. The Government was sensible enough not to declare the empire day as a public holiday. The

1. Published in *The Hindustan Review* of December 1906.

compulsory celebration of the empire day in 1906 was therefore confined to the schools, maybe, to the schools of the Punjab only. We propose to examine in this paper if the step taken was educationally sound and in any way calculated to improve the moral tone of the schools where it was, by order, enforced.

Till lately the impression was that the British were, at least, frank by nature and valued frankness and sincerity on the part of others, however distasteful and unpleasant, at times, they may be to their imperial temper. The idea was that although conscious of the unnaturalness of their rule over alien races, they aimed at making it as pleasant and benevolent as they possibly could (if ever it is possible to make subjection pleasant and benevolent) consistently with the making of the largest profit out of it for themselves. Of course, nobody having sufficient experience of human nature ever took the Britisher at his word, when the latter professed to be moved by unselfish and altruistic motives in extending his rule over other nations and countries and governing them solely for the sake of humanity and civilization.

All the same, people believed that the British administration had not lost all sense of frankness and sincerity, until the new doctrine of the white man's burden was propounded by the banjo-boards, and the jingo poets had forced their muse to sing of the great sacrifices which the white man underwent in his civilizing mission and his humane rule, undertaken for the sole benefit of the ruled. But even the jingoes, whether poets or statesmen, never thought of appealing to the subject races in the name of patriotism towards the empire, for the simple reason that in the mouths of the latter the expression was an absurdity, and a contradiction in terms. The subject races—the fact of whose subordination to Great Britain alone confers upon the latter the status and dignity of an empire—may be loyal, whether voluntarily or involuntarily, whether by free will, or by necessity, but to attempt to raise this sense of loyalty to the dignity of patriotism is sheer nonsense. No lexicographer, of any position whatsoever, will risk his reputation by speaking, even by inference, of "patriotism towards the Empire". The idea is monstrous and is for the first time being introduced into the English language by the presumptuous genius of the jingoes as an antidote towards the sacred sentiment of patriotism, in the development of which amongst the subject races, they see a dangerous enemy to their own despotic rule. The lexicographers, if they can be accepted as reliable guides, in explaining the meaning of English words to us, almost unanimously agree in expressing the general opinion, as to patriotism signifying "love of country". Johnson[2] defines it as "zeal for one's country" and Webster[3] as "the

2. Samuel Johnson (1709-1784); British author and poet.
3. Noah Webster (1758-1843); American writer and famous for his *American Dictionary of the English Language*, better known as *Webster's Dictionary*.

passion which aims to serve one's country". The *Encyclopedic Dictionary* says that patriotism is "devotion to the interest and welfare of one's country", and the *Century Dictionary* defines it as "the passion which moves a person to serve his country either in defending it from invasion or protecting its rights and maintaining its lands and institutions", and so on and so forth. But how can a subject race governed by another be patriotic towards its rulers passes one's comprehension, unless one accepts the theory that the latter rules solely for the benefit of the former. Even in this case it is love of his own country and certainly not patriotism towards the empire (signifying love for the empire) which evokes loyalty for the existing Government. Honestly speaking, the two sentiments are antagonistic, viz. loyalty to a foreign government and love for one's country, which is patriotism, unless the patriot is to reconcile his patriotism with loyalty by the idea that in loving the foreign ruler he loves his own country. It may be allowable to a patriot to soothe his conscience by identifying his loyalty with patriotism, but to carry it further and to extend it to the empire is coining a new expression with an entirely new meaning. When, therefore, in the name of the Empire, the British appeal to the patriotism of the Indians instead of to their loyalty, their object is to give a higher pedestal to the shame which every member of a subject race (having the least vestige of self-respect and honourable feeling in him) must feel at his political helplessness and at the political non-existence of his country. The object is to cover the shame of political bondage with the halo of glory that attaches to the word "patriotism" and thus to remove the sting that bites the consciences of those of the ruling race and puts to shame those among the ruled as are still open to any sense of honour.

However commendable the motive and however praiseworthy the object may be, one does not require much common sense to see through the device. The fact is that human nature with all its inherent disposition towards selfishness is always apt to find excuses for its idiosyncrasies and will not allow itself to be denied the pleasure of putting a gloss of high and pure motives on its basest and meanest acts, whereby it deprives others of the simplest rights of humanity and the priceless treasure of liberty. No wrongdoer, however educated and cultured he may be, can at times help feeling mortification at the wrongs which in the pursuit of self-interest he has inflicted or does inflict upon others, and it is then his guilty conscience runs riot in search of pleas and justifications for his wrongful conduct. Makers and rulers of empires are no exception to this general rule, which governs human nature everywhere and in every phase of life. Now empires are neither made nor maintained by right. They are made by might, both physical and intellectual, including that diplomacy and cunning without which no supremacy can ever be gained over other peoples and nations. "Only by force can empire, as a rule, be created; only by force can empire, as a rule, be maintained," rightly remarks Mr. Goddard[4] in his excellent book on *Racial Supremacy*, although instances are not wanting in which wise and sagacious empire-makers and their equally clever successors have maintained empires, for a longer period than they otherwise could, by doses of benevolence and justice in the management of their affairs. But racial supremacy is one of those necessary evils of which the world can never be purged. Its roots are deep. No amount of philosophizing and high thinking will see its complete overthrow from the world, and as long as this necessary evil exists, which is tantamount to saying that it must always exist, you cannot do away with empires and empire-makers. Still that is no reason why those who are the victims of empires and empire-makers should feel grateful to their masters for having extended their empire over them and for having included them in the category of their subjects. As to the ethics of empire-making and as to the claims of the British to the gratitude of those included in their empire, we will prefer to quote some English authorities on the subject rather than give expression to our own views.

First, as to what does "empire" signify? In the language of Mr. J.D. Goddard, a member of the new House of Commons, it "simply means rule, dominion, sway". According to Lord Rosebery,[5] empire is "the predominance of rule". According to Herbert Spencer,[6] "not the derivation of the word only but all its uses and associations imply the thought of predominance—imply a correlative subordination. Actual or potential coercion of other individuals or communities is necessarily involved in the conception". In the words of Mr. Goddard then "imperialism is the spirit of rule, ascendancy or predominance; the rule of one race of people by another race of people involving of course the subjection of the former to the latter".

Mr. J.M. Robertson,[7] another member of the House of Commons, also defines empire as "rule over other communities than his own". Mr. Joseph Chamberlain, the jingo imperialist of modern England, has, however, assured us that "the new conception of empire is of a voluntary organisation, based on community of interests and community of sacrifices, to which all should bring their contribution to the common good".

4. J.D. Goddard; Labour member of House of Commons in 1906; author of *Racial Supremacy*.
5. Archibald Philip Primrose, 5th earl of Rosebery (1847-1929); British Prime Minister, 1894-95); his advocacy of imperialist policy in Africa estranged him from Liberal Party.
6. (1820-1903); British philosopher; expounded the doctrine of laissez-faire; sub-editor, *Economist*, 1848; works include *Social Statics* (1851) and *The Principles of Psychology* (1855).
7. (1856-1933); British author and politician; connected with *National Reformer*, 1884-91 and its editor, 1891-93; Liberal M.P., 1906-18.

How far this is in accordance with existing facts has been made clear by Mr. Goddard in examining the above statement in his book referred to above. In the opinion of this writer imperialism tends to demoralise the dominant race, while it is simply the bane of the subject races. Taking the case of India as the most prominent and pertinent instance of the government of one people by another people, he concludes by saying that India is ruled in the interest of the dominant race rather than in hers and endorses the well-known remark of John Ruskin[8] that "every mutiny, every danger, every crime occurring under our Indian legislation arose directly out of our native desire to live on the loot of India". The writer further condemns imperialism on the ground that it is destructive of liberty, and applying it to the case of India he pronounces an indictment on imperialism in this country in the following terms.

> Here we have countless millions denied the rights accorded to the English agricultural labourer, taxed to pay for a Government in which they have no voice, condemned to support an army they cannot control, rack-rented for land they cultivate mainly for the benefit of others, compelled to yield interest on an expenditure they did not make, and generally reduced to the condition of hewers of wood and drawers of water, with sufferance as the badge of all their tribe.

Discussing the ethics of empire the same writer examines the claims of the dominant races in placing themselves in *quasi loco parentis* over subject races, as follows.

> The bond which unites father or mother with son and daughter is one of mutual affection and so far from self-sacrifice on the part of the dominant race being present, the opposite characteristic is manifested, and there is certainly no constant endeavour to promote the welfare of the putative child. The most serious flaw in the analogy, however, has reference to the main purpose of control. For the primary object of the parental rule of children is to develop their faculties, and that for their own benefit. *It is a temporary and not a permanent rule, devoted to the purpose of rendering the child a self-governing person, capable as manhood is reached of exercising similar rule.* The primary object of racial rule is not to *develop the faculties of the governed*; even if some development takes place, it is not for their own benefit; the rule is regarded not as temporary, but rather

8. (1819-1900); English writer and critic.

> as permanent, and it is not devoted to the purpose of rendering them capable of exercising similar rule. No doubt, in point of time, the infancy of man is incomparable to the infancy of a race, and a far larger period is requisite for development. But a dominant nation does not work for or contemplate the abrogation of its power, even in the distant future; its rooted idea is that of its own supremacy; its constant aim is to secure the maintenance, and generally the extension of that supremacy; its fundamental conception of the relations which exist is subjective and not objective. Hence, on almost all points the analogy is absolutely false and misleading. One, and one only, of the many parental functions is selected, and the rest are implicitly or explicitly ignored. The maturity of the parent and the immaturity of the child are at the outset assumed to respectively distinguish the two races; and then from a distorted simile an attempt is made to convert the temporary and qualified and specialised control which a parent exercises into a justification for the permanent and unqualified and general control which a nation claims.

Passing to the consideration of the second hypothesis of the imperialist, viz., that benevolence characterizes despotism, Mr. Goddard points out that in order to make despotism benevolent the one condition essential—that the power should be vested in one individual—is wanting in the case. Thinking on the same line I have often wished that we had been ruled by Queen Victoria[9] or by King Edward,[10] or by any other single individual exercising the power of a despotic monarch rather than by the Parliament of Great Britain and Ireland representing the British nation, for you can, at times, successfully appeal to the humanity and benevolence of individuals but to hope for justice and benevolence from a nation is hoping against hope. The rule of a foreign democracy is, in this respect, the most dangerous. The democracy is swayed by so many diverse interests and motives that it is simply impossible to expect anything like unanimity or even a preponderance of opinion in dealing justly with a subject race, because justice to a subject race often clashes or is inconsistent with the interest of some class of the ruling democracy. Whenever an attempt is therefore made to do justice to the former, the latter rise up, raise a storm and prevent the Government from doing the right thing. Looking to the history of the cotton duties in India, everyone will see the truth of my remarks. How many times have the Government of India been overruled in the matter, simply because the

9. (1819-1901); Queen of Great Britain and Ireland, 1837-1901.
10. Edward VII.

Home Government cannot afford to risk the opposition of Lancashire and incur its displeasure.[11]

As a matter of fact, we are at present ruled by a democracy which represents the British nation and in the appointing and controlling of which the Sovereign has really no hand. In my opinion the benevolence of an individual has greater chances of being effective than that of a whole nation. To me the benevolence of a whole nation seems to be nothing more than a myth and fiction, as there can never be an absolute unanimity both as to what constitutes benevolence in given circumstances, as well as to how it is to be reduced into practice. Applying the benevolence plea to the case of India and other subject races of Britain, Mr. Goddard concludes (a conclusion in which other eminent authorities agree) that the plea is simply untenable. Examining the plea of benevolence in imperial relations in the light of historical facts, Mr. Goddard says: "The truth is that whilst it does not necessarily give rise to exalting acts of cruelty, so far from its ever being largely tempered by benevolence, it has invariably one prominent characteristic, namely, the exploitation of its victims. The primary object and result of alien government is not to confer benefits upon the subject races but to obtain benefits from them." He further says that

> Perhaps . . . the most striking testimony to the virtues of benevolent despotism is seen in the employment of native races to fight our battles for us. Wild animals are sometimes lured to their doom by means of one of their kind trained to act as a decoy, and we occasionally hear setting of a thief to catch a thief. The process has been adopted with a magnificent effrontery and a grim sense of humour to the needs of aggressive imperialism, and having extended the empire by bringing the "inferior races" under our sway, by a masterstroke of grains, we utilise them to still further extend and also to defend the empire and convert them into instruments for bestowing upon their brethren the boons which they themselves have obtained. It is very largely in this way that our Indian Empire has been built up.

Then let us see what another English author, Mr. J.A. Hobson,[12] says about the sophistries of imperialism. "The idea," he says, "that we are civilizing Indians in the sense of assisting them to industrial, political, and moral progress along

11. The import duty on British cotton manufactures levied at 10 per cent *ad valorem* in 1850 and reduced to 5 per cent in 1875 was completely abolished in 1879.
12. (1858-1940); British economist, revealed economic bases of colonization in his book *Imperialism* (1902); other works include *The Evolution of Modern Capitalism and A Study of Machine Production*.

the lines either of our own or their civilization is a complete delusion, based upon a false estimate of the influence of superficial changes brought by Government and the activity of a minute group of aliens. The delusion is only sustained by the sophistry of imperialism which weaves these fallacies to cover its nakedness and the advantages which certain interests suck out of empire." Even the late Professor Seeley[s] writes in the same strain where he says: "We are not disposed to be proud of the succession of the Grand Mogul. We doubt whether with all the merits of our administration the subjects of it are happy. We may even doubt whether our rule is preparing them for a happier condition, whether it may not be sinking them lower in misery." But what Professor Seeley states in rather halting language is expressed affirmatively by another great writer on India, Mr. W.S. Lily. "The test of a people's prosperity," says Mr. Lily, "is not the extension of exports, the multiplication of manufactures or other industries, the construction of cities. No. A prosperous country is one in which the great mass of the inhabitants are able to procure with moderate toil what is necessary for living human lives, lives of frugal and assured comfort." Judged by this standard can India be called prosperous? His answer, of course, is a positive 'No'. He adds that "comfort is a relative term and that in a tropical country like India the standard is very low . . . but millions of peasants in India are struggling to live on half an acre. Their existence is a constant struggle with starvation leading too often in defeat. Their difficulty is not to live *human* lives—lives up to the level of their poor standard of comfort—*but to live at all and not die*."

Such then is the verdict of level-headed Englishmen on the results of imperial rule in India, which testimony is of hundred times greater value than the interested sayings of stock exchange brokers and speculators, whom the British system helps in hoarding up millions upon millions at the cost of the Indian peasant, the Indian labourer and the Indian handicraftsman. I could add the testimony of many more Englishmen as to the baneful effects of imperialism in India, but the fear of adding to the bulk of this paper prevents me from doing so, and I will conclude this part of the paper by adding one more quotation from the fascinating work of Mr. Goddard, wherein he shows how detrimental benevolent imperialism is to the interests of the subject races:

> The gravamen of the indictment of 'benevolent despotism' is that it tends to perpetuate the despotism. Whilst in practice the benevolence, if manifested at all, is relatively small, and whilst even if it were exhibited to the fullest extent circumstances admit, it would be no adequate justification; its supposed or actual existence obscures the facts, satisfies the conscience, and leads to acquiescence in the permanent withdrawal of liberty, instead of efforts towards its restoration.

It will be seen that in saying all this I have only discussed the general effects of imperial rule in India and have not even touched upon particular grievances. I have made no allusion to the brutal treatment we receive in South Africa, Australia and other parts of the empire, and I have made no mention of the disabilities from which we suffer in India. Is it then right to ask us to celebrate the empire day? Is it then likely to improve habits of sincerity and truthfulness amongst our boys, by compelling them to glorify the empire? Is it then honest on the part of our teachers and professors and directors to flatter us by saying that we are either the sons of the empire or its citizens, while we are neither, but are treated as the subjects of the empire—the victims of the imperial spirit that rules. Britishers may or may not glory in their empire. Perhaps from the ordinary point of view they have every reason to be proud of it and to glory in it. It tickles their fancy to think of their possessions, their dependencies and their subjects, though the sober-minded amongst them have begun to talk loudly as to the evil effects of the imperialism on the morale of their own people. The once sturdy and vigorous, both in thought and in deed, the simple but the high-minded, the reserved but stolid Britisher is perhaps exchanging his virtues for the comforts, ease and luxuries, which attend an unchecked sway of empire and the bumptiousness and the vulgar pride of unbounded intoxication of uncontrolled power. Be however as it may, we do not and we cannot object to the Britisher at home or in India celebrating his empire day, but it is nothing short of adding insult to injury to ask us and our boys to do so. Devoted patriots, as the British are, is it fair on their part to ask us to celebrate the empire day in the name of "patriotism towards the empire"—a patriotism which we do not feel, which does not inspire us with noble thoughts and which evokes neither love nor homage in our bosoms. As helpless victims of the aggressive imperialism, as servants of the Crown and as students of schools and colleges, we might silently put up with the humiliation, but I daresay I am not wrong in reading the hearts of the bulk of my educated countrymen when I say that the idea is simply revolting and extremely provoking to their sense of honour and shame. Those Britishers and Indians who thus trade in hypocrisy, and who thus would inoculate the minds of the innocent boys and girls with the serum of hypocrisy, are doing a positive injury to human nature, and to the principles of sound education without doing any good to British rule in India. In the name of loyalty we are prepared to submit to any order which the authorities issue, but we earnestly beg of them not to drag our patriotism into the mire and not to force us to compromise the same. The demands of patriotism are sacred and ennobling, which require no hypocrisy, and which evoke the deepest feelings of love for our country and for our people.

7
FAMINE

1. Evidence before the Indian Famine Commission[1]

Mr. Nicholson: You are the Honorary Secretary of the Orphanage in Ferozepore?

Answer: I am connected with other orphanages as well.

Question: Are they connected with the Arya Samaj?

A: Some are. I am connected with Hindu orphanages, whether they are connected with the Arya Samaj or not.

Q: How many orphans are there at present?

A: About 1,000; the exact numbers are given in the report.

Q: Did you collect them during the famine of 1897-98?

A: In the famine of 1897-98 there were 200 collected and in this famine 1,680.

Q: Now there are about 1,000. What has become of the remaining 880?

A: Some of them were made over to the orphanages in the North-Western Provinces, some died, some ran away.

Q: What is the age of the orphans?

A: Generally above three and less than 16.

Q: Are the bulk over ten years of age?

A: Yes.

Q: I understand they are engaged in industrial pursuits?

A: Yes.

Q. And able to earn their own living?

A. Yes.

Q: You are employing them in weaving carpets?

A: Yes.

Q: What capital do you start them upon?

A: In Amritsar no capital is required; we employ them in the factories of other people; some of them are able to earn Rs. 8 and Rs. 10 a month.

Q: What about the girls?

A: At present they are doing lace work; some are employed on hosiery work.

Q: Have you female supervision?

A: Yes.

1. Published in the *Report of the Indian Famine Commission, 1901* (Calcutta, 1908), pp. 377-80, N.A.I.

The Indian Famine Commission had been appointed by the Government of India in 1901 to enquire into the administration of famine relief during the year 1899-1900. It was presided over by A.P. Macdonnell. The other Commissioners were—F.A. Nicholson, J.A. Bourdillon and Syam Sundar Lal.

Q: Are any of a marriageable age?

A: Yes.

Q: What do you propose to do with them?

A: We give notice and dispose of them.

Q: How are they supported?

A: The numbers have increased only lately. We managed before to meet the expenditure from private subscriptions and unfunded capital.

Q: From what provinces have they come?

A: From the Hissar district, some from the Central Provinces and a considerable number from Rajputana.

Q: How did you get them?

A: We sent out emissaries and collected them.

Q: Did you collect them from houses?

A: From villages near the famine relief works.

Q: Were these children at work?

A: Purely waifs and strays.

Q: Your suggestion seems to be that no waifs and strays should be collected by non-official agency, and that they should not be taken from their Provinces, but this seems to have been done in your own case?

A: As other people acted contrary to my suggestion, so we did too.

Q: Still, I think it is your opinion that it is not advisable to remove orphans from their own Provinces?

A: Yes; that should be the general rule.

Q: There should be another condition: that a complete register should be kept up showing where the children were obtained from and where they were taken to?

A: Yes.

Q: Have you such registers?

A: Yes, we have; but they may not be complete.

Q: But you know where the children came from?

A: Yes.

Q: You have made a complaint that you made applications to the authorities in the Punjab and they didn't answer your applications?

A: Yes; except that made to the Punjab Government.

Q: Were you able to get many children from the Punjab authorities?

A: No.

Q: Are you sure of your facts regarding missionaries taking children away?

A: My authority is Lala Chuni Mal,[2] pleader.

2. Arya Samajist of Lahore: pleader of Lahore Chief Court; a close associate of Lajpat Rai in the famine relief work during 1896-97 and 1899-1900.

Q: Is it your meaning that, during the currency of a famine children should be kept under the care of Government and only distributed to certain institutions at the close of the famine?

A: Yes.

Q: In future you would be restrained from taking children from Government care except under certain conditions?

A: Yes.

Q: Would you accept the condition that, should a claimant appear, you would give up the child?

A: Yes.

Q: With regard to the suggestions you make (1) and (2) in your written evidence, the North-Western Provinces Code (shown to witness) would probably suit your idea?

A: Yes; this would in regard to one particular clause.

Q: You have also dealt with one or two other points, that of employing non-official agency on a larger scale in a future emergency. Is there any scope for this in the case of villages?

A: Yes; both in villages and towns.

Q: Was it not tried in the various towns in the Punjab?

A: Not considerably.

Q: You think it might have been more developed?

A: Major Dunlop Smith in the last famine employed it largely, but this year it was not done.

Q: Do you think it would be possible to employ non-official agency either in gratuitous relief or in supervising small village works? Have you the people there?

A: Not in the small villages themselves, but there are a number of people in the headquarters of the district who know it well and would be forth-coming.

Q: Do they know the condition of the village sufficiently?

A: Yes; some of them belong to the villages and only reside in the town.

Q: Are they available to any extent?

A: Yes.

Q: And would they act gratuitously?

A: Yes.

Q: If village works are to be developed it would be by the aid of private agency?

A: Yes.

Q: And that would prevent immorality?

A: Yes.

Q: Have you any information regarding immorality on large works; you have a serious allegation on the subject here. The agents of the Ferozepore Orphanage received 62 married girls; were these girls brought away?

A: Yes; we are now going to send agents in search of their husbands.

Q: On what information did your agents act?

A: They brought the girls from Rajputana.

The President: Did they take away grown-up girls from relief works?

A: Not exactly; it was done at their own request. My information is that they were being actually sold.

Mr. Nicholson: The Orphanage proposes to make enquiries with a view to seeing if their husbands are alive?

A: Yes; the girls were taken away simply because the idea was that if we were not to protect them they would be taken away by others.

Q: Are there no agencies which would have looked after them?

A: My instructions are that there are only one or two agencies in Rajputana where provision is made for boys only, not for girls.

Q: Were these people from Native States?

A: Yes.

The President: Were they from Native States or Ajmer-Merwara?

A: Mostly from Native States.

Mr. Nicholson: Have you organized general rescue agencies for bringing all sorts of people from all sorts of districts?

A: No; not that.

Q: Are you sure that they have no lawful guardians?

A: That was their own assertion.

Q: Were there relief works going on at the place?

A: There may have been in the neighbourhood.

Q: Why didn't they take them to the officers-in-charge?

A: The impression was that anybody could get hold of a woman and take her off.

Q: Instead of bringing them 100 miles away, why were they not taken to the Magistrate? Why were they taken out of the jurisdiction of Rajputana?

A: I have no answer to make, except that others were doing the same thing.

The President: How do you know that?

A: It was seen.

Q: Was any complaint made to the Police?

A: No.

Mr. Nicholson: Where did the girls come from?

A: From the following places. (witness read a list.)

Q: I suppose you have reports and proceedings of each girl as to where she can be found?

A: Not of each girl separately. Our agents went to certain places and collected the waifs and strays, and we then collected details.

The President: Did they rail them to you?

A: Yes; to Lahore.

Q: From Central India they were taken to Lahore?

A: Yes.

Q: Your object being to get them to their husbands?

A: Yes.

Q: Why didn't you take them to the Magistrate and point out that a large number were being removed to other provinces?

A: There was a printed appeal by a missionary lady in which she pointed out this evil.

Q: Did you make an application to the authorities that these abductions were going on?

A: No; it is with this object we have brought it to your notice.

Mr. Nicholson: Why didn't your agents go straight to the Magistrate?

A: Perhaps they were not sufficiently bold or intelligent.

The President: If these women have husbands or guardians, there was great risk in bringing them away?

A: We are prepared to give them back.

Q: If there was a government orphanage at Ajmer, would your agents have still taken the people away?

A: We would have placed them at the disposal of that Government orphanage. There are orphanages managed by the agencies where no one has any admittance.

Mr. Nicholson: Are you aware that agencies in Rajputana collected 7,000 orphans?

A: Yes; and some were sent to distant places.

Q: Then they did what you did; they sent them to another province?

A: Yes; and that is what we wanted to stop.

The President: Where do you get your funds from?

A: Private subscriptions.

Q: Do you collect all over India?

A: Only from the Punjab.

Q: What is the name of the Association?

A: The chief Association is the Arya Samaj, Ferozepore.

Q: You have a branch in Bareilly?

A: Yes.

Mr. Nicholson: Were the agents you sent out young men, or elderly men, or what?

A: Young men belonging to the college.

Q: And they were responsible for the collection of orphans, &c.?

A: Yes.

Q: And for obtaining all the information on which you acted?

A: Yes.

Q: Are they men of 20?

A: Perhaps more than that.

The President: Do they receive salaries?

A: No; nothing except some small travelling expenses.

Mr. Nicholson: Are your agents under control?

A: Yes.

Q: Do you hope to make your institution self-supporting?

A: Yes; we are trying to make a carpet factory.

Q: It is mentioned in the newspapers that it is proposed to open a joint stock company?

A: Yes.

Q: For that purpose?

A: Rupees ten thousand has been collected for the orphanage and it is proposed to collect Rs. 10,000 more.

Q: And do you mean that that should be kept there under conditions which Government might like to impose for the benefit of the orphans themselves?

A: Yes.

Q: Conditions to be imposed on the orphans?

A: No; on the employers.

The President: You say you have married some of the girls off; what class of people have they married?

A: They were married to superior castes before; this year only two or three marriages have taken place. In one case a Central Provinces boy has married a girl of the same caste, and they are making a decent livelihood.

Q: Do you give any dowry with these girls?

A: No.

Q: Don't you anticipate some difficulty in getting rid of number of girls?

A: We married them to people who were able to look after them.

Q: Will the supply be up to the demand?

A: The number of unmarried men is larger than the supply of girls.

Q: Has the man to pay the dowry or the woman?

A: In the case of low castes the man has to pay something for his wife.

Q: You don't anticipate any difficulty in the matter?

A: No.

Mr Nicholson: Is there any difficulty about castes?

A: No, not in the Punjab.

Q: Will they all become Arya Samajists?

A: No.

Q: If you take a child of three or four from a poorhouse, you don't know its caste?

A: We generally get young children from Government, and information is supplied about the caste.

Q: But if you don't know the caste?

A: They are kept separate.[3]

3. Agreeing with the views expressed by Lajpat Rai, the Commission recommended that deserted children and orphans "should not be made over to persons or institutions of a different religion until all efforts to find persons and institutions of their own religions willing to take charge of them have failed".

2. Famines and Orphans[1]

That the last two famines[2] have told very heavily upon the numerical strength of the Hindus is a fact which does not require to be established by any great array of facts and figures. The tracts mostly affected by these famines were mainly Hindu and consequently it was amongst the latter that the suffering was the most acute and the effects extremely disastrous. In these tracts the community not only lost lacs by death, but an immensely large number have so seriously deteriorated in physique, that though not totally incapable of bearing children, the offspring which they might bring forth must be small in number and extremely weak in body. Besides actual losses by death many a family has been deprived of the means of continuity of line by the survival of women doomed to life-long widowhood. Even men who have survived their wives are not seen to be remarried. Add to this the loss by conversion to other religions, which have been sufficiently numerous to cause a gap which will not be easily filled up. However true it may be that people whom sheer want of food and drink forced to accept the protection of other religions in these periods of dire calamity can hardly be called converts, but it is a fact all the same that they are lost to Hinduism. The Hindu is conservative to the core, and loves his religion and nationality, above everything else. To him the loss of religion is worse than death itself, but what is he to do when starvation and other privations

1. Reproduced from *Lala Lajpat Rai—The Man in His Word* (Madras, 1907), pp. 44-54.
2. The famine of 1899-1900 caused by the failure of monsoon in 1898 and 1899 was much more severe than that of 1897-98 and it affected large areas in Punjab, Rajputana, Kathiawar and the Central Provinces.

following in the train of grinding poverty root out the very idea of religion from his mind. It was only in extreme agony that they sacrificed their beliefs to the necessity of keeping body and soul together. The choice lay between two agonies—one of starvation, the other of loss of every sentiment and connection that was dear and sacred—and it is no wonder that many succumbed to the second, though only after they had reached the last stage of suffering beyond which there was only the yawning abyss of annihilation. Many must have willingly preferred death to the acceptance of relief at such a heavy cost, but how can we blame even those who, fearing the pangs of slow dissolution, exchanged life for religion. Be what it may, it is a fact that in these calamitous scarcities which have held the country in their squeezing grip for the last five years consecutively, a very large number of men and women have been lost to Hinduism, which otherwise would have been a source of strength and power generally as well as a source of increase to its numbers. Then again numerous families have been ruined and have practically (at least from a Hindu point of view) ended, by their young ones having been taken away to long distances from their homes, and kept in charge of organisations which are beyond the reach of their parents and relatives, if any living. These children, though living, are for all purposes dead to their parents, their relatives, their caste and their community. We are talking not of orphans only but even of those who were either deserted by their parents in the vicissitudes of famine or who strayed away from their homes either in search of food or in search of absent parents who had already left to labour, and who while thus straying were collected and relieved, as they say, by benevolent philanthropists belonging to other denominations. These children were principally the victims of that short-sighted policy, which in the first instance, allowed very large numbers of relief seekers to accumulate on large works distant from their homes and their villages, and then allowed philanthropy to take charge of other people's children during the pendency of the famine, either from the Government poorhouses, and Government orphanages by the authority of Government Officers or from the streets etc., when they were straying in search of food or relatives. In plain words the truth is that the various missions engaged in the work of famine relief purchased so many converts to their faith at an awfully cheaper price per head than it ordinarily costs them to evangelize one non-Christian soul in India in years of normal rainfall. It is an open secret that even ordinary methods of sale and purchase were resorted to. Children, boys and girls were sold and purchased at a few annas, or a few pices per head.

Don't you be thinking, gentle reader, that these are imaginary statements. We know what we state and we can prove it, if necessary, to the hilt. Why, quotations from Christian papers themselves will bear out the truth of our statement. What, then, does it amount to? Briefly told it amounts to this, that a

Christian Government, with its anti-slavery laws, allowed the missionaries of its own faith to take charge of deserted children, in many cases with parents living, and in some cases to purchase them from parents themselves, with the ostensible object of converting them to Christianity in lieu of supporting them with food and water, in the time of famine. Ah! But for fallen Hinduism, the state of things should have been the reverse. A Hindu would gladly feed and clothe any number of the poor of other religions, in times of famine, or no famine and would never think of taking advantage of other people's misfortunes and troubles and poverty but when he requires the help of others he has to pay for it dearly. Neither a Mahommedan nor a Christian will feed him except at the price of his religion. Even in this famine, if well-to-do Hindus had used some discrimination in the distribution of their charities they could have saved thousands of their people and their little ones being sent out of the bosom of Hinduism for ever. Rich Hindus swelled the lists of Famine Charitable Funds, a decent portion of which was spent through the Christian missionary who used it in the Christian interest as effectively as he could. Broad-mindedness and charity to the poor, without any distinction of creed and caste is a noble trait of character of which Hinduism might be proud, *in the abstract*, but in this world of sects and creeds and in these days of struggle and competition between creed and creed, it does not pay. If over-rich, superfluously rich, resourceful Christianity cannot stand it, how can poverty-stricken, slavery-ridden, helpless Hinduism afford to indulge in it? But we have digressed. It was not our object to read a sermon to the Hindus. We meant to state facts and to comment upon them a little.

To resume, in Rajputana alone, Hinduism lost seventy thousand of these unfortunate children, who were collected by Christian Missions of various denominations and dispatched to distant places in various parts of India. The Arya Samajists took charge of about 1,000 and sailed them off to the Punjab. There were some married girls amongst the latter who had been deserted by their husbands and who would have joined the seventy thousand mentioned above, but for their timely rescue by the Arya Samajists. The latter are now searching their husbands and using all possible means of restoring them to their families, but those whom the Christians took away, are gone for good, whether married, or unmarried, orphan or no orphan. The Arya Samajists removed these children to the Punjab because they could not maintain them on the spot. They depended entirely upon local support in their own province which they could not have got but by the removal of the children to the land of five rivers. No amount of descriptive rhetoric, short of the actual sight of misery, would have moved our people to the necessity of taxing their scanty means. The removal of the famine-stricken children to the various districts in the Punjab was an effective appeal which touched more successfully the heart of every

Hindu who could save even a little out of his own necessities. Then the question of maintaining and training them after the famine was another difficulty in the way of providing relief on the spot. In the case of orphans at least, it was out of the question to give them temporary relief during the pendency of the famine, unless the relieving agencies were prepared to make permanent arrangements for bringing them up as useful members of society who could, in the course of time, earn their own livelihood. Of course, all these ends could be achieved even in Rajputana, if the Arya Samajists could command the same amount of funded help as was at the back of Christian Missions. Failing this, mere necessity forced them to remove the children to their province. But there was no such difficulty in the way of the *Padri*. He got his funds from England, America or other parts of Europe. To him Rajputana was as good as the Punjab, Bengal, Madras, Bombay, or any other place in India, still there might be some justification for those missions who had their permanent orphanages and buildings at the places to which they removed the famine-stricken children of Rajputana or the Central Provinces. But what possible justification could there be for the transfer of these children to distant places by those missions who had to keep them in hired buildings? At Lahore itself, two of the mission orphanages, one containing more than 100 boys and the other more than a 100 girls are located in hired buildings. Is it not, then, reasonable to infer, that besides the avowed facilities of management and economy, there was another object too, which induced our philanthropic Missionaries to remove these children to places distant from their homes? Whatever be the object, however, there can be no denial of the fact that this action of theirs has resulted in the complete loss of those children to their families and homes, at least of such who have parents or other relatives living and willing to take them back. And this has taken place under the policy of neutrality followed by the Government. The truth is that with these recurring famines, which have become an almost permanent feature of this ill-fated country, this system of orphan relief is a standing menace to Hinduism, and it is therefore with great satisfaction that we have read the recommendations of the last Famine Commission on this subject. Our gratification enhances still more when we remember that in 1898 even a strong conscientious ruler like Sir Antony MacDonnell[3] failed to carry into practice the principles now so clearly enunciated in this report. In 1898 Sir Antony allowed Christian Missions to remove Hindu orphans of the N.W.P. and Oudh to distant parts of India, while he had practically refused the same privilege to the Arya Samajists of the Punjab, a few months before. Consequently

3. Sir Antony Patrick MacDonnell (1844-1925); entered Indian Civil Service in 1865; Chief Commissioner, Central Provinces, 1891; member, Council of Viceroy, 1893-95; Lieutenant-Governor of North-Western Provinces and Chief Commissioner of Oudh, 1895-1901.

we are glad to find that the last Famine Commission have recognised the great importance of this question and have recommended that the "policy of the Government in regard to orphans, should be formulated in Provincial Codes, *beyond risk of misconception either by its officers or by the public*". So far as the principles of this policy are concerned, we believe they have been the same all this time *on paper* at least. What we are thankful for is the unambiguous and clear language which the Commissioners have used in making their recommendations. Should the Local-Government formulate their policy in the Provincial Codes in similar style, we feel sure, much of the misapprehension hitherto caused would be removed, and much unnecessary discontent would be stopped. The Hindus will know what they can do to keep children of their community within the pale of their religion. The following recommendations should therefore be hailed with delight by the whole Hindu community, as they are the persons principally affected by these rules, the Mahomedans being sufficiently powerful, united and influential to allow the destitute children of their community to be taken away with impunity by persons and Associations of other denominations.

Para 234 of the Report recommends that the following policy be adopted by Government with regard to orphans or destitute children, viz. that "the State should be, in times of famine, the temporary guardian of children whom it finds deserted and should not, in our opinion, divest itself of the care of them until a reasonable time has elapsed after the close of the famine, during which efforts should be made to discover the natural protectors of the children or, failing these, respectable persons of the same religion who are willing to adopt them". According to this recommendation it is the duty of the State henceforth to discover respectable persons of the same religion who may be willing to adopt children whose natural protectors have either died or cannot be found out. Failing such respectable persons the deserted children are not to be made over to persons or institutions of different religions "*until all efforts to find persons and institutions of their own religion willing to take charge of them have failed*". This is a most substantial concession for which we are heartily thankful to Sir Antony and his colleagues on the Commission. The next important recommendation is contained in para 235, which proposes to place certain obligations upon private orphanages with a view to enable the District Magistrate to institute the enquiries contemplated by the 1st part of para 234 i.e. the search for natural protectors, and also to enable the parents and relatives of lost children to trace out their children in such orphanages. This recommendation requires the private orphanages to maintain a register containing full particulars regarding the children in these orphanages and also further that "a copy of the register should be periodically forwarded to the District Magistrate in order that he may make enquiries for the parents or relatives of such children". But the most substantial part of these latter recommendations consists in recognizing the right of the ostensible parents and relatives of the inmates of famine orphanages to free access to such institutions in order to reclaim their little ones. The hasty removal of the children to places distant from their homes is proposed to be stopped or checked by the rule "*that no unclaimed child be removed from the district in which it is found until a period of three months has elapsed after the close of relief operations in the district*".

Categorically put, the Commissioners first admit:

1—That the action of European and native philanthropists in having taken charge of deserted children and in some instances in despatching them "to private orphanages" and homes in distant parts of the country has given rise to "misunderstanding".

2ndly—That "it is of great importance that the policy of the Government in regard to orphans should be formulated in Provincial Codes, beyond risk of misconception either by its officers or by the public".

3rdly—That "it is common experience that besides those children who are true orphans, others are deserted by their parents or relatives in the stress of famine, and reclaimed when it is over".

4thly—That "it is also common experience that relatives and caste-fellows and sometimes co-religionists are ready to adopt children at the end of a famine".

And then they make the recommendations we have already referred to above. We hope Hindus all over India will profit by these recommendations and exert as they can to relieve and protect the orphans and other deserted children of their community in times of famine. Nay, we think, it is only fair that the recommendations contained in para 235, at least, should be given a retrospective effect and persons claiming as relatives and guardians should be allowed free access to all orphanages to find their lost children or the children of their deceased relatives. The Hindus of different provinces should combine and make a joint representation to Government to achieve this end.

In the end beyond thanking the Commission for their clear recommendations as far as they go, we have to express our disappointment at the absence of a suggestion that during the pendency of a famine all orphans or deserted children whether found by Government or other private charitable agencies be brought to government orphanages, and be not allowed to be detained or admitted into private orphanages except after the requirements of para 234 had been complied with.

8
KANGRA VALLEY EARTHQUAKE

1. To G.K. Gokhale[1]

Lahore
10 April 1905

Dear Mr. Gokhale,

To-day's *Panjabee* will give you some idea of the terrible disaster that has befallen the Punjab and its people on account of the earthquake.[2] You will also find an account of what we are doing. All the same this does not seem to me to be sufficiently good ground for warranting the abandonment of your visit nor do we contemplate the postponement of the ceremony of laying down the foundation stone of our College in the Easter. My only fear is that distracted and awfully engaged as we are so we may not be able to give you a suitable reception and to make your stay very comfortable. Some of our workers are going to the scene of disaster and I am myself thinking of doing so if I can escape from Lahore for a few days. I was very anxious to have you here in the Easter because that would have given you an opportunity of seeing most of the Punjab's leading men and also seeing some of our work. But under the present circumstances I am afraid I must ask you to come a week or two later. May is not likely to be very warm this year. We have been thinking of giving you a grand reception and my people will not pardon me if I were to propose a quiet visit. The boys here were making all sorts of preparations, addresses and triumphal arches, etc. I do not now know what to say to them now. Even this morning a number of them saw me and enquired the date of your arrival and wanted instructions for reception, etc. Please do let me know, therefore, if you can come over in the beginning of May and whether that is likely to upset your plans. In the meantime we have called a meeting of the Indian Association for Tuesday and I shall wire to you if the Association decides to have you in Easter and not later.

With a heavy heart.
I remain

Yours sincerely,
Lajpat Rai

1. G.K. Gokhale Papers (microfilm), N.A.I.
2. The Kangra district in Punjab (now in Himachal Pradesh) was rocked by a severe earthquake on 4 April 1905 resulting in large-scale damage to property and loss of life in Dharamsala, Kangra and many other towns and villages. Lajpat Rai visited the affected areas on 8 April and, on behalf of the Arya Samaj and as Secretary of the Kangra Valley Relief Committee, Lahore, organised relief work.

P.S.—My girl[3] has broken her thigh bone on the day of the earthquake and my friend Lala Hansrajji has lost a sister who was buried alive with her husband, two sons, daughter, daughter-in-law and granddaughter. Only the husband, a son and daughter-in-law have been rescued. All others are dead. And similar or even worse has been the fate of many families at Dharamsala, Kangra and other places. I have just received a telegram from Wacha saying you are sailing on the 13th and that I should accompany you. But here the matters are proceeding very slowly. Harkishen Lal is waging a war against the proposal. Others are lethargic while I cannot move actively. Under the circumstances your visit would have been simply invaluable. I shall see and wire later on.

Yours,
Lajpat Rai

P.S.—I am very busy with relief work. Can't you come for next Saturday and Sunday at Lahore (i.e. 29th and 30th)? Will the following programme suit you?

27th Umballa, 28th Amritsar
29th to 30th Lahore

Lajpat Rai

3. Parbati.

2. The Kangra Valley Relief Committee[1]

Sir, Will you allow a space in your columns for the following brief report of the above Committee's work? Since writing to you last amongst other smaller items I have received the following:

		Rs.
A Christian lady (anonymous)	...	100
A friend from Lahore (anonymous)	...	300
A friend from Bombay (anonymous)	...	50

1. Letter to the editor published in *The Tribune* of 15 April 1905.

Lala Ram Saran Das of Lahore	...	200
Rai Sahib Mohan Lal	...	100
Lala Niranjan Das, Pleader	...	100
Sardar Buta Singh from Rawalpindi	...	100

(2) Lala Mulk Raj Bhalla,[2] the elder brother of Lala Hans Raj, has reached Kangra and is cooperating with Bakhshi Sohan Lal and other friends who have gone from Lahore.

(3) We are sending two hospital assistants, five *chhouldaries*, a stock of medicines, blankets, clothes &c. &c. by this evening's train.

(4) The reports from Kangra lay great stress upon the paucity of labourers there, and we are trying to send about 50 labourers also.

(5) We have by this time sent from Lahore Rs 1,000 cash to the scene of disaster and about two dozen workers.

(6) The following telegram from Lala Mulk Raj speaks for itself:

"Conditions awful. Towns, villages levelled to the ground; population houseless; gigantic measure needed."

(7) I went to Amritsar yesterday, delivered a speech at a meeting presided over by Rai Diwan Chand, M.A., LL.B., Judge, Small Cause Court, in the Theatre of Lala Kanhaya Lal, after which a subscription list was opened. Subscription lists have been opened by the Muffassil Arya Samajes also.

Lajpat Rai

2. B. 1876; businessman who started a spinning and weaving mill in Lahore in 1897; Municipal Commissioner of Lahore for eighteen years; appointed by the Government as Joint Secretary of the Kangra Valley Earthquake Relief Work in 1905; awarded 'Kaiser-i-Hind' gold medal in 1914; President, Punjab Sanatan Dharma Pratinidhi Sabha; elected to Punjab Legislative Council, and, later in 1920, to Council of State.

3. Relief Work in Villages in Kangra Valley[1]

For some days past I have not been able to send you any report of our work in the Kangra valley as I was otherwise very busy. The work has been progressing very well. Funds are coming, and workers are being added or substituted. I am

1. Letter to the editor published in *The Panjabee* of 1 May 1905.

now sending a number of carpenters and masons. Some doctors have also been employed and will proceed immediately.

The following extracts from the last three reports of Bakhshi Sohan Lal are sent for favour of publication in your paper. . . .[2]

2. The three reports, dated 23, 24 and 25 April, sent by Bakshi Sohan Lal, a prominent Arya Samajist, social worker and philanthropist of Lahore, which are not reproduced here, contained accounts mainly of medical help being provided by doctors and social workers in Kangra and neighbouring villages. The last report of 25 April emphasized the need for "able men who might visit the stricken district and make correct estimates of losses to individuals" so that they could be placed "before the authorities to obtain compensation in order to restart such persons in life".

4. Donations to Kangra Valley Relief Fund[1]

Sir, Will you please convey my thanks to all those who have so nobly responded to my appeal for the Kangra Valley Relief Fund? Press of business has not allowed me to acknowledge each donation personally and individually, but I have asked Bakhshi Tek Chand[2] to send receipts to all. Moreover, printed lists of donations can also be had from him for the mere asking. In future all money orders, cheques, & c., should be drawn in favour of Bakhshi Siban Lal[3], who has been appointed Secretary of the Committee. All remittances should be made payable to him or to Bakhshi Tek Chand, M.A., the Assistant Secretary.

Yours &c.,
Lajpat Rai

1. Letter to the editor, dated Lahore, 9 May, published in *The Tribune* of 11 May 1905.
2. Son of Jaisi Ram and eminent Arya Samajist of Lahore; worked as Assistant Secretary of Kangra Valley Relief Committee; Secretary of D.A.V. College Managing Committee for a number of years.
3. A prominent Arya Samajist of Lahore, philanthropist and social worker; Secretary of Kangra Valley Relief Committee.

5. Ruin and Devastation in Kangra District[1]

I have just returned from a visit to Dharamsala, Kangra and the neighbouring villages.[2] Below I beg to give my impressions of what I saw, observed and came to know by careful enquiries made from trustworthy and reliable persons.

(a) General Description

Devastation by earthquake in the Kangra district

The ruin and devastation caused by earthquake in the Kangra district is too vast and extensive to be described by pen or to be imagined by those who have not seen the affected area with their own eyes. In less than a minute, Nature seems to have done what could not possibly be done by man even in centuries. Populous and large towns have been converted into heaps of ruins and present an appalling sight. Buildings, small and low, *kachcha* or *pakka*, of bricks or of stones, built on the rock, hill or below, have all crumbled down and are lying in such a state as if the whole thing had been crushed into pieces by numerous hammers from top to bottom bringing down wood, iron, bricks, stone, mortar or mud together, and making one heap of all of them. It was a strange and painful look that the devastated towns presented especially to me who had seen them before the earthquake. The grander, the loftier, the more substantial a building, the more complete and sudden has been its fall and the greater the loss it inflicted in coming down on its owners or occupiers.

In towns having hundreds of buildings not a single structure is left to give shelter to man or animal. Impossible as it is to describe the general look of places affected and brought down by the earthquake, the following facts might serve to give the reader a general idea of the loss caused.

(b) Area Affected

The area affected consists of 3 complete Tehsils, viz. Palampur, Kangra and Kulu; parts of Tehsils Dera and Hamirpur, and the native States of Mandi and Lambagraon.

Kangra Tehsil consists of 134 villages including 1,028 *Tikas* (hamlets).

1. Published in *The Panjabee* of 15 May 1905.
2. Lajpat Rai visited these places on 8 May.

Palampur Tehsil consists of 114 villages including about 1,000 *Tikas*.

Sir Charles Rivaz[3] estimates the area to be 700 square miles but I am afraid he had not by that time (i.e. when he wrote his reports) full information about the Sub-Division of Kulu. Even now the information about Kulu is not very full, and each day brings to light the greater extent of the damage done and the larger area affected therein. According to my estimate the number of villages and *Tikas* affected will come to over 3,000. The Kangra Tehsil consists of 1,028 *Tikas*, all of which have been affected. The same may be said of Palampur. If the hamlets affected in other Tehsils be added, the total number may exceed 3,000. The affected area includes the towns of Dharamsala, Kangra, Jwalamukhi, Dera, Sujanpur, Palampur, Kulu, Baij Nath, Paprola, Bhawana, Nagrola and Dowlatpur.

Loss of Life and Property in Kangra Tehsil

It is difficult to give even an approximate estimate of the loss of life as returns and figures are yet coming in and there are places in the Sub-Division of Kulu of which we have little information, if any, at all. The Tehsil of Kangra alone, excluding the town of Kangra and the civil and military stations at Dharamsala, is said to have lost no less than 10,257 human beings.The loss of life at Kangra is roughly estimated to be in no case less than 2,000.The official returns do not take into account the large number of pilgrims that were there on account of the days being particularly auspicious for the worship of the goddess. The civil and military stations of Dharamsala are said to have lost about 3,000 persons.

To this may be added the loss of cattle which is over 20,000. Excluding the towns of Kangra (with Bhavan and the civil and military stations of Dharamsala) the number of houses fallen in the Kangra Tehsil is believed to be over 40 thousand. The loss of property in Kangra town could not be less than 20 lacs.

In the Palampur Tehsil the loss of human lives is said to be about 6,000 souls and that of cattle very near 16,000. I was informed by a friend that in one revenue circle consisting of 14 villages the loss to property was estimated at a figure exceeding 9 lacs.

3. Lieutenant-Governor of Punjab.

Sujanpur

In Sujanpur town the number of houses fallen is estimated by a gentleman, who is acting as the secretary of a local relief committee, to be 1,600.

From this one may form some idea of the loss of life and property caused by the earthquake. My own idea is that when full information is available the figures of loss will be appalling.

Relief Measures

The official measures taken for the relief of districts have been given in detail by H.E. the Lieutenant-Governor in his report published in the *Civil and Military Gazette* of the 5th May.

All I intend to do is to add a few more facts which will throw additional light on the relief measures hitherto taken; but before I do so I would like to give expression to the sense of gratitude which the people in the Valley feel towards His Excellency, who exhibited his sympathy by personally inspecting the worst part of the affected area, and whose kind enquiries of the people and promises of help went a great deal in putting heart into them. Amongst European officials the next name which is being freely mixed with that of Sir Charles Rivaz in the blessings of the population is that of Major Lane, the Civil Surgeon of Dharamsala. Amongst Indian officials the man who has given substantial proof of his having right royal blood worthy of the historic community to which he belongs is Ticca Rajindra Pal. But for him and the indefatigable exertions of Dr. Vaishno Ram many lives that have been saved would have been lost. I am sure many more Indians could have been saved out of the debris if some more of the brave Gorkhas could have been spared in time to dig out the living interred, several of those who had been buried were heard crying for help but in vain as there was no one ready at hand to dig them out. This is about Dharamsala.

At Kangra the only influential person left to do the work of rescue was Lala Diwan Chand, Contractor. Diwan Bishan Das, Bar-at-Law, however, reached the place on the evening of the 4th and both of these gentlemen did what they could to help the survivors and dig out the living buried. No official help reached except on the evening of the 7th, when Major Smith arrived at Kangra with the necessary authority to do the work of rescue but unfortunately he had only one *chhouldarie* with him, no labourers, no provisions and no tools. The Tahsilder of Dera was the first man to reach there with 50 labourers on the morning of the 8th. On his arrival on the evening of the 7th, Major Smith found that the Treasury was intact and guarded by the two or three surviving police constables, the only ones remaining alive of the whole police force on duty in that police station. On the morning of the 8th commenced the work of rescue and relief, on the 9th a woman was dug out alive, on the 14th a living goat and on the 27th a living *chikor* were dug out, which shows that many more lives could have been saved if diggers had been found in time. It is impossible to tell how many lives were lost for failure or inadequacy of digging hands and tools. Of the private relief parties the first to reach Dharamsala and Kangra was that of Bakhshi Sohan Lal of the Lahore Arya Samaj. He reached Shahpur on the 7th April, Dharamsala on the 9th and Kangra on the 10th, i.e. only two days after the Government relief operations began. How far the Government rose equal to the occasion, at Kangra at least, may be judged from the fact that bodies are being dug out there even up to this day. Two were dug out in my presence on the 6th of May, i.e., 32 days after the earthquake. It is believed that a large number of bodies are still lying in Bhavan close to the temple. The work of digging out bodies is being creditably shared by private relief parties. In the villages too a large number of cattle are still lying buried in the debris. It appears that no relief in the way of help for the digging out of corpses of human beings and dead cattle has been given in the villages. On my way to Kangra from Dharamsala I passed through a village, Mataur by name. There I happened to meet a family of agriculturists consisting of one female and two males. Of the males one was an old man of about 60 and the other a young man of about 30. The latter had his leg broken and the former his shoulder bone dislocated. Both these were set right and planted by the Arya Samaj doctors, but when I saw them the old man had removed his splint and had an extremely dirty bandage of old torn rags round his arms. The woman had her foot burned. All three were thus incapable of doing any digging work, and so the courtyard where they were sitting was full of bad odour and emitted a most nauseating and sickening smell. On enquiry I found that a bullock was buried under the debris and the members of the family being incapable to dig him out no extraneous help was forthcoming to do the needful. Now this was a typical case of neglect. Very little if anything at all seems to have been done for the villages. It is true that in some places medical aid has been provided; in others a few maunds of rations and a few hundred *sirkis* have been distributed, but beyond this no help has been given to the villages generally, except in a number of roadside villages, to exhume the dead bodies of men and cattle and to build their houses. It is true that in most of the villages the people have done this for themselves. Being so near the rains (in fact it has several times rained since the earthquake) they are very anxious to have some sort of shelter for themselves and their children, and therefore at almost every step in this desolate area you find signs of resigned activity in building huts and shelters. The people seem to have forgotten all their losses and appear to be too grateful for what has been saved. From Dharamsala to Kangra, a distance of 12 miles, which I walked on foot from 3.30 P.M. up to 8 P.M., I heard no cries of woe nor any signs of mourning. But it broke my heart to observe that this time the roadside gave a look of being lonely and deserted, having no little ones to break the monotony of Nature with their gay songs, playful jovialities and freaks of childish ingenousness which I witnessed on the previous occasion when I passed through that area in 1903. The fact is that children seemed to have suffered the most. Even the womenfolk seemed to be resigned to God's will. In the whole affected area traversed by me I saw no mourning except when I reached the Kangra bazaar where for the first time I saw an old woman crying piteously, and a little further on in the same locality I noticed a middle-aged woman with a child in her lap sitting on the ruins of her house and weeping bitterly for the loss of her dear ones, Oh! What a sight!! It was sufficient to melt a heart of stone. What a population to have as subjects! Any government on the face of the globe would be proud to have people like this and would be prepared to do everything possible for the amelioration of their miserable state, but is not our Government very humane, wise and liberal as they let these people live in peace and security? Should they not be grateful because they are allowed to cultivate their lands and sell the produce to the highest bidder in the market? But this is only by the way. To resume my narrative, I have grave reasons to doubt if the liberal concessions ordered by Sir Charles Rivaz and the Punjab Government will really benefit the people. Some of them have already built their huts, others are actually building the same; the Revenue officer is said to be pressing hard for repairs to *Kulds* (natural water courses) being completed by the people themselves. Till now nothing has been done to help the people in cutting their crops and bringing the produce home before the rains set in. No pecuniary help has yet been given to any Indian, whether in towns or villages. In some places the entreaties for help are reported to have been met with a show of temper and a shower of abuse on the part of an officer who may better remain unnamed.

May we beg of the Government of Sir Denzil Ibbetson[4] to depute some experienced native E.A.C.s who know the district well, such as Lala Nathu Ram who was for many years the Superintendent of the Jullundur Commissioner's Office or Lala Sansar Chand or Lala Amar Chand Johar, or others whose names are better known to the Government than to us. At this time it will be more in keeping with the sympathetic policy laid down by the Government to have old, experienced, hard-working and sympathetic native officers than young civilians who do not know much of the country and its people or their habits and who quite unconsciously and unwillingly may even in small

4. (1847-1908); I.C.S.; member of Viceroy's Executive Council; Lieutenant-Governor of Punjab in 1907.

matters be liable to injure the tender feelings of a suffering population and thus make the situation more painful for those who are already afflicted with the wrath of heaven. If there was ever a great need of relief being administered with sympathy and considerate it is now, and if there was ever an afflicted area which required extremely considerate treatment it is the district of Kangra in its present trouble. That the people in this district are not yet completely demoralised and do still preserve some remnants of noble Aryan instincts will be more than clear from the fact that many cases have come to my notice in which old and decrepit men and women, and naked starving youths every inch needy and in trouble, have refused to accept charity on the ground of religious scruples. Can there be much danger of charity being misapplied and misused in a population like this? Several of our workers have related to me with tears in their eyes the stories of charity being absolutely refused by men and women, who were themselves in absolute destitution and did not know how and wherefrom to make a meal and how to cover their bodies. Bravo! Noble souls! Hinduism is proud of you and will, I trust, leave nothing undone to help you in your affliction.

9
HINDUISM

1. Hindu Nationalism[1]

I have read with considerable interest the article by a "Hindu Nationalist", on the "Creation of a Hindu Nationality", in the June number of the *Samachar*, as also the contribution on the same subject, in the last number of this journal, by my friend Pandit Madho Ram. While I heartily join in the "Hindu Nationalist's" appeal to the educated Hindus, yet I do not share his opinion that "the idea of nationality is an essentially European and modern idea", nor can I agree with his reading of the facts of history relied upon by him in support of his assertion. In my humble opinion the ideas of "nationality" and "patriotism" are as old as the different countries into which the earth is divided, as ancient as the distinctions of race and religion that have been existing in the world from time immemorial, and are pre-historic. They may have been more phenomenal in one epoch than in another. Their hold on different races and nations may have varied in intensity or extent, but that the ideas have always been there, as fixed and immutable as those of truth and falsehood, is my firm belief. It is not, however, my intention to enter into a speculative or a historical controversy with the "Hindu Nationalist" on the origin of the sentiments of nationality and patriotism. Suffice it to say that I agree with most of the conclusions and am prepared to generally endorse the remedies suggested. In fact, some of the thoughts expressed in his article were, as if, foreshadowed by me in my article on the Congress published in the *Samachar* of October 1901. This reference has been made not to suggest any borrowing on the part of the "Hindu Nationalist", but to show that these thoughts are just now uppermost in the minds of all such Hindus as claim to love their people and to think of the means of their progress.

The "Nationalist" begins by bemoaning the absence of the idea of nationality amongst Hindus, and ascribes all our misfortunes, past and present, to the same fact. "The Hindus," he says, "offer a curious instance of a people without any feeling of nationality." Having thus laid down the proposition he appeals to the pages of history to support his conclusion and apparently seems to have made out a strong case. But he has evidently missed the fact that his own proposition assumes the existence of a people having a common name, who have made history by that name. Quite unconsciously he assumes the existence of a Hindu nationality when he talks of the unsuccessful efforts of the Rajputs and the Mahrattas to throw off the foreign yoke and to found a Hindu empire. What he complains of is that these efforts were spasmodic, not

1 *Lala Lajpat Rai—The Man in His Word* (Madras, 1907), pp. 54-66; originally published in *Hindustan Review and Kayastha Samachar*, September-October 1902, pp. 249-54.

supported by the general body of the people, and therefore not quite national, but all the time he admits by implication that there was a nation which could and should have made a combined effort. Otherwise what can he possibly mean by saying that "the Mahrattas were left to fight the last battle of the Hindus alone, unaided by the Sesodia or the Rathore?" He admits that "if allowed to grow unchecked the Mahratta confederacy might have developed into a national empire". In the face of these facts we cannot deny the existence of a nation simply because all the members of that nation did not join the struggle for defence, or that some of them seceded or proved traitors, or joined the enemy's camp. Nor can we deny the existence of the sentiment of nationality, because that sentiment was not sufficiently strong and marked to overcome all differences among the different members of that nation to enable them to stand as one man in defence of national interests. In the next place, why ignore the united front presented by the Hindus of all classes to repel the fourth invasion of Mahmud of Ghazni, and why forget the empires of the Pandavas, of Asoka, of Siladittya, Vikram, Bhoja, and others? Even the ill-fated Prithvi Raj, the last of the Hindu emperors, who paid the penalty of the empire in the battle of Thaneswar,[2] could twice command the united services of almost the whole nation in his noble and valiant defense of the empire and the motherland? Who knows that but for the treachery of that fratricide of a Jai Chand, history would have been made otherwise? But the treachery of Jai Chand and the defeat of Prithvi Raj do not detract from the character of the heroic stand which the nation made against the foreigner. Victories and defeats are not solely made by man but are regulated by many a cause some of which may be quite outside the control of the parties at war. If in 1192 Providence decreed the fall of the Hindus, that alone is not sufficient to justify us in damning the Hindus of that period as men who were totally bereft of the sentiment of nationality. Then, as I have already hinted, the very fact of our people being known to other peoples by a distinctive name is a proof of the existence of Hindu nationality.

I am too old now to continue to believe that the name Hindu was for the first time given to us as one involving abuse, contempt and reproach by our Mohammedan invaders. Rather, I believe that our fall and degradation helped the fall of the word also, and perhaps a peep into the philological history of the word might prove that all the bad meanings that are now assigned to the word in the Persian lexicon were of a comparatively later origin, and an outcome of the fall of the Hindu nation. Long before the Mohammedan invasion, and perhaps long before the advent of the Prophet of Islam, we were known to the people of other countries as Hindus. If so, what did this name signify? Was it a tribal distinction? I say, no, because the Hindus were of many tribes. Was it a

2. In 1192.

racial name? I again say, no, because Persians of Iran, too, belonged to the same race. Was it then a religious designation? Yes, partly religious no doubt, but mainly national, and in evidence I can produce a number of quotations from the productions of early Greek historians and Mohammedan writers. For example, in what other sense does the Homer of Persia, the gifted Firdausi,[3] who has immortalized the struggle for supremacy between the Iranians and Turanians, use the expression Hindu in the following verses, which I pick at random from his great work, the *Shahnama*.[4]

Then we find many references to our people as Hindus in the sacred books of the Parsis, the Vindidad and others. So far as the name is concerned, our only difficulty arises when we fail to find any trace of it in our own literature where our people are invariably styled as Aryas. But here again we find enough traces of the sentiment of nationality in the passages in which the *Rishis* ordained all Aryas to combine against the attacks of *Dasyus*, *Chandalas* and *Mlechhas*. God is often invoked for protection against the latter. As for indications of an imperial spirit amongst the Hindus, the *Ramayana* and the *Mahabharata* are full of evidences of the same. What was king Yudhishthira's *Rajsuya Yajna* and by what name would you style the ambitious scheme of Jarasindhu?

The fact is that the best and the most glorious period of Aryan supremacy is yet a closed chapter to us. Almost the whole of the pre-Buddhist period is shrouded in mystery. Even the literature that has reached us is so full of allusions, enigmas, signs and names and is written in such an archaic language that the whole thing seems to be a mystery. According to the best of European authorities, the language of the Vedas is so full of obsolete and archaic forms and expressions that the whole seems to be a cipher which with the best of efforts might yet take years to decipher. Still we know and understand enough to be proud of, and to glory in, the heritage which has descended to us from our "barbarian"(?) ancestors in the shape of national literature. And this must be the fulcrum of the lever with which we are to rise as a nation. It will not do to be unjust to our forefathers and to deny the idea of national love in them. No, they were patriots according to the best of their own lights. The history of our country, from the standpoint of a Hindu, has yet to be written and till that is done, let us suspend judgement, remembering that the men whom we desire to judge and whom we are sometimes inclined to hastily condemn (often unheard) were masterminds, whose productions and teachings are the loftiest in the whole range of written or known thoughts. We, the English-educated Hindus of the present day, who claim to have imbibed the new spirit of nationality and patriotism from the West, would really do well to study a few chapters of the

3. Mansur Abdul Qasim Firdausi (935-1020); Persian poet; known for his classic epic *Shahnama*.
4. Not reproduced here.

Vedic literature with care and thought, and I am confident that this study will open a panorama of new ideas to our view. Such a study will, I am sure, enable us to see that the keynote of the pre-Buddhistic *Vedic* religion was the *sacrifice of all for all*. True, that the genius of a jealous and perverted, sometimes corrupt and selfish, priesthood built such a vast and stupendous superstructure of conventionalities and formalities, with an almost interminable labyrinth of rituals and ceremonials obscured by which the true spirit of the religion was practically lost and could no longer be the mainstay of the nation.

It is this submergence of the true spirit of the ancient Hindu faith under the load of conventional rituals and formal ceremonials that has since been the bane of the Hindus and not the entire absence of the idea of nationality. But you might say that we have been producing martyrs and no one can be a martyr except by the strength of faith. How can a nation destitute of faith produce martyrs? Is there a nation who have shown more of faith in their religion, in their individuality, in their sacred laws than the Hindus? How can you otherwise explain their tenacity in clinging to their forms of religion, their pertinacity to stick to their customs? I purposely say, *forms of religion* became real religion—the religion that guides and moulds a man, or a nation, and that elevates and ennobles them, that raises them to high ideals, that evokes the highest of sacrifices, has long ago disappeared from us. In fact, it was never in the post-Buddhistic period restored to its altar in the temple of hearts. True, martyrs we have certainly been producing, ever and anon, and sometimes in numbers, but when I accuse the Hindus of want of faith, I do not mean *individual faith*, but that *social faith* which is the parent of victory; the faith that arouses the multitudes; faith in their own destiny, in their own mission and in the mission of the epoch; the faith that leads on to struggle; the faith that enlightens and bids men advance fearlessly in the ways of God and Humanity, with their religion in their heart and their future progress as their goal. It is such a faith that we have been wanting since the time of Buddha and it is such a faith that we require to become a nation again.

I shall now discuss the observations of Mr. Madho Ram and I shall remark at the outset that even admitting for argument's sake the absolute accuracy of all his statements and facts, and also the correctness of the inferences he draws therefrom, I would beg to differ from him in a *matter of principle*. My esteemed friend seems to think that all these internecine quarrels, strife and sectarian struggles which he records at such great length in the course of his article largely take away "the chance for the progress of Hindu Nationalism in our country" or to be more accurate in quoting his words, he questions the Hindu Nationalist, if in the face of circumstances stated by him "there is much chance for the progress of Hindu Nationalism in our country". I answer the question in the affirmative. What I am anxious to point out is, that the existence of these quarrels and strife is neither a bar to the progress of Hindu Nationalism nor is it sufficient proof of the absence of the idea of nationality amongst the Hindus. And this, for the simple reason that the idea of nationality does not necessarily imply a complete union amongst all its members on all matters, social, religious or political; nor does it suggest the existence of a state of perfect concord and harmony among its members or leaders, or the freedom of the latter from all human weaknesses such as lead personalities to indulge in strong or even abusive language amongst, and towards, each other. Has there been any nation in the past, or is there any nation now living, which has been or is free from these differences or quarrels? Surely, Roman, Grecian and Mohammedan histories must be admitted to present splendid and noble types of nationality and nationalism, and the present times cannot furnish better and nobler types of nationality than the English, the German, and the American and the French, not to speak of others equally noble though not so influential and powerful, such as the Swiss, the Italian and the Dutch. Religious and social differences have played a prominent part in the histories of these nations and even now they are not free from the same. A mere glance at the English and Irish papers, a perusal of the speeches in Parliament and out of Parliament by political men, a study of the literature of different religious sects in the West and the perusal of the biographies of the public men in these countries will show that the incidents narrated by my friend altogether lose in significance and weight in the presence of the more vituperative and sometimes highly abusive differences and quarrels of these magnates of the European world. The truth is that honest differences, controversial discussions, and criticisms of public men by public men, are absolutely necessary for the healthy growth and progress of nationality. Then we must be prepared to meet with human weaknesses, partialities, jealousies, personalities, insinuations, innuendoes, use of strong language etc., in these discussions and controversies. Carried beyond a certain degree and limit they might retard the growth of nationalism, or might bring down an already completed edifice of nationality. I am not, however, prepared to admit that the differences and the disputes amongst the different classes of educated Hindus at the present moment exceed that limit. It is wrong to suppose that the idea of nationalism or nationality requires a complete union in all details of religious, social, economic, or political life, or that it requires a complete freedom from sectarian quarrels or disputes or jealousies. To expect so is to expect what is an impossibility and what entirely ignores human nature. In my humble opinion it is sufficient for the growth of nationality, if the different parts that claim the shelter of its ways have a sense of unity, which is sufficient to make them combine against a common enemy and a common danger. Run on a few basal principles in religion, on the community of a sacred language, and on the community of interests, the Hindus ought to foster the growth of a national sentiment which should be sufficiently strong to enable them to work for the common good in the different ways and according to the lights vouchsafed to each. Let us keep one ideal before us. Let our ideal be sufficiently high to cover all, sufficiently broad and extensive to include all, who take pride in one common name, a common ancestry, a common history, a common religion, a common language and a common future.

We will not advance the cause of nationality by one inch if we decide to preserve an attitude of silent quietude and non-disturbing peace in all matters, religious and social. Such an attitude can only mean stagnation and gradual extinction. Struggle, hard struggle, is the law of progress. Yes, struggle we must, both *inter se* as well others. There must be a struggle between truth and untruth, between vice and virtue, between honesty and dishonesty, between expediency and righteousness, between indolence and energy, between enterprise and a spirit of lethargy and between time-serving selfishness and noble disinterestedness. Without this struggle no nation can ever aspire to be great and influential. This struggle we have just entered upon. We have just emerged out of stagnation, and it is no wonder that we are sometimes apt to exceed the limits of propriety or to irresistibly throw in more of sectarianism and personality, where more or much less is needed. But national delinquencies or faults are not made up or remedied in a day. Let us not be impatient of what in my humble opinion seems to be a healthy sign of growth. Let us not strangle it by drawing its undesirable concomitants in high colours or by attaching undue importance to the same. Then there are men and men in all public bodies, religious and social. Because there are some violent men, some bad-tempered, some dishonest men, some traitors and time-servers in our public associations, it is no reason to record a wholesale condemnation of the same or to be disappointed with them. Public opinion in this country has yet to grow. It is a very feeble plant yet. Its growth must cause some unpleasant friction and struggle. Let us not be impatient of it. The country has yet to foster a bold spirit of disinterested, fearless criticism. Few people in this country are guided by purely public interests. Fewer still are those who can be moved to take interest in things which do not concern them exclusively and in which they have little at stake. The interests of others do not move them. What little criticism exists in the country is at once dubbed as sectarian, as interested, or as the outcome of jealousy or personal animosity. The criticism, that potent weapon, which alone can effectually check the vicious or selfish tendencies of great and powerful men, is discouraged and strangled. What we should aim at is not the silencing of criticism but the purging it out of personalities, jealousies, abuse and vituperation. This will take time, but so long as this is not achieved, let us not discourage, run down and do away with criticism altogether. At any rate, in my humble opinion impatience at, or silencing of mutual, criticism, or absence of all controversy will not necessarily mean unity or a healthy progress of nationalism. Having thus disposed of to the best of my power the objections of the "Hindu Nationalist" based, to my mind, on a wrong view of our ancient history, and that of Pandit Madho Ram who has, in my opinion, drawn erroneous inferences from the facts detailed by him and the accuracy of which I have assumed for the sake of argument, I conclude this article with a hope that I may be able to return to the subject in a later issue and discuss the present condition and prospects of Hindu Nationalism, the evidence of its progress and the chances of its future growth.

2. Social Genius of Hinduism[1]

An idea seems to be gaining ground amongst Hindus educated on Western lines that the genius of Hinduism is essentially individualistic and anti-social and that therefore no substantial reform in social life can come out of a revival of the past, and that we can only draw on the West and take light therefrom. They do not place much faith in reform on national lines and would rather go in for wholesale or bodily adoption of most at least, if not all, of the social institutions of the West. They would rather build a new social edifice on *rationality*, as distinguished from *nationality*, in religious and in social life. Again, there are a large number of Hindus who, although they are prepared to grant that there is much in our national religion as handed down to us in our sacred literature which may satisfy even the highest cravings of the human mind, whether in the sphere of the spirit, intellect or morals, cannot yet see the existence of a spirit of nationality among the old Hindus or the old Aryans (as I will prefer to style the pre-*Pauranic* ancestors of the Hindus).

1. This article written in three parts was published in *The Hindustan Review and Kayastha Samachar* of Apirl 1904

   At the end of the article Lajpat Rai has written: "In the above article I have relied upon the English translation of the Sanskrit text by European scholars so that there may be no occasion for a charge of straining the words or of extorting meanings or of inventing theories of my own, although I do not believe that these translations are the best that could be done." And as regards the italics and capital letters in the article, he has noted: "The italics and capital letters are everywhere mine."

The current impression of the educated Hindus has very much been strengthened by the utterances of some eminent Hindus of the western Presidency, whose learning, scholarship and devotion to the cause of the country entitle them to be heard with respect and admiration. They are supposed to say that Hinduism was wanting in the social principle being ostensibly individualistic.

It is very unfortunate to have to differ in any point from men of such vast erudition, deep learning and great reputation. Ordinarily any man will shrink from such an unpleasant and risky task however strong and cogent his reasons may be for that difference of opinion. Still, what sometimes deters men of deep learning and great reputation, may not stand in the way of a man who, though possessed of lesser qualifications, is possessed of a stronger faith in the truth of his cause and believes that the question is of vital importance to the cause of progress and reform amongst his people. It is therefore upon the strength of this faith, though with the greatest possible diffidence and hesitation, that I venture to express an opinion on the question raised in the opening sentences of this paper. Let me however make it clear that I quite concur with the opinion expressed by so many eminent social reformers that the question of social reform is one of *paramount national importance*. There can be no doubt that the whole future of the nation depends upon the amount of social efficiency we secure and display, but I do not at the same time share the general belief that socially the ancient Hindus were a very inferior people and had no, or a very poor notion of social or national responsibilities. In one of my papers on a similar subject, I have already expressed an opinion, giving my reasons and proofs, that the old Hindus were not entirely devoid of the idea of nationality or patriotism. In this paper I propose to discuss their social ideals and standards. I am prepared to grant that the tendency of the prevailing Hindu beliefs (which are generally styled orthodox and *Pauranic*) has a greater leaning towards individualism and appeals more to the interest and well-being of the individual than to that of the society to which the believers belong. But beyond this I cannot go. I do not share the commonly accepted opinion that Hinduism as a whole is either essentially or even principally individualistic at the cost of the social principles or at the sacrifice of the social obligations. No religion can be worth its name which does not take sufficient care of the individual. The development of the individual soul and its attainment of spiritual beatitude must be the goal of all religions. There can be no religion without this object. A religion without the teaching of spirituality is a misnomer and a lever without a fulcrum. All purely spiritual development must, from the very nature of things, be individualistic, and it should be the ambition of every human being to strive after the elevation and refinement of the spirit in him and thereby secure spiritual perfection resulting in perfect bliss, or (as some religions style it) salvation. No religion can, therefore, be condemned as individualistic, because it attaches great importance to the unfolding and developing of the spiritual side of men, nor can any religion be extolled as socialistic which either ignores the spirit altogether or gives it only a subordinate or secondary position. In judging of a religion or of a system of religious beliefs, what has to be seen is whether it gives sufficient importance to the different requirements and the different sides of human nature without sacrificing one for another. To be a perfect and sound religion, it must make adequate provision for the harmonious development of all those sides of human nature which are to form the basis of the upward progress of man. Such a religion cannot afford to neglect even the physical side, much less can it throw into the background the social.

But before we proceed further we should like to clear the ground by first examining the social ideal which our English-educated friends have set before themselves. The social ideal of Herbert Spencer is stated to be "a state of things in which the antagonism between societies having utterly ceased on the one hand and the conciliation between the interests of the individual and those of the social organism having been perfectly attained to, on the other, the individual also will have reached a stage of development in which it will afford him the highest pleasure to act in a manner conducive to the good of the social organism, and this even where such conduct is to all appearance directly antagonistic to his own material interests, just as at present the highest happiness is often obtained in parental sacrifice". He expects that this altruistic instinct will, in course of time, "attain a level at which it will be like parental altruism in spontaneity" and so lead the individual to obtaining the highest of all satisfactions in voluntarily sacrificing himself in the interests of the social organism. In his *Data of Ethics*, Spencer professes to see in the process of social evolution going on around us a reconciliation taking place "between the interests of each citizen and the interests of citizens at large, tending ever towards a state in which the two become merged in one and in which the feelings answering to them respectively fall into complete concord".

Leaving out of consideration for the present that social millennium of Spencer in which the antagonism between societies shall entirely cease, we are just now concerned with the internal social efficiency of our own social organism. The point to be seen is whether the religion and the laws that have guided the formation and development of that social organism do or do not contain the germ of that principle by which members may be required to sacrifice what to them appear to be their best interests as individuals for the interests of the organism to which they belong, or, to put it more accurately, whether Hinduism as a religion, in its teachings and in its system of laws, contemplates that concord between the interests of its individual members and those of the community at large which, according to Spencer, is the key-note of the process of social evolution going on around us and which he so admiringly holds up as affording prospects of that social millennium which, according to him, will soon be established on earth.

In the opinion of Mr. Benjamin Kidd,[2] the Darwinian science of evolution, as it is now understood, does not afford "any warrant for anticipating the arrival of that state of society contemplated by Mr. Herbert Spencer". Further, he rejects his conception of the process of social evolution (quoted above from his *Data of Ethics*) "as being inconsistent with the teachings of evolutionary science".

Admitting that "the forces, which are at work in the evolution of society, are certainly, on the whole, working out the greatest good of the greatest number in a progressive community", he takes care to point out that the earlier utilitarian conception of the greatest number being related merely to the majority of the existing members of society at any time, has now given way to the greatest number being "*comprised of the number of generations yet unborn and unthought of, to whose interests* the existing individuals are absolutely indifferent". And in the process of social evolution which the race is undergoing, says he, "it is these latter interests which are always in the ascendant". Applying the principle to the limited sphere of a particular social organism, it comes to this that the social efficiency of the latter depends not only on the subordination or merging of the individual interests of its members to or in the interests of the whole, but also in looking forward to and guarding the interests of the generations yet unborn. A social organism can therefore be considered as efficient, only if, beyond requiring its members to sacrifice what to them seems to tend to their individual good, happiness or prosperity, if the same clashes or is inconsistent with the good of the whole, it also takes sufficient care of the interests of the generations yet unborn so as to guarantee the continuance of that state of efficiency in the future. The social system of a nation is perfect or imperfect, complete or incomplete, natural or unnatural, progressive or retrogressive, according as it does or does not fulfil the requirements set forth above. But before we proceed to examine the social system of the ancient Hindus in the light of these considerations, we prefer to clear two more points. The first is that there must surely be something wrong with a social system from which had developed the modern civilization of Europe, which has evoked strong and sweeping condemnation from so eminent a scholar and scientist as Professor Huxley.[3]

"Even the best of modern civilizations," he says, "appears to me to exhibit

2. (1858-1916); British philosopher; special correspondent of the *Times*; works include *Social Evolution* (1894) and *Principles of Western Civilization* (1902).
3. Thomas Henry Huxley (1825-1895); British biologist and exponent of Darwin's theory of evolution; dealt in his writings with the conflict between traditional religion and science.

a condition of mankind which neither embodies any further ideal nor even possesses the merit of stability. I do not hesitate to express the opinion that, if there is no hope of a large improvement of the condition of the greater part of the human family, if it is true that the increase of knowledge, the winning of a greater dominion over nature which is its consequence, and the wealth which follows upon that dominion, are to make no difference in the extent and the intensity of the want with its concomitant physical and moral degradation amongst the masses of the people I should hail the advent of some kindly comet which would sweep the whole affair away as a desirable consummation."

What Prof. Huxley says about the whole human family can more or less be said of the internal state of every great nation of Europe.

The solution of the social problem of India therefore does not necessarily lie in the wholesale imitation of the West to the entire neglect of its past, with its glorious heritage of laws and principles which might shine even with greater splendour if studied in the light of modern science and modern history. We do not mean to say that we should decline to take any light from the West or be prejudiced against it because it is of the West. But what I do maintain is that social reform should only proceed on safe and, as far as possible, on reasonable and national lines. The best and safest social reformer will be he who can read the ancient system of the Hindus in the light of the modern knowledge thrown upon it and who out of this joint study can recommend the line of action which he considers likely to lead to true social progress (felicity). I may at once say that I do not believe in the possibility of a wholesale bringing back or revival of the past such as perhaps some of the Theosophists and also some of the Arya Samajists contemplate. Such a thing is impossible and it will be a waste of energy to try to achieve what is impossible. It is very important that my co-religionists should realize the impossibility and also the futility of this attempt, and should desist from doing or saying anything which may tend to lead the Hindus astray and make them direct their energies into unprofitable or doubtful channels. I have already said that the *first* necessity of the Hindus of today is the acquistion of that degree of social efficiency which alone can enable them to hold their own in the stress and strife of this world of competition. No nation can as such be spiritually high or pure which is socially currupt, degraded or *inefficient*.

What I aim at in the present paper is to show that there is a great deal in our past which can rightly inspire or guide us in the building up of our future social edifice, or in the mending of the existing one, and that we should be going equally astray if in our anxiety to copy the West we ignore or neglect our own laws and the lessons which a study of our past alone can impress upon us.

The second point which I want to clear up is that it is not by reliance on unguided and uncontrolled reason that we can get at the true principles of social progress. Reason, when uncontrolled, is styled by Kidd to be "the most profoundly individualistic, anti-social and anti-evolutionary of all human qualities". In his opinion the central feature of our evolution has always been the supreme struggle in which the control of this disintegrating influence is being continually effected in the interests of society first, and of the race in the next place; and that the function of the immense and characteristic class of social phenomena which we have in our religious system is to secure the necessary subordination of the present interests of the self-assertive individual to the general interests of the process of evolution that is in progress. "It would be impossible," adds he, "to conceive any altruistic feeling of this kind which could exceed in strength the parental instinct. *Yet one of the plainest facts of our time and of past history is the perversion of this instinct under the influence of rationalism* and the suspension of its operation in furthering the evolution the race is undergoing." We have discussions proceeding in the literature of the time in which rationalism, with reiterated emphasis, points out, to use the phrase already quoted, that "there is something pathetically absurd in this sacrifice to their children of generation after generation of grown-up people". No observant person, who has watched the signs of the times, can have the least doubt that, *in a state of unrestricted rationalism, the institution of marriage and the family would undergo modifications incompatible with the continuance of that process of simple self-sacrifice with which the interests of the race are bound up.* We have unmistakable evidence of the perversion of the parental feelings amongst the Greeks and Romans under such rationalistic influences. Speaking of the decay of the Athenian people, Mr. Francis Galton[4] says, "We know, and may guess something more, of the reason why this marvellously gifted race declined. Social morality grew exceedingly lax; marriage became unfashionable and was avoided; many of the more ambitious and accomplished women were avowed courtesans, and consequently infertile, and the mothers of the incoming population were of a heterogeneous class." The same state of popular feeling with respect to marriage prevailed during the decline of the Roman Empire. "The courtesans," says Mr. Lecky,[5] "were raised in popular estimation to an unexampled elevation, and aversion to marriage became very general." And we have at the present day that striking example . . . of the

4. (1822-1911); honorary fellow of Trinity College; Secretary, British Association, 1863-68; member, Meteorological Council, 1868-1901; President, Anthropological Institute, London, 1885-88; publications include *Hereditary Genius* (1869), *Englishmen of Science—Their Nature and Nurture* (1874), *Human Faculty* (1883) and *Finger Prints* (1893).

5. William Edward Lecky (1838-1903); British historian; works include *History of the Rise and Influence of Patriotism in Europe, History of European Morals from Augustus to Charlesmagne* and *History of England in Eighteenth Century.*

perversion, under similar circumstances, of the parental feelings amongst the most brilliant and able race amongst the European peoples and the consequent failure of that race to maintain its place amongst others in the evolution which is proceeding under our eyes in the civilization in which we are living.

It will, I hope, be now clearly seen how dangerous it is to give undue prominence to "rationalism" in any program of social reform and to divorce it from religion. We are, in any case, in a position now to judge of the wisdom of the ancient Aryans in developing all the social laws on the basis of religion and in making the latter so comprehensive as to include everything that is necessary for the right progress of man, as a member of a family, as a member of a social organism and last but not least as a member of his race.

II

With these introductory remarks I proceed to produce evidences of the social conception of the Hindus, showing the idea of social unity in their religion and in their rules of life. Firstly, in my opinion one could hardly come across a more beautiful, a more comprehensive and a truer view of the unity of the social organism than is expressed in the idea of the division of castes—the much abused, much maligned and much misunderstood idea of the four castes representing the different parts of the Creator's body—*the Sharir of the Purusha.* To take the earliest and the highest authority, first, *Rigveda* X. 90, verses 11 and 12, literally translated into English by Dr. Griffiths,[6] run as follows:

> "11. When they divided *Purusha* how many portions did they make? What do they call his mouth, his arm? What do they call his thighs and feet?"
>
> "12. The Brahman was his mouth, of both his arms was the *Rajanya* made. His thighs became the *Vaishya*, from his feet the *Shudra* was produced."

These verses give expression to two of the sublimest truths about the social relations of man with man as an individual and with mankind as a whole. They establish the oneness of humanity in the body of the Lord and they explain away the phenomena of differences in the capacities, powers and faculties of

6. Ralph Thomas Hotchkin Griffiths (1826-1906); professor of English literature at Benares College, 1854-62, and its Principal, 1863-78; Director, Public Instruction, North-Western Provinces and Oudh (later United Provinces and now Uttar Pradesh), 1878-85; founder-editor of *The Pandit*, a Sanskrit journal, for about 8 years; works include *Scenes from the Ramayana* and *The Ramayana* of Valmiki (5 vols).

individuals. As parts of the same whole, they are to sustain, support, supplement, help and co-operate with each other. As individual units of one organism, they have, each of them, their own separate functions to perform. Applying this to particular social organism as distinguished from general humanity, they form the basis of a complete system of social duties. In no other way could one better express the mutual interdependence of all parts of society upon one another, be they high or low, and also the essential oneness of the whole.

Taking it in another and a higher sense, it is a better and more effectual representation of collective Humanity representing God Himself, than any put forward by the Prophets of the Religion of Humanity from Auguste Comte[7] downwards. Read in that light, the verses standing by themselves explain only a partial or a relative truth. For the whole truth, you must read the whole hymn together. It was our misfortune that such a grand exposition of the greatest of social truths should have so degenerated in the hands of an interested priesthood as to be made the basis of the present-day inhuman, ingenious, corrupt, invidious and demoralising distinctions between man and man. But this experience is not so very exceptionally confined to Hinduism only. The evil genius of man has in this and other countries, and in this and other systems of religion, more than occasionally subverted and distorted some of the sublimest truths taught to him by God and nature with a view to advance the interests of particular individuals or of particular classes and to oppress others. Take the history of any great religion, be it the humility-professing Christianity, militant Islam or Buddhism, you will find similar distortions in abundance, thus showing that the tendencies of priesthood have been almost the same everywhere. Then the same idea of the good of the whole runs through the various duties that the Hindu *Shastras* assign to the four orders. *Manu Smriti* (a treatise on laws, the compilation of which the European scholars fix at about 200 B.C.) is one of those books which lay great stress on caste distinctions, and advocate vast and rather astounding inequalities of treatment between the Brahmans and the *Shudras*, verging in some places almost on inhumanity and cruelty. It is a book held in universal esteem by the orthodox Hindus, be they of any sect or school. As such we shall be on the safe side in giving quotations from it, supporting the original social conception of the caste system. Verses 88-91 prescribe the duties of the different *Varnas*:

"88. To Brahmans he (Manu) assigned teaching and studying (the Veda), sacrificing for their own benefit and for others, giving and accepting (of alms).

7. (1798-1857); French philosopher, exponent of positivism; rejected metaphysics in favour of modern science; works include *Course de Philosophic Positive.*

89. The *Kshatriya* he commanded to protect the people, to bestow gifts, to offer sacrifices, to study (the Veda), and to abstain from attaching himself to worldly pleasures.

90. The *Vaishya* to tend cattle, to bestow gifts, to offer sacrifices, to study (the Veda), to trade, to lend money, and to cultivate land.

91. One occupation only the Lord prescribed to the *Shudra*, to serve meekly even these (other) three castes."[8]

The one note that runs throughout these rules is the *service of others* and the social good and the prosperity of the whole community. The Brahman is enjoined to study not for the benefit of his soul only, but to *teach others* as a purely social duty. In the same way, it was the duty of the *Kshatriyas* to *protect the people.*

Mark, please, the distinction between *ruling* and *protecting*. The same may be said about the duties assigned to the *Vaishyas* and the *Shudras*. We may, here, for a moment take the liberty of drawing the attention of the promoters of the different caste conferences and caste organisations to these rules of Manu. These rules show that each of these castes was understood to exist and work for the benefit of all, and not for the benefit of their own caste-people only. If it was the duty of a Brahman to teach *all*, a *Kshatriya* to protect *all*, similarly the duty of a *Vaishya* was to produce and to trade for *all* and that of a *Shudra* to labour for *all.*

From the division into *varnas* (castes) we might proceed to the division of an Aryan life into the four *Ashramas*, and there also you will find the same idea running through the duties and obligations assigned to each. For instance, wherein can you find such a system of free and compulsory education deeply interwoven with religious merit as amongst the Hindus? Every twice-born Hindu was bound to educate his children unless he intended to degrade them to the level of a *Shudra*, and every Aryan householder was threatened with severe religious demerit if he refused food or alms to a *Vidyarthi*. The various rules laying down the respect that it was the privilege of the teacher to command, show the great importance which the old Aryans attached to the position and

8. The Sanskrit texts of the verses are as follows:

श्रध्यापनमध्ययनं यजनं याजनं तथा
दानं प्रतिग्रहं चैव ब्राह्मात्वानांमकरपयत्।। 88
प्रजानां रक्षकं दानभिज्याध्ययनमेव च।
विषयेष्वप्रसक्तिष्चक्षन्निस्य विषानतः।। 89
पषूनां रक्षतं दाननिष्याध्ययनमेव च।
वणिक पथं कुसीदं च वैश्यस्य कृषिमेव च।। 90
एकमेव तु शूद्रस्य प्रभुः कर्म समादिशत्।
एतेपामेव वर्सानां शुसु षामवसू यथा ।। 91

the profession of a teacher. *Shloka* II, 165, lays down the obligation of studying the Veda for all Aryans: "An Arya must study the whole Veda together with the *Rahasyas*, performing at the same time various kinds of austerities and the vows prescribed by the rules of the Veda."

Shloka 154 gives precedence to one who has learnt the Veda, over all those whose claim to respect lies either "through years", i.e. age, or "through white hair", i.e. old age, or "through wealth" or "through powerful kinsmen".

A householder destitute of the knowledge of the Veda was looked down upon as unfit for social intercourse with the twice-born. A student was not to accept food from the house of anyone who was deficient in the knowledge of the Veda or in performing sacrifices or who were not known as earning their livelihood by lawful means. Similarly at the time of the selection of a wife, a good man was ordained to "avoid the ten following families, be *they ever so great or rich* in kinc, horses, grain or (other) property". "(viz) One which neglects the sacred rites, one in which no male children (are born), *one in which the Veda is not studied*, one (the members of) which have thick hair on the body, those which are subject to haemorrhoids, phthisis, weakness of digestion, epilepsy, or white and black leprosy." The same idea is again prominent in III, 63: "By low marriages, by omitting (the performance of) sacred rites, *by neglecting the study of the Veda*, and by irreverence towards Brahmanas, (great) families sink low."

In the case of Brahmanas it is so very pronounced in the following verses:

"II, 197. The oblations to gods and manes, made by men ignorant (of the law of gifts), are lost if the givers in their folly present (shares of them) to Brahmanas *who are mere ashes*. . . .

"III, 198. As a fire of dry grass is (unable to consume the offerings and is quickly) extinguished, even so (is it with) an unlearned Brahmana; sacrificial food must not be given to him, *since it (would be) offered to ashes*."

See also 133 and 142.

Texts to this effect, full of similar sentiments and breathing the same spirit, can be multiplied by hundreds, not only from the *Manu Smriti* but from the other *Sutras* and *Smritis* as well.

Looking to the life of a Hindu *Grihastha* (householder), what ideals of altruistic sentiments are set forth by the texts that describe his daily duties? Where, on earth, will you find rules such as those which are so explicitly laid down by the epics, the *Puranas*, and others containing pictures of ancient Aryan life, and which rules were scrupulously observed in olden times? The five great daily duties of the Hindus are well known. In English phraseology they are styled "sacrifices". In Sanskrit they are called *Maha* (great) *Yajnas*. Tracing back their origin you find the germs and the ideals in the Veda *Mantras*, but in the *Shatapatha Brahmana*, one of the most ancient Hindu *Shastras*, whose place in antiquity is, by common consent, only next to the Vedas themselves, you see them in a more organised shape. We quote from the translations of Julius Eggling, published in the *Sacred Books of the East* series, Vol. XII, pp. 190 and 191.

> 1. Verily, whoever exists, he, in being born, is born as (owing) a debt to the gods, to the *Rishis*, to the fathers and to men.
>
> 2. For, inasmuch as he is bound to sacrifice, for that reason he is born (owing) a debt to the gods; hence when he sacrifices to them, when he makes offerings to them, he does this (in discharge of his debt) to them.
>
> 3. And further, inasmuch as he is bound to study (the Vedas), for that reason he is born as (owing) a debt to the *Rishis*; hence it is to them that he does this; for one who has studied (the Vedas) they call the *Rishis* 'treasure-warden'.
>
> 4. And further, inasmuch as he is bound to wish for offspring, for that reason he is born as (owing) a debt to the fathers; hence when there is (provided by him) a continued, uninterrupted lineage, it is for them that he does this.
>
> 5. And further, inasmuch as he is bound to practise hospitality, for that reason he is born as (owing) a debt to men; hence when he harbours them, when he offers food to them, it is (in discharge of his debt) to them that he does so. Whoever does all these things has discharged his duties; by him all is obtained, all is conquered.
>
> 6. And, accordingly, in that he is born as owing a debt to the gods, in regard to that he satisfies (*avadan*) them by sacrificing; and when he makes offering in the fire, he thereby satisfies them in regard to that (debt); hence, whatever they offer up in the fire, is called *avadanam* (sacrificial portion).

This quotation speaks only of the four *yajnas*. But the *Sutras* and the *Smritis*, which are mostly of later date, speak of five, adding a fifth debt which man owes to the animals and plants, &c. The *Smriti*, which goes after the name of Manu and is by European scholars believed to be a compilation of about 200 B.C., also speaks of five and ascribes the rule to the necessity of expiating the sins committed by each householder, in the use of hearth, the grinding stone, the broom, the pestle and mortar.

Below I give all the verses bearing on the subject, a comparison of which with the quotation given from the *Satpatha* will give the reader a very clear idea of the difference between the two ideals of the pre-Buddhistic and post-Buddhistic periods of Aryan civilization.

III, 67. With the sacred fire, kindled at the wedding, a householder shall perform according to the law the domestic ceremonies and the five (great) sacrifices and (with that) he shall daily cook his food.

68. A householder *has five slaughter-houses* (as it were, viz. the hearth, the grinding stone, the broom, the pestle and mortar, the water vessel, by using which he is bound (with the fetters of sin.)

69. *In order to successively expiate (the offences committed by means) of all these (five)* the great sages have prescribed for householders the daily (performance of the five) great sacrifices.

70. Teaching (and studying) is the sacrifice (offered) to Brahmana, the (offerings of water and food called) *Tarpana* the sacrifice to the manes, the burnt oblation, the sacrifice offered to the gods, the *bali* offering that is offered to the *Bhutas*, and the hospitable reception of guests the offering to men.

71. He who neglects not these five great sacrifices, while he is able (to perform them), is not tainted by the sins (committed) in the five places of slaughter, though he constantly lives in the (order of householders).

72. But he who does not feed these five, the gods, his guests, those whom he is bound to maintain, the manes, and himself, *lives not, though he breathes*.

The idea expressed in 68, 69 and 71 is peculiar to this *Smriti* and other later books and is entirely foreign to the spirit as well as the letter of the earlier law books. It seems to be essentially Jainist. The truth and sentiment expressed in 72 is both lofty and beautiful.

The same idea pervades the whole chapter which lays down the duties of the order of householders. *Shloka* 76 explains how the sacrifice to gods (i.e. the *Agnihotra*) is also based on an altruistic conception of man's duty towards all other living creatures:

"76. An oblation duly thrown into the fire reaches the sun; from the sun comes rain, from rain food, therefrom the living creatures (derive their subsistence)."[9]

In the same way *Shlokas* 77 and 78 proceed to show the prime importance of the order of the householders, thereby expressing a very high standard of the social conception of the Aryas:

9. The Sanskrit text is as follows:
अमौ प्रात्वाहुतिः सम्यगात्यिमुपति ।
आदित्या ब्यापते वृष्टिक्तरकं ततः प्रजाः ।। 76

"77. As all living creatures subsist by receiving support from air, even so (the members of) all orders subsist by receiving support from the householder.

78. Because men of the three (other) orders are daily supported by the householder with (gifts of) sacred knowledge and food, therefore the (order of) householders is the most excellent order."

Shloka 79 promises a noble reward for the due performance of these duties and lays particular stress on the necessity of the householder cultivating strength:

"79. *(The duties of) this order, which cannot be practised by men with weak organs,* must be carefully observed by him who desires imperishable (bliss in) heaven, and constant happiness in this (life)."[10]

Could there be a higher conception and could it be more forcibly expressed than in III, 118? The idea is common to most Hindu *Shastras*. In the *Bhagavad Gita*, Sri Krishna gives expression to the same in IV. 31.

"118. He who prepares food for himself (alone), eats nothing but sin; for it is ordained that the food which remains after (the performance of) the sacrifices shall be the meal of virtuous men."

Then look at the following detailed rules about the entertainment of guests and the distribution of food to dependents and you will be at once in a position to know why the Hindus (the bulk of them) have been proverbially hospitable.

"III, 105. A guest who is sent by the (setting) sun in the evening, must not be driven away by a householder; whether he has come at supper time or at an inopportune moment, *he must not stay in* the house without *entertainment* (i.e. without being fed and looked after).

114. Without hesitation he may give food, even before his guests, to the following persons, (viz). to newly married women, to the infants, to the sick, and to the pregnant women.

115. But the foolish man who eats without having given food to these (persons) does, while he crams, not know that (after death) he himself will be devoured by dogs and vultures.

10. The Sanskrit text is as follows:

स संधार्यः प्रयत्नेन स्वर्गमक्षयमिच्छता। ।
सुख चेहेच्छता नित्यं योऽधार्यो दुर्बलेन्द्रियैः ।। 76

116. After the Brahmanas, the kinsmen, and the servants have dined, the householder and his wife may afterwards eat what remains.

IV, 32. A householder may give (as much food) as he is able (to spare) *to those who do not cook for themselves*, and to all beings one must distribute food without detriment (to one's own interest)"[11]

Even now every Hindu of the twice-born caste thinks it obligatory to give a part of his cooked food in charity, be it only one cake, to a Brahman. It was these rules which when practised left no room for public poorhouses, orphanages, &c., &c.

The following *shlokas* lay down a high standard of regard for women, which it was the duty of every Arya to maintain and respect.

III, 55. Women must be honoured and adored by their fathers, brothers, husbands,and brothers-in-law who desire their own welfare.

56. Where women are honoured, there the gods are pleased; but where they are not honoured, no sacred rite yields rewards.

57. Where the female relations live in grief the family soon wholly perishes; but that family where they are not unhappy, ever prospers.

58. The houses in which female relations, not being duly honoured, pronounce a curse, perish completely, as destroyed by magic.

59. Hence men, who seek (their own welfare), should always honour women on holidays and festivals with (gifts of) ornaments, clothes, and (dainty) food.

60. In that family, where the husband is pleased with his wife, and the wife with her husband, happiness will as surely be lasting.

61. For, if the wife is not radiant with beauty, she will not attract her husband; but if she has no attractions for him, no children will be born.

62. If the wife is radiant with beauty, the whole house is bright; but if she is destitute of beauty, all will appear dismal.

The following *shloka* lays down the consequences of a householder's (a married man's) neglect to earn his livelihood and of his dependence upon others for the same:

11. Lajpat Rai has noted: "This would include ascetics, sannyasis, *vidyarthis*, oprhans and other destitute people."

"III, 104. Those foolish householders who constantly seek (to live on) the food of others, become, in consequence of that (baseness), after death the cattle of those who give them food."[12]

The following prayer is a fitting sequel to the *Shastric* life of a *Grihastha* as explained above and shows the high standard of altruistic morality that prevailed amongst the Aryas:

"III, 259. *May liberal men abound with us!* May (our knowledge of) the Vedas and (our) progeny increase! May faith not forsake us! May we have much to give to the needy!"

The following are the principles in accordance with which Brahmanas and other twice-born people were ordained to control the great and inevitable struggle for life. They represent a high state of national righteousness.

"IV, 2. A Brahmana must seek a means of subsistence which either causes no, or at least little, pain (to others), and live by that except in times of distress.

"IV, 17. Let him avoid all (means of acquiring) wealth which impede the study of the Veda; let him maintain himself anyhow, but study (because that) devotion to the Veda-study secures the realisation of his aims.

"IV, 18. Let him walk here (on earth), bringing his dress, speech, and thought to a conformity with his age, his occupation, his sacred learning and HIS RACE."[13]

"IV, 170-174. Neither a man who (lives) unrighteously nor he who (acquires) wealth (by telling) falsehoods, nor he who always delights in doing injury ever attains happiness in this world. Let him, though suffering in consequence of his righteousness, never turn his heart to unrighteousness; for he will see the speedy overthrow of the unrighteous, wicked men.

"Unrighteousness, practised in this world, does not at once produce its fruit, like a cow; but advancing slowly, it cuts off of the roots of him who committed it.

12. The Sanskrit text is as follows:

उपासते ये ग्रहस्थाः परपकमबुद्धय ।।
वेनते प्रेत्य पशुतां ब्रचन्त्यडगदिदायिनाम् ।। 104

13. The Sanskrit text is as follows:

वयसः कर्मणोऽर्थस्य श्रु तस्यभिजनस्य च ।
वे षवाग्बुद्धिसारुप्यमाचरम्बिचरेदिह ।। 18

"If (the punishment falls) not on (the offender) himself, (it falls) on his sons, if not on sons, (at least) on his grandsons, but an iniquity once committed never fails to produce fruit to him who wrought it.

"He prospers for a while through unrighteousness, then he gains great good fortune, next he conquers his enemies, but (at last) he perishes (branch and) root.

"IV, 176. Let him avoid the acquisition of wealth and the gratification of his desires if they are opposed to the sacred law, and even lawful acts which may cause pain in the future or are offensive to men."[14]

The following lay down a perfect standard of charity:

"IV, 190. A Brahmana who neither performs austerities nor studies the Veda, yet delights in accepting the gifts, sinks (with the donor) into hell just as (he who attempts to cross over in) a boat made of stones (is submerged) in the water.

"191. Hence an ignorant (man) should be afraid of accepting any presents; for by reason of a very small (gift) even a fool sinks (into hell) as low into a morass.

"192. (A man) who knows the law should not offer even water to a Brahmana who acts like a cat, nor to a Brahmana who acts like a heron, nor to one who is unacquainted with the Veda." (For definitions of cats and herons see 195 and 196).

"193. For property, though earned in accordance with prescribed rules, which is given to these three (persons), CAUSES IN THE NEXT WORLD MISERY BOTH TO THE GIVER AND THE RECIPIENT.

"194. *As he who (attempts to) cross water in a boat of stone sinks (to the bottom), even so* AN IGNORANT DONOR AND AN IGNORANT DONEE SINK LOW.

"195. (A man) who, ever covetous, displays the flag of virtue, (who is) a hypocrite, a deceiver of the people, intent on doing injury, (and) a detractor (from the merits) of all men, one must know to be one who acts like a cat.

"196. That Brahmana, who with downcast look, of a cruel disposition, is solely intent on attaining his own ends, dishonest and falsely gentle, is one who acts like a heron.

"197. Those Brahmanas who act like herons, and those who display

14. The Sanskrit text is as follows:

तरित्यजेदर्थकामौ यौस्यातां धर्मवर्जितौ ।
धर्म चाप्यसुखोदर्कंलोकविकुषुश्रेव च ।। 176

the characteristics of cats, fall in consequence of that wicked mode of acting into (the hell called) *Andhatamisra*."

The following *shlokas* will show how the social and national interests of the community were guarded against an undue and unseasoned desire towards abnegation and ascetic life.

"VI, 35. When he has paid the three debts, let him apply his mind to the attainment of final liberation; he who seeks it without having paid (his debts) sinks downwards.

36. Having studied the Vedas in accordance with the rule, having begot sons according to the sacred law, and having offered sacrifices according to his ability, he may direct his mind to (the attainment of) final liberation.

37. A TWICE-BORN MAN WHO SEEKS LIBERATION WITHOUT HAVING STUDIED THE VEDAS, WITHOUT HAVING BEGOTTEN SONS, AND WITHOUT HAVING OFFERED SACRIFICES, SINKS DOWNWARDS."

The following extracts will show how strongly that the ancient Aryas felt and believed in the unity of a political or social organism.

In their opinion the safety and welfare of all consisted in the righteousness of all. Any failure of duty by individuals operated to corrupt the whole society, and if ever the number of those who failed to fulfil their obligations or act in accordance with law increased, it was considered a sure sign of the decay of the national power, strength and virtue. The king representing the commonwealth was required to protect his people, always to keep their interests in view, to see that all orders and classes and individuals performed their respective obligations properly. His neglect or failure to secure the due performance of everyone's duty was calculated to result in disaster to the whole community.

There are numerous texts in *Manu* and other *Shastras* which can be quoted in support of the above position, but, I am afraid, I will be only increasing the length and size of the paper if I did so. I will therefore confine myself only to a few, by way of example, in which the idea stated by me seems to be sufficiently prominent.

VIII, 22. Foretells the ruin of a commonwealth by *famine and disease in* which the number of the twice-born decreases and which principally consists of *Shudras* (i.e. labourers and menial classes). How can a nation

> continue to exist which has no brain to guide the organism, no arms to protect it, and no traders and manufacturers to maintain and increase its wealth? No one can conceive of a self-governed community consisting of labourers only. An increase of the labouring classes with a corresponding decrease of the learned, the fighting and the producing classes, is a sure index of decay and *coming ruin.*

"That kingdom," says Manu, "where *Shudras* are very numerous, which is infested by atheists, and *destitute* of twice-born (inhabitants), soon entirely perishes, afflicted by famine and disease."[15]

Being "destitute of twice-born" is equivalent to being destitute of knowledge, power and wealth. A nation not possessing these cannot exist as a nation and is bound to lose its position as such. Famine and disease are sure to follow in the train of ignorance, weakness and poverty. Let my countrymen ponder over the sublime truth preached in this verse and it shall at once dawn on them as to why they are such frequent victims of famine and disease. The true course then to be followed in order to uproot them is to increase the stock of national knowledge, national strength and national wealth. That is the best, the safest, the most effective, and the only cure of these national afflictions of ours. Here is a remedy, an unfailing remedy, pointed out by the son of Swayambhuva himself, the great Manu. Let us apply it with faith, and it is sure to drive away the diseases with which we, each and all of us (both individually and socially), are at the present moment afflicted.

The idea of the ruling class being only a part of the whole social organism and of its earning merit or demerit by the actions of the whole is beautifully and with characteristic force expressed in the following four *shlokas* which we quote from chapter VIII:

> "304. A king who (duly) protects (his subjects), receives from each and all the sixth part of their spiritual merit, if he does not protect them, the sixth part of their demerit also (will fall on him).
>
> "305. Whatever (merit a man gains by) reading the Vedas, by sacrificing, by charitable gifts, (or by) worshipping (*Gurus* and Gods), the king obtains a sixth part of that in consequence of his duly protecting (his kingdom).
>
> "306. A king who protects the created beings in accordance with the sacred law and smites those worthy of corporal punishment, daily offers (as it were) sacrifices at which hundred-thousands (are given as) fees.

15. The Sanskrit text is as follows:

यद्राष्ट्रं शूद्र भूयिष्ठं नास्तिकान्तमद्विषम् ।
विनश्यत्याशू तत्कृत्सनं दुर्भिक्षव्याधिपीडितम् ।। 122

"307. A king who does not afford protection, yet takes his share in kind, in taxes, tolls and duties, daily presents and fines, will, after death, soon sink into hell."

There are many more texts which similarly tell us of an advanced political science, including political economy, having been developed by the Hindus. Elaborate rules and provisions are laid down for the appointment of state officials, the imposition of taxes, tolls and fines, the regulating of state expenditure, the administration of civil and criminal justice, the control of revenues, the necessity of paying special attention to agriculture, trade, commerce and manufactures, &c., &c.

These all give one an idea of the social position of the Hindus. There are among them some rules which undoubtedly appear to be very invidious, childish, and grotesque but they form only the exceptions even if we were to grant that they are not subsequent interpolations or additions by interested priests. That they are later interpolations can be proved in many ways and by the testimony of the best scholars. However, this is only by the way.

Before I have done with the laws of Manu, I should like to point out that there are various texts in *Manu* which bespeak an anxiety for the welfare of the unborn generations. Amongst Hindus, marriage is a sacred duty and a sacrament, and as such it is regulated very strictly and with the greatest regard for the interests of the unborn generations. The rules as to *Brahmacharya*, marriage, and its consummation are all framed with that express object in view. It is the procreation of good, virtuous and strong progeny which is the object of an Aryan marriage according to the Aryan laws. Hence all marriages are regulated accordingly. "Let him," says Manu, "who desires To Raise His Race, even form connections with the most excellent (women) and shun all low ones."

With these laws before us, it is surely unjust to say that the genius of Hinduism is essentially individualistic.

I have given these quotations from *ManuSmriti* alone, although most of these rules and many more similar to these are also to be found in other books on the laws of the Aryas. Some of the rules are to be found expressed in almost the same language in every book on Hindu law.

III

From the laws of Manu, we proceed to examine the *Vedic* literature for traces of the social idea therein. Taking the *Rigveda* first, which is (according to European scholars) the most ancient of all the Vedas, or for the matter of that, the oldest book in the Library of the Aryan race, we find the following exhortations in the 10th *Mandala*, Hymn CXCI.

> "2. Assemble, speak together: let your minds be all of one accord as ancient Gods unanimous sit down to their appointed share.
>
> "3. The place is common, common the assembly, common the mind; be so their thoughts united. A common purpose do I lay before you, and worship with your general oblation.
>
> "4. One and the same be your resolve, and be your minds of one accord. United be the thoughts of all that may happily agree."

The translation is that by Dr. Griffiths, but that there is a mistake or a misprint is clear from a comparison of the third stanza as given above with the original Sanskrit.[16]

The word मन्त्रः (*mantrah*) means scripture or *Vedic* hymn—"A portion of the Veda including the *Samhita* and distinguished from the *Brahmana*,"—a charm, a prayer, a revelation or plan or policy (see Dr. Apte's *Dictionary*, p. 842). I fail to find any authority for its being translated by "place".

The 1st stanza, which we have not reproduced, is a prayer to God (*Agni*) in which the Lord is asked to bring about the gathering of all friendly creatures round the common altar.

The translation of the second stanza, 2nd line, seems to imply that none should encroach upon others' rights and all should peaceably enjoy their shares.

In the second line of the third stanza again, the original gives the idea of a common worship.

The teaching of the hymn is reproduced in *Atharvaveda*, Book VI, 64, which Dr. Griffiths translates as below:

> "1. Agree and be united: let your minds be all of one accord. Even as the Gods of ancient days, unanimous, await their share.
>
> "2. The rede is common, common the assembly, common the law, so be their thoughts united.
>
> I offer up your general oblation: together entertain one common purpose.
>
> "3. One and the same be your resolve, be all your hearts in harmony; one and the same be all your minds that all may happily consent."

In this translation the word *mantrah* is rendered into "rede" and the idea of a "common law" is expressly given out.

16. The Sanskrit text is as follows:

 समानो मन्त्रः समितिः समानीः समानं मनः सह चित्त मेषाम् ।
 समानं यन्त्रमभि मन्त्र्येवः सुभानिन वो इविषा जुहोसि ।।

In my opinion these two *Mantras* inculcate the conditions of an effective social organisation which is thus made to depend upon—

(a) community of language.

"Speak together or speak alike."

(b) Respect for individual rights.

(c) Common scriptures, common social life and common laws.

(d) A common (national) purpose or mission.

The same idea is more clearly and still more beautifully expressed in *Atharvaveda*, III. 30, which, as translated by Dr. Griffiths, runs as follows:

> "1. Freedom from hate I bring to you, concord and unanimity. Love one another as the cow loveth the calf that she hath borne.
>
> "2. One-minded with his mother, let the son be loyal to his sire. Let the wife, calm and gentle, speak words sweet as honey to her lord.
>
> "3. No brother hate his brother, no sister to sister be unkind. Unanimous, with one intent, speak ye your speech in friendliness.
>
> "4. That spell through which Gods sever not, nor ever hear each other hate, that spell we lay upon your home, a bond of union for the men.
>
> "5. Intelligent, submissive, rest united, friendly and kind, bearing the yoke together. Come, speaking sweetly each one to the other, I make you one-intentioned and one-minded.[17]
>
> "6. Let what you drink, your share of food be common: together, with one common bond I bind you.
>
> Serve *Agni*, gathered round him like the spokes about the chariot nave.
>
> "7. With binding charm I make you all united, obeying one sole leader and one-minded even as the gods who watch and guard the *Amrita*, at morn and ever may ye be kindly-hearted."

The same spirit runs through *Atharva*, VI, 73 and 74.

> "1. Let *Varun* come hither, *Soma, Agni, Brihaspati* come hither with the *Vasus*. Unanimous, ye kinsmen, come united, come to the glory of this mighty guardian.
>
> "2. The inclination, which your hearts have harboured, the purpose which hath occupied your spirits.

17. Bloomfield's translation of this stanza, printed in *Sacred Books of the East*, Vol. XVII, p. 134, reads as follows: "Following your leader, of (the same) mind, do ye not hold yourselves apart. Do ye come here, co-operating, going along the same waggon-pole, speaking agreeably to one another render you of the same mind."

"This I annul with sacrifice and butter. In me be your sweet resting place, O kinsmen.

"3. Stand even here; forsake me not. Before us may *Pushan* make your path unfit to travel.

"Vastoshpati incessantly recall you! In me be your sweet resting place, O kinsmen!"

"1. Close gathered be your bodies: be your minds and vows in union! Here present *Brahmanspati* and *Bhoga* have assembled you.

"2. Let there be union of your minds, let there be union of your hearts: all that is troubled in your lot, with this I mend and harmonise.

"3. As, free from jealousy, the strong *Adityas* have been the *Vishnu's* and the *Rudra's* fellows, so free from jealousy, Lord of three titles! Cause thou these people here to be one-minded."

Passages like these are to be found in abundance in the *Vedic* literature (*Sacred Books of the East*, Vol. XIII, p. 360) and can be multiplied at pleasure. For the actual working of this spirit of unity you may study the *Ramayana* and the *Mahabharata*. In the latter you find a Devayani being appealed to sacrifice all her *Kshatriya* pride, anger and dignity for the welfare of all of her race with success.

In its pages you find many interesting and instructive sermons on political science, the most noteworthy of which are those given by Bhisma on his death-bed.

Then the celebrated Chanakya also says in his *Niti Shastra*:

त्यजेदेकं कुलस्यार्थे ग्रामस्यार्थे कुलं त्यजेत्।
ग्रामं जनमदस्यार्थे आत्मार्थे पृथिवी त्यजेत्।। 3-10

Sacrifice a member for the sake of the family, a family for the sake of a village, a village for the sake of a district, and even the earth for the welfare of the soul.

There are other treatises on political science which promulgate the same truth. These quotations are only relied on to show that the sacred books of the Hindus contain the germs and the foundations of the highest social ideals and testify to the prevalence of a very high standard of social life amongst them with all the duties and obligations that such a life involves and implies.

It is not my intention to suggest that we can or need learn nothing from the Europeans, but my object is only to show that there is sufficient in our sacred books round which we can rally for social strength and reform, and that with all our eagerness to sit at the feet of European savants and scholars we need neither discredit our ancestors nor indulge in general lamentations for want of social ideals in our past.

3. Reform or Revival?[1]

We thought that with the fall of the old class of Pandits we had done with those wars of words which were formerly carried on with all the weight of great learning and accompanied by a demonstrative show of deep erudition, but we had evidently counted without our hosts, the great body of Indian reformers that are the products of English education, who owe nothing to the old school of Pandits and for whom the old school of Pandits have incurred no responsibility whatever. Before the spread of English education in this country there were only two classes of public literary or intellectual entertainments to which the people were treated now and then and which supplied some diversion from the otherwise dull, monotonous or in some places extremely hazardous lives which they generally led. The one was the most popular and useful practice of reciting the *kathas* to a mixed and general audience consisting of all classes of people, from old men to boys and from old ladies to young girls. The ancient epics of the land—the chronicles of life of Rama and his consort, and the great *Mahabharata*—were very often the books that were thus recited.

These *Kathas* were greatly instrumental in keeping the national spark alive through so many vicissitudes of national fortune, when on occasion it had almost reached the point of total extinction. The second were the periodical religious discussions, which in most instances originated with the advent of a learned Pandit from the outside.

Very often the new Pandit's discourses had caught the popular ears and the local Pandit or Pandits thought their dignity, prestige and even emoluments were in danger, to prevent which calamity they considered it their duty to come out and give a challenge to the newly-arrived to prove his superiority in the knowledge of the *Shastras* by an open discussion. Or it might be that the newcomer thought his success depended on drawing out the local theologian and giving him a defeat. Be that as it may, the invariable result was that the discussion began with words, the accuracy of certain expressions used by one or the other, the applicability or the non-applicability of certain rules of grammar and ended often if not always in heated words and sometimes in blows. I am

1. *The Hindustan Review and Kayastha Samachar*, Vol. X, 1904, pp. 474-82.

sorry to observe that the present quarrel over "reform or revival" between the reformers seems to me to resemble, at least in part, the above-mentioned wordy polemics between the Pandits. The reformers claim to be the leaders of the community. They have occupied the place of the Pandits and divines of former times. They profess to lay down rules for the guidance of the general mass of people. They are agreed that the state of Hindu society is bad and rotten, that it needs great and radical changes, and that without these changes the whole social fabric stands in danger of giving way and burying the nation down in its debris. They have remedies, ready, patent and infallible. On most of these they agree, only to differ on the name by which the same is to be styled. Their agreement as to the remedy disappears in their differences about the wordy habitat to be given to the proposed and contemplated changes. One class of people who have already established a name for themselves do not like to give up the name they have patented and by which they have gained distinction. These latter gentlemen call themselves reformers and insist upon certain social changes being introduced in the name of "reform" and reform only. The other class who have lately come into prominence call themselves "revivalists", and they swear that any change in the social customs and institutions of the community can only be introduced under the shadow of revival. They think they cannot tolerate reform. The result is that while the former taunt the latter as "revivalists and reactionaries", the latter mock the former as "reformers and revolutionists". Both classes contain amongst them great and good men, men with pure motives and noble intentions. They are generally prominent men—well-read and deep in the lore of history. Both classes are to all appearances sincere in their convictions and efforts, but to the great misfortune of the country and the nation they cannot join their heads and work amicably. The wordy weapons are sometimes changed, and while the reformers take their stand on "reform on rational lines", the revivalists plead for "reform on national lines". Here for once at least they seem to agree on reform, as the force of the difference is centered on the words "rational" and "national". The result is that much ink and paper are uselessly spent in dilating upon the necessary soundness of reform and the danger and risk of revival, and *vice versa*. Unfortunately, no one ever sees and deplores the great waste of valuable time and precious energy which this quarrel involves—time and energy which could be usefully employed in, nay, which is imperatively demanded by, so many other things that are the *sine qua non* of national progress and that should be done but are not done for want of working hands. On both sides are arrayed tough warriors armed with the knowledge and experience which is gathered by deep study and growing years. On both sides are arrayed sturdy and stout soldiers possessed of and carried by the enthusiasm of youth, full of ambition, and proud of credentials gained by academic success and literary achievements. On both sides the pen and the tongue are being used with strength and vigour not totally devoid of grace. It is very perilous to come between such daring, bold and determined fighters specially for a comparatively ill-provided and poorly circumstanced man like myself who can wield neither the pen with the dexterity that comes of practice, nor the tongue with that skill which is the outcome of discipline. In fact, I am rather inclined to think that it is positively dangerous for recruits who have not had the advantage of regular lessons in drill or of the discipline that comes out of exercises at the manoeuvres, to interfere between such veteran combatants. But the interests at stake are so great, the field is so vast, the workers in the field are so few and far between, the amount of energy available is so little and the resources are so limited, that on better thought I have decided to take the risk and raise my voice against what to me looks sheer waste of opportunities and misapplication of energy.

I will begin by examining into the respective programmes of reformers and the revivalists and see if there are any vital and real differences which justify so much contemptuous talk of each other. On both sides, I believe that the social reform programme begins, and very rightly too, with the question of early marriage. I confess I am unaware of any radical difference between the views of the reformers and the revivalists on the point. In provinces other than the Punjab Mrs. Besant is believed to be the leader of the latter. Now, who does not know that she is opposed to early marriages and denounces them as *unshastric* and disastrous? She has in fact taken pains not only to definitely pronounce against this evil custom, but, to give force to her utterances, has shut the doors of a department of her school at Benares against those who might have been or might be by the improvidence of their guardians married at a tender age. The Arya Samajists also may to a certain extent be called revivalists, but in this matter of early marriage and the marriageable ages of boys and girls they go a step further than even the most radical reformer is prepared to go just now. They say and preach, and try to enforce their precept, that no girl be married under 16 and no boy under 25. Now let us ask if there is anything irrational in saying that the institution of child marriage is not only condemnable by reason, but is actually opposed to the letter as well as the spirit of the *Shastras*. From the question of child marriage we may proceed to the great evil of the present divisions and sub-divisions of castes. Mrs. Besant and her school have already pronounced against the sub-divisions in the main castes. Her defence of the original Hindu conception of four castes principally coincides with the views of the Arya Samajists in the matter and practically knocks the present caste system on the head, though in theory only. In practice neither the Arya Samajists nor the reformers can go further than denunciation. All of them agree that a beginning should be made with the sub-divisions. The sub-divisions having been swept away (which is not likely to be achieved very soon or very easily) the time will then come to think of the remoulding or the fusion of the main castes on *Shastric* or rational lines. For the present we are all agreed that the existing arrangement is an unmixed evil, and the sooner it is done away with the better. From castes let us proceed to the question of foreign travel, and here again we find a practical unanimity. Of course, there are and there shall continue to be ultra-orthodox people who will not give up their opposition to any of these measures and will continue to say that they are un-Hindus; but just now we are not concerned with them, as we daresay there is no one who can justly or even contemptuously be called a revivalist who condemns foreign travel on the plea of revival and no reform. Then let us take up the great question of female education. I know of no sensible man in the country, not to speak of the revivalists only, who is a man of culture and education, who is opposed to it. The school of Mrs. Besant, the Arya Samajists, and the reformers are all pledged to it. There may be and there are practical difficulties in the way of educating our girls and sisters and wives, but nobody questions the desirability, nay the necessity of giving, if possible, the very highest education to girls. People nay differ on the *modus operandi* or may have different views about schemes of education to be enforced in the case of females, but there are no two opinions on the question of principle. There may be some among the so-called revivalists who are not favourably disposed to an exact copy of European customs and usages relating to females being adopted by the Hindus, but surely there is none who can in the name of revival defend the existing *Purdah* system or the universal ignorance of women.

Similarly, we do not think there is much difference of opinion, at least so far as practical measures feasible at present are concerned, on the necessity of raising the social status and bettering the condition of low castes, if Hinduism is not bent upon suicidal indifference and mad neglect of vital interests which might result in disastrous consequences. With the exception of some apparently spurious passages in *Manu* and other *Smritis*, there is absolutely nothing in the more ancient literature to justify the inhuman and cruel treatment to which the low castes are at present or were till lately subjected. We think we have almost exhausted the list of prominent subjects comprised in the list of reforms advocated by the social reformers, having reserved one important matter to be discussed last, viz. the question of widow remarriage.

On this question there exists undoubtedly real difference of opinion between the so-called reformers and the so-called revivalists. We grant that the question is a very important one, but still we are not prepared to admit that a difference on this single question justifies all that bitterness which characterises the writings of these two classes about one another. The real and important difference are on questions of religion and worship which the social reformers profess to exclude from their curriculum of school and college education. Here in the Punjab, fortunately we have been spared that bitter fight over these words which is going on in the western and southern Presidencies, although we are not unaware that of late attempts have not been wanting to introduce it in collegiate and inter-collegiate debates. We cannot but deprecate these unwise attempts and will warn our young men from throwing themselves into the vortex of this absolutely unnecessary and uncalled for fight over words. We may be pardoned for pointing out that to us the fight seems to be generally on the same lines and on the same grounds which marked the polemics of the old class of Pandits. The real truth is that the so-called reformers are mostly in faith and in religion Brahmos. They were the earliest in the field and fought for reform when the revivalists had not yet come into existence. The revivalists are the products of a wider diffusion of Sanskrit literature, which has taken place principally within the last quarter of a century. This study has afforded them sufficient and strong evidence of their ancestors having enjoyed a great and glorious civilization from which most of the present evil practices and customs that are the bane of modern Hinduism were absent. They, therefore, naturally look to the past for light and guidance and plead that a revival might lead them into that haven of progress, which is the object of all. They have found that most of the social evils existing in their society were not to be found in the ancient Hindu race and they have, therefore, begun to appeal to the authority of the past and the *Shastras* for the introduction of these very reforms for which reformers had been pleading with much force though with scanty success on grounds of utility and natural justice. The revivalists are naturally popular in Hindu society as they take their stand on the authority of the Hindu *Shastras* and thus threaten to oust the reformers from their hard-earned position. Then, to add insult to injury, their exposition of the popular religious beliefs of the Hindus is so injurious and cunning as to justify a reasonable fear in the minds of the reformers that they are taking the nation back to superstitions and low and debased forms of worship from which English education, contact with Western religion, and a study of the masterminds of the West was just extracting them with so desirable a success. The reformers had thus based their religious propaganda on the same basis on which their social programme rested, viz. grounds of rationality. The revivalists, having taken to the defence of the so-called national, have extended the same base to the removal of social evils and thus the fight began between "reform on rational lines" and "reform on national lines". But, as I have pointed out above, so far as real social reform is considered, both lines of work lead to a common conclusion. It is not, therefore, fair to entangle social reform in this quarrel which is really based on differences in religious views. Let the "reformers" by all means, if they like, ridicule the religious views of the "revivalists", and criticise or hold them to derision, but it is not, to say the least, graceful and fair to talk of them contemptuously in matters of social reform. The same should we say to the revivalists. Happily here in the Punjab, as we have already said, there is not much difference between reform and revival. By far the strongest reforming agency in the Punjab appears to accept both. To them reform is revival and revival is reform. It is true they attach much importance to nationality or to national lines, but subject to the important proviso *that they are not irrational.* The Arya Samajists shall have nothing *irrational* though it may even have the look of being national. They want everything national which is rational as well. They even go in for things *national* if only they are not irrational, but no further. According to them nothing can be either national or rational which is against the letter or the spirit of the Vedas. So far there seems to be no danger of the Punjab being involved in the meaningless distinction between reform and revival, but we think it is better to take time by the forelock and sound this note of warning to guard against any contemplated or impending mischief. But over and above that, it is our earnest request to the leaders of the Hindu community in the eastern and the southern provinces to abjure this absurd distinction and to work harmoniously for social reform, at least so far as all are agreed upon. Lately I had occasion to listen to an address on social progress by an esteemed friend of mine who is a pronounced social reformer. In the course of his remarks he treated the revivalists with scant respect, and in support of his views read the following quotation from the Amraoti speech of that great reformer—the late Mr. Justice Ranade.[2]

> On the other side, some of our orthodox friends find fault with us, not because of the particular reforms we have in view, but on account of the methods we follow. While the new religious sects condemn us for being too orthodox, the extreme orthodox section denounces us for being too revolutionary in our methods. According to these last, our efforts should be directed to revive and not to reform. I have many friends in this camp of extreme orthodoxy and their watchword is that revival and not reform should be our motto. They advocate a return to the old ways, and appeal to the old authorities and the old sanctions. Here also, as in the instance quoted above, people speak without realising the full significance of their own words. When we are asked to revive our institutions and customs, people seem to be very much at sea as to what it is they seem to revive.

2. This speech was delivered by Ranade at the eleventh session of the Indian Social Conference held at Amraoti in December 1897.

   Mahadev Govind Ranade (1842-1901); author, social reformer, historian and economist; professor of English at Elphinstone College, Bombay, 1868-71; joined Bombay Judicial Service in 1871; started *Sarvajanik Sabha Quarterly Journal* in 1878; member, Bombay Legislative Council, 1885-87 and 1891-92; Judge, Bombay High Court, 1893-1901; works include; *Essays on Indian Economics* (1899) and *Rise of Mahratta Power* (1900).

What particular period of our history is to be taken as the old? Whether the period of the Vedas, of the *Smritis*, of the *Puranas*, or of the Mohammedan or modern Hindu times? Our usages have been changed from time to time by a slow process of growth, and in some cases, of decay and corruption, and we cannot stop at a particular period without breaking the continuity of the whole. When my revivalist friend presses his argument upon me, he has to seek recourse in some subterfuge which really furnishes no reply to the question: What shall we revive? Shall we revive the old habits of our people when the most sacred of our castes indulged in all the abominations, as we now understand them, animal food and drink which exhausted every section of our country's zoology and botany? The men and gods of those old days ate and drank forbidden things to excess in a way no revivalist will now venture to recommend. Shall we revive the twelve forms of sons, or eight forms of marriage which included capture, and recognised mixed and illegitimate intercourse? Shall we revive the *Niyoga* system of procreating sons *on* our brothers' wives when widowed ? Shall we revive the old liberties taken by the *Rishis* and by the wives of the *Rishis* with the marital tie? Shall we revive the hecatombs of animals sacrificed from year's end to year's end, and in which human beings were not spared as propitiatory offerings? Shall we revive the *Shakti* worship of the *left hand* with its indecencies and practical debaucheries? Shall we revive the *sati* and infanticide customs, or the flinging of living men into rivers, or over rocks, or hook-swinging, or the crushing beneath the Jagannath car? Shall we revive the internecine wars of the Brahmans and *Kshatriyas* or the cruel persecution and degradation of the aboriginal population? Shall we revive the custom of many husbands to one wife or of many wives to one husband? Shall we require our Brahmans to cease to be landlords and gentlemen, and turn into beggars and dependants upon the king as in olden times? These instances will suffice to show that the plan of reviving the ancient usages and customs will not work out salvation, and is not practicable. If these usages were good and beneficial, why were they altered by our wise ancestors? If they were bad and injurious, how can any claim be put forward for their restoration after so many ages? Besides, it seems to be forgotten that in a living organism, as society is, no revival is possible. The dead and the buried or burnt are dead, buried, and burnt once for all, and the dead past cannot, therefore, be revived except by a reformation of the old materials into new organised beings.

Now, if it be permissible for a comparatively young and inexperienced man without laying himself open to a charge of disrespect for one of our revered leaders whose great wisdom, deep learning, and general judicial-mindedness are accepted all round, I will, with due deference to the late Mr. Ranade, beg to point out the injustice of the observations quoted above. Cannot a revivalist, arguing in the same strain, ask the reformers into what they wish to reform us? Whether they want us to be reformed on the pattern of the English or the French? Whether they want us to accept the divorce laws of Christian society or the temporary marriages that are now so much in favour in France or America? Whether they want to make men of our women by putting them into those avocations for which nature never meant them? Whether they want us to substitute the legal *niyoga* of the *Mahabharata* period with the illegal and immoral *niyoga* that is now-a-days rampant in European society? Whether they want us to reform into Sunday drinkers of brandy and promiscuous eaters of beef? In short, whether they want to revolutionise our society by an outlandish imitation of European customs and manners and an undiminished adoption of European vice? The revivalists do not admit that the institutions which they want to revive are dead, burnt and gone. The very fact that they wish to revive them goes to show that they believe that there is still some life left in them and that, given the proper remedy, their present unhealthy and abnormal state is sure to disappear and result in the bringing about of the normal and healthy condition of affairs. In fact, in an earlier part of the same address, Mr. Ranade summed up the position of the revivalists in a few well-chosen and apt words when he admitted that, "In the case of our society especially, the usages which at present prevail amongst us are admittedly not those which obtained in the most glorious periods of our history. On most of the points which are included in our programme our own record of the past shows that there has been a decided change for the worse and it is surely within the range of practical possibilities for us to hope that we may work up our way back to a better state of things without stirring up the rancorous hostilities which religious differences have a tendency to create and foster." It is exactly this working up our way back which the revivalists aim at. No revivalist has ever pleaded for the institutions selected by Mr. Justice Ranade as the butt end of this attack against them.

The real significance of these words—"reform" and 'revival", if any, seems to be in the authority or authorities from which the reformers and the revivalists respectively seek their inspiration for guidance in matters social. The former are bent on relying more upon reason and the experience of European society, while the latter are disposed to primarily look at their *Shastras* and the past history and the traditions of their people and the ancient institutions of the land which were in vogue when the nation was at the zenith of its glory. On our part we here in the Punjab are prepared to take our inspiration from both these sources, though we prefer to begin with the latter and call in the assistance of the former mainly to understand and explain what is not clear and ambiguous in the latter. But so long as our conclusions are principally the same, I think the fight is not worth being continued and may be dropped for good.

4. Hinduism and Common Nationality[1]

It is often said that Hinduism is not the name of a particular religion, nor that of a religious nationality, and that it does not represent one set of beliefs, common to all who call themselves Hindus, and that therefore it is perfectly idle to appeal to the Hindus in the name of a common nationality. It has become almost a fashion to insist that the term Hinduism is too vague to be properly defined, and that there is hardly anything substantially common which binds one Hindu to another in the ties of national brotherhood. Hinduism, in short, is said to be more of a congeries of different religions and sects holding diverse and not unoften diametrically opposite views on matters of faith and doctrine. Hinduism is said to include and cover almost every form of religious faith known to or practised by mankind, from the purest monotheism to the lowest form of animism, polytheism, hedonism, pantheism, in fact all sorts of *isms*. There is a fairly large class of Hindus who suffer from want of faith in the potentialities of their religion to unite them or to inspire them to the lofty ideals of a great religious platform whereupon to bring together a Hindu union. To many the idea of a Hindu union seems to be nothing more than an unrealizable dream. In their opinion, the talk of a Hindu nationality is a senseless talk, and the attempt to bring about a union amongst Hindus on the basis of religion is extremely impracticable. Some even go further and opine that the religious difficulties of the Hindus cannot be met with, removed or solved, by an appeal to the *Shastras*, and that amongst Hindus religious reform, too, must proceed on lines and ideas borrowed from the West. We confess we are unable to subscribe to these views, and are rather inclined to hold just the otherwise. We have substantial reasons to maintain that Hinduism is at least as much a religious nationality as its sister faiths—Christianity or Islam. These two latter contain as many varieties and shades of religious beliefs and doctrines in themselves, if not more, as Hinduism does, of course, giving due consideration to the ages of these three religions. If the Hindus have got their *Vedantists*, the Muhammadans have their *Sufis* and

1. Article published in *Lala Lajpat Rai—The Man in His Word* (Madras, 1907), pp. 99-107.

the Christians have those who have raised the banner of higher Christianity. If Hindus have their Trinity in Brahma, Vishnu and Shiva, the Christians have theirs in Father, Son and Holy Ghost. If the Hindus have got their *Avatars*, the Christians have (besides the great incarnation of God in the body of Christ) their Popes and Saints. If the Hindus believe in different deities, there are Muhammadans and Christians who believe in Saints, *Walis*, *Mahdis*, &c., &c. If the Hindus have their sacrifices, the Muhammadans and Christians have theirs also. If there are Hindus who are steeped in superstitious beliefs and observe many gross forms of worship, there are millions and millions of Muhammadans and Christians also, particularly the latter, whose religious practices are as gross as those of the multitude of Hindus. If there are fables in the *Puranas*, there are equally ridiculous stories in the Quran and the Bible. What is, then, that deprives Hinduism of that binding force which knits together the different discordant elements in Islam and Christianity? What are the special features of the latter that are absent in the former? Is Hinduism entirely devoid of any basal principles on which the foundations of a church national could be laid? It is these latter that we at first propose to take in hand and examine touching upon the former whenever it is relevant to do so. Our first contention is that like the general mass of Muhammadans and Christians, the Hindus, likewise, directly or indirectly, profess to accept the Vedas as their religious scriptures. The great bulk of the latter, like the great bulk of the former, believe that their scriptures are the word of God, and are infallible. There are learned Muhammadans and Christians who cannot go so far and do not believe that the Quran and the Bible are the word of God. On the question of the exact authority of the scriptures in these great religions of the world there are as many schools and shades of thought with all their varieties and niceties in one as in the other. There are scoffers, agnostics and skeptics everywhere. Everywhere there are men who do not care a jot for the scriptures, make no secret of their views, but still cling to the outer form of religion, the very essence of which they take pleasure in decrying. The number of such Christians is legion who do not believe that Christ was the son of God or the son of the Virgin, or that the Bible is the revealed word of God, but who do not still care to go out of the pale of outward Christianity. For the purposes of religious rites and ceremonies, for the purposes of baptism, marriage, etc. they are as much Christians as those who believe that every letter of the Bible was spoken by God Himself.

We have said all this not with the intention of disparaging either Islam or Christianity but only in support of our contention that in these respects the religious difficulties of the Hindus are in no way greater in extent, or larger in volume, than those of the Muhammadans and Christians. We know there are some people who are so hopeless of Hindu unity, or who are so much perplexed with the endless variety of religious beliefs in Hinduism that in moments of despondency they have been heard to apostrophize if it would not be better for India if all Hindus were to accept Christianity. But irrespective of spiritual efficiency or inefficiency of Christianity, we are afraid, even from the unity point of view we will not thereby be nearer the desired millennium. That such is the opinion of all impartial and disinterested observers will be amply borne out by the following quotations which we cull from a paper written by the late Professor Theodore Goldstucker[2] on the "Religious Difficulties of India". In the paper under reference were noticed certain (then) recent publications by two learned Hindu converts to Christianity,[3] criticizing the Hindu religion and philosophy and exhorting their late co-religionists to solve their religious problems by embracing Christianity.

After giving copious extracts from these publications containing the views of these learned *Padris* on the inconsistencies and anomalies of the Hindu religion and Hindu philosophy, with his own comments thereupon, the learned Professor says:

> There is another serious perplexity into which our learned authors must be aware that they will throw even those Hindus who may be clever enough to overcome all these difficulties, but it has as little been removed by them as indeed any difficulty which besets the solution of the religious problem in India. Their object, as we have seen, is to persuade their countrymen to embrace the Christian religion, but they have neither explained to them what the Christian religion is, nor where it may be found. Any Hindu, who follows the deductions of Mr. Bannerjee, would simply infer that there is but one Christian religion, which a devout student of the Bible might easily acquire from a perusal of the sacred book. Let him descend, however, from the region of abstraction into that of reality, and he will soon discover the endless variety of opinions which may be founded on the apparently so intelligible scriptural text, and he will soon learn that, so far from this being a mere possibility, hundreds of creeds have sprung up from this same scriptural soil, every one of which claims to be in exclusive possession of Christianity. *And if he be disposed to investigate historically the mutual relation of all these creeds he will find that their difference is so essential that it was strong enough to perpetuate the most inveterate*

2. (1821-1872); professor of Sanskrit at University College, London, 1850-1872; member of London Indian Society.
3. The reference was to *Dialogues on Hindu Philosophy* written by K.M. Banerji, professor of Sanskrit at Bishop College, Calcutta, and to *A Rational Refutation of Hindu Philosophical Systems* written by Nilakantha Shastri Gore.

animosities and to result in wars the like of which cannot be traced in the history of any other creed.

We have no desire to enlarge upon this theme, for we have said enough to explain why we hold the solution proposed by Mr. Bannerjee to be an impossibility. Attempts of conversion are too frequently made without examining the limits within which they are possible and the result in which their momentary success may end. If a man derives his religious views from his own individual information or from sources which are void of authoritative influence, he may yield them to the views which are of a higher range without causing injury to the nobler part of himself. *But if the creed of an individual is founded on texts held sacred and authoritative, it is a national creed; no individual can abandon it without severing himself from the national stem; no nation can surrender it without laying the axe to its own root. For religion, based on texts believed sacred, embodies the whole history of the nation which professes it; it is the shortest abbreviation of all that ennobles nation's mind, is most dear to its memory and most essential to its life.* No religion has better illustrated this truth than the religion founded on the Bible. It could be, and was successfully, introduced amongst all nations which possess no texts supposed to be divinely inspired, and therefore of general authority, and whenever a nation possessing merely the semblance of such a text adopted it, it thereby decreed its own end. The Romans and Greeks, when becoming Christians, ceased to be the continuation of the classical Romans and Greeks, in history, in literature, in character. Their political importance based on the conditions of the past was brought to a close, and they had to grow into another nationality. The condition under which this religion introduced itself into the countries of Europe was always the absence of book ascribed to divine authorship. When Mr. Banerjee speaks of the Jews, he has chosen an exact counter-instance which goes far to prove that even a people without land, without any history which can be called their own, that a people exposed to all the horrors of persecution and all the allurements of seduction did not and do not espouse that very religion which exercises the most powerful influence on their actual destinies and which it even supports and favours amongst those who profess it. The Jews do not become Christians, simply because they believe that their *Testament* is a sacred book.

Having expressed these views as to the undesirability and impossibility of converting Hindus to Christianity, Professor Goldstucker further addresses the Hindus themselves, and lays down what, in his opinion, is the true key to the solution of their religious difficulty. We cannot do better than once more quote his words which are full of significance and pregnant with great meaning to all educated Hindus.

> We have been carried, however, with these remarks to the point where we cannot shrink from expressing the views which we entertain of the duties of the Brahmanical Hindus of our own days. We need not emphasise more than we have already done, that we reject as unwise and unpractical any attempt to persuade them to become Christians or to adopt the Biblical scriptures as their spiritual code. We want them to become a nation worthy of their ancestors and worthy of the great role, which in ancient times they have acted in the history of the human race, and we are satisfied that they cannot regain that position by breaking the spring ties of their life, and by exchanging their own religious uncertainty for that of any other creed. It is necessary, however, that they should realize the condition in which they are. We need not prove to them that the minds of the enlightened portion of their nation are estranged from the sectarian worship as it is practised now, but who could satisfy them that they are utterly remiss in examining where the root of the evil lies?
>
> Every Brahmanical believer, if asked, will tell that the mode of his worship is founded on the Vedas. He refers us, it is true, occasionally to the *Puranas* and *Tantras*, but he himself admits that these works have no authoritative powers unless they can prove that the tenets they contain are drawn from the *Vedic* source. The pivot, then, on which all religious questions of India turn, is and remains—the Veda. Philosophers and non-Philosophers, *Vishnuits* and *Sivaits*, all echo the word Veda. . . .

Forty years have clapsed since these words were written by one of the profoundest Sanskrit scholars and one of the most competent and shrewd students of comparative religions, which Europe produced, but the words hold as good, as true and as forcible today as they ever were. In fact, the events of these forty years have, instead of showing any flaw either in the arguments or in the sentiments of the learned Professor, proved, if any further proof was needed, how accurately did he grasp the real situation and how truly did he lay down the solution.

We repeat, therefore, before we close, for the present, that the pivot on which all religious questions of Hindu India rest is, and remains—the Veda. To the Veda, therefore, we must go for light and guidance in our religious troubles, and in the Veda we shall find our solace.

5. Hinduism and Social Responsibility[1]

A question has often haunted us, asleep or awake, as to why is it that notwithstanding the presence amongst us of great vigorous and elevating religious truths, and of the very highest conception of morality, we have been a subject race, held down for so many centuries by sets of people who were neither physically nor spiritually nor even intellectually so superior to us as a *fortiori* to demand our subjection.

We do not require a Herbert Spencer to tell us that the social efficiency of a social organism as such, depends upon the sense of social responsibility amongst the members of such an organism. The greater and the intenser the sense of responsibility amongst the individual members, regarding the safety and the welfare of the whole, the greater and the stronger the efficiency of the organism.

It is precisely this sense which is wanting in us and which stands in our way as a nation. Physically we are the equals of any people on earth. Barring those high-class Hindus who think their glory consists in weak constitutions, delicate limbs and womanly features or who are given to determine their position in society by the amount of fat on their body and by the amount of physical inactivity which attends their business in life, the majority of our countrymen possess fine physiques and are able to withstand any amount of hardship and struggle. Even with the little they get to satisfy their meagre wants, with their coarse food, scanty clothing and ill-ventilated and excessively crowded homesteads they produce a soldiery which ranks amongst the best in the world. Whether it be the Rajput, the Jat, the Sikh, the Gorkha, the Purbia, the Marahatta, or the Punjabi Mussulman, the view expressed above holds equally good in the case of all. All of them have, by turns, earned the highest praises of military experts under whom they had occasion to serve beneath the British flag. Whatever may be said of the many mistakes of head and heart by which they lost their own battles before the advent of the British, no one can question their bravery and valour. History is full of their deeds. Intellectually, too, given the opportunities, the sons of India have given no occasion to shame their mother country. The Hindu civilization, the Buddhistic achievements are standing monuments of their high intellectual calibre. Under Mohammadan rule as well, when, according to the celebrated Alberuni, the elite of the Hindu community sought the safety of the remotest and the farthest parts of the country to be secure from the molestation of the fanatically disposed Mohammadans, the

1. Article published in *Lala Lajpat Rai—The Man in His Word* (Madras, 1907), pp. 108-14.

country continued to produce intellectual giants whose names still shed lustre on the country of their birth. Under the British, too, with the few opportunities that are possessed by the Indian scholar to distinguish himself, the country has produced a Bose, a Paranjpye, a Ranade, and many others whose names are the common property of all Indians. Then if we look at the domain of religion we stand also unequalled. Which country in Europe can show the equals of the unknown authors of the *Upanishads*, the Buddha, and Shankaracharya? From religion if we come down to the regions of philosophy, where in one country could we find such a galaxy of truth-loving, honest and bold thinkers, as the immortal authors of the six *Darshanas*, and some of their commentators and elucidators? Again, glancing at the history of chivalry and noble deeds, does not the history of the Rajputs read like a romance? Why, then, are we so low in the scale of nations? What is it that keeps us down and does not allow us to raise our head above the waters? We are not wanting in flexibility or adaptability. Where on earth will you find another case parallel to Hinduism? Notwithstanding 12 centuries of Islamic propaganda backed by all the forces of political ascendancy and of that moral superiority which is the anchor sheet of a virgin religion and a conquering creed, notwithstanding again of 100 years of active evangelical work done in the name of Christ by devoted missionaries, Hinduism still reigns supreme in the land and baffles all attempts, made from time to time, to displace and overthrow it. How is it then, that, with all the education we have received during the one century of British rule, with frantic professions of patriotism that are the natural result of a knowledge of our degradation and helplessness, with wild cries of nationality in danger, with pathetic appeals for reforms in the administration of the country, we have so far failed to gain anything substantial in our quest for national liberty? How is it that our cries make no impression, our appeals go unheeded and our professions turn out to be of no avail? While sparing no occasion or means of criticizing government measures, very often offering right and sensible criticism, with that amount of persistency which sometimes we show, why are we yet powerless to obtain even the smallest measure of reform either in constitution or in administration, or even of remedial justice? Why, leaving the political sphere aside, how is it that even in matters of social reform, which being in our hands no government prevents us from giving effect to, we have so far failed to achieve that amount of success which the Herculean efforts of men like Rammohun Roy,[2] Dayanand Saraswati, Ishwar Chandra

2. (1772-1833); religious and social reformer of Bengal who founded Brahmo Samaj in 1828; campaigned for the abolition of *sati* until it was abolished by law in 1829; advocated English and scientific education; served East India Company in several capacities from 1803 to 1815; advocated political freedom; works include English translations of *Upanishads* and a thesis on Hindu theism.

Vidyasagar[3] and Mahadev Govind Ranade deserved? The reply is the same as we have already given above. We are individually wanting in that sense of social responsibility which requires each and every member of the organism to place the interests of the community or the nation over and above those of his own. Amongst us selfishness, greed and calculation reign supreme. Most of us cannot even think of the society or the community or the nation. But even those who can think and do profess to care for them do not care a farthing for the same, when their own individual interests seem to clash with the interests of the society. Most of us, including some of the very highly educated men, who do not fail to exhibit often an unpardonable pride in the amount of learning locked in their brains, who very readily spend hours in finding fault with the commas and semi-colons of less gifted brethren, who do not fail to parade their knowledge of the philosophy of Herbert Spencer, of the science of Huxley or of the fine poetic genius of a Shelley or a Tennyson are utterly devoid of a sense of social responsibility.

We know that men who denounced the institution of child marriage in the most vehement language they could command, were at the same time conscious of the fact that they had themselves already fixed a date for the marriage of their seven years old girl with a boy of a similarly tender age. We have known men whose professions of patriotism were often the most profuse, giving a point-blank refusal to any demand of help for any national institution. We have known of great patriots rolling in wealth, possessing palatial residences, enjoying the blessing of a good fixed income, never moving their finger to reduce misery that was next door to them. We have seen great patriotic Indians passing by in a spirit of perfect indifference, when another countryman of theirs was being cruelly beaten by a European. No Indian is supposed to make any move unless such a move pays or benefits him in cash or in kind in any way. If you go to a gentleman to ask him to join such and such an association or to do such and such a thing, the question that he puts to you or, if he has not the courage to do so openly, to himself is, what shall he gain thereby? We know that people give subscriptions, attend meetings, join associations and *Samajes* and do a lot of other things that have the look of public spirit or national help but how many of them, may we ask, except when moved by religion, do so by a sense of public duty and individual responsibility for the national cause? It is very unpleasant to speak ill of one's own countrymen or to appear to be

3. (1820-1891); educationist and social reformer of Bengal; taught Sanskrit at Fort William College, Calcutta, 1841-45; conferred the title of "Vidyasagar" by Sanskrit College, Calcutta, in 1841, later taught at Sanskrit College and became its Principal; made honorary member of Royal Asiatic Society in 1864; wrote *Sitar Binobas* in 1861 and edited Kalidas's *Kumar Sambhavam*, *Meghadutam* and *Abhijnan Shakuntalam*.

ungrateful to those estimable gentlemen who do keep public movements going, but to be truthful we shall be failing in our duty if we were to pretend a belief in their patriotism. It is our firm belief that if the country could have claimed the one-tenth part of that patriotism which is often paraded and assumed, the state of things would have been different and no government could have ignored the existence or the demands of such patriotism. But the facts are otherwise; not that the social ideals taught by our religion are low and mean, not that this rank selfishness and base calculation of self-interest is countenanced by the teachings of our great men, not that this sense of national and public duty is entirely absent from the teachings of our *Shastras*. No. Political degradation for so long has practically extinguished the very germs of this noble sentiment from our blood. Our immediate ancestors did not possess it, so we could not inherit it from them. As for its inculcation from without, we are sorry that the advantages of Western culture have not been unmixed. While very few have imbibed its noble sentiments, a large number have taken and adopted in life its materialistic tendencies. We know that we require the latter, too, rather badly but we cannot forget that, if we once allow ourselves to be possessed of these only without the other necessary and counteracting tendencies, we are done for. The country may grow rich, it may extend its commerce, it might even begin to manufacture for other countries, but unless all this is accompanied by a sense of public duty in the people of this country, all this will not avail us, nay, might be the very foundation of future fall, if further fall is yet possible. Yes, we want all this, but first and foremost of all we want the habit and sense of subordinating our individual interests to the interests of the community at large. In short, what we pre-eminently want is that every Indian may be sufficiently patriotic and dutiful to believe and act up to the belief that the interests of the country are paramount and must override all private considerations. We want this to be regularly taught as the highest religion that will bring about the salvation of India. To promulgate this we want faithful and true preachers who may be living examples of the truth of their propaganda and who can show the power of their faith in their own persons. Let each province produce a number of such preachers and we are convinced that patriotism will gain firm ground in the country and the cause of nationality will advance by leaps and bounds. Without this we may go on crying for decades and decades but we shall not advance an inch.

10
ARYA SAMAJ

1. Call to the Youth to Make Sacrifices for Progress of the Nation[1]

Brethren, you have come here as our guests and I am ashamed to find that we are unable to show the hospitality of providing you sufficient accommodation here. This poverty of ours is an index of the poverty of our country. However, there is no occasion for anyone to complain. We have been doing whatever is within our power, but for that which is beyond our means there can be no help, and we therefore ask your forgiveness.

This morning I had begun by saying that while I was in Europe I tried to search for a solution to the question: What is the secret of the progress of Europe? What are the causes which have raised the sun of prosperity of Europe to its zenith? How is it that, although the Europeans are a few in number, they reign supreme in the whole world and nobody dare disobey their command? From the day I set foot on European soil I began to ponder over questions such as these. He who has his eyes open can have a clear insight into the truth behind them. As soon as you land on European soil, you observe things working in a way which itself suggests the solution to the problem. Soon you begin to have a clearer perception that the Europeans are far more intelligent than we are. In their system of education, their arts, industries and their commerce what strikes us is that there exists organization everywhere, i.e. the quality of doing a thing systematically and in a sustained manner. Every man by his very nature, then, is fond of organization, and no one dares to interfere with the law of organization. You find working of this law not only in navies, armies and other departments of Western Governments, but also in their homes. The home of a European typifies the marvellous system of organization that prevails in the West, and from his very childhood he grows up under its influence. There is not a single man who is not privy to some sort of organization. In short, it is organization which rules supreme in Europe. But, gentlemen, what forms the backbone of organization is education. If anyone wishes to see the practical manifestation of the maxim that knowledge is power and that even the elements, i.e. earth, air, fire, water etc. have come under the sway of man, let him go and see the ships or the machinery being manufactured in the factories of Europe. Then alone will the truth begin to dawn upon him that how successful they have been in harnessing the stupendous powers of nature to provide for the

1. Speech delivered on the occasion of the anniversary of Arya Samaj, Lahore, (College party) on 26 November 1905. This speech was used by the Government to arrest and deport Lajpat Rai in May 1907. *Lala Lajpat Rai—The Man in His Word* (Madras, 1907), pp. 235-52; also published in *The Panjabee* of 27 November and *Paisa Akhbar* of 12 December 1905.

comforts of man! But the secret of all this power lies in the system of education which obtains there.

All the nations of Europe are not equally great. While some are of ordinary standing, some others are highly advanced and powerful by virtue of the vastness of their empires and the power and influence they wield over the world. Admittedly the extent of power and influence of the various nations of Europe is dependent upon their respective systems of education though in the educational scheme of a country like Switzerland there is little room for military preparations to infringe upon the liberty of any other nation. The system of education prevalent in Europe is on the whole calculated to develop intelligence and make a man adventurous and daring. In Europe, the current notion about education is that it should equip a man to meet personal and national requirements, that while, on the one hand, it should develop personal qualities in him, it should, on the other, help in making him a true and sincere lover of his country.

A man is a creature of his surroundings. No one is immune to the influence of his environment. Even autogenous plants and trees that grow in the jungle reach their fruition by absorbing from the soil the elements conducive to their growth. Nothing in nature can escape or obviate the effect of the environment. The development of each individual also depends to a great extent on his environment. European children are fortunate in being born of civilized parents, and as such are motivated, to a high degree, for their civilisational values. As soon as a child attains the school-going age, he, in a way, ceases to require the protection of his parents, and another agency with vast and unbounded resources steps in to take upon itself the responsibility of bringing up the child. This agency is the Government of the country. In cases, where parents are not in a position to satisfactorily discharge their duty of giving proper education to their children, the Government takes this task upon itself, the fulfilment of which it considers the supreme aim of its existence.

The Government there represents the people; it is the executive of the nation and is composed of representatives chosen by the people. The state is responsible for the prosperity and protection of its people. The Government deems it its duty to ensure that no child grows up in ignorance and, therefore, legislates that education up to a certain age is compulsory for all children, whether male or female. In the education of their children, parents are relieved of the burden of providing them with books, pens, ink and fees. The children are not required to carry these things with them to school; rather they are supplied to them there free of charge. Now they have gone a step further inasmuch as students who are needy and poor are supplied with nourishing food on behalf of the school. Seeing that the poor children are placed at a disadvantage as compared to the children of the rich, and that mental work tends to tell upon the physique of the former as a result of which they cannot derive the maximum benefit from their education, the state has stepped in to provide food to such children free of cost. When this question came up for consideration before the Governments of the various self-governing countries of Europe, the French Government was the first to offer a solution to this problem. It went ahead to lay down that the state ought to provide for the care and nutrition of those children whose parents cannot afford it. In England also the London County Council has introduced a similar system in schools under its charge. There girls are taught cookery, handicrafts, needlework and singing as part of the educational curriculum.

In the course of holding classes in cookery they are also taught chemistry and told about the ingredients and properties of various foods and such other details as the quantity of oxygen and hydrogen that go into making them. In one room they receive theoretical instruction on the subject and in another arrangements exist for a practical demonstration in which girls are actually made to cook food with their own hands. The food thus prepared is given to those boys and girls who cannot afford it by themselves.

This would suffice to show how keenly the Europeans feel and realise the importance of education. We here in India wish to provide the cheapest form of education to our children, unmindful of its influence. And yet with all this we Indians want to imitate and excel those Europeans who at present are the rulers of the world. In Europe no problem is considered of such paramount importance as the educational one. In India the function of a teacher ends when the school-time is over and with it also ends the relation between the teacher and the taught. But in every European country a large class of great thinkers and experts is always busy in devising new ways and means for improving and perfecting the educational system of the nation. Some of the best intellects of the country are paid high salaries in order that they might go and study the educational systems of other countries and compare them with their own with a view to finding out the shortcomings of their own system and devising schemes for their removal. The findings of such studies are published in reports for the information and edification of the people. They are widely discussed among the people and much-needed conclusions are drawn from them. A large number of experts are always busy in thinking over educational matters, their chief concern being that the country should not lag behind in any area of national advancement.

Here in India it has become customary for the teacher to resort to the use of the cane as soon as the boy begins his alphabet. But in Europe it is not so. The children there are given oral instruction for 2 or 3 years and are also made to draw pictures as an entertainment. They are taught how to use their hands and feet by engaging them in outdoor activities like walking, running, etc. and after this they are taught the alphabet. Drawing of sketches and figures, music and physical culture are considered among the most essential ingredients of elementary education. Boys brought up in these schools are never morbid or morose. No power can hold them back from serving their country. The sense of responsibility towards the nation is so much developed in them that they can never become indifferent to it. Patriotism and love of the nation is ingrained in their minds through music. They are taught colour painting as soon as they learn the elements of drawing, needlework and cookery. The minds of the pupils are not unnecessarily burdened with useless bits of information. They are told the names and colours of flowers and other details about them. This is done to teach them to distinguish colours, and learn elementary arithmetic. The teacher places various things upon the table and asks the pupils to tell their names, colours and number. In Europe, children have not to read at home after school hours. They think, and it is no doubt true, that the imposition of excessive burdens can stunt the mental and physical growth of children. In Europe the number of subjects taught in primary schools is not less than what is taught here, but the method of teaching there is such that it does not cause much mental strain to the student. The result is that after receiving instruction for 5 or 7 years the child can use his hands, feet and brain to good advantage and he is in a position to adopt any profession he likes later in life. The grounding in education that he has received stands him in good stead everywhere. On the other hand, we, too, receive theoretical education in geometry, but in practice we are unable to draw a straight line correctly. An Englishman, who begins his education with drawing, can draw good pictures with the least effort. In Europe, in one place, a teacher lectures theoretically, say, upon the art of making a table and the materials required for it, and in another place the children are afforded the opportunity of translating theory into practice by direct manipulation. After receiving this sort of elementary education up to the fourteenth year, they have to decide how they are to make a living in the world. The arrangements for this purpose are wonderful indeed; some boys study for five hours and spend the rest of the time earning their livelihood. Facilities for higher education are provided for those who wish to work in the day and study at night. Even the best equipped educational institution in India does not possess the apparatus, which every night school of the London County Council does. There in England absence of pecuniary support from one's home does not necessarily mean that he will be deprived of higher education. Here, on the contrary, those who are intelligent but poor have quite often, after a time, to give up their education and prematurely search for sources of livelihood, thus hampering their advancement in life. This involves loss of talent and the nation is deprived of the valuable services of such individuals would have rendered to the nation by occupying eminent positions in life. In Europe steps have been taken to avert this national and individual loss. The education the people receive there is, moreover, meant to make them honest, high-minded, religious and patriotic, besides making them capable of earning their livelihood by honourable and industrious means. Some of the officials here frequently remark that Indians do not acquire education for its own sake, but as a means of earning livelihood; but if such a remark were made in Europe, people would ask in amazement, what on earth is the object of education if it is not to make one better able to earn a living?

A great struggle for supremacy is going on in Europe; every nation is trying to march ahead of the rest. Every nation fears that if its educational system atrophies and becomes flawed and consequently its members are superseded by others in the matter of sending the cheapest and the best wares to the world markets it will suffer a loss of position in the field of commerce. The chief object of each country's respective educational system is to keep its people ahead of the others in industry and commerce. The competition coming from Germany and America is at present threatening to weaken the commercial ascendancy of England. It is undeniably true that the educational system of Germany is much superior to that of any other country in Europe but after careful research great changes have been introduced into the educational system of England during the last five or six years. Now every school in England possesses a workshop for practical training. The English are taking measures to ensure that they do not lag behind the Germans in industry, trade and commerce.

The object of educating a child is that in addition to being useful to himself and to the society, he should be imbued with patriotic feelings in no way inferior to those of any other nation. Europeans in general and the English in particular are ardent admirers of liberty. They cannot tolerate a single word directed against their nation. They hate the word "ruler". Although they have got their own King and Parliament, they look upon them as mere advisers, helpers and leaders in national advancement. A recently published book, *Struggle Against the Monarchy*, which is included in the curriculum for young students, drives home the point that whatever rights and privileges the English enjoy have been obtained after countless sacrifices.

As was stated above, music is an essential part of their elementary training. Boys and girls assemble in the halls of the schools to sing such patriotic songs as create this impression on their minds that they are future custodians of national interest.

Here in India physical exercise is considered a thing of minor importance, whereas in Europe it is part and parcel of the school instruction. The bodies of children are developed by means of physical exercises and games so that in times of emergency they may be able to render service to the state.

Europeans regard this world as a paradise and a place worth living in. They consider it the finest manifestation of the workmanship of the Almighty Creator. They want to live in this world thinking it to be fine and splendid. They think it their duty to prolong their lives as much as they can, no matter how. We also pray daily for a life of hundred years, but we regard the world as a place of misery, hence we achieve little. Unless we look upon this world as a place of bliss we can never be prepared to make sacrifices to attain happiness here and now. So long as we do not consider the world as the abode of external happiness and joy we can make no progress. Europeans impress upon the minds of their children that the world is vast and is full of happiness. Hence they teach them to be prepared for all sorts of struggles in their onward march. They point to the limitless vistas before them and exhort them to go ahead and achieve glory and honour for themselves and for their nation.

In Europe no mother bothers as to what her son will do in life. They love their children no less than we do but they realize and make their sons also realize that just as this universe is infinite so their courage too should be vast and boundless. It is our duty, therefore, to emulate and absorb this spirit from Europe. Besides, they have established schools for imparting technical education. Our rulers here show signs of impatience at the establishment of four or five universities and the number of boys to be educated therein, but in the West there exists a university in every big town, and still the Governments there are not seen to be impatient in devising ways and means for reducing the number of students. On the contrary, their chief concern is to improve and perfect their existing educational system by removing whatever defects they could detect therein. The universities there are authorized to impart education in all departments of learning and confer degrees in banking, commerce and other branches of industrial and technical education. Then the question that arises is, can we do anything for ourselves or for that matter how can we help ourselves? If you really wish that industrial development may be accelerated and you may not be dependent for your necessaries upon foreign countries, then you should prepare your young men for the task. It is fortunate that there are a number of schools here, but they are not sufficiently equipped for the purpose. It is necessary for us to send our young men to foreign countries—especially the men of means among you should do so—to enable them to receive industrial training. Instead of bequeathing huge sums of money and a large quantity of gold for your children at the time of death, it is better that you should give them education of the kind which might enable them to earn their living wherever they may happen to be. This world presents great possibilities and immense opportunities before you. If there are not sufficient manufactories in India to provide jobs for those who return after doing a technical course in foreign countries, then why should you not go and gain a living in the factories of other countries? In America, people of Arabic, Japanese, Chinese and Austrian origin labour during the day and receive education at night. They are not bothered in the least about what work they shall have to do on return to their own country. One who knows a craft should have no anxiety about the capital needed to execute his schemes. Indians who go abroad expect that on their return others should start factories for them. But a trained man should not complain on that score. I think of the day when there will be habitations of Indian expatriates in all parts of the world and they will not only pray for the welfare of India and the Indians, but also at times of need render them assistance. The very thought gives me immense pleasure that if five hundred Indians trained in any art are settled in other countries they will at any point of time be fully equipped to meet at short notice all our requirements with respect to that particular art. If the Indians spread themselves out into the whole world and learn various arts and engage in industrial pursuits, then what is it that they will not be able to achieve? For instance, how important ship-building is for all nations on the march? Now, if there be Indians who have learnt the art of ship-building in the great ship-making factories of the world, they can be of great help to India, and to a great extent meet her maritime requirements.

A number of factories already exist in Punjab, but they are not progressing satisfactorily. The reason is that those who run these factories do not have sufficient skill and efficiency required for it. If the proprietors of these factories form a conclave and send a number of young men to other countries for technical training on condition of the latter working in these factories on their return, then both the factories and the students will be benefited. Preferably such young men should not be married persons. If they recognize the value of the dignity of labour, then nothing can stand in the way of their receiving the requisite training and skills. In America even an unskilled labourer who has not received any special training in any particular art or industry, gets at least $ 1.50 or Rs. 4-8 as daily wages. If a sufficient number of young men gird up their loins to acquire technical education in other countries by sustaining themselves through hard work and if an organisation is formed to defray their passage-money and meet their preliminary expenses as well as to render them assistance whenever they are ill or out of job, a great deal can be done in this direction.

The test of our progress, our advancement, our prosperity, nay, our very existence, is education. Twenty years ago the Arya Samaj put forward swadeshi and national education as the two tests of advancement in the national struggle, and now you find Bengal demonstrating practically that the program which the Arya Samaj had adopted in this respect was the right one. The scheme of the Dayanand College, which was framed after long and careful consideration of the needs of the nation, and taking into account the direction in which events were happening in India, has been proved to be correct. The ideal of education put forward by the founders of the Dayanand College is the same which Europe has now adopted. Japan too says that we cannot continue to live and thrive until we do all that appeals to our souls keeping in view our past greatness and draw the people's attention to our ancient values, literature and civilisation. This does not mean that we should blindly follow whatever is there in our ancient civilisation. I have pondered deeply over the question and I have come to the conclusion that the ancient civilisation of India was superior to the modern civilisation of Europe and if I were asked to express my opinion about the two I would unhesitatingly say so. But, my friends, it is not in our power to be totally immune to the influence of modern Western civilisation, for Western civilisation is a gigantic force and one wonders how we can protect ourselves from its advancing march. We can wage a struggle against this civilisation only with the help of modern devices and techniques. Ancient weapons shall not be able to check its progress in the least. We have to face it with Western methods and Western instruments. We are part of this world; we live within the globe and not outside it. Therefore we cannot do without coming to terms with the forces that are working in the world. It is, therefore, desirable that, while protecting ourselves from the evils to which the West has fallen prey, we should at the same time imbibe its virtues. In short, in this struggle against the Western civilisation we can hardly make any progress without adopting the means and methods of the West.

The education of females is linked with the education of males. A nation can never be great until its mothers are great. Regrettably our country does not now produce forth noble and valiant women like the mothers of Jaimal, Fatta and other Rajputs. These days we do not get the same sort of nourishing and invigorating milk from the breasts of our mothers as our ancestors did from theirs. The path of progress is straight, but so long as our country does not have spirited and patriotic mothers any talk of advancement is a mere pipe dream. What can the sons of mothers who do not allow their children to stir outside the four walls of their house do as compared to the sons of those broad-minded women who are not afraid of the roar of the oceans? In Europe women have virtues as well as vices; and so is the case here. If we want to make progress we should try to shun their vices and imbibe their virtues, thus making the greatness of women the test of our national advancement.

Come, let us all try to make the Dayanand Anglo-Vedic College a model for all other schools and colleges. Let it have well-equipped apparatus and well-paid teachers. Let us all come forward and help the cause of the Dayanand College because it is the custodian of our honour. This institution is the center of all our national activities for educational advancement and the soul of our nation. The Dayanand College is also the head and heart of Punjab. If the head and heart get weak or palsied how can the body be expected to survive for long? This College is your own and it can satisfy all your requirements. Others have no hand in its working and cannot interfere with it in any way.

I was extremely pleased to learn in England that the number of new admissions in the College this year has been larger than it was last year. The students have in this way given a resounding rebuff to those who are bent upon ruining the College. The students have thus shown that the designs of the latter cannot succeed in this matter. National progress is proceeding on the right lines and no power on earth can stop its advance. We prize university degrees and we all are helping our young men to obtain them. But if insurmountable difficulties are placed in their way, then the better course would be to give up the craving for these degrees. The Dayanand Anglo-Vedic College is a national institution. If you have to choose between a university degree and national honour, you should without the least hesitation forsake the former and accept the latter.

I wish the world was full of young students from Punjab. There is perhaps no other province in India which can excel Punjab in determination and daring. Those who possess these qualities prosper everywhere. Young men, step forward, spread over France, Germany, Japan and Canada. You will then see how you are rewarded by them. Those who now despise us and try to crush us will then respect us. The wide world is before you, the Aryan blood runs in your veins. None can stop your progress. You are the descendants of great *rishis* and sages who imparted knowledge to the whole world. Have you fallen so low now that you are unfit even to learn from others? Those among us who marry off their children at an early age and thus stunt their development by putting the heavy load of family life round their necks, ruin their children. Pray, keep your children free from these trammels and let them spread their wings and soar to great heights, thereby growing to full potential of their manhood. Do not clip their wings and, like featherless birds, casue them to be trampled down by others.

Gentlemen, may I appeal to you in the name of nationality? Alas, where is nationality? This congeries of sects and creeds holding different systems of beliefs cannot but be altogether wanting in the sentiment of nationality. Then why do we look upon our kith and kin as our enemies, and other non-Hindus as our friends? Why do we despise our own kith and kin and worship others? Alas, if we could but set aside our internecine quarrels and put up a united front to the outer non-Hindu world! The true meaning of nationality will dawn upon us only when in the name of 'nationality' we all are united to face the adversary. It is saddening to think that we have entirely lost the sense of national honour. As you know, Ramabai is blaspheming against the entire Indian womanhood by declaring in America that no Indian girl of 13 or 14 years of age can boast of her chastity. But are there not many even in this assembly who unashamedly admire the same Ramabai? Had we possessed any sense of national honour, could anyone dare crush us or hurl such calumnies at us? How can we claim national honour when 70 million of the children are found starving and where girls are made over to outsiders—Christian missionaries or Muslim divines—to save them from starvation?

You youths of Punjab, there is one thing alone in the name of which I can appeal to you, and that is the D.A.V. College which was founded in 1886. You have already shown signs of life by contributing heartily to its success and I appeal to your same spirit. Come, let us spurn all worldly desires and stick to our pledge. We should not leave undone what we have once taken in hand. A wave of national advancement in the sphere of education has arisen in another province in the form of the Bengal Association which has been founded for the advancement of scientific and industrial education. There money is pouring in and young men are coming forward to carry on the mission. O young men, your blood is warm and it is required for watering the national tree, for the tree of freedom can only be nurtured by the blood of martyrs. History writes in letters of blood the account of the intellectual advancement of a nation. It has been ordained by God that a country can advance intellectually only if its members practise the virtues of self-sacrifice and self-abnegation. Your sacrifices will leave indelible marks on the history of the world. Concrete is required to strengthen the foundations of a building. Let us throw ourselves like concrete to lay the foundations of the national edifice. Let us forget our own problems in the interests of the national progress. O, ye students of Punjab, remember that students have written the history of the world in letters of gold. Old men can never accomplish what young men can do. Come, let us crown our national institutions with spires of our sacrifices, so that a time may come when we may also take our rightful place among the nations of the world. If the young men of this nation of ours can brace themselves for forthcoming challenges our dignified existence will be ensured and nobody will dare debase or harm us.

2. To G.K. Gokhale[1]

Lahore
12 March 1906

Dear Mr. Gokhale,

Thanks many for your kind letter of the 9th and its contents. I have so far entirely ignored the attacks made upon me by my opponents in the Arya Samaj

1. G.K. Gokhale Papers (microfilm), N.A.I.

but I thought it better to inform you of the same so as to reverse all chances of any misapprehension arising in your mind on the subject. At present I have no intention of taking any further notice of the same.

Will you please let me know the probable date of your departure to England? Are the Bengalees going to send a deputation? If so, when? Have you idea of who the delegates are likely to be? The Council session will probably end in a few days and you will probably be going back to Poona to prepare for your intended trip to England. If it may not be presumptuous on my part, may I enquire if you expect any tangible concession from the Liberal Government?

With kindest regards,

Believe me to be

Yours very sincerely,
Lajpat Rai

3. On the Charge of Arya Samaj Being a Political Body[1]

It has become quite a fashion with the enemies of the Arya Samaj (particularly of that section of it which is known by the name of the College section, or the Anarkali Arya Samaj, and to which the writer has the honour to belong)[2] to charge it with the heinous crime of being a political body, whenever any or some of them have any reason to fall out with a prominent worker or member thereof. It is a common phenomenon in this world of ours that the success or supposed success of a particular man or group of men necessarily arouses the worst passions of those who have lagged behind in the march of progress or who have failed to achieve a similar amount of success or who are disposed to think that to the success of the former are to be ascribed the want of success, the failures or the misfortunes of themselves. Success always evokes jealousy, and jealousy breeds hatred and opposition. The Arya Samaj is believed to have been successful and as such was bound to arouse jealousy and opposition. The Arya Samajists are credited with a strong and fanatic bent of mind with determination to achieve their aims *at any cost*, unmindful of the opinion and the goodwill or the opposition of those with whom they happen to come into conflict. Hence the desperate nature of the opposition they meet and the hatred they arouse.

1. Published in *The Panjabee* of 4 July 1906.
2. Lajpat Rai was President of the Anarkali Arya Samaj which was formed after the split in the Arya Samaj in 1893.

Let us try to understand the position more definitely.

(1) A great number of the members of this Samaj hold strong and uncompromising views on the desirability of checking and counteracting all encroachments on the efficiency and numerical strength of Hinduism both as a cult as well as a distinct religious community. They have always shown a bold and uncompromising front to the Christian missionaries and have, whether by reclaiming the Hindu converts or by starting orphanages or by taking other steps by which Hindus may be guarded against the onslaughts of Christianity, incurred the direct displeasure and hatred of the Christian missionaries as well as of the native Christians. The latter have a grievance against the Arya Samaj, insofar as the Samaj would not allow their numbers to grow so largely as they would quite naturally desire, and more so because by putting obstacles in the way of the conversion of the respectable classes of Hindus they prevent suitable matrimonial matches being formed of the marriageable boys and girls of native Christians. Even Christianity has failed in uprooting caste prejudices altogether from the minds of Indian Christians, and high caste Hindus converted to Christianity have always been very eager to find matches for their boys and girls in equally respectable convert families. Converts from lower classes are generally neither respectable nor handsome. Hence, of late, the desperate measures which the Christian propagandists have everywhere been adopting to get hold of Hindu females generally and unmarried girls and widows particularly. The Arya Samajists are determined to withstand it and to oppose it. Hence the hostile attitude of Christians to the Arya Samaj. The Anarkali Arya Samajists are the most active, at times seemingly offensive, in this opposition to Christian propagandists. They are generally the first in the field to thwart the Christian missionary from reaping his harvest where the misfortunes of the people favour the chances of success to the Christian philanthropists and propagandists. Both are actuated by the best of motives from their own standpoints but where interests clash, judgement generally gets warped and it is hopeless to expect generosity from combatants in war.

(2) The Arya Samajists have similarly incurred the displeasure of the Mohammadans by their attempts to re-convert Hindu youths; but the real reason of the hostility of the English-educated Mohammadans to the Arya Samajists is to be sought in their belief that the Arya Samajists stand between them and the pro-Mohammadan policy of the Government. The educated Mohammadans believe that but for the Arya Samajists, the English who want to patronise the Mohammadans will have a freer hand. Any agitation carried on by the Hindus for the protection of the interests of their *co-religionists,* or any attempt made to expose those official jobberies and vagaries which are likely to result in injury to Hindus, are put to the credit of the Arya Samajists. And as pro-

Mohammadanism is just now rampant the occasions for this conflict happen to be many.

The Mohammadans and the Christians are under the impression that non-Arya Samajist Hindus (or such of them as occupy positions of prominence and are taken as leaders) are as a rule indifferent in this matter or at any rate are no so keen over it. Hence the whole of their hostility and dislike is directed against the Arya Samajists and amongst the Arya Samajists on the College section of the same. How far they are right in this attitude and how far their beliefs are well-founded are questions which admit of diversity of opinion.

(3) Then again there are some classes of Hindus who have real grievances against the Anarkali Aryas. The same may be divided into the following sub-heads.

(a) Those of them who have not been allowed to have their own way in the management of public concerns, whether industrial or charitable, and feel that their ambitions have been foiled and their plans disconcerted.

(b) Those whose designs on some concerns have been *defeated* by the activity and energy of some amongst the Aryas and who have been beaten on their own ground. This class includes those who have been forced to leave concerns upon which they had fixed their minds and which they intended to use freely *for their own private ends* or for the aggrandisement of selves and their friends.

(c) Those who are grieved because of the rival institutions that have been started by *some* again amongst the Aryas in competition with their pet concerns. Their monopoly having been thus interfered with, they assume that they have a grievance against the party which they think has made it impossible for their rival schemes to succeed. Some people feel that they were the sole-anointed of the Lord to do certain things, and naturally when they find that others have the audacity of doing the same and perhaps in a better way and on better principles, they feel inclined to damn these interlopers and to curse them for their audacity.

(d) Lastly, those who are prepared to pass as Hindus whenever they have to get anything (appointment, position, title, honour, &c.) but who, on other occasions, disclaim their connection with Hinduism and openly maintain that they are not Hindus. The Anarkali Aryas have always identified themselves with Hindus and Hinduism. They are one and all strong on this point. Very naturally some of them think it wrong to allow these estimable gentlemen to play a double game with the community which they are disposed to own or disown as it suits them. Some of the Anarkali Aryas never lose an opportunity of warning the community against these double-faced gentlemen and this accounts for their hatred against the former. In fact, at times one is inclined to think that this class harbours the bitterest, the most uncompromising and the deadliest feelings of hatred against the Aryas. They malign individuals, they calumniate institutions, they backbite, they provoke the other communities and they carry tales to the officials and it is amongst these that the Anarkali Arya Samajists have their most dangerous, most desperate and never-sparing enemies. These good men always ignore that it is wrong and unjust to hold a whole community responsible for the real or supposed opponent's behaviour of its individual members. They know it very well that there are large numbers of Arya Samajists (both amongst commoners as well as leaders) who take no interest in most of the affairs which have from time to time aroused their opposition. But they do not care to distinguish between the acts of individuals and those of organisations. They do not stop to enquire if the act or acts complained of have been done by individuals in their individual capacity or in their representative capacity. They at once rush to the conclusion that every act done by an Anarkali Arya Samajist has been done after consultation with the whole body or with the majority of its leaders and workers and they at once direct their attacks against the Samaj as a whole. They are not even content to attack the Anarkali Samaj but in the intensity of their desire to injure the organisation involve the *whole party* known as the College party which includes a number of Samajes situated hundreds of miles apart from one another. They also know that it is not always that unanimity of opinion prevails amongst the College party of the Arya Samaj. Some of them have positive knowledge that at times the widest diversity of opinion prevails amongst the leaders and the rank and file of the party on several important questions of the day or with regard to the conduct or behaviour of a certain member which has elicited the opposition of non-Arya Samajists. But no! these estimable opponents of the Samaj ignore all this and hold the whole party responsible for every single act of every single individual, which is in their eyes fairness *par excellence*. Just let me take one or two cases in point and illustrate what I mean.

1. Everyone knows that in the probate case of the late Sardar Dyal Singh's Will[3] while two leading Aryas appeared and conducted the case for the Rani two of the leading Aryas appeared and helped the executors. In the party itself there was a wide difference of opinion on the propriety of the conduct of those gentlemen who had taken up the case for the Rani. At the present moment the Rani's case is being conducted by a leader of the Mahatma section but still our enemies will persist in making the whole College party responsible for this litigation. How far this is fair I leave the reader to judge for himself.

2. Then let us examine the *bona fides* of the charge that is made against

3. Dyal Singh Majithia, founder of the *Tribune*, in his will, had made Lala Harkishen Lal a trustee of the paper, who since then controlled the paper.

the Samaj in connection with the *Panjabee*. Everyone knows that Lala Jaswant Rai is the sole proprietor of the paper, that the paper has absolutely nothing to do with Samajic propaganda and *that its policy or its tone is not shared by even all the leading Anarkali Aryas, still our enemies, including the well-informed patron of the Panjabee,* styling himself *an Arya*, insist on fastening the responsibility of what appears in the *Panjabee* on the whole College party.

3. Then again, look at the charge with which I began this paper, viz. that the Arya Samaj is a political body. Now our enemies are fully aware that amongst the members of the Samaj there is a very large number of Government servants some of them holding the highest posts under the Government which are open to the natives of this country. They know as a matter of fact that by the very terms of their service the government servants cannot take any part in political movements, and if they were to do so they will make themselves liable to dismissal. These *friends* also know that the Samaj as a body never discusses or deals in politics. Some of them know *as a fact* that the comparatively recent activity of the writer in connection with the Congress has been the subject of unfavourable comment amongst Samajic circles and has been not only disapproved but actually denounced by *several leading men*, one of whom has prominently been mentioned in one of the letters that have lately appeared in the columns of the *Tribune* against our party. If one were to look at the leading workers of the Anarkali Arya Samaj he shall find that the alleged political activity of the party is confined to only one or two prominent workers of the Samaj.

(a) Everyone knows that Lala Hans Raj is the acknowledged leader of the College section of the Arya Samaj and that he has never attended any political meeting or joined any political propaganda.

(b) That Lala Ram Prashad,[4] the secretary of our Pratinidhi Sabha, has never done so.

(c) That none of the Professors of the D.A.V. College have ever done so.

(d) That Lala Lal Chand[5] whose soundness and sobriety is acknowledged on all hands has never taken any active part in the Congress movement. In fact, our opponents know that even before his elevation to the Bench he never showed any fondness for the Congress or its methods and that excepting on the occasion of its sittings at Lahore he never attended any of its meetings held elsewhere.

4. Eminent Arya Samajist and Secretary of Arya Pratinidhi Sabha, Lahore, from 1909 to 1910.
5. (1852-1912): lawyer of Lahore; joined Arya Samaj in 1877; elected President of D.A.V. College Managing Committee in 1886 and held the post for several years; one of the founders of Punjab National Bank (1895); founded Punjab Hindu Sabha in 1909 and became its President; author of *Self-Abnegation in Politics*.

(e) That the same may *mutatis mutandis* be said of Lala Ishwar Das[6] who has succeeded Lala Lal Chand in the Presidentship of the Managing Committee of the D.A.V. College.

(f) That next to the D.A.V. College the most important institution maintained and managed by the Anarkali Arya Samajists is the Ferozepur Orphanage and that the two leading Arya Samajists who are devoted heart and soul to the cause of the Orphanage have never taken any part in political propaganda (I mean Lala Kanshi Ram[7] and Chaudhri Bishen Sahai[8]).

(g) That the Anglo-Sanskrit Schools at Abbottabad, Multan, Jullundhur and Hoshiarpur are managed by men who have never evinced any political propensities.

In fact, from amongst the whole party if you were to search for men who have ever been *active* in political work you won't find more than 2 or 3 including the writer. Now, on these facts to give out that the Arya Samaj is a political body is a most bare-faced lie that could be invented by the most ingenious of mischief-makers. Still our enemies do not scruple to repeat this charge against the Samaj whenever there is the slightest occasion for differences between us. Recently the occasion for differences between the *Panjabee* and the *Tribune* was the latter's change of policy. Now the question at issue was, whether the policy of that paper had undergone a change at the hands of the new Editor,[9] and, if so, whether it had changed for the worse or for the better. *The Panjabee* maintained and maintains that it has changed for the worse. The native Christians, the Mohammadans and the European officials maintain that it has changed for the better. The Trustees, evidently, maintain that there has been no change. The former advances the evidence of the columns of the *Tribune* itself. The latter reply by cursing the Arya Samajists and by arousing the worst passions of the different cliques that hold no goodwill towards the Anarkali Arya Samaj and by systematic efforts to discredit the latter in the eyes of the Government. Suppose that our opponents succeed in proving that we are the greatest blackguards on earth, that might shake our credit but will that be good evidence in favour of the *Tribune*? But our opponents are shrewd, clever men of the world. They place their faith in the well-known adage of winning a case by abusing the adversary and by rousing the very worst passions of the judge and

6. Eminent Arya Samajist and President of D.A.V. College Managing Committee, 1895-1900 and 1903-06.
7. Pleader of Ferozepur and an Arya Samajist; member of D.A.V. College Managing Committee in 1906.
8. An Arya Samajist of Ferozepur who supported the Cultural section or College party led by Lala Hans Raj during Arya Samaj split in 1892-93.
9. Alfred Nundy

the jury. Even this though not honourable may be excusable. But suppose it is proved that the Anarkali Arya Samaj is a political body opposed to the Government will that help the *Tribune* or our opponents in any way? Apparently our opponents have good reasons to believe that it will help their cause. They perhaps hope to win the favour of the officials and the Government by giving the latter a handle to injure the Arya Samaj for their supposed and alleged misbehaviour against the Government. Are we then to assume that in their anxiety to wreak vengeance on the Anarkali Arya Samaj our opponents, including the conductors of the *Tribune* and their correspondents, are anxious to see the said Samaj crushed by the Government even if they have to stoop so low as to make false assertions by ignoring facts and throwing dust in the eyes of all concerned?

In the Punjab the Arya Samaj has done a great deal of educational work and as Lord Curzon has unfortunately thrown a great deal of political tinge into education it may perhaps be explicable that the officers of the Education Department look with disfavour upon all these efforts which the Arya Samaj in carrying on its educational work makes to resist official interference and to avoid absolute conformity with official ideas. The Mohammadans and native Christians may also have good reasons of their own to look upon it with disfavour but how except on the ground of treachery can one explain the conduct of these professed Hindus including "an Arya" who denounce it as a political body and try to make the position of government officials amongst the members of the Arya Samaj liable to misconstruction. But it is time that we should definitely know what our friends really aim at. Do they want these officials to leave the Samaj or do they want them to vacate their offices for their Mohammadan and Christian rivals? Or do our critics want me to give up all connection with political work? A few years ago we were as a class being openly charged with neglecting political work and with having given a death blow to the political movement in this province. Now that one of us has shown some activity in political work the whole Samaj is threatened with destruction because of the political activity of that one man. How patriotic, how noble, and how generous it is, we leave the reader to judge for himself. If that is the value which our opponents attach to political work, the country may well cry "save me from my friends".

In the end, although we know that our opponents find it most *convenient* to involve the whole party and to attack it as a body and to hold it to the ridicule, contempt and hatred of others, as well as the Government for the faults or alleged faults of its individuals, experience should have shown them by this time that this was a most short-sighted policy and that they had played their tactics very badly. If they would confine their attacks to the particular individual or individuals who offend them or against whom they have a grievance, they may have greater chances of gaining their object of bringing their adversary into disrepute or of inflicting a defeat on him. But *this mischievous* and *ill-advised* policy of involving the whole party and the attempt to attack and injure the organisation often, if not always, fails in its principal object and every time the Samaj is attacked, it emerges out stronger, better-organised and in a state of greater efficiency to carry on war with its enemies. At times one fails to comprehend the real objects of these opponents of the Arya Samaj in following this line of action but to believe that good and substantial grounds do not exist at the bottom of this particular line of action, will be denying them that amount of intelligence and foresight which they without doubt possess.

That their object in involving the whole body of Anarkali Arya Samajists in quarrels for which only individuals may be responsible and for making the former responsible for the conduct and actions of the latter, cannot be honest and free from mischief is transparent.

11
ECONOMIC PROBLEMS
1. Swadeshi

1. Increasing Demand for Swadeshi Goods[1]

I would like to draw your attention and that of your readers to the evil and growing practice of disposing of imported goods by falsely stating that the same are country-made and indigenous. Now that Swadeshism has taken a hold over the public some selfish and short-sighted men have commenced to resort to this practice. I came to know of several instances of this malpractice, in one of which a glass lamp was sold as Ambala Glass Factory-made in a mofussil station and, in another, imported woollen cloth was similarly sold as Dhariwal-made.

Up to now the Indian manufacturers, knowing perhaps that their goods could not sell, if so marked in preference to the imported goods, did not consider it necessary to stamp them "Made in India".

But now the scales have been turned, and what was a couple of months or two before the pride and boast of people to say "the article was *wilayati*", has now become a thing to be ashamed of, and they say "it was bought long ago", and it is therefore necessary that all goods made in India should be marked to avoid fraud, as otherwise it would be very difficult and almost impossible to distinguish one class of goods from another, which has already become a perplexing question to the buyer.

I hope you will see the importance of the suggestion and call attention to it.

1. Letter to the editor published in *The Panjabee* of 4 December 1905.

2. Appeal to Make Swadeshi Movement a Success[1]

One week before the boycott movement was started in Bengal, I, while addressing a Manchester audience, drew their attention to the fact that the last weapon in the hands of Indians to awaken the English to their sense of duty

1. Speech at a public meeting held in the compound of Bradlaugh Hall, Lahore, published in *The Panjabee* of 4 December 1905.

was to boycott English goods.[2] To my utter amazement, a week after this utterance telegrams were received in England that the Bengalees had vowed to abjure English goods, the only effective measure which could be adopted to revive the dead industries of our motherland as well as to give a fresh and vigorous start to the political life in India. The Swadeshi movement no doubt should be looked upon as a divine dispensation.

During his seven years' Viceroyalty, Lord Curzon passed the most repressive and reactionary measures. The Official Secrets Bill, the University Bill, the University Validation and the Partition of Bengal Bills were passed into laws in the teeth of opposition by the most enlightened section of the Indian community who are in a better position to judge what measures will suit the people and under what circumstances. Lord Curzon's rule has turned the country topsy-turvy and it is now convulsed by the agonies of the nation. History tells that at such a moment there comes a change in the political life of a country. Fortune has thrown in our lot a rare opportunity in that a wave of Swadeshism has sprung up in every Indian heart. The boycott movement is a weapon which, if wielded with tact and wisdom, will cow down all the enemies of the industries of our motherland and will drive out of the land that scourge which carries away yearly millions of people from this poorest country in the world. We should devote our heart and soul to the Swadeshi cause with a view to achieving the desired end. But I am afraid we, the Punjabis, lack patience and perseverance and are always guilty of not acting with the same amount of zeal throughout a movement with which we give it a start. Yes, certainly this is a charge which cannot be denied. But, oh, you Punjabis, are you not ashamed of being stamped as habitual offenders in this respect? When will you be awake to the sense of duty which you owe to your motherland? Do you not feel it disgraceful to just make a promise and then to break it without any sense of shame? Lahore is to lead the whole of the Punjab in this matter. At the Swadeshi meetings held in this town and attended by thousands of men the people declared through their leaders that they would not use foreign articles in future. Now the shops in Dabbi Bazaar and Bazaar Hatta are greatly flooded with foreign goods. I have been frequenting these bazaars to watch with interest how far the people are true to their cause. In the beginning the people showed a great hatred towards foreign goods and would not purchase any but countrymade articles. But now their enthusiasm is showing signs of abatement. They come and ask for countrymade cloths in a half-hearted manner. The shopkeepers depict the so-called dark side of the picture. They tell their Swadeshi customers that the countrymade cloths are coarse, unfashionable, bad-looking, very dear and so

2. Lajpat Rai visited England as a Congress delegate from mid-May to mid-November 1905. See also *ante*, section 4.

on. These men yield to the silly arguments of the shopkeepers and buy foreign cloths without feeling any shame whatsoever. So long as we are not prepared to shun the idea of having fashionable articles we doubt very much the success of the movement. Let us make a fashion of wearing coarse cloths and if a sufficiently large number of men take to this habit the time will come when the people, clad in coarse cloths, will be considered more fashionable than those who appear in fine Manchester cloths. Let me also warn the public of what the shopkeepers are doing these days. They are regularly cheating the public by representing the foreign goods as countrymade. Our fashionable gentlemen and especially the students hanker after Dhariwal and Cawnpore flannels. Let me give them a warning also. For the last two years Germany is sending out here flannels of the same pattern and colour as manufactured by the Dhariwal and Cawnpore mills. They are freely passed as turned out by these mills and no wonder if, as is rumoured in the commercial circle, they too have imported a lot of such goods from Bombay and other Indian markets to meet the especially heavy demand this year. The conduct of the shopkeepers is excusable to some extent. They have already imported foreign goods worth thousands of rupees. They should naturally be expected to devise some means to dispose of their stocks. To put an end to this regular cheating on the part of the merchant class I would suggest the Punjab Swadeshi Association should invite the representatives of the Cloth Merchants Association, Lahore, to confer with them on this subject and to devise measures best suited for the advancement of the Swadeshi cause. Lala Ramji Das of Bazaar Hatta is the Secretary of the above Association.

3. Swadeshi Movement Essential for Salvation of the Country[1]

It is commonly supposed that there are two sides of the Swadeshi movement, one, the political and the other the economic. Pure Swadeshi, as some of the Anglo-Indians choose to call it, is an economic movement and they profess to have great sympathy for the same. Boycott of foreign-made goods is held to be a political weapon upon the uses and ethics of which there is a great divergence of opinion. The Anglo-Indians can see nothing but mischief in it. In their opinion

1. Published in *Indian Review* of May 1906.

it is morally wrong, politically pernicious and economically unsound and impracticable. But there are a number of Europeans and Americans who see nothing pernicious in it and consider it not only a perfectly legitimate weapon but a very powerful and effective one to bring pressure upon any imperial race having commerce as its principal business. Amongst the Indians themselves different classes of people look at it from different points of view. Firstly, there is that class who can never see differently from their Anglo-Indian patrons. The opinions of this class do not count for much and need not be considered at all. Secondly, there are those, who both by nature and habit are in favour of peace at any cost. They cannot approve of any methods which are calculated to cause the least disturbance in the relations of the different persons and communities, whether Indians or aliens, who are in some way or other interested in India. These good people have great faith in moral persuasion and prayers—prayers addressed to the Great Ruler of the Universe as well as to our rulers in affairs mundane. They believe that a combined force of these two is sure to bring about a quiet, bloodless, moral revolution in India which will set matters right and remove all the political disqualifications and disabilities from which the Indians at present suffer and which result in so much hardship, oppression and wrong to the people of this country. Personally, I am a believer in the efficacy of prayer as an instrument of religious discipline but it will require a great stretch of imagination and inconceivable amount of credulity on my part to accept that prayers to the Almighty, coupled with prayers to the ruling nation, are likely to lead to any practicable results in matters, political and international. Prayers to the Almighty may be useful in intensifying your desire for political liberty and political privileges. Prayers to the ruling nation may be useful to you in proving the uselessness of appealing to the higher sense of man in matters political, where the interests of one nation clash with those of another, and in driving you to the conclusion that human nature, constituted as it is, is extremely selfish and is not likely to change or bend unless the force of circumstances compels it to do so in spite of itself. But beyond this I cannot pin my faith on prayers. The third class of Indians consists of those estimable gentlemen who believe in the righteousness of the British nation as represented by the electors of Great Britain and Ireland and who are afraid of offending them by the boycott of English-made goods. If there are any two classes into which the British nation can roughly be divided they are either manufacturers or working men. Both of them are interested in keeping the Indian market open for the sale and consumption of their manufactures. Any movement aiming at the closing or contracting of this market is sure to offend them. They are said to be our only friends to whom we can appeal against the injustice of the Anglo-Indian bureaucracy. Offend them, say these friends, and you are undone. You lose the goodwill of the only class who can help you and who are prepared to listen to your grievances. But these good friends forget that, boycott or no boycott, any movement calculated to increase the manufacturing power of India is likely to incur the displeasure of the British elector. The latter is a very well-educated animal, a keen man of business who can at once see through things that are likely to affect his pocket, however cleverly they might be put or arranged by those who hold an interest which is really adverse to his. He is not likely to be hoodwinked by the cry of Swadeshi minus the boycott, because really speaking if effectively worked and organised both are one and the same.

The Swadeshi aims at the production of those articles at home, which are at present imported from abroad. The boycott means the discontinuance of the consumption of those articles which are not made in this country. So far, then, it is not likely to be of much use to drop the boycott in order to secure for us the continuation of the friendly attitude of the British elector. But then we may go a step further and maintain that up till now the alleged friendliness of the British elector has been of no good to us. Past experience shows that they have more than once stood between the people of India and some of its more noble-minded Anglo-Indian rulers whenever the latter tried to obtain economic justice for the former. The latter from their knowledge of the growing seriousness of the economic situation in India have now and then taken a bold stand for justice to India against the demands of the British manufacturer, but they have almost always had to give in because the latter proved too strong for them. Here then we are on the horns of a dilemma. To our wrongs the British elector is indifferent, to our rights, even if supported by good Englishmen in India, they have been opposed. The British elector has no doubt a sympathetic ear to the tales of wrong and oppression that you may carry to England, but unfortunately he is too busy and too absorbed in his own affairs to spare any time to listen to your tales or to take a serious view of them. The burden of the empire is too heavy to be conveniently shifted from the shoulders of a few magnificently-paid for the work to those of the English people. The struggle for wealth, for luxury, is too keen and too intense to leave the latter any leisure or inclination for the study of the ethics of imperialism. Under the circumstances, the sympathy of the British elector is for the present at least a negligible quantity. The question directly put comes to this: Are the British prepared to give us full political privileges in exchange for open markets for their goods? Any attempt to answer this in the affirmative must be put down as chimerical. But even granting that the argument has some force, is it not worth our while to impress upon the Britons at home the enormity of the wrongs inflicted upon us by their representatives here in this country, by supplementing the Swadeshi by boycott? Admitting that Englishmen at home have the power to set matters right, how are you to force their attention to the state of things in India except by directly threatening their pockets? The logic of losing business is more likely to impress this nation of shopkeepers than any arguments based on the ethics of justice and fair play. The British people are not a spiritual people. They are either a fighting race or a commercial nation. It will be like throwing pearls before swine to appeal to them in the name of higher morality or justice or on ethical grounds. They are a self-reliant, haughty people, who can appreciate self-respect and self-reliance even in their opponents. It is then for the Indians to decide whether they mean to continue to appeal to them in the name of political justice, fair play or whether they intend to attract their attention to the existing intolerable condition of things in India by inflicting losses in business and by adopting an attitude of retaliatory self-reliance.

But then there is another class of Indians who tread on more solid ground than any of those spoken of above. This is the class who oppose the boycott on economic grounds. Here we feel we are on more substantial grounds. There is no plea of expediency, nor does it arise out of fear of the authorities in India or of the British elector at home. Their warning note has a scientific basis and deserves the most careful and attentive consideration of all patriotic Indians. Whether free trader or protectionist, you cannot dismiss them off-hand nor treat their reasoning with contempt. They may be faddists (a term which in their turn they apply to Swadeshists), but they are neither cowards nor traitors. Speaking for myself, I am an out-and-out Swadeshist and have been so for the last twenty-five years, in fact ever since I learnt for the first time the true meaning of the word patriotism. For me the words Swadeshi and patriotism are synonymous though I do not maintain or insinuate that those who are free traders are not patriots. I advisedly do not say "not Swadeshists", because I am not prepared to say that those Indians who are free traders are not necessarily Swadeshists. Be it as it may, I am personally inclined to attach the greatest importance possible to the Swadeshi movement. I look upon it as the remedy on the right and continued use of which depends the alleviation of the sufferings of our country. I regard it as the salvation of my country. The Swadeshi ought to make us self-respecting, self-reliant, self-supporting, self-sacrificing and last, but not least, manly. The Swadeshi ought to teach us how to organise our capital, our resources, our labour, our energies and our talents to the greatest good of all Indians, irrespective of creed, colour or caste. It ought to unite us, our religious and denominational differences notwithstanding. It ought to furnish us with an altar before which we can all stand in the fullest sincerity of our hearts and in the deepest strength of faith to pray for the good of our common motherland, with a determination to stand together and work together. In my opinion the Swadeshi ought to be the common religion of united India. But all this notwithstanding, as a practical Swadeshist, I want a better understanding of the economic needs and requirements of the country and a practical programme of industrial development based on scientific calculations. As an indication of the lines upon which I shall like this programme to be framed, I cannot do better than quote from a very famed paper, from the journal of the Royal Economic Society of London for the month of March 1906, under the heading "Protection of Infant Industries". Discussing the economic effects of a protective tariff, the writer remarks:

> We see that when the import of goods is checked, the exchanges are affected in a way which tends to raise prices at home; and that this rise continues until importation is again possible, unless such heavy duties are imposed that the country can be cut off both from importation and from exportation, and so become entirely self-contained. We find also in this process the explanation of the fact that the relief afforded by a protective tariff is frequently of a somewhat temporary character. For a few months the home producer has the field to himself; then his costs of production gradually rise; at last he finds foreign competition pressing on him once more; and finally he falls back upon the fatal demand for more protection.
>
> But this—the common course of protection in both the new and the old countries—is not the only possible course in theory. It is caused, so far as I can see, principally by the attempt to do too much at once. Your new country is inclined to be generous to its home manufacturers, and to start manufacturing in all lines at once; by so doing it fritters away energy, and spreads expenditure over a wide field which if concentrated might produce imposing results.
>
> For, supposing that a new country would consent to do one or two things at a time, its difficulties would probably be far less. If it started, for instance, by attempting to found one textile or one branch of metallurgical industry, it could afford to give to its infant for a few years a genuine and important assistance. Gold prices would, of course, still be to some extent affected, but in an infinitely smaller degree than when a dead set is made against all manufactured goods at once. And by concentrating the money which is available on one end instead of dividing it among several hundreds, more real progress would indubitably be made. After all, under modern conditions, no industry ought to remain an infant for more than five years; during those years it probably needs more assistance than can be easily given to it under a general protective system; later on, the less help it has, the better.
>
> Other important gains could be made—both political and economic—by this system of concentration. In the first place, the opportunities for logrolling would certainly be diminished. If the system were once established, a most salutary division of the protectionist forces would assuredly take place; as it is, the tendency in many countries is for

> everybody to favour protection on the off-chance that he may make more by it than he loses; on the system proposed everybody would know that only one or two industries were to be protected at a time, and those only for a few years. Again, the present certainty that a protective system will last much longer than there is any need for it, would be removed. For, as only one or two industries would receive help at any one time, all the other industries would combine to reduce that time to a minimum in the hope that their turn would come next.

In my opinion, the leaders of the Swadeshi movement, including men actually engaged in business, ought to put their heads together and promulgate an industrial pronouncement for the next five years, prepared on the lines indicated in the above extract.

4. Implications of Swadeshi Movement[1]

The Swadeshi movement had its genesis at the same time as God created the universe and divided the earth in several segments inhabiting mankind in them. The same God who put milk in the mother's breast and instinctively induced the child towards it also taught him to utter the word 'mother' so that whenever the child was in trouble he should draw solace by uttering this word. Again, the same God created the idea of swadeshi for man to seek repose in his home after coming back from the day's hard grind and in order that while wandering over the far-flung regions of the earth he should not forget his native land. The same elements which formed his body also gave rise to the swadeshi movement. The omnipotent God who sowed in man's heart the seed of love for his country also nurtured the plant of swadeshi in him. The power that taught man to distinguish his own people from aliens and love his own people in preference to others and fight with them, if need be, the same power created the idea of swadeshi in man's heart.

We Indians may not have the privilege of being called a political entity but we have the same sentiments and feelings as the people of Europe. We also love our own people, claim to be members of the same fraternity and make sacrifices for one another, which is our inborn trait. But ironically enough, as if by our own volition, we have changed our mode of thinking in such a manner

1. *Zamana*, August 1906 (translated from Urdu).

that we have come to believe that we are born to serve others, and those whom we serve have no hesitation in subscribing to this view. But unwittingly when we started uttering the word Swadeshi, those to whom we were subservient were taken by surprise. "What's going on here?" they asked. "We regarded them as our chattels, and here they are making tall claims," they exclaimed. Aliens were no doubt surprised but we ourselves were also not less surprised. "Are we sleeping or awake?" we asked ourselves. It was as if mountain had crashed upon us. We looked around warily.

Swadeshi, what an endearing word! Was our brain addled that we had dared to mouth such a sweet word? When we talk of swadeshi we get up and peep out of the room lest somebody should be hearing us. It is a strange state of affairs in our country. What is normal and common for others is abnormal and uncommon for us. Those among us who are a little daring or reckless shout "Swadeshi, Swadeshi", but those who are timid are afraid of uttering the word swadeshi lest our foreign rulers should feel offended. As for our foreign rulers, no doubt they say that there is nothing wrong about it, but in the heart of hearts they feel that it is a diabolical move which is likely to take hold of the people's mind. And that it could cause a serious setback to their trade and commerce. Among them those who are fair-minded feel really sad at the fate of our poverty-stricken country. In their opinion the salvation of the country lies in producing consumer goods indigenously and they approve of the swadeshi movement and praise it. But the majority of Englishmen and bureaucrats are no more than birds of passage in this country and have predominantly the interests of their own country at heart. They do not take a broader view of things and attach little importance to the welfare of Indians. They are averse to the idea of swadeshi at heart and only make a pretence of subscribing to it.

Swadeshi is a Hindi word which means "of one's own country". The followers of this movement believe that one should use things made in one's own country. But the question is, why should Indians do so? In plain words, one might say that we Indians have given up the use of things Indian since a long time. But how did it happen and why? The pages of history are replete with replies to these questions. The British conquest of India created such conditions that the production of indigenously made goods which fetched lakhs of rupees continuously for thousands of years gradually diminished. Their production became uneconomic and the demand for them ceased. On the one hand, the authorities that be of the imperial country imposed heavy import duties and other restrictions on the import of Indian goods into Britain, and on the other they also imposed a heavy duty on the goods exported from their own country to outside destinations. As a result of these dual duties the indigenous commodities went out of production. With the decline in foreign demand, the production of goods at competitive prices was substantially reduced and on account of higher overhead costs, because of smaller quantities, their prices went up. Consequently, the imported goods came to be sold at lower prices and the indigenous products were driven out of the market. To achieve their purpose the authorities reduced the import duty on the incoming goods with the result that our countrymen preferred foreign stuff to things produced indigenously. With the fall in production of Indian goods our craftsmen and workers became idle. A time came when manufacturing completely stopped and the workers became daily-wage earners. The rate of wages being lower than the cost of raw material, the workers for want of jobs started dying of starvation. On top of that capital started moving out of the country and the Indians were reduced to extreme poverty.

Under these dire circumstances the slogan of swadeshi implied that our people should give preference to indigenous products over imported ones. It meant we Indians should totally eschew the use of foreign articles. The eschewing of the use of foreign goods in common parlance was "boycott" and the use of Indian goods in general was known as swadeshi. To a large extent these words, viz. swadeshi and boycott, denote action and reaction. The aftermath of swadeshi is automatic boycott. One has no meaning or significance without the other.

One can also look at the swadeshi movement from another angle. Is it not incumbent upon the natives of a country to buy things made in their own country? The sense of patriotism too enjoins this. They should not allow foreign goods to enter their country. If the English people do not allow the import of wheat and other food products into their country they will die of starvation. If they do not import cotton their textile mills will go out of production. Under the circumstances, their sense of patriotism demands that they should import things from outside their country out of necessity and as a matter of policy for survival. Consider a similar analogy. If the demand for British textiles goes down and foreign cloth being cheaper is dumped in their country so that their manufacturers are not able to compete with imported goods, will they not resort to their own brand of Swadeshi movement?

Reverting to our subject, it would be pertinent to ask what should be the dimensions of boycott. Should it be confined to specific commodities and, if so, which ones? The question can be viewed from two aspects—economic and political. From the economic angle we should assess which commodities and which countries, when brought within the ambit of boycott, would yield best results. It is a matter of bare statistics in which anger, prejudice, pressure or retribution should play no role. As for the political boycott, it is based on such factors as retaliation, or pressurising an antagonist country. Many of our discerning and sagacious men assert that between swadeshi and boycott only political boycott can be called boycott in the true sense of the word. All the same, I have taken pains to point out that Swadeshi is meaningless without inducting boycott into it. Our friends who are opposed to the word boycott have perhaps something in their mind to define the limits and extent of boycott. As regards its limitations, according to them, political boycott perhaps is the only meaningful word. Now what remains to be decided is whether boycott is morally justified and if so for what purpose and to what extent and under what circumstances.

The countries which are independent or deal on equal terms with other countries can resort to boycott by imposing import duty on foreign goods. But as regards those countries which cannot be regarded as politically equal, the question of boycott does not arise. In the first category come the United States of America and China and in the second category come England and Ireland. Recently when political relations between America and China deteriorated the Chinese business community, unable to persuade its own government to impose import duty on American goods, itself resorted to the boycott of American goods as a result of which a change occurred in the attitude of America towards China.

As for Ireland, although in political terms it is not independent, to all intents and purposes it is not subservient to England either. An Irishman named Boycott who represented Ireland in the British Parliament suggested to his countrymen that they should stop buying British goods. This is how the word "boycott" came into vogue. It is difficult to assess as to what extent the Irish people succeeded in their objective. We have the example of a similar case between England and America. Towards the close of the eighteenth century when England imposed a tax on American goods America considered it unjustified and expressed its displeasure by refusing to buy British goods. In the same manner quite recently Hungary boycotted Austrian goods to express its displeasure. There are various ways of expressing political displeasure. The first step or stage is a simple agitation through memorials and adopting political resolutions. If these do not prove effective the aggrieved nation may resort to boycott which is considered an extreme measure.

There cannot be two opinions about the legal justification of boycott. But whether boycott can be used as a weapon for expressing displeasure is a highly subjective matter, depending on the situation obtaining at that time. For instance, those of us who think that England is exploiting our country in utter disregard of our own national interests can be justified in recommending boycott of British goods.

They may consider it not only desirable but a veritable necessity. On the contrary, those who think that England has always given us a fair deal and has been watchful of our country's interests may question the legitimacy of boycott as a weapon to be used against England.

We must remember that under the present conditions we cannot meet our requirements only from our own resources. Secondly, the Government of the day can, on one pretext or the other, put a ban on the trade with other countries, specially when India's doors are open for import of all sorts of commodities, particularly such commodities as are not available in our own country and which are indispensable for us. Taking into account the economic aspect, it may become necessary to continue boycott within certain limits. To make boycott effective we may put an embargo on one or two commodities to begin with, keeping in mind which commodities we cannot produce indigenously and the production of which commodities can be increased with the passage of time. For instance, we have been manufacturing cotton textiles in our country for a long time. We made very fine cloth which was exported in huge quantities and which valued at millions of rupees. Even today the Indian cloth of a special variety is exported to China and other countries. The same can be said about sugar. Here we are taking the economic aspect into consideration which has nothing to do with politics. As it is apparent, this kind of boycott would apply to all countries equally and its objective will be to safeguard our economic interests. But in case we want to use boycott as a political weapon the axe would inevitably fall on British textiles so that the British Government may realise that we are not happy with them and that we strongly deprecate their attitude towards us. Personally, too, I am not opposed to this kind of boycott though there are many who do not see eye to eye with me. They fear it would make the British more hostile towards us and they might further hurt our interests. To my mind, such objections have no validity. The English people are by and large a nation of traders. So long as the Indian market is open to them as an avenue for their economic prosperity they are not concerned with the ethics of their Government. They are only concerned with their profits. But if they face an economic setback even for a year or two they will feel the pinch and try to probe the reason behind our anger. This may lend strength to our constitutional agitation. But as things stand, so long as we Indians hold conflicting opinions and keep pulling in different directions it would be difficult to give boycott a practical shape.

The call of swadeshi is bound to buoy up our patriotic zeal, inculcate in our people a sense of fortitude to bear hardships and create in them a spirit of sacrifice. A man who takes to wearing coarse cloth on principle by discarding fine foreign cloth with which he is in love, and thus makes a great sacrifice has the best interests of the country at heart. In the same way one who goes questing for swadeshi goods and has predilection for them even if they are costlier than foreign goods is also serving the country in his own way. A man who is sowing the seeds of swadeshi in the minds of the womenfolk, which in turn percolates through to the minds of the children of the family, is also promoting a noble cause. To propagate the cult of swadeshi is a sacred task like taking a sacred vow for the advancement of the country's interests.

Some people think that swadeshi is a kind of bigotry. I think that for a poor country like ours which is groaning under foreign rule bigotry is far better than broadmindedness of a doubtful variety which cannot pull us out of the mire of sloth and indigence. Swadeshi will also bring Hindus and Muslims closer to each other since they will be working for a common cause. In this connection I would like to reproduce a few stray thoughts which I had penned down for *Paisa Akhbar* on its editor's request.

> One benefit of the swadeshi movement would be that the rift between Hindus and Muslims which has kept them apart and which has been a source of mistrust between them would gradually vanish. The rivalry between the educated Hindus and Muslims for higher government posts has been largely responsible for the bitterness between them. The swadeshi movement would divert their minds from government jobs by opening up new and lucrative avenues in the fields of business and enterprise. This will at least weaken if not completely eliminate the sense of rivalry between the two communities. In business there can be a constant give and take which is not possible in government jobs. The swadeshi movement will also create more avenues of employment for the Muslim working class comprising a large number of skilled workers who sit idle for want of suitable work. The resultant prosperity will also enhance their sense of self-respect. Even if there is a competition between Hindus and Muslims, the benefits will accrue to the country as a whole. Thus more wealth will be created which will benefit both the Hindu and Muslim inhabitants of the land, and thus both will be equally vigilant to take effective steps to see that the wealth created by their hands is not drained out of the country.
>
> After dwelling on the swadeshi movement in somewhat general terms I deem it necessary to point out, in passing, its economic aspects. This requires a practical approach which again has two aspects, viz. producing raw materials to feed an industry and providing the means to finance it. This also implies sound and smooth distribution of goods. The success of an industry depends on the following factors.
>
> (1) Adequate availability of finance,
> (2) Technical knowledge or know-how of production,
> (3) Efficient industrial manpower,

(4) Comprehension of joint stock operations and awareness of their pitfalls, and

(5) Publication of commercial and industrial bulletins and handbooks.

Each aspect of this multi-dimensional topic requires a detailed study which I reserve for some future issue of the magazine.

11

ECONOMIC PROBLEMS

II. The Punjab National Bank

1. Directorship of Punjab National Bank[1]

Sir, I confess it was a mistake of judgment on the part of the shareholders to propose me for one of the vacancies in the Directorate of the Punjab National Bank.[2] They failed to see that the outgoing Director—unwilling as he was to leave the Bank—was bound to have his revenge both upon the Bank as well as upon the person who was proposed to replace him and was sure to twist it into a Samajic move.

The mistake has had its fruits by catching the fancy of many a friend of the Arya Samaj, specially of the ironically styled "cultured" section of it. Herein they have found a fit opportunity for reviling and "damning" the cultured Hindus, as they call this section of the Arya Samaj, to their heart's content. Under the circumstances, I think the best course for me is to withdraw my consent to act as a Director. And when I say this I mean what I say. I do not intend to change my mind on pressure being brought to bear upon me by any dependent of mine or by other friends.

In the interests of truth and fair play I will join with Mr. Gulab Din[3] in appealing to Babu K.P. Roy[4] to let the public know, why and under what circumstances he resigned the Directorship of the Bank. The Arya Samajists have now proposed his name.

In the interest of the Bank I may be permitted to add that in case certain shareholders be inclined to accept Mr. Harkishen Lal's suggestion for the sale of their shares, they will find a ready market. A number of gentlemen are prepared to purchase all the shares that may be in the market for sale.[5]

Yours &c.,
Lajpat Rai

1. Letter to the editor published in *The Tribune* of 1 March 1902.
2. The Punjab National Bank was founded in 1895 by Harkishen Lal and Lajpat Rai as the first joint-stock bank in Punjab. Dyal Singh Majithia was the first Chairman of the Board of Directors and Harkishen Lal the Secretary. Lajpat Rai was elected as a Director in 1898. However, he resigned in May 1907 but was again appointed as the Director of the Bank.
3. A shareholder of the Punjab National Bank.
4. A leader of the Lahore Indian Association; member, Board of Directors, Punjab National Bank, 1895-1900; President, Punjab Congress Committee, 1897-1900; Chairman, Reception Committee of Lahore Congress, 1900.
5. Later Lajpat Rai informed the shareholders that K.P. Roy had not agreed to become the Director of the Bank and that he was leaving Lahore for some time.

2. Controversy about Punjab National Bank[1]

Sir, In connection with the controversy that is now raging about the Punjab National Bank, Lahore, I intend to give a few specimens of Mr. Harkishen Lal's business capacities as evidenced from public records and other documents accessible to members of the public in one capacity or another.

(1) Lala Harkishen Lal (with the concurrence of Mr. Jussawala)[2] advanced a loan of Rs. 15,000 to Diwan Lakshman Das, while under the rules of the Bank neither he alone, nor he with the consent of another Director, had any power to do so. The Bank had eventually to sue for the amount, and it is after a lengthy and expensive litigation, extending over a period of 2 to 3 years, that the case has just ended in favour of the Bank in the Chief Court.

(2) This loan was advanced under the verbal instructions of Mr. Harkishen Lal, no written order to that effect being given to the Manager, as stated by him in his statement in Court. This loan has a history of its own which throws enormous light on the ways of business adopted by Mr. Harkishen Lal. We reserve the history of the loan with extracts from the documents that are in the record of this case for another letter.

(3) Mr. Harkishen Lal (of course, with the consent of his colleagues on the Board of the Bharat Insurance Company),[3] built the Congress Hall by spending the money of the Bharat Insurance Company. This loan has not yet received the sanction of the Congress Committee. No security for this amount has yet been taken, nor has the Congress Committee yet accepted liability of this amount. About Rs. 12,000 of the Bharat Insurance Company have been invested in this industry.

On a proposal of accounts being audited and examined there were scenes in the Congress Committee which are well known to the members and had better be left unmentioned here. Motives were imputed to the President, Babu K.P. Roy, which will not bear comparison with those which are now alleged against the Arya Samajists.

(4) A part of this loan was advanced in 1900, when the Hall was being built, but in the balance-sheet for the year ending December 1900, it was not shown as such and was probably disguised as a loan to "other companies".

(5) Out of the total working capital of the Bharat Insurance Company, to the extent of about 1½ lacs, about one lac has been invested in the Lahore

1. Letter to the editor published in *The Tribune* of 6 March 1902.
2. One of the Directors of the Punjab National Bank in 1902.
3. The Bharat Insurance Company was founded by Lala Harkishen Lal and Rai Mul Raj at Lahore in 1896.

Weaving and Spinning Mills Company[4] at Shahdara, on 6 per cent per annum. The amount up to the last general meeting was Rs. 78,000. Since then it has risen to about a lac and valuable securities have been disposed of to patronise the Lahore Weaving and Spinning Mills and find funds for the same. The Bharat Insurance Company has a second lien on the property of the company, the first lien being that of the Punjab National Bank for another lac of rupees on a rate higher than 6 per cent. The Bank advanced money to this company long after the latter had already utilised large sums of the former.

(6) Some 6,000 rupees of this company (the Bharat) are due from the Punjab Publishing and Stationery Company,[5] another flourishing concern, which gives no dividends. The Bharat holds no securities beyond *hundis*.

(7) Some 7,000 rupees of this company, i.e. the Bharat, are due from the Punjab Hosiery and Manufacturing Company which has stopped work since the last six months and owes debts of the value of about 22,000 rupees against a paid up capital of about Rs. 15,000. This company too has given no dividends for several years past. The Bharat Insurance Company holds no securities beyond *hundis*.

(8) Since Lala Harkishen Lal found it necessary to develop his ideas about banking by means of the People's Banking Company[6] all these companies have substituted the latter, as their bankers, in place of the Punjab National Bank Company Limited.

This will do for the present issue. More in my next. These facts, I suppose, need no comments.

Yours &c.,
Lajpat Rai

4. The Lahore Weaving and Spinning Mills Company was started by Lala Ram Saran Das in 1897.
5. It was started by Lala Harkishen Lal and others in 1896 at Lahore.
6. The reference was to the People's Bank of India which was started in 1901 by Lala Harkishen Lal and had nearly 70 branches. However, during the banking crisis of 1913 it was closed down.

11

ECONOMIC PROBLEMS

III. General

Industrial Development and Joint Stock System[1]

There can be no denial of the fact that the industrial and economic future of our country mainly depends upon the introduction and successful working of the joint stock system. Gifted with vast natural resources, which can produce any amount of raw material, and with an enormous and ever-increasing population which is always in want of employment, India can achieve wonders in the line of manufacturing industries, only if it has the necessary capital and the still more necessary skill at its command. Of artistic skill it has plenty. What it lacks is the power and capacity of calling in the assistance of modern science and modern appliances in the refining of its arts, and the production of larger quantities, at lesser cost, of its articles of art. Precious little has up to this time been done in the way of enabling qualified Indians to acquire this skill. Beyond providing some facilities for acquiring an elementary and mainly theoretical knowledge of modern science in connection with the Arts Colleges, the Government has done practically nothing in the way of enabling or encouraging Indian youths to acquire mechanical skill with a view to the industrial development of the country. It was not perhaps to the interest of the British to take steps which might have eventually closed the Indian markets to English goods. If so, they probably did not foresee that the doctrine of free trade might drive even the English goods out of Indian markets in favour of countries better placed in their natural resources and in their populations than the British Isles. Thus their neglect has not only injured India, but brought no permanent benefit to Great Britain. Is it not a fact that English goods are being driven out of markets by the cheaper productions of Germany, United States, France and Japan? But in the absence of Government initiative in the matter, we, Indians, too have not done much to provide facilities for the acquisition of mechanical skill by our youths, because of want of foresight and power of organisation in us. Instead of putting the horse before the cart we have been all this time busy in making the cart go with the horse behind. Instead of applying most of our humble resources in equipping our countrymen with mechanical skill in order to enable them to stop the exploitation of this country by foreigners, we have been spending lacs upon fruitless agitation for political enfranchisement. It never occurred to us that in these days of science and machinery a nation poor in economics and skill could never be politically great or free. Thank God that after a lot of dissipation of energies we have been awakened to a sense of our duty in this direction and on all sides there is a demand

1. First printed in *Kayastha Samachar* of August 1901 and reprinted in *Lala Lajpat Rai—The Man in His Word* (Madras, 1907), pp. 39-44.

for technical training and industrial education. But few of those who cry for technical education and are even prepared to incur some amount of expenditure and sacrifice for the same know what technical education is, and how it can be introduced in this country.

The movement therefore is suffering for want of expert knowledge and no amount of agitation or enthusiasm can make up for that unless the latter is accompanied by earnest efforts to provide means to Indian youths to acquire this knowledge. Many an industry can be made to flourish if we had only technical knowledge to work it up. The first thing therefore to do is to send Indian youths to Europe and America to be trained as experts. Let each province send one youth every year to learn all that is required to start and successfully work up a particular industry. Japan has done the same through its Government, because there the Government represents the country. In India the case is different and the country will have to do this by itself what in Japan has been done by its Government.

Capital is the second important factor in the development of industries. Individual wealth is powerless before the accumulated wealth of millionaires who have joined together on the joint stock principles. Rich citizens can no doubt do a lot by investing their riches in factories and industries which can be run by them with their own resources. But joint stock enterprise must be met by similar combinations and these combinations, to be successful, must be organised on sound principles and with perfect confidence in those who are at the helm of affairs. This confidence can only be begotten by the promoters themselves being men of substance having substantial risks in the enterprise, and of acknowledged integrity and honesty of purpose. Joint stock enterprise in India is yet an infant of very tender age; it is a foreign plant that has yet to grow and take root before it fructifies and as such it requires great care and caution to watch its growth and secure it as a fruitful crop. The friends of industrial development need not be told how suspicious and indolent the people of this country are.

Our lacking in enterprise is mainly due to want of faith in each other and unwillingness to co-operate for common good. It is therefore of the greatest importance that the business of company-promoting in this country should be entirely above suspicion. There seems to be no room for encouraging individual speculations under the sense of company-promoting. The English company-promoters of whom we have of late read so much in British journals, must not be allowed to abuse the confidence of those Indians who are disposed to give a fair trial to joint stock system and who if once deceived are not likely to enter the lists again. But equally vigilant must we be against the Indian company-promoters, if there are any, who may be disposed to copy their British colleagues and make a profession of company-promoting at the cost of those who might be willing to invest a portion or the whole of their hard-earned savings in a business or businesses which is or are likely to be of profit to themselves as well as to the country at large.

The Indian shareholder is generally a sleeping partner and prone to leave the business to those, relying upon whose name and fame, he signed his application for shares. He is no good for control or check and therefore gives carte blanche to the managers. If he is proved to have been unfortunate in placing his confidence all that he shall do will be to curse his stars and nothing further. He will not move an inch to see that those who have played fast and loose with his money, receive their deserts and thus deter others from similar acts of treachery and bad faith. Much less is he to be moved by considerations of public good or the good of the country. Under these circumstances the friends of industrial development cannot be too vigilant against this class of company-promoters. In England itself a cry has already been raised to the effect that the existing laws do not sufficiently protect the shareholder from the devices of a cunning and sharp director. A writer in the *Contemporary Review* of June 1901, while reviewing the causes of the economic decay of Great Britain, pens the dirge on the company law of England. Says he, "Our company law is a most excellent law in favour of cunning company-promoters, financiers, stockbrokers and of everyone who wishes to rob the nation of its accumulated saving." After giving a table of figures showing the amount of capital involved in companies liquidated from 1892 to 1899 as ranging between 34 million sterling and 77 millions, he quotes the following remarks of the Inspector-General of Companies in liquidation: "It appears that the total number of abortive and liquidating companies during 1899 were in proportion to the new companies registered, *60 per cent as against 56 per cent during the previous year.*" To explain it still more he is believed to have further said, "*About 37 per cent of the capital belongs to the more or less solvent class while the remaining three-fourths in number or 63 per cent of capital wanted represent the insolvent class.*" The italics are ours. Upon this data the writer bases the following pregnant remarks of his own—"Whilst the thrifty part of our population has been robbed within a few years of several hundred pounds earned by millions of British toilers during a lifetime of patient labour, none of the company-promoters who perpetrated these enormous frauds on the nation, nor their satellites, have been imprisoned with hard labour. The new company law is not designed to protect the unsuspecting public but to protect the company-promoter and his associates. . . . It is a law in favour of the strong against the weak. In consequence of this immunity from punishment for fraud, in consequence of the growing difficulty of making an honest living by productive industry and in consequence of the ease by which company frauds may be perpetrated under the shelter of our company law, the popularity of promoting swindling companies is on the increase."

The Indian company law is much the same as the English, in fact almost a copy of it, and the rapidity with which companies here too are being floated and then wound up or sold at considerable loss to the shareholders raises an apprehension in our mind lest in a few years the state of affairs here might justify the same strictness as we have quoted above about the class of professional company-promoters in England. Let us hope at any rate that the occasion for such a complaint may not arise soon, although signs are already visible which excite our worst fears.

12
MISCELLANEOUS

1. The Sun Has Risen in the East[1]

The *Public Magazine* (Amritsar), of the 26th September 1904, reprints from the *Arya Gazette* an article headed "The Sun has risen in the East", and contributed to the latter paper by Lala Lajpat Rai. The writer says that it was Asia which taught Europe not only religion but the rudiments of that civilisation which has enabled Europeans to obtain the sovereignty of the world. The vicissitudes of fortune have, however, laid Asia low, so much so that Europe has reduced Asiatics to the position of hewers of wood and drawers of water. Their only hope now centres on Japan, to which the light, which went out to Europe from the Asiatic continent in days of yore, has come back.[2] God grant that the light may not prove illusory, and that it may impart new life to the people of Asia!

1. *Selections from the Native Newspapers Published in the Punjab*, Vol. XVII, No. 43, pp. 253-54.
2. Japan, a country with a feudal society, became a world power with its victory over China in 1894 when it captured the island of Formosa. In 1904 it again fought a war against Russia and won it.

2. Russo-Japanese War[1]

The *Arya Gazette* (Lahore), of the 15th December 1904, publishes an article from the pen of Lala Lajpat Rai, who, in continuation of his previous remarks,[2] says that only forty years back the tiny island of Japan was not of much consequence even among Asiatic kingdoms, let alone its being reckoned among the civilised countries of the world. Today, however, it absorbs the attention of the entire world, and the spirit of patriotism and rare gallantry displayed by its people in the war with Russia have raised a feeling of fear in Europe. It is difficult to believe that it is puny Japan which has brought to the dust the colossal bear of which even the strongest country in the world was afraid.[3] Europeans, who are highly civilized, who have degraded the peoples of other

1. *Selections from the Native Newspapers Published in the Punjab*, Vol. XVII, No. 51, pp. 303-04.
2. See the preceding item.
3. In the war against Russia, Japan took part of Korea in 1904 and thus established itself on the mainland of Asia.

continents, and who used, in their arrogance, to regard others as inferior human beings, who have been sucking the life-blood of weak, poor and ignorant nations and bringing the latter into their power by force or fraud, who were beginning to believe that the world and all it contained was made for them, who had come to believe that they were created by God to rule over the rest of mankind, are looking on the struggle with astonished eyes. The writer adds that what he would draw the particular attention of his fellow countrymen to are the high traits in the national character of the Japanese which the war in the Far East has brought into prominence. The most prominent of these characteristics is the intense patriotism of the Japanese, a patriotism for which there is no parallel in the history of the world. After referring to some episodes which point to the existence of this feeling amongst the ancient *Kshatriyas* and Rajputs, the writer observes that Japan has reminded Europe that there is a limit to high-handedness and that a time comes when even the worm turns. She has also strengthened the conviction that God always fights on the side of those who take up arms in defence of their rights.

3. To G.K. Gokhale[1]

Lahore
9 April 1906

Dear Mr. Gokhale,

The bearer of this letter is one of the leading Arya Samajists in this province and a valued friend of mine. His son is going to England to study for the bar and the commerce. He is sailing by the same steamer by which you are going. He takes his wife with him. The lady goes to study medicine. I have a great regard both for the boy and the girl and I commend them to your care. Any advice or help given to them will be considered a personal favour done to me.

Yours very sincerely,
Lajpat Rai

1. G.K. Gokhale Papers (microfilm), N.A.I.

4. Petition for Transfer of Murder Case against Police Officers of Jullundur Cantonment[1]

Kundan Lal of Jullundur Cantonment, complainant–petitioner, versus Mr. Schofield, Police Inspector, and others of Cantonment, Jullundur, accused.

Complaint under Sections 301, 166, 357, 452, 456 and 107, I.P. Code.

Petition under Section 526 C.P. Code for transfer of the case on the following grounds:

(1) The petitioner, son of Lala Sheokarn Dass, banker at Jullundur Cantonment, has filed a complaint under Sections 304, 166, 357, 456 and Indian Penal Code, against Mr. Schofield, Inspector of Police, and others of the Jullundur Cantonment, for having caused the death of the petitioner's nephew by certain illegal acts specified in the complaint.

(2) The complaint is being enquired into by the District Magistrate of Jullundur. The petitioner's preliminary examination took place on the 6th of April 1906 on the close of which the District Magistrate recorded that the complainant's demeanour was not a favourable one and that he seemed to be actuated by some ulterior motives (*vide* copy of the order attached).

(3) The petitioner apprehends that he cannot expect a fair and impartial trial in that court for the following reasons:

(a) That the complaint calls in question the legality of certain orders of Major Cowie, the Cantonment Magistrate, under whose authority the accused professed to have committed the acts complained of. The petitioner believes that the District Magistrate, Major Burlton and Major Cowie have been on friendly terms and that Major Cowie must have been talking to the District Magistrate about the incident forming the subject of the complaint in private and that Major Burlton must have already formed some opinion about the same.

(b) That there has been a departmental enquiry into the said incident consequent on a question being put about the same in the Supreme Legislative Council by the Hon'ble Mr. G.K. Gokhale and the petitioner believes that the District Magistrate must have been part in the said enquiry or must have talked over it with his superior officers and formed some opinion about the same.

(c) That the case having been originally fixed for the 25th of April 1906, the date of hearing was suddenly changed to the 10th April 1906.

1. Filed by Lajpat Rai as pleader of the petitioner in the Chief Court, Lahore, on 24 April 1906. *The Panjabee*, 2 May 1906.

(d) That being a brother officer in the district it will be impossible for the Magistrate to preserve an attitude of strict impartiality in a case of this nature which materially affects the reputation of an officer of almost equal standing and position.

(e) That the District Magistrate has already rejected the complainant's application for arranging the suspension or transfer of the accused police officers, pending enquiry into charges brought by the complainant.

(4) That the petitioner's father, L. Sheokarn Dass, was prosecuted under Section 177 of the Cantonment Act for not having given the information of his grandson's being ill with small pox in due time in which case the District Magistrate has already adjudged the defence to be false and punished Sheokarn Dass. That the findings arrived at in that case very materially affect this case.

(5) That the case is likely to give rise to difficult questions of law.

(6) That in the interest of justice it is expedient that the case be heard outside the district before an officer of much higher position and standing than Major Cowie.

The petitioner therefore prays that further proceedings be stayed and the case be transferred to Lahore or some other district at the discretion of the Chief Court.[2]

2. The petition was, however, rejected by the Chief Court.

5. Letter to Editor of *The Tribune*[1]

Lahore
27 June 1906

Sir,

I have no intention to stoop so low as to attempt a full reply to L. Harkishen Lal's letter which appeared in your issue of today, but there is one statement of fact therein which I cannot let go unchallenged and which refers to the speech of Mr. Justice Lal Chand, delivered at the last prize distribution day of the

1. *The Tribune*, 28 June 1906.

D.A.V. College.[2] It is true that as soon as Lala Lal Chand had finished delivering this speech, Kali Babu[3] took the speech from him. But before he left the compound, I asked him if he intended to publish the speech *in extenso* in the *Tribune*, as we wanted a *verbatim* report of it in the press. Kali Babu said that it was hardly possible as Mr. Nundy was not likely to do it. Upon this I asked him to return the speech to me, as I would manage to have it reported *verbatim*. He, however, did not return it to me then and there but took it away on the understanding that after taking notes of it for the purposes of editorial comments in the *Tribune*, he will return it to me sometime in the course of the day. He probably also added that he would show it to Mr. Nundy but I am not sure about it. As a matter of fact, the speech was with him for several hours and he did not return it till late in the afternoon. All we know of what took place in the office of the *Tribune* relating to it is that a report of the meeting appeared in the columns of the *Tribune*, "as supplied by a correspondent". The editorial columns were studiously silent about the speech or the meeting.

Yours &c.,
Lajpat Rai

2. Harkishen Lal, in his letter, had written: "It is said that the present *The Tribune* represents me and my friends and not others. . . . The only section of the people of the Punjab who have been unkind to me and who disown me is the Rai Mul Raj section of the Arya Samaj, and there is no arguing with them. They tilted the Khalsa College, they bowled the Dyal Singh College, they appropriated the Punjab National Bank and usurped the Hindu orphanages, and if *The Tribune* has not become quite the Lajpat Rai trumpet and the D.A.V. College gazette, many must be glad though a few must be sorry." As regards Lal Chand's speech, he had alleged that Lajpat Rai had snatched the text of the speech from the man through whom it was sent for publication in *The Tribune*.
3. K.P. Roy.

6. On Sarala Devi Choudharani's Charge of Betrayal of Confidence[1]

Sir, With reference to the letter of Mrs. Choudhry[2] that appeared in your last issue I regret the sex of the writer prevents me from giving a proper reply. I may, however, be permitted to say this much that I have never betrayed any

1. *The Panjabee*, 3 November 1906.
2. Sarala Devi Choudharani; wife of Rambhaj Dutt Choudhari, a prominent Arya Samajist and Congressman of Punjab.

confidence that Mrs. Choudhry was ever pleased to repose in me, nor I hope I shall ever be guilty of doing so in future, under any circumstances whatsoever.[3] I hope Mrs. Choudhry may have ample opportunities of finding out the real traitor in her camp, whoever he may be. I have nothing more to add to the statement of facts made by you, Mr. Editor, in your footnote.[4]

Your &c.,
Lajpat Rai

3. In her letter published in *The Panjabee* of 31 October 1906, Sarala Devi Choudharani had charged Lajpat Rai with having divulged the contents of a letter written by her to him in England on account of which, she added, it was alleged that she had changed her political views and criticized Bepin Chandra Pal.
4. Refuting the charge laid against Lajpat Rai, the editor of *The Panjabee* had written: "We became aware of the letter she addressed to him in England for the first time from her own confession. Lalaji never spoke to us a single syllable about the letter itself or its contents or even the political views ever held by Mr. and Mrs. Choudhry."

7. What Is Religion?[1]

A consideration of the religious problem must begin with a consideration of the primary question, viz. "what is religion?" One would think that, universal as the idea of religion is, there must not be any difference about its meaning and conception and that everybody, all over the world, must have the same notion about it. But, strange to say, there is no other subject upon which there exists a greater want of unanimity than that on religion. There are great, important, wide and extensive differences in men's conceptions of religion. No two communities understand quite the same thing from it. Professor Max Muller[2] says, "If there is a word that has changed from century to century and has a different aspect in every country in which it is used—nay, which conveys peculiar shades of meaning as it is used by every man, woman or child—it is religion." Still, a comparative study of religions will disclose a fair amount of agreement or at least some salient points which form the fundamental basis of

1. *Lala Lajpat Rai—The Man in His Word* (Madras, 1907), pp. 128-34.
2. (1823-1900); German Orientalist and linguistic scholar, professor at Oxford, 1868; edited the *Sacred Books of the East* (51 volumes), wrote on Indian philosophy and encouraged search for Oriental manuscripts and inscriptions.

most of the great religions of the world. Before we come to these common salient points we think we might profitably consider the various definitions of religion, that have from time to time been attempted by those who have discussed the subject and thrown light upon the same. We might begin with the root-meaning of the word and its etymological derivation, though perhaps we may not gain much therefrom. Unfortunately, even here we fail to find a unanimity. Some amongst them whose derivation has been accepted by Max Muller derive it from Latin *re-legere*, to gather up again, to take up, to consider, to ponder—opposed to *nec-legere*, to neglect. According to this derivation, religion originally meant attention, regard, reverence and awe and was not restricted to reverence for the gods. Very soon, however, it became more and more restricted to reverence for the gods and divine beings. People began to speak of man's religion, meaning his piety, his faith in the gods, his observance of ceremonies till at last an entire system was called religious or religion. There are others who derive religion from *religare*, to bind up, to fasten, to moor, i.e. what binds or holds us up. But it is quite clear that if *religio* or religion originally meant attention, regard or reverence it did not continue to retain that simple meaning. The word has had such a vast and varied use that it is almost hopeless to invent such a comprehensive definition as to cover the meanings of all those who have used it, discussed it and lived by it. With some the word has been synonymous with all that is good and noble in this world, with others it had nothing to do with the affairs of the world. With some it was only another name for morality, with others it overlapped morality and expressed a sense of spiritual ecstasy. With some it expressed the relationship of the spirit of man with that Universal Spirit, God. With others it directed a number of ideas in which God had no place at all, while there were others whose conception of religion even directed the existence of what we call human soul or spirit. By way of illustration we will notice a few of these attempts at defining religion.

Kant,[3] for instance, one of the greatest European savants, says, "religion is morality". According to him, looking upon all our moral duties as divine commands is religion. To the question whence originates the building force of those moral duties, Kant has no satisfactory reply. Having no faith in revelation, he cannot ascribe this authorship to God. What then does he mean by asking us to look upon moral duties as divine commands? He calls them divine because in his opinion we are directly conscious of them. In the words of Professor Max Muller, any outward divine authority is, in the eyes of a Kantian philosopher, mere phenomenal or, as we should say, a mere confession of human

3. Immanuel Kant (1724-1804); German philosopher; works include *Critique of Pure Reason* (1781) and *Foundations of the Metaphysics of Ethics* (1785).

weakness. Fichte,[4] however, an equally great name in European philosophy, takes an exactly opposite view. He denies that religion is morality because he says religion is never practical and was never intended to influence life. In his opinion pure morality serves the latter purpose and religion is knowledge which gives man a clear insight into himself, answers the highest questions and thus imparts to us a complete harmony with ourselves and a thorough satisfaction to our mind. Apparently this seems to be very much like the *Gyan* of the Indian *Vedanti* of the school of Swami Shankaracharya.

Then there are the two definitions of Schleiermacher[5] and Hegel[6] expressing two opposite views. According to the former, "religion consists in our consciousness of absolute dependence on something which though it determines us we cannot determine it in turn". The latter, however, declares that "the feeling of dependence is the very opposite of religion". According to Hegel, "religion is or ought to be perfect freedom", for it is, according to him, nothing more nor less than the Divine Spirit becoming conscious of Himself through the finite spirit. This again sounds like *Vedantism*.

The next step from this was taken by Comte who has taught that man is "not only the subject but also the object of religion and religious worship". We are told that man cannot know anything higher than man; that man therefore is the only true object of religious knowledge and worship, "not only man as an individual but man as a class". This last qualification is the keynote of Comte's philosophy and no doubt reads very solemn, even sublime. But it was reserved to Feuerbach to give the last of the brush and remove even "this last mystic hold" off the brow of religion. According to him, "self-love is a necessary, indestructible, universal law and principle and inseparable from every kind of love. Religion must and does confirm this on very page of its history. Wherever man tries to resist that human egoism, in the sense in which we explained it, whether in religion, philosophy or politics, he sinks into pure nonsense and insanity, for the sense which forms the foundation of all human instincts, desires and actions is the satisfaction of the human being, the satisfaction of human egoism." Hegel's rough but curt criticism of this definition is so pertinent that we cannot resist the temptation of quoting it. He says that if the feeling of dependence were the sole test of religion then a dog would be the most religious of all creatures.

4. J.G. Fichte (1762-1814); German philosopher who developed Kantian ethics in his book *Critique of Religious Revolution* (1792).
5. F.D.E. Schleiermacher (1768-1834); German philosopher and Protestant theologian who attacked rationalism and orthodoxy in *The Christian Faith* (1821-22).
6. (1770-1831); German philosopher; formulated concept of historical dialectic; works include *Phenomenology of Mind* (1807) and *Science of Logic* (1812-16).

Thus if universal philanthropy or humanity is religion according to Comte, pure selfishness is religion according to Feuerbach. To the same school belongs the definition of Gruppe who says that "religious belief is a doctrine professing to be able to produce union with a being or the attainment of a state which, properly speaking, lies beyond the sphere of human striving and attainment". According to him, "religion is a pure invention of somebody's imagination, the acceptance of which is due to the unconscious vanity of its founders, a belief in the happiness which it procures to its believers and the substantial advantages which society derives from it".

From the philosophers' definitions of religion we next proceed to the definitions of European theologians.

Martineau describes it as "A belief in an ever-living God, i.e. a Divine Mind and Will ruling the universe, and holding moral relations with mankind." Professor Flint defines it as "man's belief in a being or beings, mightier than himself, and accessible to his senses, but not indifferent to his sentiments and actions with the feelings and practices which form such a belief". Spinoza[7] says, "religion is the love of God founded on a knowledge of this divine perfections". According to Reville, "Religion is the determination of human life by the sentiment of a bond uniting the human mind to that mysterious mind whose dominations of the world and of itself it recognises and to whom it delights in feeling itself united." These definitions are objected to because they exclude certain systems of belief and practice which, although universally recognised as religious, yet ignore the existence of God or gods (such as Buddhism). Consequently, an attempt has been made by Professor Max Muller and some other writers to invent definitions of religion which may be sufficiently wide and comprehensive to include all that has till now been known or styled as religion. He defines it to be "a mental faculty which independent, nay, in spite of sense and reason enables man to apprehend the Infinite, under different names, and under varying disguises". In anticipation of criticism he has taken pains to point out that by "Infinite" he does not mean God but "Indefinite", thereby including Buddhism as well. With great deference to these great names we cannot help remarking that we have quite failed to realize the necessity of finding such a definition of religion as may cover all those forms of belief or faith that have to this day been, whether rightly or wrongly, described or styled as religions. This, in our humble opinion, is not the correct way of teaching "what is religion?" It may be a suitable definition for historical purposes but certainly not for theological or ethical or moral purposes.

7. B. Spinoza (1632-1677); Dutch philosopher; propounded that "all life is embraced by infinite God (or Nature)"; excommunicated from native Jewish sect in 1656 for unorthodoxy of thought; works include *Ethics* (1677).

CHRONOLOGY

1865	28 January	Birth at Dhudike, a village in Ferozepore district in Punjab
1874		Admission to District Board School, Rupar
1877		Married Radha Devi
1878		Passed Middle School examination
1880		Joined Mission High School, Ludhiana
1881	January	Passed entrance examinations of Calcutta University and Punjab University
	February	Joined Government College, Lahore
		Joined Law School, Lahore
1882		Joined Brahmo Samaj
		Qualified as *Mukhtar*
	December	Joined Arya Samaj
1883	January	Started legal practice as a *Mukhtar* at Jagraon
		Started *The Regenerator of Aryavarta* (English weekly) and *Deshopkarak* (Urdu weekly)
	31 October	Addressed a condolence meeting at Lahore on the death of Swami Dayanand
1884		Moved to Rohtak and continued legal practice as a *Mukhtar*
		Elected Secretary of Rohtak Arya Samaj
1885		Passed law examination and started practising law as a *Vakil* at Rohtak
1886		Shifted to Hissar and continued legal practice there till 1892
		Associated with the founding of D.A.V. School at Lahore which became a college in June 1889
1888	26-9 December	Attended Allahabad Congress as a delegate from Hissar

1889		Elected member of Hissar Municipal Committee and also served as its Honorary Secretary
		Attended Congress session at Bombay and supported resolution on reform of Legislative Councils
1891		Elected Corresponding Secretary of D.A.V. College Managing Committee
1892		Moved to Lahore and started legal practice at Chief Court
		Elected Honorary Secretary of D.A.V. College Managing Committee, Lahore
		Supported College Party as against Mahatma Party in the Lahore Arya Samaj conflict
1893	September	Elected President of Anarkali Arya Samaj founded after the split in Lahore Arya Samaj
		Started *Dayanand Anglo-Vedic College Samachar* (Urdu monthly)
	December	Member of Reception Committee of Lahore Congress
		Met B.G. Tilak and G.K. Gokhale for first time at Lahore Congress
1895		Started Swadeshi movement in Punjab
		Founded, along with Lala Harkishen Lal, Punjab National Bank at Lahore
1896		Began writing books in the series 'Great Men of the World'
		Took active part in famine relief work in north India
1897	February	Organized famine relief work in Central Provinces
		Started Hindu Orphan Relief Movement in Central Provinces
		Led a campaign at Lahore for raising funds for the legal defence of B.G. Tilak

1898		Elected Director of Punjab National Bank
	June	Death of younger brother, Dalpat Rai
		Decided to curtail his work at Bar and devote time to public work
1899-1900		Took active part in famine relief work in Rajputana, Kathiawar and Central Provinces
1900		Death of mother, Gulab Devi
	December	Attended Lahore Congress and elected member of Industrial and Educational Committees
1901		Elected member of All India Congress Committee
		Gave evidence before Indian Famine Commission
		Attended Calcutta Congress
1902		Gave evidence before Indian Universities Commission and submitted a memorandum relating to Punjab University
1904	October	Started *The Panjabee*, a weekly, at Lahore
		Attended Bombay Congress
1905	January	Visited Ceylon and, on return, south India
	February	Met G.K. Gokhale at Calcutta
		Met Sister Nivedita at Calcutta
	April	Engaged in relief work during the Kangra Valley earthquake and founded Kangra Valley Relief Committee
	13 May	Left for England as a Congress delegate
	10 June	Reached London and stayed at India House
	27 July	Addressed a meeting at Stockport Labour Church, Lancashire
	September	Visited America and delivered lectures at New York, Philadelphia and Boston
	October	Went back to London
	1 November	Left England for India
	17 November	Reached Bombay

	22 November	Arrived at Lahore
	26 November	Delivered a speech on the occasion of the anniversary of Anarkali Arya Samaj at Lahore which was used, in May 1907, for his arrest and deportation to Mandalay, Burma (now Myanmar)
	29 December	Attended Banaras Congress and supported the resolution protesting against repressive measures in Bengal
1906		Took active part in agitation against the partition of Bengal
	30 September	Attended Punjab Provincial Political Conference at Ambala
	December	Attended Calcutta Congress
		Death of son-in-law, Dr Jai Chand (husband of Parbati Devi)
1907		Took part in agitation against the Punjab Colonisation of Government Lands Bill and the Punjab Land Alienation Act (Amendment) Bill
	9 May	Arrested under Regulation III of 1818 and deported to Mandalay
	16 May	Lodged in Mandalay Fort prison (Fort Dufferin)
	29 June	Sent a memorial to Governor-General protesting against his arrest
	22 September	Sent another memorial to Secretary of State for India
	11 November	Taken from Mandalay Fort prison to Lahore Central Jail
	18 November	Released at Lahore
	26 December	Attended Surat Congress and withdrew his nomination for Presidentship
	27 December	Attended National Convention convened by Moderates at Surat
	30 December	Presided over All India Swadeshi Conference at Surat

1908	February	Visited Bombay, Calcutta, Delhi and several towns of U.P. to organize famine relief work
	4 May	Set out on a second tour of famine-affected areas in U.P.
	29 August	Sailed for England
1909		Attended a dinner given by Indian Majlis at Cambridge and met Indian students, including Jawaharlal Nehru
	March	Returned to India
	October	Founded Hindu Elementary Education League to promote education of Hindu children
1910	March	Third visit to England
	June	Attended Conference on Nationalities and Subject Races in London
	September	Returned to India
1911	March	Death of his second son, Pyare Krishna
		Elected to Lahore Municipal Committee
		Established Punjab Shiksha Sangh and opened schools for primary education
1912	18 October	Delivered presidential speech at All India Arya Kumar Sammelan held at Saharanpur (U.P.)
		Attended Bankipur (Patna) Congress and advocated the cause of Indians in South Africa
1913		Founded Radha Kishan High School, named after his father, at Jagraon
	May	Presided over Depressed Classes Conference at Gurukul Kangri
	December	Attended Karachi Congress and spoke on 'Indian nationals in South Africa'
1914	April	Left for England as a Congress delegate
	17 May	Reached London
	14 November	Left England for New York
	21 November	Reached New York

1915	April	Reached San Francisco
	3 July	Left San Francisco for Yokohama, Japan
	19 July	Reached Yokohama
		Met Japanese Prime Minister, Count Okuma
		Made a speech suggesting formation of a sort of Asian federation at a banquet given in his honour by the journalists of Tokyo
		Met Chinese leader Sun Yat Sen who, after the abortive second Chinese Revolution of July 1913, had taken refuge in Japan
		Met Rash Behari Bose in Tokyo
	27 November	Presided over the banquet given by the Indian community to celebrate the coronation of Emperor Taisho
	12 December	Left Yokohama for San Francisco
	27 December	Reached San Francisco
1917	22 October	Founded Indian Home Rule League of America in New York with himself as President and J.T. Sunderland as Vice-President
1918	January	Started *Young India*, a monthly journal of Home Rule League of America
		Established Hindustan Information Service Association in New York
		Wrote out a memorandum on India's case which was presented before the Foreign Relations Committee of the American Senate
1919	24 December	Left New York for London on way to India
1920	20 February	Reached Bombay
	May	Started *Bande Mataram* (Urdu daily) at Lahore
	4 September	Presided over special session of Calcutta Congress
	7 November	Presided over first All India Trade Union Congress at Bombay

	December	Founded Tilak School of Politics at Lahore
		Attended Nagpur Congress and supported Gandhiji's resolution on non-cooperation
		Founded Dwarka Das Library at Lahore (later shifted to Chandigarh)
	25 December	Presided over All India College Students' Conference at Nagpur
1921	March	Founded Servants of the People Society
	May	Established Qaumi Vidyapeeth at Lahore
	3 December	Arrested for taking part in non-cooperation movement and sentenced to 18 months' imprisonment
1922	31 January	Released and re-arrested
	20 February	Sentenced to two years' rigorous imprisonment
1923		Death of father, Radha Kishan
	16 August	Released from Lahore Central Jail
	December	Presided over Punjab Provincial Conference at Jaranwala
	27 December	Presided over All India Cow Protection Conference at Nagpur
1924	January	Visited Mahatma Gandhi in hospital at Poona
	9 April	Left Bombay for England
		Joined Independent Labour Party of Britain
	June	Visited Switzerland
	August	Visited Constantinople
	September	Returned to India
	December	Attended Belgaum Congress
1925	11 April	Presided over Calcutta session of Hindu Mahasabha
	July	Started *The People*, a weekly, at Lahore
	5 December	Presided over Bombay Provincial Hindu Conference at Bombay
	20 December	Gave evidence before Punjab Jails Inquiry Committee

	25 December	Attended Kanpur Congress
	December	Elected to Central Legislative Assembly
1926	January	Joined Swaraj Party and elected its Deputy Leader in Central Legislative Assembly
	26 January	Made a speech in Central Legislative Assembly supporting the resolution demanding release of political prisoners
	May	Left for Europe
	7 May	Arrived at Marseilles and left for Paris
		Visited London for a week
	26 May	Attended Eighth International Labour Conference at Geneva
	2 June	Spoke at International Labour Conference on the existence of *begar* (forced labour) in India
		Met Shyamji Krishna Varma at Geneva
		Met Jawaharlal Nehru, who was at this time in Switzerland and called on him at Geneva
		Paid visits to Romain Rolland at Geneva
		Attended World Parliaments Union at Geneva
		Went back to London and addressed World Migration Congress
	13 August	Returned to India
	24 August	Resigned from Swaraj Party
	14 September	Founded, along with Madan Mohan Malaviya, Independent Congress Party (Nationalist Party)
		Elected to Central Legislative Assembly from two constituencies
1927	9 January	Presided over first session of Burma Provincial Hindu Sabha held at Rangoon
	April	Met Mahatma Gandhi at Sabarmati
	May	Left for Europe
	19 August	Returned to India

	December	Attended Madras Congress and supported resolution advocating boycott of Simon Commission
		Founded Gulab Devi Memorial Trust
1928	16 February	Moved resolution in Central Legislative Assembly refusing co-operation with Simon Commission
	March	Founded Shraddhanand Achhut Uddhar Ashram at Lahore
	28-30 August	Attended All Parties Conference at Lucknow at which Nehru Report was adopted
	27-8 October	Presided over Agra Provincial Hindu Conference at Etawah (U.P.)
	30 October	Led a procession demonstrating against Simon Commission at Lahore and received lathi blows from the police
		Addressed a public meeting the same evening
	3-4 November	Attended AICC meeting at Delhi
	17 November	Death at Lahore

INDEX

(Biographical footnotes are italicized)